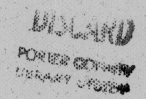

RISING UP FROM INDIAN COUNTRY

RISING UP FROM INDIAN COUNTRY

The Battle of Fort Dearborn and the Birth of Chicago

ANN DURKIN KEATING | THE UNIVERSITY OF CHICAGO PRESS
Chicago and London

Ann Durkin Keating is professor of history at North Central College in Naperville, Illinois. She is coeditor of *The Encyclopedia of Chicago* and author of several books, including *Chicagoland: City and Suburbs in the Railroad Age* and *Chicago Neighborhoods and Suburbs: A Historical Guide.*

The University of Chicago Press, Chicago 60637
The University of Chicago Press, Ltd., London
© 2012 by The University of Chicago
All rights reserved. Published 2012.
Printed in the United States of America
21 20 19 18 17 16 15 14 13 12   1 2 3 4 5

ISBN-13: 978-0-226-42896-3 (cloth)
ISBN-10: 0-226-42896-6 (cloth)
ISBN-13: 978-0-226-42898-7 (e-book)
ISBN-10: 0-226-42898-2 (e-book)

Library of Congress Cataloging-in-Publication Data

Keating, Ann Durkin.
  Rising up from Indian country: the battle of Fort Dearborn and the birth of Chicago / Ann Durkin Keating.
     pages cm.
  Includes bibliographical references and index.
    ISBN 978-0-226-42896-3 (cloth: alk. paper) — ISBN 0-226-42896-6 (cloth: alk. paper) — ISBN 978-0-226-42898-7 (e-book) — ISBN 0-226-42898-2 (e-book)   1. Fort Dearborn Massacre, Chicago, Ill., 1812.   2. Kinzie, John, 1763–1828.   3. Chicago (Ill.)—History—19th century.   I. Title.
    E356.C53K43 2012
    977.3'1103—dc23   2012006703

Contents

John Kinzie Timeline

1763   Birth in Quebec to John and Emily (Tyne) McKenzie; father dies

1764   Mother marries William Forsyth; family moves to New York City

1766   Family in Detroit

1771   Half-brother, Thomas Forsyth, born

1770s   Trains as a silversmith

1780s   At British trading outpost, Kekionga, as a silversmith and
trader; common-law marriage with Margaret McKenzie

1788   Son William born

1791   Kinzie family burned out of Kekionga, flee to Au
Glaize, rebuild house; daughter Elizabeth born

1793   Son James born at Au Glaize

1794   Au Glaize destroyed as part of Fallen Timbers
offensive; family flees to Detroit

1796–97   Margaret McKenzie returns to her Virginia
childhood home with their children

1798   Marries Eleanor Lytle McKillip

1796–1804   At St. Joseph working for William Burnett
and with Thomas Forsyth

1800   Witnesses sale of Point de Sable holdings at Chicago

1803   Son John Harris born

1803   Purchases Point de Sable house

1804–12   Kinzie & Forsyth operate from Chicago and Peoria

1804   Moves with his wife to Chicago; daughter Ellen Marion born

1807   Daughter Maria Indiana born; sutler to Fort
Dearborn with Lt. William Whistler

1810   Son Robert Allen born

1812   Reappointed sutler to Fort Dearborn; kills Jean
Lalime; aids United States on August 15

1812–16   Family lives at Detroit

1813   Accused of treason and imprisoned by the British

1814 Appointed interpreter by the United States

1816 Returns to Chicago from Detroit with his
      wife, Eleanor, and three children

1818 Appointed subagent for Indian Affairs at Chicago

1825 Elected justice of the peace for Peoria County (including Illinois)

1828 Dies at Chicago

General Timeline

1754–63 Seven Years' War (French and Indian War)

1763 Treaty of Paris; France cedes Canada, Illinois, and Louisiana to Britain

1763 Pontiac's War

1776–83 American Revolution

1783 Treaty of Paris; British cede land in trans-Appalachian West to United States

1787 Northwest Ordinance

1790 President George Washington inaugurated

1786–94 Maumee-Wabash Confederacy War

1794 Jay Treaty

1795 Greenville Treaty

1796 Western forts turned over to Americans from British

1797 President John Adams inaugurated in Philadelphia

1801 President Thomas Jefferson inaugurated in Washington, D.C.

1803 Louisiana Purchase; foundation of Fort Dearborn

1808 Establishment of Prophetstown at Tippecanoe

1809 Treaty of Fort Wayne; Illinois Territory established

1809 President James Madison inaugurated

1811 Battle of Tippecanoe

1812 Fort Dearborn destroyed; war between Great Britain and the United States

1815 Formal end of the War of 1812

1816 U.S. Army rebuilds Fort Dearborn

1816 Indiana statehood

1817 President James Monroe inaugurated

1818 Illinois statehood

1821 Treaty of Chicago

1825 President John Quincy Adams inaugurated

1828 Winnebago War

1829 Treaty of Prairie du Chien

1829 President Andrew Jackson inaugurated

1831 Cook County established

1832 Black Hawk War

1833 Treaty of Chicago; Chicago town incorporation

A Mobile Cast of Characters

KEKIONGA, 1790 (destroyed by U.S. attack in October)

Alexander McKee, British Indian agent

Matthew Elliott, British trader who had emigrated from western
Pennsylvania

Simon Girty, British trader

John Kinzie, a British silversmith and trader

> **Margaret McKenzie**, his common-law wife who had been a
> Shawnee captive
>
> **William McKenzie**, their son

John Clark, John Kinzie's trading partner

> **Elizabeth McKenzie Clark**, his wife who had been a Shawnee captive

TURTLETOWN, 1791

Little Turtle, Miami village leader, successful against U.S. attack in
November 1791

> **Sweet Breeze**, his daughter
>
> **Apekonit (William Wells)**, raised as a Wea captive, husband of
> Sweet Breeze

CHICAGO, 1798

Jean Baptiste Point de Sable, trader and farmer of African descent

> **Catherine**, his Indian wife
>
> **Jean**, their son
>
> **Suzanne**, their daughter
>
> **Jean Baptiste Pelletier**, trader husband of Suzanne
>
> **Eulalie Marie**, daughter of Suzanne Pelletier

Antoine Ouilmette, a French trader and farmer

> **Archange Marie Chevalier**, his métis (French and Potawatomi
> descent) wife

François Le Mai, a métis trader probably from Cahokia

> **Marie Therese Roy**, his Potawatomi wife

Jean Lalime, a French trader associated with William Burnett

> **Nokenoqua**, his Potawatomi wife

ST. JOSEPH VILLAGES, 1798

Topinbee, a Potawatomi village leader

Chebanse, his half-brother

Kakima, their sister

    William Burnett, American trader married to Kakima

    James Burnett, their son (at school in Detroit)

    John Burnett, their son (at school in Detroit)

    Isaac Burnett, their son

    Rebecca Burnett, their daughter

DETROIT, 1798

William Forsyth, British subject, farmer and innkeeper at Sandwich, stepbrother of John Kinzie

    Margaret Lytle Forsyth, his wife, and a former Shawnee captive

John Kinzie, trading for William Burnett and others

    Eleanor Lytle McKillip Kinzie, sister of Margaret, former Shawnee captive, bride of John Kinzie

    Margaret McKillip, Eleanor's daughter with British officer David McKillip

Robert Forsyth, British subject, stepbrother and intermittent trading partner of John Kinzie

Thomas Forsyth, half-brother and trading partner of John Kinzie

James Forsyth, stepbrother and intermittent trading partner of John Kinzie

John Lytle, father of Eleanor, British subject

Robert Lytle, brother of Eleanor, British subject

FORT DEARBORN, 1806

Captain John Whistler, Irish-born U.S. Army officer, builds Fort Dearborn 1803–4

    Ann Whistler, his wife

    Lt. William Whistler, their son, served under his father at Fort Dearborn

    Mary Julia Whistler, married William Whistler in 1802 and came to Chicago from Detroit

    Meriwether Lewis Whistler, son of William Whistler, grandson of Captain Whistler

    John Harrison Whistler, son of William Whistler, grandson of Captain Whistler

    John Whistler, son of Captain Whistler

    George Washington Whistler, young son of Captain Whistler

    Catherine Whistler Hamilton, daughter of Captain Whistler

    Lt. Thomas Hamilton, husband of Catherine

Thomas Hayward, U.S. factor
James Leigh, recruiting sergeant for U.S. garrison at Chicago
Surgeon's Mate John Cooper

CHICAGO, 1806

Archange and Antoine Ouilmette family
François Le Mai and family
Jean Lalime and his wife, Nokenoqua
Louis and Angelique Pettell family
John and Eleanor Kinzie family (son John Harris Kinzie and daughter
    Ellen Marion)

CALUMET REGION AND FOX RIVER, 1806

Naunongee, Potawatomi warrior
    Chopa (Marianne), his daughter
    François Chevalier, her husband
    Catherine Chevalier, their daughter, sister of Archange
Joseph Bailly, British-allied trader
Alexander Robinson, métis employee of Joseph Bailly
Shabbona, Ottawa warrior heading a Potawatomi village
    Mah-naw-bun-no-quah, his daughter
    Jean Baptiste Beaubien, her husband, a French trader working for
        Joseph Bailly

PEORIA AND VICINITY, 1806

Thomas Forsyth, partner in Kinzie & Forsyth and half-brother of John
    Kinzie
    Keziah Malott Forsyth, his wife, and a former Shawnee captive
    John Kinzie Forsyth, their son
    Robert Allen Forsyth, their son
Louis Buisson, French trader
    Sheshi (Suzanne) Chevalier Buisson, his wife, and sister of
        Archange Ouilmette
    Louis Pierre Buisson Jr., their son
Mucktypoke (Black Partridge), Potawatomi village leader
Waubansee (Foggy Day), Potawatomi warrior and Mucktypoke's
    brother
Main Poc, Potawatomi warrior
Nuscotomeg (Mad Sturgeon), Main Poc's brother-in-law and
    Potawatomi warrior
Wabinewa (White Sturgeon), his brother
    La Nanette, Wabinewa's daughter
    Billy Caldwell, Kinzie & Forsyth clerk and La Nanette's husband

Gomo, Potawatomi warrior and village leader
Senajiwan, Potawatomi warrior and Gomo's brother

FORT DEARBORN, AUGUST 1812

Captain Nathan Heald, U.S. commander
    Rebekah Wells Heald, his wife, and niece of William Wells
    Cicely, enslaved by Heald, as well as her infant
Lt. Linai Helm, officer at Fort Dearborn
    Margaret McKillip Helm, his wife, and daughter of Eleanor Kinzie
Ensign George Ronan
Surgeon's Mate Isaac Van Voorhis

CHICAGO, AUGUST 1812

William Russell, retired U.S. soldier
    Martha Leigh, wife of James Leigh, daughter of William Russell
    John Leigh, her son
    Lilly, her daughter
    Mary, her daughter
    infant, her daughter
Thomas Burns, U.S. soldier at Fort Dearborn to 1811
    Mary Cooper Burns, widow recently married to Thomas Burns
    James Cooper, son of Mary Burns, stepson of Thomas Burns
    Anne Cooper, daughter of Mary Burns and stepdaughter of
        Thomas Burns
    Frances Cooper, daughter of Mary Burns and stepdaughter of
        Thomas Burns
    Isabella Cooper, daughter of Mary Burns and stepdaughter of
        Thomas Burns
    Catherine Burns, infant daughter of Mary and Thomas Burns
Archange Ouilmette, métis householder
    Sheshi Chevalier Buisson, her sister
John Kinzie, official sutler and partner Kinzie & Forsyth
    Eleanor Kinzie, his wife, and their children
    J. B. Chandonnai, clerk for Kinzie & Forsyth
    Athena, enslaved member of Kinzie household
    Black Jim, enslaved member of Kinzie household
    Pepper, enslaved member of Kinzie household
    Henry, enslaved member of Kinzie household

CHICAGO, 1814

Antoine and Archange Ouilmette family
Louis and Sheshi Buisson family
François Des Pins, British-allied trader

Martha Leigh Des Pins, his wife
Mary Leigh, her daughter

ST. LOUIS, 1813

Thomas Forsyth, U.S. subagent for Indian Affairs, Missouri Territory
Keziah Forsyth, his wife
John Kinzie Forsyth, their son
Robert Allen Forsyth, their son

DETROIT, 1814

John Kinzie, interpreter for U.S. government
Eleanor Kinzie, his wife, and their children
William Forsyth, her brother-in-law and Kinzie's stepbrother, British-allied farmer
Margaret Lytle Forsyth, his wife, and Eleanor Kinzie's sister

FORT DEARBORN, 1823

Alexander Wolcott, U.S. Indian agent
Ellen Marion Kinzie Wolcott, his wife, and daughter of John Kinzie
John Kinzie, U.S. Indian subagent
Eleanor Kinzie, his wife, and their children Maria Indiana and
Robert Allen

CHICAGO, 1823

Jean Baptiste Beaubien, trader working from the former U.S. Trading Post
Josette Beaubien, his wife
James Kinzie, son of John Kinzie and Margaret McKenzie
John Crafts, representative of the American Fur Company at Chicago
Jean Baptiste Chandonnai
Angelique Ouellett Pettell, widow of Louis Pettell
Michael Pettell, her son
Antoine Ouilmette, farmer
Archange Ouilmette, his wife
Alexander Robinson (Che-Che-Pin-Qua), trader
Catherine Chevalier Robinson, his wife, and sister of Archange Ouilmette
Billy Caldwell, trader for John Kinzie
Joseph LaFramboise, farmer and trader at Hardscrabble (Leigh Farm)
Therese Pelletier LaFramboise, his métis wife

Maps

Figure 1. There is no extant image of John Kinzie, but examples of his silverwork, like this silver cross made around 1820, provide a tangible link to his life. (Chicago History Museum, ICHi-64676)

Preface: John Kinzie's World

I did not set out to write a biography of John Kinzie, nor have I done so here. In-stead, I have used Kinzie's life as a means to better understand the early history of the place that becomes Chicago. John Kinzie was not someone I wanted to spend time studying. Far from it. My first encounter with him was in a fourth-grade classroom, where he was presented as "the Father of Chicago."

Kinzie was born in Montreal to British-born parents near the end of the Seven Years' War just as the French were forced out of North America. He grew up next door to the British fort in Detroit. In the late 1780s, he used his family's business and military ties to establish himself as a silversmith, trader, and head of a household south of Detroit at Kekionga. In 1804 Kinzie relocated to Chicago after the construction of Fort Dearborn. He developed close ties to U.S. officials as well as to area Potawatomis.

When the Potawatomis attacked the retreating garrison in August 1812, John Kinzie put his life on the line to mitigate the violence and secure the safe passage of the commanding officer at Fort Dearborn. While the battle at Chicago was a complete victory for the Potawatomis and their allies, it was not a portent of the future. Instead, it was a final Pyrrhic victory for those who wanted to maintain a permanent Indian Country in the region of Chicago. After the war the United States completed the conquest of this region, and alternative futures were quashed. Chicago as we know it today could not exist without this conquest and the end of the Indian Country in the western Great Lakes.

When I returned recently to research the early history of the Chicago region, I encountered many compelling reasons not to focus on Kinzie or perpetuate the booster narrative of manifest destiny. After all, Jean Baptiste Point de Sable was living at Chicago well before Kinzie, and we now know that many other men and women were central to early Chicago, such

as Archange Ouilmette, Naunongee, Black Partridge, Jean Lalime, and Nokenoqua. Why bring Kinzie to the forefront once again?

Kinzie was not even the staunch American supporter that later histories
suggest. He never wanted or envisioned the growth of Chicago as an industrial metropolis, so it is hard to see him as Chicago's John Smith. Kinzie
never embraced the U.S. vision of conquest and assimilation of the Indian
Country in which Chicago was located. Instead, he hoped for a permanent
Indian Country around Chicago where he could trade and where his children could live out their lives as he had.

On top of this, Kinzie was not a likable fellow—he killed a longtime
associate and double-crossed countless friends and family members. All
those he came in contact with were well advised to keep a close eye on
him. He was often drunk and made his living selling liquor to Potawatomis
and traders who could ill afford it. His first wife and small children left him
when the opportunity arose. He was denounced as a traitor by Tecumseh
and convicted of treason by the British. He saved himself from debtors'
prison only by selling his stepfather's home and not sharing the proceeds
with other family members.

Still, there is another side to Kinzie. He was married for more than thirty
years to his second wife, Eleanor McKillip Kinzie, who stayed with him
through thick and thin. He helped all his children as they entered adulthood. He developed long and deep friendships with the Potawatomi warriors Topinbee and Black Partridge, who would rescue him on several occa-
sions. Kinzie also had loyal associates, like Billy Caldwell and Jean Baptiste
Chandonnai, who assisted him long after they left his employ.

Kinzie embodied the complexities and contradictions at the center of
Chicago's founding in 1812. The Potawatomis and their allies won the battle on August 15, 1812, but the Americans came back and never left. Kinzie
was a reluctant American who would not have become one if he could
have avoided it. But in 1812 he was forced to make a decision, and he made
it—not based on ideology but on personal and business circumstances. In
the end, Kinzie did not get what he wanted, and over time a more familiar
Chicago emerged, set in a country with recognizable boundaries and an
ideology that we now celebrate.

Just as Kinzie was a reluctant American, I have reluctantly come to see
his usefulness in understanding Chicago's early history. He was present at
so much of the story between 1795 and 1833 that his life provides a cru-

cial point of reference. So that is what I have done here—used Kinzie's life to orient the reader through a world that was far more complicated than we might imagine. This is not the simple story of manifest destiny laid out to me in fourth grade. Kinzie allows us to move beyond the simplistic conquest narrative drawn by nineteenth-century boosters and rejected by twentieth-century academic historians.

Acknowledgments

My debts of gratitude on this project are many. Pierre Lebeau, my colleague at North Central College, first encouraged me to think about early Chicago. During the long years of work on the *Encyclopedia of Chicago,* my coeditors, Jan Reiff and Jim Grossman, supported my explorations in the history of Chicago before 1833 for our project. Through the encyclopedia, I had the opportunity to work with the late Helen Hornbeck Tanner, whose scholarship profoundly influenced me.

Many people have read and commented on the manuscript. I want to give special thanks to Fred Hoxie for his thoughtful suggestions and encouragement, as well as to Lamar Murphy, who read the whole of this at a critical early stage and then again in its final draft form. I also would like to thank all those who advised me and/or read portions of the manuscript, including Joe Bigott, Michael H. Ebner, Ellen Eslinger, Susan Gray, Suellen Hoy, Ted Karamanski, Betsy Keating, John J. Keating, Julie Martin, Walter Nugent, John Reda, Ellen Skerrett, and Alexis Smith.

I am deeply grateful, as I have been for many years, to Dennis McClendon of Chicago Cartographics, for designing the rich maps found in the following pages. I am indebted to family members who took photographs for this project: Betsy Keating, John J. Keating, and Margaret Durkin Roche. I have benefited from many conversations with John Swenson, a retired Chicago attorney who has avidly studied early Illinois history, and the late Mary Hammersmith, a longtime volunteer at the Newberry Library, who investigated the Beaubien family. I am most appreciative of the ready welcome from the Glenn Black Laboratory at Indiana University.

A special thanks to Lesley Martin at the Chicago History Museum in helping me to track down photographs of *The Fort Dearborn Massacre* monument and to Con Buckley for helping me to see the monument again. I am grateful to Tom Gill at North Central College for taking digital images of the historical photographs in this book and to Kim Butler, the North Central College archivist, for help with scanning. I also want to thank Diane Grosse at Duke University Press; Kathy Hussey-Arnston and Patrick Leahy at the Wilmette Historical Society; Kathy Atwell at the Tippecanoe County Historical Association; and Jessica Herczeg-Konecny at the Chicago History Museum for help with photographs and permissions.

I am indebted to the support of Robert Devens at the University of Chicago Press. My sincerest appreciation goes to Russell Damian, who shepherded this project from manuscript to book, and to Erin DeWitt, whose editorial suggestions much improved this work. I am also grateful to North Central College for institutional support including Summer Faculty Professional Development Grants, the Senior Faculty Enhancement Program, and Toenniges Chair funds.

As always, I have relied on the support of my family, especially my husband, John, and our children, Betsy and Jack. There are no words to express my profound gratitude to you all.

Introduction

Chicago in the Indian Country of the Western Great Lakes

When the United States declared war against Great Britain in June 1812, the hope was for a quick invasion of Canada. Instead, British forces, with the help of Indian allies, took Michilimackinac and Detroit with little fighting. Buoyed by the quick success at Michilimackinac, at least a thousand Potawatomis and their allies gathered around Fort Dearborn by early August 1812. It was an easy target, far from U.S. help and racked by internal dissension. After Captain Nathan Heald received orders to withdraw to Fort Wayne, he distributed food to the Indians but destroyed the stockpiles of alcohol and ammunition after consulting with John Kinzie, the most influential trader at Chicago.

On August 15, 1812, Captain Heald led the evacuation of 56 U.S. soldiers, 12 militia members, 9 women, and 18 children south along Lake Michigan from Fort Dearborn to Fort Wayne. Kinzie and William Wells, the former Indian agent at Fort Wayne, accompanied the group with some Miami warriors. They all came under attack by 500 Potawatomi warriors a mile and a half from the fort. In under an hour, Wells, some of his Miami escort, and 52 of 95 members of Heald's group were dead. The Potawatomi warriors claimed those still alive as prisoners of war, burned Fort Dearborn, and returned to their villages. Kinzie, with the help of Potawatomi warriors Black Partridge and Topinbee, ransomed Captain Heald and his wife, while his neighbor Archange Ouilmette protected Kinzie's stepdaughter Margaret Helm.

Within weeks U.S. officials and newspapers were reporting the battle as a massacre. The use of the word "massacre" by Americans made great sense, as it assigned blame for the event squarely at the feet of a savage enemy, neatly ignoring the fact that it was a battle lost by the United States. It turned the rout at Chicago into a rallying cry for raising support for the War of 1812, especially for recruiting volunteers for western militia units.[1]

Figure 2. Mrs. John H. (Juliette) Kinzie, after the publication of *Wau-Bun.* (Chicago History Museum, ICH, 10968)

Perhaps even more problematic, now nearly two hundred years later, most still remember it as a "massacre." It remains a potent image in Chicago's mythic past. The first star in the Chicago flag represents Fort Dearborn, and the battle in August 1812 has been memorialized many times in history and in fiction. No version is better known than Juliette M. Kinzie's 1856 reminiscence, *Wau-Bun: The "Early Day" in the North-West.*

Recounting the stories of her husband's family around August 1812, Juliette Kinzie wove a fanciful tale of intrigues, shifting loyalties, as well as personal and professional betrayals. Not surprisingly, Juliette highlighted her father-in-law, John Kinzie, and the heroic actions of her sister-in-law Margaret Helm, who was married to a young lieutenant at Fort Dearborn and was taken prisoner in the attack. At the height of the battle, Margaret remembered that "a young Indian raised his tomahawk on me. . . . I was dragged from his grasp by another and older Indian . . . Black Partridge."[2]

Helm's recollections served as the basis for the 1893 monument, *The Fort Dearborn Massacre*. Originally located near the site of the battle on Prairie Avenue at Eighteenth Street, for more than fifty years it was the first and largest image of Chicago history that visiting schoolchildren encountered at the Chicago Historical Society (now the Chicago History Museum). However, since 1998 the monument has been out of public sight and largely out of mind.[3]

Figure 3. The Fort Dearborn Massacre monument at its original site at Prairie Avenue and Eighteenth Street. (Chicago History Museum, 38949)

Figure 4. In 1931 the Chicago Historical Society (now the Chicago History Museum) installed *The Fort Dearborn Massacre* monument (without its base) in the entranceway of their new Lincoln Park building. In 1987 the historical society returned the monument, and it was installed near its original site on Prairie Avenue in 1987, only to be de-installed and placed in storage in 1998. (Chicago History Museum, ICHi-36553)

RETHINKING AUGUST 15, 1812

Today historians often breeze over 1812 as prelude to their accounts of Chicago's dramatic rise with the railroad and industrialization, much as the War of 1812 itself is marginalized in U.S. history. The August 1812 attack at Chicago is dismissed as "too remote to have a decisive effect on the outcome of the war."[4] The critical actions took place to the east, from Detroit across the Great Lakes to the St. Lawrence River. In turn, the War of 1812 was itself a side story in the nearly two decades of European fighting known as the Napoleonic Wars. During the summer of 1812, Napoleon led half a million soldiers into Russia, while French armies continued to fight against the British in Spain.[5]

Still, this Indian victory remains interesting as the only battle fought at Chicago for at least 250 years, most certainly through the whole of the time that the United States has claimed the region. Moreover, the U.S. military lost that battle badly. Hiding the monument and forgetting the episode seems self-serving to a local and national history that focuses on the successes of the United States and its political and economic systems.

The Potawatomis and their allies who fought against the United States at Chicago in August 1812 had their own motivations that were related to, but not the same as, those of the United States or Great Britain. They were fighting to reduce the influence of the United States in their country by driving the United States out entirely—or at least those settlers intent on destroying Indian Country. The Potawatomis and their allies did not see the arrival of American settlers and institutions as progress, but as catastrophe.

From this perspective, Chicago did not develop first from a resource-rich agricultural hinterland that "called forth" a great city. There were no railroads or stockyards or steel mills. Instead, Chicago emerged from the imperial rivalries of the trans-Appalachian West—at the crossroads of multiracial and multi-ethnic communities. It is not a story of the heartland, but of a time when Chicago was part of the borderland between competing colonial and tribal claims. The Chicago that emerges from this story results from a uniquely American mix of peoples and shifting circumstances, whose advantages only came into focus when American sovereignty successfully overcame alternatives like a permanent Indian Country or an extended period of British colonial rule. Chicago developed because of American conquest. It is as much a part of the narrative of manifest destiny as the vast expanses of the Great West.[6]

Over the last few decades, scholars have created a rich literature about Native Americans, borderlands, and the trans-Appalachian West. They suggest that we look at the region around Chicago not just as the Northwest Territory, but also as an Indian Country that was highly contested. The western Great Lakes during these years were, historian Andrew Cayton suggests, "the cockpit of the continent."[7]

To study Chicago in Indian Country requires, as historian Michael A. McDonnell has recently noted, an "imaginative leap of perspective" to see back to the last indigenous era in Chicago history. Taking that imaginative leap allows us to reconsider the events of August 15, 1812, as a crucial victory in

Map 1. Indian Settlement Pattern in the Chicago Region, circa 1830. Rather than an uninhabited region, the Indian Country around Chicago was an ever-changing system of villages and colonial outposts. This map is a snapshot of the region in 1830 and is based on a map by Michael Conzen and Helen Hornbeck Tanner in the *Encyclopedia of Chicago* (Dennis McClendon, Chicago Cartographics)

an attempt by local Indians to stave off American conquest and invasion and to maintain Chicago in Indian Country. To make this leap, we must begin to see the region around Chicago not as empty, uninhabited space, as portrayed in textbooks and histories, but as an ever-changing weave of native villages and colonial outposts that together made up Indian Country in and around Chicago in August 1812.[8]

To be sure, this was not yet Chicago. In fact, there were no urban places across the western Great Lakes that we would recognize today as cities. Today we purchase real estate and build permanent structures—for our homes, our work, and our institutions. We organize our lives and our world around the order of places.

The Indian Country in the western Great Lakes was dramatically different. Villages regularly relocated in the face of changing seasons and conditions. People built housing not to last for a lifetime or more, but for a season or two. Real estate was not bought and sold. Instead, the control of resources ordered society (and led to many of its conflicts).

The general absence of a permanent built landscape did not mean, however, that the Native and non-Native peoples who lived in this Indian Country did so without dense webs of relationships. In fact, Indian Country was built on deep tribal, national, personal, and trade networks. As people moved around the region, their locations changed, but their relationships were not necessarily broken. Of course, this is as true today as it was back then, but permanent places often blind us to these connections, which are indeed the real sinew that holds our urban lives together. We think of where we live and work as basic definers of ourselves. But behind these places that we can mark in the landscape are human relationships and connections, much the same as those found in the Indian Country of the western Great Lakes.

One of the imaginative leaps that we must take to understand this Indian Country is to step away from the usual kinds of questions we ask— where someone lives or works—and instead focus on the relationships that individuals cultivated over their lifetimes. Most people who lived in this Indian Country moved easily across it, forming and re-forming networks of family, trade, tribe, and visions of the future. Understanding the complex weave of these relationships is essential to understanding Indian Country.

CHICAGO IN INDIAN COUNTRY

Before the arrival of Europeans in North America, there was no such thing as Indian Country, because the whole of the continent was under Native control. The idea of Indian Country emerged to describe that territory not under the direct power of Euro-American colonies. This Indian Country evolved from the first arrival of trade goods and then Euro-Americans into a middle ground, still controlled by local Indians but influenced by Euro-American currents through the fur trade, missionary activity, and ongoing colonization.

Even before the arrival of Joliet and Marquette in this region in 1673, the fur trade had begun to shape the Indian Country in the western Great Lakes. The Iroquois Confederacy, a major partner of the Dutch and then the British in the fur trade, pushed many Algonquian tribes westward into the Great Lakes in their quest to control the available supply of beaver skins. Groups like the Potawatomis, who had lived around the St. Lawrence River, found themselves refugees on the western shore of Lake Michigan. The French offered aid from Green Bay, eventually the Iroquois threat was quelled, and the Potawatomis and their allies moved southward and eastward.

During the first half of the eighteenth century, Britain, France, and Spain vied for colonial control of the western Great Lakes, while Indian groups repopulated the area. The British influence emanated from its colonies along the Atlantic seaboard from Maine to Georgia. The French claimed a far-ranging territory that included Canada (centered at Quebec along the St. Lawrence River), Louisiana (with New Orleans as its hub), and the Illinois Country (with St. Louis established in 1764). The Spanish colonial authority was strongest in Florida and west of the Mississippi River.

In the North American theater of the Seven Years' War (1754–63), fighting radiated from the Indian Country north of the Ohio River and south of the Great Lakes. In the 1763 treaty ending that war, the French relinquished

Map 2. European Colonial Claims in North America before 1763. The European claims are overlaid on tribal spheres of influence. (Dennis McClendon, Chicago Cartographics)
Map 3. European Colonial Claims in North America after 1763. (Dennis McClendon, Chicago Cartographics)
Map 4. Euro-American Colonial Claims in North America in 1796. Based on maps by Helen Hornbeck Tanner and Miklos Pinther. (Dennis McClendon, Chicago Cartographics)

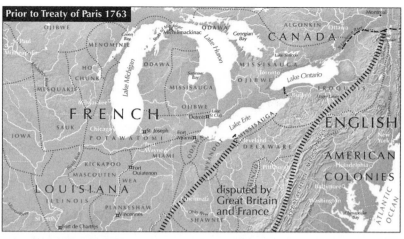

Prior to Treaty of Paris 1763

After Treaty of Paris 1763

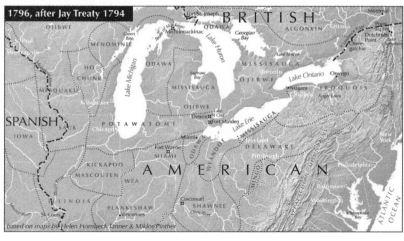

1796, after Jay Treaty 1794

based on maps by Helen Hornbeck Tanner & Miklos Pinther

all colonial claims in North America. While the French gave up these lands and withdrew their troops, many French civilians chose to remain in North America—east of the Mississippi River in territory then held by the British, or west of the Mississippi River in Spanish Louisiana.

Detroit was one of a string of forts across Ohio and the Illinois Country established by the French and turned over to the British as part of the 1763 Treaty of Paris. Other forts included Fort Edward Augustus (Green Bay), Fort Sandusky (Toledo), Fort St. Joseph (near Niles, Michigan), Fort Miami (Fort Wayne), Fort Ouiatenon (near Lafayette, Indiana), and Fort Michilimackinac. However, before the British could take control, Pontiac, an Odawa war chief, led a pan-Indian force that included Odawas (Ottawas), Potawatomis, Ojibwas (Chippewas), and Wyandots to try to expel the British as well. Pontiac was moved into action by the Delaware prophet Neolin, who called for the Indians to drive out all Euro-Americans as well as their goods and customs. While Pontiac did not win the war against the British, the British came to understand that it was best to make the Indians allies instead of a subject people in an Indian Country.[9]

THE PEOPLE OF INDIAN COUNTRY

Miamis

While the colonial story is often viewed from the perspective of the French, British, Spanish, and American occupations, Pontiac's War is a clear reminder of the peril of ignoring the perspective from Indian Country. Indian tribes swept in and out of the western Great Lakes over the eighteenth century, reshaping the pattern of settlements. By 1768 the Great Lakes had become home to many groups, from the Ho-Chunks (Winnebagos), Sauks, Illinois, and Kickapoos to the west, to the Shawnees and Delawares to the east. By then, the Miamis controlled much of what would become Ohio and Indiana.

The Miamis, along with many other Algonquian-speaking neighbors, had been pushed westward under waves of attacks by the Iroquois before 1700. The area between the Ohio River and the Great Lakes saw a dramatic population decline during these Iroquois onslaughts.

The Miamis were among the Algonquian-speaking groups who clustered in a wide circle around Green Bay until the French brokered peace with the

Figure 5. Little Turtle, longtime Miami leader. (Joseph Kirkland, *The Chicago Massacre of 1812* [1893])

Iroquois in 1701. Then the Miamis began moving slowly eastward into the Ohio River Valley.[10] This may seem counterintuitive, but the Miamis and other Algonquian-speaking groups moved east over the eighteenth century. By the 1780s, Miami villages dotted northern Indiana and western Ohio. At the same time, American expansion into western Pennsylvania, western Virginia, Kentucky, and southeastern Ohio meant that Indian refugees from those areas, especially the Shawnees and the Delawares, settled into the same lands in western Ohio as the Miamis. Delaware, Shawnee, and Miami villages soon were interspersed across the region.

Little Turtle (Meshekunnoghquoh) was born in the late 1740s at a Miami village in northeastern Indiana. He grew up during the Seven Years' War and witnessed the British wrest control of Detroit and other western outposts from the French. During the Revolutionary War, as Little Turtle came to adulthood, he showed his alliance with the British by wiping out a detachment of French soldiers set on capturing Detroit from the British. After this successful attack, Little Turtle became a war chief among the Miamis.[11]

Potawatomis, Odawas, and Ojibwas

Like the Miamis, the Potawatomis, Odawas (long identified as Ottawas), and Ojibwas (long identified as Chippewas) had been pushed into the western Great Lakes during fighting with the Iroquois in the late seventeenth century. Over the first half of the eighteenth century, they began moving eastward, planting villages across southern Michigan and trading with the French. After the withdrawal of the French from North America following the Treaty of Paris in 1763, the Potawatomis continued to trade—but now increasingly with the British and then Americans. Some of the Potawatomi converts also traveled great distances to seek out Catholic priests at Detroit, Cahokia, and St. Louis.[12]

There were at least half a dozen Potawatomi villages along the St. Joseph River and the Elkhart River inland from the southeastern shore of Lake Michigan. Each village had between ten and forty men, making for general populations of between forty and two hundred people in each. Topinbee

Figure 6. *Potawatomi Camp Scene, Crooked Creek*, painted by George Winter in late summer 1837. (Tippecanoe County Historical Association, Lafayette, Indiana)

and his half-brother, Chebanse, were the most prominent chiefs at St. Joseph. The two brothers often worked closely with Five Medals, an older chief, and Metea (Sulker), a younger warrior who rose up as an orator.[13]

While many Potawatomi warriors resisted Euro-American incursions into their region, they lived amicably among villages established by other tribes. The Potawatomis, Odawas, and Ojibwas shared control of Lake Michigan by 1800. The Ojibwa villages were primarily centered in a small arc southeast and southwest from Mackinac. The Odawa villages were primarily on the northeast side of Lake Michigan along the shore, especially at outlets of rivers. There were Odawa villages every thirty to seventy miles along the eastern shore of Lake Michigan from Mackinac to the Kalamazoo and Grand Rivers. Then the Odawas and Potawatomis shared villages south to the St. Joseph River, after which Potawatomis clustered along the southern lakeshore. The Potawatomis also had a string of villages on the western shore of Lake Michigan. Plotted about thirty to seventy miles apart (something of a mirror image of the Odawa settlements on the eastern shore), these villages extended from the Door Peninsula to the Calumet region in what is now northwest Indiana.[14]

While conflicts did occur, most of these groups lived peaceably alongside one another. The Odawas, Ojibwas, and Potawatomis shared population within many of their villages, especially along the western shore of Lake Michigan. As historian Helen Tanner has explained, Indian villages were "always composed of people from more than one tribe, even though they generally identified with only one particular tribe."[15] Because of long-standing ties to Odawas and Ojibwas, Potawatomi villages often contained members of these groups.

Shabbona was an Odawa who journeyed into Illinois on horseback as a young man with two Odawa prophets. They were promoting a nativist religion that called for the renunciation of European culture and institutions. During these travels, Shabbona married the daughter of a Potawatomi village leader, Spotka, on the Illinois River. Upon Spotka's death, Shabbona became a village chief. He was an Odawa, tied by family and career to the Potawatomis, and drawn to nativist teachings throughout all of his life.[16]

The Potawatomis also moved south and west, creating villages beside the Fox, Illinois, Kankakee, and Tippecanoe Rivers in what would become Indiana and Illinois. Essential to this extension was the widespread introduction of horses among the Potawatomis that came at the end of the Seven Years' War. Until then the Potawatomis moved on foot or used canoes across rivers and lakes. After 1763 they acquired horses in large numbers from retreating armies (both British and French). With horses, the Potawatomis began to abandon "their frail bark canoes," and few "were willing to travel in them if they had horses." Western Potawatomis began to use horses to hunt buffalo, stage Indian raids against their enemies, and establish villages at a distance from their base in southern Michigan.[17]

The area between the St. Joseph River on the eastern shore of Lake Michigan and south to the portage at the Kankakee River grew as a center for Potawatomi settlement. There were concentrations of Potawatomi villages outside Detroit along the Huron River and around the shores of Lake Michigan from the mouth of the St. Joseph River on the southeast to all along the lakeshore west and northward to Green Bay. By the early 1790s, the Potawatomis controlled eighteen million acres of land in a wide band running from Detroit across Lake Michigan to Milwaukee.

The Potawatomis expanded village by village, along the Wabash, Tippecanoe, Kankakee, Des Plaines, and Illinois Rivers, into areas that had once been home to the Illinois and other Indians. Throughout this western growth, the Potawatomis maintained the autonomy of individual villages. There was no central authority. Concerted action required cooperation among the leadership in different villages.[18]

For instance, Gomo was also among the first generation of Potawatomis who traveled on horseback to the Illinois River from St. Joseph. He built a substantial village nestled into "the timbered sections along the rivers and creeks" near present-day Peoria. Gomo's own lodge was quite substantial, "a bark building 25 by 50 feet inside, tenanting about 30 people." Scaffolds all along the walls of the lodge served as places for Gomo and his family to sit and sleep. Gomo maintained connections with Potawatomis and traders from St. Joseph years after he moved west. However, he also made new links to traders in Kaskaskia, Cahokia, and St. Louis.[19]

Ho-Chunks, Sauks, and Kickapoos

By the late eighteenth century, the Ho-Chunks (long known as the Winnebagos), were northern neighbors of the Potawatomis and shared some villages around Milwaukee. The Winnebagos had many villages in southern Wisconsin and along the Rock River in northern Illinois. They spoke a

Siouan language, which was quite distinct from the Algonquian language spoken by the Potawatomis, Odawas, and Ojibwas. In contrast to the Potawatomis, the Winnebagos did not give up their canoes for horses. One observer attributed Winnebago success in battle to the fact that "should they be attacked they can immediately embark in their canoes and go up or down a river, or into a swamp or marsh."[20]

Nearby the Winnebago villages and stretching westward across Illinois were Sauk villages. With the deep decline of the Illinois Confederacy after the Seven Years' War, the Sauks moved into an area around the Rock River and soon overlapped in territory with the Potawatomis, Winnebagos, Fox (Mesquakie), and Kickapoos. Saukenauk was their great settlement at the confluence of the Rock and Mississippi Rivers. More than a thousand Sauks gathered there in the late spring, rather than in the smaller villages favored by the Potawatomis. Of central importance to all Sauks, Saukenauk was "where they held their most important feasts and festivals, and where their dead were laid to rest on the brow of a long ridge that arose just beyond the town."[21]

Among the most notable of Sauk leaders was Black Hawk. Born in 1767, he was "an unyielding traditionalist," cherishing "the old customs and ways, never wearing white people's clothing or tasting their alcohol in any form." While supporting pan-Indian movements that offered self-determination, Black Hawk also found friendship with traders and agents who passed through his lands.[22] He was not old enough to remember Neolin's vision and Pontiac's War, but Black Hawk embraced their strong call for pan-Indian solidarity throughout his lifetime.

The Kickapoos also lived along the rivers of Illinois, generally to the south of the Sauks around the Illinois River at Peoria and the Sangamon River. Some of the Kickapoos moved eastward toward the Vermilion and Wabash Rivers in Indiana during the late eighteenth century. They spoke an Algonquian language closely related to that of the Sauks and Potawatomis. And like these tribes, the Kickapoos seized horses from Spanish, American, and French traders and settlers when the opportunity arose. With horses, they transformed their lives on the Illinois prairie.[23]

Together these groups inhabited an Indian Country in the western Great Lakes. The estimated population of the Miamis, Ojibwas, Odawas, Potawatomis, Sauks, Winnebagos, Kickapoos, and Illinois living in the western Great Lakes was around thirty thousand in 1768 (sixty thousand across the

Great Lakes more broadly). Over the following decades, Indians relocated across this region, but the general population remained about the same.[24]

It was not a static place, but one constantly changing and evolving, responding both to internal change as well as to wider colonial currents. With the American Revolution, the United States became another colonial partner in this Indian Country. However, unlike the French and British periods in the western Great Lakes, where the fur trade fostered a rich Indian Country, the American government and its settlers would challenge the existence and continuation of Indian Country.

BEFORE CHICAGO WAS CHICAGO

Set in this context, the battle of August 15, 1812, at Chicago was part of a much larger struggle for regional control that served as a victory for the Potawatomis within the wider American conquest of Indian Country. Most centrally, this book is concerned with the transfer of the western Great Lakes from Indian to American control through a combination of treaties and military conquest.[25]

In 1795, after the Greenville Treaty, Chicago was a small U.S. reserve in Indian Country. In 1804 the U.S. government completed Fort Dearborn as an outpost at the mouth of the Chicago River. For years it was an island in Indian Country, but during the War of 1812, Potawatomi warriors tried to push the United States from the region. While the western Indians won the battle at Chicago in August 1812, they lost the wider war when the British abandoned them to negotiate on their own with the United States.

Between 1815 and 1833, the Potawatomis ceded all of their lands, some five million acres, to the United States. They accepted reservation lands in U.S. territory, while only forty years before the U.S. government had sought outposts in Indian Country. In 1795 the Greenville Treaty reflected a sense that "two peoples could inhabit America as neighbors." The 1833 Chicago Treaty replaced that vision with the idea that "everyone was better off with a lot of distance between them."[26]

In retrospect, this story seems inevitable, as the United States would eventually become a continental empire. However, this was not at all certain at the time, either to the people living within this Indian Country or to the American farmers heading west. What was evident was that the region could not accommodate both the visions of American settlers and that of

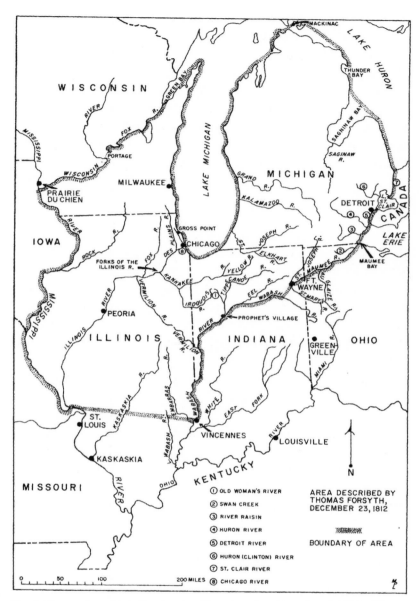

Map 5. Thomas Forsyth's Indian Country, December 1812. (From Dorothy Libby, "Thomas Forsyth to William Clark, St. Louis, December 23, 1812," *Ethnohistory* 8, no. 2 [Spring 1961].)

the Potawatomis and their allies. American settlers wanted the U.S. government to divest the Indians of their land as quickly as possible. At the other extreme were strident Indian nationalists (nativists) who sought to expel all Euro-Americans and Euro-American influences from the region.[27]

Whether Potawatomi warrior, métis trader, or U.S. soldier, the fact was that most people at Chicago on August 15, 1812, envisioned a future somewhere in between. Most Potawatomi warriors saw the value in American trade items, especially ammunition, blankets, pots, and whiskey. Métis traders wanted to provide those goods. Even U.S. soldiers understood that their jobs were rooted in the continued existence of Indian Country. There would be no need for them in a territory exclusively held by American settlers.

John Kinzie was part of a majority at Chicago who wished to see Indian Country maintained. He seldom made decisions based on ideology or national allegiance, but instead calculated what was best to preserve the Indian Country that was his home. His skills and his way of life stood in stark contrast to American settlers who staked a claim to land and continued the westward push of contiguous settlement from the Atlantic coast. Kinzie moved across a wide region, developing a trading network with his half-brother Thomas Forsyth (across what is today Michigan, Wisconsin, Illinois, Indiana, western Ohio, and Ontario). Forsyth described this region, their home, simply as "the Country":

> From the mouth of the Illinois River across the Country to Vincennes, thence up the Wabash to Fort Wayne, down the Miami of the lakes [Maumee River] to its mouth, along Lake Erie to Detroit, thence up Detroit River, through Lake and River St. Clair to Lake Huron, thence along the West side of said Lake to Makinaw [Mackinac] from thence along the East-side of Lake Michigan to Chicago, and thence along the West-side of said Lake to Green Bay, up Fox River to the Portage into the Ouisconsin [Wisconsin] River, thence down said River to its mouth; thence down the Mississippi River to the Mouth of the Illinois River, the place of beginning.[28]

Neither Forsyth nor Kinzie were much concerned with who held colonial control. They cared primarily that the colonial power would protect Indian Country.

PART ONE

The United States
and the Indian Country
of the Western
Great Lakes

1 John Kinzie and the Traders in the Indian Country of the Western Great Lakes, 1763–1812

John Kinzie was born in 1763 in Quebec at one of the most significant moments in American colonial history. He would grow up in a world turned upside down by 1763, as new alliances and opportunities emerged in British colonial territory resting uneasily on an Indian Country. His mother, Emily (Anne) Tyne, came to North America as the wife of a British army chaplain, William Haliburton, and mother (or mother-to-be) of an infant daughter, Alice. They were part of the first British force to occupy Quebec after the impressive victory of General James Wolfe over the Marquis de Montcalm in September 1759. While British troops secured their hold on New France in 1760 by capturing Montreal, Kinzie's mother dealt with the death of her first husband. Alone in a war-besieged land, Emily married a surgeon in the British army in 1861, and John Kinzie was born two years later. The senior John Kinzie (Kenzie) died soon after his son's birth. Emily Kinzie, with two small children, had little choice but to seek out a third husband.[1]

John's mother, widowed twice, married William Forsyth Sr. in 1765. Forsyth was a widower with four young sons (William Jr., Philip, Robert, and George) who had served in the British military and worked in the fur trade. Their blended family included Kinzie and his half-sister, Alice Haliburton, a half-brother, Thomas, born in 1771, and his stepfather's four older sons.[2]

Initially, the family lived in New York City, where John Kinzie and two of his stepbrothers attended school. By 1768, however, the family had moved to Detroit, where William Forsyth purchased a tavern next to the fort and set up a thriving business selling liquor and other goods to the hundred-odd British soldiers stationed there. Forsyth and his sons constructed a ball field adjacent to their inn to draw in even more business.

Living at Detroit, the teenage Kinzie was not affected much by the Revolutionary War (1776–83), which was a distant distraction. Detroit, with about three hundred residents, was a British stronghold, "the very center of British military and governmental power in the western country." As well, Detroit was important to the fur trade in the Indian Country to the west. Traders traveled to Indian villages, but Indians also came to Detroit, where British gifts solidified their colonial hold on the region.[3]

John Kinzie, seeking to make his way in this world, apprenticed with a silversmith, learning a craft in demand both by British colonists and in the fur trade. Silversmiths made buckles, cups, and other silver items for Euro-American families, as well as reworking silver pieces made in other colonies or in Europe. They also made silver ornaments and trinkets for the fur trade.[4] By 1785 the twenty-two-year-old Kinzie was making wristbands, large crosses, armbands, and broaches to Indian tastes, as well as repairing silverwork for leading Detroit families.[5]

Kinzie's skills as a silversmith helped him develop relationships with Indian traders and agents, some of whom he probably met as a youth at the Forsyth tavern.[6] He made connections with some of the most prominent British traders in town, including Alexander McKee (the British Indian agent), John Hay (deputy Indian agent), Matthew Elliott, and Simon Girty. These men had left western Pennsylvania during the Revolution as Loyalists, and Kinzie allied himself deliberately with them.[7]

Kinzie could have stayed at Detroit, but his opportunities were limited—the fur trade drew him into Indian Country. The people he would meet along the way shaped his understanding of Indian Country and his place in it.

TRADERS IN THE INDIAN COUNTRY

John Kinzie did not move into an undifferentiated wilderness. The core of the Indian Country in the western Great Lakes was a dense, ever-changing system of tribal villages. Also, several networks of non-Native places including administrative, military, and trade centers operated within (or adjacent to) Indian Country during the colonial period.

In a traditional view of the "wilderness" of the American frontier, there was little room for the systems of villages and towns that served the disparate peoples of the Indian Country of the western Great Lakes. According to this imagined view of the past, only as Americans moved westward were there urban or proto-urban settlements. As historian Richard C. Wade writes, places like Pittsburgh, Lexington, Cincinnati, Louisville, and St. Louis were "planted far in advance of the line of settlement and they held the West for the approaching population . . . through the wilderness." Wade persuasively argues for a central role for cities in the frontier. However, he ignores the networks of Native and non-Native places that made up Indian Country well before the arrival of American settlers on the scene.[8]

There was, in fact, a broad range of settlements across the region well in advance of any Americans. Most villages were small, comprising just four or five extended families, but a few reached substantial size. Saukenauk, the summer town of the Sauks along the Mississippi, had a population of over a thousand. To the south along the river, Kaskaskia, long the French administrative center for the Illinois Country, also had a population of over two thousand by 1750. These networks of Native and non-Native villages and outposts ebbed and flowed with the seasons and over time, but remained a vital part of Indian Country.

Over the first half of the eighteenth century, the French established colonial administrative and trade centers in Quebec, Louisiana, and Illinois Country. Forts at Detroit, St. Joseph, Michilimackinac, Ouiatenon, and Vincennes, as well as Fort Chartres and Fort Miami, anchored the French colonial presence in the region between Quebec and Louisiana. Kaskaskia and later St. Louis became important centers along the Mississippi River, connecting the region to New Orleans, while Detroit became the northeast entrepôt, with connections to Montreal and Quebec.

After 1763 the British took nominal control of these administrative and trade centers in Quebec and Illinois, while the Spanish gained colonial control over New Orleans and St. Louis. The British also took over the former French forts across the western Indian Country, eventually abandoning St. Joseph, Ouiatenon, and Fort Chartres. Like the French before them, fewer than a hundred British soldiers staffed the smaller forts, while Detroit grew into several hundred residents.

As well as these deliberately planted colonial settlements, there were dozens of trading posts founded by French, British, and American traders across the western Great Lakes. Without a doubt, the fur trade led most non-Native people into Indian Country.

The fur trade had been an integral part of the western Great Lakes for more than a century. French traders traveled to Indian villages and sold their goods in exchange for beaver, otter, bear, and deerskins. The fur trade brought cloth, blankets, guns, iron implements, and alcohol to Indian tribes. These goods were both utilitarian and ceremonial: they were immediately useful to everyday life, but they also cemented a ceremonial relationship with newcomers.[9]

French traders sought out Indian women as their wives because their ties to specific Indian villages and tribes were strengthened through marriage to local women. And these Indian women brought their skills as cooks, guides, herbal physicians, farmers, and household managers.[10] The mixed-race children of these traders and their Indian wives were known as métis. The métis population grew with the fur trade, where their intermediary role gave them possible advantages over both their Indian and European counterparts. Métis women generally either married other métis men in a village or married incoming Euro-American traders.

Métis played a critical role in the Great Lakes fur trade. While some traders moved into their wife's Indian village, others established separate settlements that were distinct from those of either their Indian or Euro-American neighbors. Their buildings were often a composite of Indian and French styles, set in a rambling style in contrast to the rectangular grids of the European towns. Land ownership was not significant, with land titles rare in métis villages. Many métis families adhered to Roman Catholicism, but it evolved more as a house religion than a congregational one by the late eighteenth century.[11]

Dress, language, and food reflected the melding of two distinctive cultural traditions. Métis wore a combination of European and Indian styles that could include the blue pantaloons and capote of their French forebears, coupled with moccasins and feathers drawn from their Indian heritage. Most métis children became fluent in French as well as the Algonquian language of their mothers. Young métis women learned to farm, but the methods and crops reflected both Indian and European traditions. French plows, wheat, and dairy cows were found alongside fields of corn, squash, and beans.

French fur traders continued to trade in the expanding territory of the Potawatomis and their allies long after the official exit of France in 1763. However, British traders also began to make their way to Potawatomi villages, vying for trade that had once been almost exclusively in French

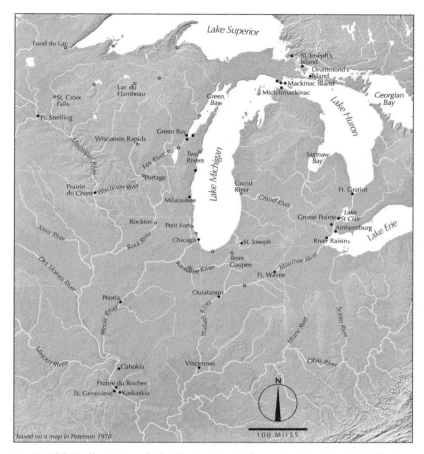

Map 6. Métis Trading Centers in the Western Great Lakes, 1763–1830. (Dennis McClendon, Chicago Cartographics, based on information from Jacqueline Peterson "Prelude to Red River: A Social Portrait of the Great Lakes Metis," *Ethnohistory* 25, no. 1 [Winter 1978]: 44.)

hands. After the American Revolution, American traders joined into the mix, in a trade conducted in various Algonquian dialects, French, and English. Those with facility in all these languages had the greatest access across Potawatomi country.

By the 1780s, some two dozen villages along the upper Great Lakes and the rivers that fed into them served as centers for the fur trade, including Milwaukee, Peoria, St. Joseph, Chicago, Kekionga, River Raisin, and Sault Sainte Marie. These settlements were near Indian villages but were not

Indian villages. They were also closely tied to the larger trading outposts at Michilimackinac, Detroit, and Vincennes, but were not so tightly under colonial administration.[12]

French, British, and American traders continued to move into Indian Country to seek their fortunes. They gravitated to established fur-trading outposts in the western Great Lakes. Among them was John Kinzie, who would tie his fortune to Indian Country. Kinzie was closely associated with three fur-trading outposts during his career: Kekionga, St. Joseph, and Chicago. As he moved to each of these places, his life would become intertwined not only with local Indians, but also with other traders, most especially with William Burnett and Jean Baptiste Point de Sable.

KEKIONGA

John Kinzie began trading south of Detroit at Kekionga in partnership with John Clark. Kekionga was a political and military outpost in the Indian Country in the western Great Lakes. There were at least six Shawnee, Delaware, Potawatomi, and Miami villages in the vicinity. The Delawares and Shawnees living near Kekionga were refugees from the expansion of the new United States into the trans-Appalachian West as American settlers moved into Kentucky and southern Ohio. The Shawnees, Delawares, and Miamis attacked American farmsteads in the hopes of stanching further migration. Their raiding parties destroyed farms, killed settlers, and took others captive, all with the hope of driving Americans back east.[13]

While Kinzie was far from most of this fighting, he traded with Shawnee, Miami, and Delaware villages that included young American captives who had been taken as children and raised as members of Indian families. Kinzie no doubt encountered these captives, particularly in the Shawnee and Delaware villages in which he traded. One of these captives was Margaret McKenzie.

Over a decade before, while Margaret's father was away from their western Virginia farm, a Shawnee war party killed her mother and younger siblings, and took Margaret and her sister Elizabeth as captives. Both sisters grew up together among the Shawnees, and they met John Kinzie and his partner John Clark while they traded at Kekionga. The partners set up households with the sisters, affording them close connections within the Shawnee villages. Kinzie fathered three children (William, Elizabeth, and

James) with Margaret McKenzie between 1788 and 1793. They made a life in Indian Country, where their neighbors included other British traders, but also Shawnee, Delaware, Potawatomi, and Miami villagers.

Little Turtle lived almost all of his life just to the west of Kekionga. While his village had traded with the French for generations, his family shifted their allegiance to the British before the Seven Years' War. During the Revolutionary War, as Little Turtle came to adulthood, he fought alongside the British against the Americans and became a war chief. Little Turtle watched with trepidation as American settlers poured into western Pennsylvania, western Virginia, Kentucky, and southeastern Ohio. Shawnee and Delaware refugees from these areas settled into villages nearby Little Turtle's village, and the British established Kekionga as a trading outpost in this increasingly dense and heterogeneous Indian Country. Like Kinzie, Little Turtle maintained his alliance with the British as he raised a family that included his daughter Sweet Breeze. He no doubt knew Kinzie and perhaps traded with him, although Kinzie had stronger ties to the Shawnees than to the Miamis around Kekionga.

ST. JOSEPH

To the northwest of Kekionga, St. Joseph flourished near the eastern shore of Lake Michigan. The French established a fort and Catholic mission in the area, drawing people to the area. When they relinquished the fort in 1761, Pontiac and his allies took it until the British negotiated for control. For the next two decades, the British held the fort, while the remaining French traders prospered in trade with area Potawatomi villages. After the American Revolution, the British abandoned the fort—leaving the region to Potawatomi villagers and their traders.

Kakima was a Potawatomi woman born near the St. Joseph River around 1763, the year of John Kinzie's birth and the year that Pontiac's forces attacked nearby Fort St. Joseph. She was the sister of two Potawatomi leaders, Topinbee and Chebanse. Her parents brought her to Detroit for a Catholic baptism as an infant, as the mission was abandoned when the French left the region. As a result of generations of trade, Kakima no longer wore traditional Potawatomi clothing. Instead, she dressed in purchased cloth, decorated with trade ornaments.[14]

Kakima's marriage to an American trader, William Burnett, in 1782 continued a long tradition among the St. Joseph Potawatomis where Indian women married traders. The couple traveled to Detroit to have their marriage performed by a Catholic priest, and they would later bring their children there to be baptized. Their household developed into a burgeoning trading outpost with a large house, a barn, storehouses, a blacksmith shop, and a bakery.

In addition to managing their trade while Burnett was away, Kakima was responsible for the successful farming operation. Like most Potawatomi women, she was a skilled horticulturalist. She cultivated fields of corn and wheat, as well as apple, peach, quince, and cherry orchards. Kakima also packed maple syrup in tradable baskets (*mokucks*). The farm surplus was often a substantial part of the trade goods that Burnett offered. For instance, in 1791 Burnett had "a great deal of corn" for sale, enough to fill three canoes (of a size that required three men in each). With their profits from farming, Burnett financed "adventures": a canoe loaded with goods that traders took to distant Indian villages. The monies from their agricultural surplus also paid for better equipment, such as a light French plow that Kakima could use, as well as for items like tea and salt.

While Burnett was clearly a shrewd trader, he relied heavily on Kakima's family connections. In turn, her extended family came to rely on Burnett's business associates to get the goods and services that they needed. She had many brothers and sisters, uncles, aunts, and cousins in the vicinity, which provided a ready market for their trade goods. In February 1790, when Burnett arrived back at St. Joseph from his winter post along the Kankakee River, he found that Kakima, "his Indian woman," had "done on her part in the trading very, very well."[15]

CHICAGO

Kakima's husband, William Burnett, turned increasingly westward in his trading "adventures," following the Potawatomis as they moved southwest of Lake Michigan. Chicago became a strategic point for trade, linking the St. Joseph Potawatomis to their relatives moving west into the Illinois River valley.

Jean Baptiste Point de Sable was part of Burnett's successful trading enterprises. He was one of the few persons of African descent who were

Figure 7. There is no image of Jean Baptiste Point de Sable from his lifetime, but this recent bust builds on available descriptions. It is located adjacent to the northeast corner pylon of the Michigan Avenue Bridge in Pioneer Court. (Margaret Durkin Roche)

not enslaved. Point de Sable was a French-speaking, mixed-race, practicing Catholic who married an Indian woman and traded around Lake Michigan for nearly thirty years.

While there continues to be controversy about Point de Sable's origins, evidence suggests that he was born before 1746 in or near Kaskaskia, a French settlement along the Illinois River. Kaskaskia was among the first French outposts, settled in 1703, with an economy that rested on trade and farming the rich bottomlands. Surplus wheat and other agricultural staples were sold into the Louisiana colony, while furs and hides were shipped north to Canada. Enslaved Africans were among the trade goods sent back north on the Mississippi River. By 1750 Kaskaskia had 1,000 French residents, 300 black slaves, 60 Indian slaves, and 800 Kaskaskia Indians living in nearby villages.[16]

Among the French residents was Jean Jacques Brunet dit Bourbonnais, who was born in 1673 in Montreal. He was a successful trader who married French immigrant Elisabeth Deshayes. The couple held as slaves a woman named Catherine and her son Jean. In 1746 they successfully petitioned the French colonial government for permission to emancipate Catherine and her son upon their deaths. It is quite possible that Catherine's son was in fact Jean Baptiste Point de Sable. He bore the same first name, was the right age, long maintained connections in Kaskaskia, and was later described as a free black man.[17]

Regardless of his early history, Point de Sable found a career in the fur trade after the Seven Years' War, when Frenchmen still controlled many of the key outposts despite the transfer of imperial control to the British. As a young man, he began trading with partners who had connections in Montreal, Kaskaskia, and Cahokia. Point de Sable traded at Michigan City (at the southernmost part of the eastern shore of Lake Michigan) during the American Revolution. Accused of being an American sympathizer, he was arrested in 1779 by the British commander at Mackinac, along with other French traders around Lake Michigan. Within a year, though, that same British officer had appointed Point de Sable as the manager of a British post north of Detroit (the Pinery).

Point de Sable established a métis family with his marriage to Catherine (Kittihawa, who may have been Potawatomi). By 1788 they had a home and trading outpost at Chicago. Jean Baptiste and Catherine Point de Sable lived at Chicago with their children, Suzanne and Jean. Suzanne married a trader, Jean Baptiste Pelletier, in 1790. They solemnized their marriage at the Catholic Church in Cahokia and returned there for the baptism of their daughter, Eulalie Marie.

The family made significant improvements at Chicago over the dozen years they lived there. They built a one-and-a-half-story French-style house on the north bank of the Chicago River. The house had a long piazza, an entrance hall, and two rooms on either side. Among their possessions inside the house were four glass doors, eleven copper kettles, and a French walnut cabinet. None were manufactured locally, and the glass in particular was brought to Chicago with great difficulty. The glass doors must have been particularly prized because they offered some protection from the sand that blew over everything. A later account described how "there was sand here, there, and every where."[18]

The house anchored a complex of buildings that included those related to a substantial farm: two barns, a bake house, a poultry house, a smoke-house, a blacksmith shop, and outhouses. There were also storehouses for furs and trade goods. Inside these buildings, the family accumulated farm equipment, including carts, plows, scythes, and sickles. They ran a thriving, well-equipped farm and raised dozens of cattle, hogs, and hens. The number of livestock suggests that the operation went beyond self-sufficiency to market production, not unlike the Burnett household at St. Joseph.

The métis outpost at Chicago grew beyond Point de Sable and his family. Antoine and Archange Ouilmette, François and Marie Therese Le Mai, and Louis and Angelique Pettell were among the other métis couples who came to Chicago in the 1790s. Chicago was a small but thriving métis outpost.

Living next door to Catherine and Jean Point de Sable were Archange and Antoine Ouilmette. Antoine was born near Montreal in 1760 in the midst of the Seven Years' War, so it is not surprising that he sought his fortune in the West.[19] Ouilmette claimed to have come to Chicago in 1790 as a voyageur, a manual laborer in the fur trade. Voyageurs paddled the canoes, portaged the supplies, and loaded/unloaded packs. They served under a clerk or licensed independent trader. After settling at Chicago, Ouilmette continued the often-backbreaking work of transporting travelers and their baggage across the Chicago portage (linking the south branch of the Chicago River to the Des Plaines River through an area known as Mud Lake). Later accounts stated that Ouilmette was a fair man who did not cheat travelers, but he was illiterate, which would have been a serious impediment to his working as an independent trader.[20]

In 1796 Antoine formed a métis household with his marriage to Archange Marie Chevalier, a French-Potawatomi woman then living in the Calumet region with her parents, François and Marianne Chevalier. The Chevalier family was one of the most powerful métis families in the Great Lakes fur trade in the mid-eighteenth century, and Ouilmette tied himself to an extensive kin network. They would have eight children over the course of their long marriage.[21]

Over John Kinzie's life, he would live at Kekionga, St. Joseph, and Chicago as his career took him westward. Each of these trading outposts flourished in the 1780s and 1790s in the western Great Lakes. The destruction of

Kekionga is a reminder that these trading outposts were also flashpoints for violence in Indian Country, places where the interests of many groups intersected. The respective British, American, and French roots of John Kinzie, William Burnett, and Jean Baptiste Point de Sable show the wide range of men involved in the fur trade. Their strategic marriages point to the importance of family connections to success as a fur trader in this era.

2 The Greenville Treaty and the American Era, 1789–1800

The 1783 Treaty of Paris that ended the American Revolution had little immediate effect in the western Great Lakes. While the United States claimed most of this territory, the British did not relinquish control of their northwestern forts, including those at Detroit and Michilimackinac. For most Potawatomi villagers and traders like John Kinzie, William Burnett, and Jean Baptiste Point de Sable, life continued as before.

However, the transition to an American era threatened the continuation of this region as an Indian Country. The Confederation Congress had taken up the question of relations with western Indians in the 1787 Northwest Ordinance. There the new nation presented a conciliatory tone to Indians, promising: "The utmost good faith shall always be observed towards the Indians, their lands and property shall never be taken from them without their consent." While ostensibly seeking common ground, the ordinance assumed that the U.S. government would be acquiring Indian land and turning it into real estate. To do so would replace the diverse mix of Native and non-Native settlements that constituted the Indian Country with American farmers and settlers.[1]

President George Washington fully supported this transformation. By 1790 there were 73,000 non-native settlers in Kentucky, 121,000 in western New York, 92,000 in western Pennsylvania, and another 36,000 in western Virginia.[2] Under Washington's administration, Kentucky was admitted as the first state west of the Appalachian Mountains. Despite Indian attacks on white settlements, the populations continued to expand into territory north of the Ohio River. These settlers demanded that the U.S. government protect their interests. President Washington helped to organize a U.S. Army whose purpose was to protect the rights of American settlers as much as to maintain peace. Among those who moved across the Appalachian Mountains were Virginians who had served in the Continental army under General Washington: Hayden Wells, William Pope, and William Oldham.

WILLIAM WELLS

Hayden Wells and his family were among a vanguard of American families who showed their independence from Great Britain by moving west into Kentucky. The Declaration of Independence included a complaint that the king "endeavored to bring on the inhabitants of our frontiers the merciless

Figure 8. Miniature portrait of William Wells. (Chicago History Museum, ICHi-14160)

Indian savages."[3] During the Revolutionary War, the Wells family and thousands of others moved into what had been territory reserved by the British as Indian Country. William Wells, born in 1770, was among the youngest members of the family to move into Kentucky.

The Revolutionary War followed the families westward. George Rogers Clark, the American commander in the West, established a military post at Louisville as a base of operations for his military assault on the British in 1778. William Wells's brother Samuel served with George Rogers Clark in 1780 and 1782. Their father, Hayden, was killed while serving with a militia unit that fought off a British incursion south across the Ohio River into Kentucky in 1781.[4]

In 1784, three years after the death of his father, fourteen-year-old William was abducted by a Miami war party while he played near the Ohio River. He became one of the many captives taken in the ongoing skirmishing between Indians and American settlers moving into their lands. William was taken to a Miami town about 150 miles southwest of Little Turtle's village. Like Margaret McKenzie, his captors treated young Wells as their own child. The village chief adopted Wells and gave him the name Apekonit, "wild carrot," because of his red hair. Soon Apekonit was serving as a decoy in war parties on the Ohio River, luring American travelers by his fair skin and red hair. Wells's birth family tried to ransom him back, but he chose to return to his Miami home, where he married and fought alongside the western Indians against U.S. settlers and soldiers.[5]

WESTERN WAR

When the American government sought cessions from Indians in Ohio in 1788 and 1789, they hoped to obtain more land for American settlers by reducing the extent of Indian Country. Warriors from the Miami villages of Little Turtle and his allies saw little reason to cede their lands to the U.S. government. With negotiations stalled, the U.S. Army began building a line of forts, beginning in 1790 at Fort Washington (now Cincinnati) on the Ohio River, directly south from the Miami towns where Little Turtle, William Wells, and John Kinzie lived.

From the base of these forts, U.S. general Joseph Harmar attacked Kekionga and other neighboring villages. Little Turtle and his allies learned of his plans, and Harmar arrived at the abandoned villages, where he burned

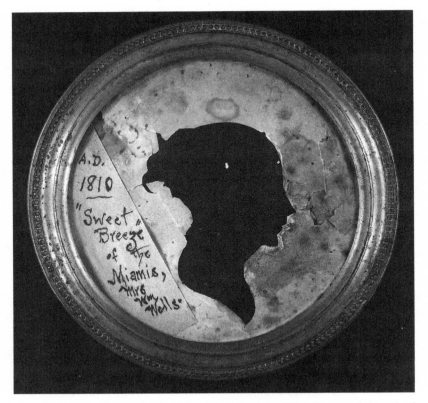

Figure 9. Sweet Breeze was the daughter of the Miami chief Little Turtle and the wife of William Wells. (Chicago History Museum, ICHi-12872)

three hundred houses and twenty thousand bushels of corn.[6] Harmar's troops destroyed Kinzie's home at Kekionga, although his family was able to flee to safety. Along with other British traders, Kinzie rebuilt his home about thirty miles northwest at Au Glaize.

William Wells was also homeless, after U.S. troops destroyed his village on the Wabash. The Americans took his Miami wife and child captive, and Wells became a refugee in Little Turtle's village. Soon after arriving in Turtletown, while his first wife remained a U.S. captive, Wells married Little Turtle's daughter Sweet Breeze and began another family in the midst of war.

Little Turtle successfully organized a confederation of warriors drawn from across the region to respond to these attacks. Alongside his Miamis were Potawatomi warriors like Black Partridge. They sought to repel the American advance and maintain their Indian Country. In November 1791, in a battle without a familiar name (perhaps because it was so devastating to the new U.S. Army), the American forces suffered a great defeat. Wells fought alongside Little Turtle and his confederation in this victory over General Arthur St. Clair's forces where six hundred U.S. soldiers lost their lives. Unbeknownst to Wells, his brother Samuel was a member of the Kentucky militia also fighting in the battle.

After the late 1791 victory, Wells tried to ransom back his first wife and child. He must have been filled with contradictory impulses. He had two wives (a child with one and a child on the way with the other), one an American captive and the other in the path of the American troops. He had fought alongside Little Turtle and other Miami warriors, but also against his brother. While he had traveled south away from his second wife, Sweet Breeze, to try to ransom his first wife and child, he detoured to Louisville to visit his brother.

While in Louisville, Wells chose to give up "his Indian life." However, his next step was to go to Cincinnati, where his first wife was held. In the course of negotiations, U.S. officers realized the considerable knowledge and skills that Wells possessed. In exchange for the release of his wife and child, Wells agreed to serve as a U.S. interpreter and representative.[7]

The U.S. Army worked hard to recoup the damaging loss at Little Turtle's hands in November 1791. The Department of War expanded the size and training of the army in order to be better prepared for battle. They also sought better intelligence about Indian plans. During the fall of 1793, General Anthony Wayne offered Wells the command of a U.S. scouting company, as he prepared for an attack on Turtletown, Kekionga, Au Glaize, and other villages in the Maumee Valley. Wells offered his insights as well as collecting intelligence. Among those who provided Wells with information on the British was a young John Kinzie.

In contrast to 1791, when Little Turtle actively recruited warriors and led them into battle, he advised against fighting a U.S. force of over three thousand regular troops, scouts, and Kentucky militia: "We have beaten the enemy twice under different commanders. We cannot expect the same good fortune to attend us always . . . it would be prudent to listen to his offers of peace."[8] Instead, in 1794 the Shawnee Blue Jacket led two thousand warriors to defeat at Fallen Timbers in a battle that lasted only an hour in the shadow of the British Fort Miami. In a crushing blow, the British troops closed the gates of the fort as the Indians retreated, refusing them any aid. John Kinzie, along with many other British traders, found his home destroyed for a second time in three years. Just months later, at the 1795 Treaty of Greenville, the United States government would press for land cessions that cut deeply into the Indian Country around Kekionga and began a transformation of the trading world that had dominated this region for more than a century.

LITTLE TURTLE AND THE GREENVILLE TREATY

After the U.S. victory at Fallen Timbers, General Wayne negotiated with western Indians from a position of strength. In August 1795 Wayne headed a U.S. delegation that met with members of the Miamis, Wyandots (Hurons), Delawares, Odawas, Ojibwas, Weas, Piankashaws, Kaskaskias, Kickapoos, Shawnees, and Potawatomis at Greenville, Ohio. These same tribes had together held the territory north of the Ohio River since halting Iroquois expansion with French help in 1701. Now they faced the prospect of making cessions that would turn over most of Ohio and southeast Indiana.

Western Indians continued to look to the British for support. Not until 1796, under the terms of the Jay Treaty, did the British finally evacuate western forts, including Detroit and Michilimackinac. While Great Britain established new forts at St. Joseph Island (near Mackinac) and at Malden (near Detroit), the Jay Treaty signaled a tighter control of the region by the United States.[9]

It is no wonder that there was considerable debate among the leadership of the western Indian Confederacy about signing the Greenville Treaty. While the U.S. government demanded large cessions, they agreed to "relinquish their claims to all other Indian lands, northward of the river Ohio, eastward of the Mississippi, and westward and southward of the Great Lakes, and the waters uniting them."[10] To some, it seemed that the United States was affirming a permanent Indian Country. But others were not so sanguine. They understood that the 1787 Northwest Ordinance proffered a different vision for the future where there would eventually be no Indian Country. Those Indian leaders who held this view saw Greenville not as a final solution, but only a first step toward total divestiture of their lands.

Regardless of their understanding of the future, General Wayne de-

Figure 10. A 1795 painting depicting the "Indian Treaty of Greenville." The artist was believed to be an officer in General Anthony Wayne's staff. (Chicago History Museum, ICHi-64806)

manded what are now the eastern and southern sections of Ohio, as well as an area around Vincennes (now in southeastern Indiana). Wayne also negotiated for sixteen other reservations in Indian Country that could be used for military purposes, including a tract at the mouth of the Chicago River.

While the immediate terms of the U.S. government were straightforward, the negotiations surrounding the treaty were complicated by dissension among Indian leaders, villages, and tribes who did not agree what land was theirs to cede.[11]

With William Wells as Wayne's interpreter, Little Turtle became a principal Indian voice in the negotiations, which revolved around which group owned what land (thus determining which groups received the most annuities). Perhaps not surprisingly, Little Turtle emerged in a privileged position with the United States and the object of considerable envy among his peers.[12]

After negotiating the Greenville Treaty, Little Turtle and William Wells made two trips to Philadelphia to secure further support among Americans, including President George Washington and President John Adams. Philadelphia served as the temporary capital and was the country's largest city, with forty-five thousand people, and here they were embraced as celebrities. Little Turtle was inoculated for smallpox by Benjamin Rush, sat for a portrait by Gilbert Stuart (destroyed by the British in 1814), and met Revolutionary War hero Thaddeus Kosciusko, who honored Little Turtle with a set of his pistols.[13]

While Little Turtle was feted, Wells was rewarded. In addition to a U.S. pension for his service at Fallen Timbers, President Adams appointed Wells as interpreter and deputy Indian agent in the Northwest Territory. Both men were seen as critical to the success of the United States in the West.[14] Little Turtle and Wells returned home with the continuing hope that the Greenville Treaty would provide a framework for good relations with the U.S. government.

THE POTAWATOMIS AND THE GREENVILLE TREATY

Greenville presented to the Potawatomis, especially those at St. Joseph, an opportunity to reach a peace with the United States. Twenty-three Potawatomis signed the Greenville Treaty—including Gomo, Siggenauk, Black Partridge, Topinbee, and Five Medals—who saw it as a template for future relations with the United States. Like Little Turtle and William Wells, they understood that change was coming. These warriors hoped that settling a boundary line with the United States would resolve relations with the Americans well into the future.

Aside from the tract of land six miles square at the mouth of the Chicago River and others at Vincennes, Ouiatenon, and Fort Wayne, the Potawatomis were not asked to give up any territory. Nonetheless, they began receiving annuity payments from the U.S. government for their recognition of American sovereignty. The money flowed in, providing Potawatomi villages with extra goods (including a considerable amount of alcohol). The Potawatomi leaders who had signed the Greenville Treaty seemed to have struck a good bargain with the Americans—only a few tracts of land in exchange for considerable annuities.

There remained, however, groups of Potawatomi warriors who were strongly anti-American, while others simply sought to avoid contact or confrontation with this new imperial power. Especially after Greenville, established Potawatomi leaders at St. Joseph encouraged disaffected young men to move west and start their own villages. Young warriors who found they could not become chiefs at St. Joseph "[flew] to the woods" and created new villages in what would become northern Indiana and Illinois.[15] Such migration reduced tension within the St. Joseph villages themselves while at the same time moving a younger generation westward (and hopefully beyond the reach of American incursions).

Main Poc was one of those troublesome young men. He was born in a St. Joseph village during the 1760s (around the same time as John Kinzie) without a thumb or fingers on his left hand. While this might seem quite a disability in a world where men became hunters and warriors, Main Poc embraced his deformed left hand as a "special sign of favor from the Great Spirit" and emerged as a shaman who was a *wabeno*, or "firehandler."[16]

While growing up at St. Joseph, Main Poc trained as a hunter and a warrior. He fought against the Americans at Fallen Timbers and was outraged when an older generation of Potawatomi leaders signed the Greenville Treaty. He was among those militant young warriors who established villages along the Wabash, Kankakee, and Illinois Rivers. Nuscotomeg and his brother White Sturgeon (Wabinewa) joined Main Poc, establishing villages along the Kankakee that became centers of anti-American activity.[17]

Main Poc also found allies among the Potawatomis at Milwaukee and in the Calumet region to the north and south of Chicago along Lake Michigan. About sixty miles west of St. Joseph by horseback, the long, meandering Little Calumet River paralleled the southern shore of Lake Michigan adjacent to three smaller lakes, the largest named Lake Calumet. Campignan, who aligned with the British, headed one Potawatomi village on Lake Calumet. Another Potawatomi warrior at Calumet was Naunongee. His daughter Marianne married François Chevalier, and his granddaughter Archange married another French trader, Antoine Ouilmette, and was living at Chicago by 1796. Both Campignan and Naunongee opposed American expansion into the region.[18] At Milwaukee, the younger Siggenauk (Blackbird) rejected his father's alliance with the United States. Instead, the young warrior joined Main Poc in raiding against the Osages and American settlements in southern Illinois.[19]

The Spanish at St. Louis who controlled the Louisiana Territory encouraged Potawatomi warriors like Blackbird and Main Poc to attack the Osages, with whom they were both embroiled in an ongoing border war. They offered Main Poc and others arms and some protection for these raids. When Spain ended their war with the Osages, they found that they could not stop the Potawatomis from their raids across the Mississippi River. Instead, Main Poc and others found that "the war against the Osages offered young warriors an opportunity to assert their manhood." In addition to attacks on the Osages, the Potawatomis also began attacks on American parties traveling in southern Illinois. They made travel in southern Indiana and Illinois very dangerous.[20]

Not all of the Potawatomi villages established along the Illinois River harbored militants. Gomo had been living near Peoria from the 1780s. He allied with the American government as early as 1792 when he signed a treaty of peace with the United States at Vincennes and was part of the first delegation of Northwest Indians, which included Little Turtle and William Wells, to travel to Philadelphia to meet with President Washington and other leaders after Fallen Timbers.[21]

Black Partridge (Mucktypoke) became a near neighbor of Gomo as well as a staunch ally of the Americans. One friend described Black Partridge as "a man of unusual intelligence," though later accounts emphasized his fondness for drinking and were more disparaging of his character. While Black Partridge fought against the Americans at Fallen Timbers, boasting of having taken American scalps, he was part of the Potawatomi contingent at the Treaty of Greenville in 1795. There, he received a medal for his new loyalty to the Americans. After the Greenville Treaty, Black Partridge joined other St. Joseph Potawatomis who moved westward into the Illinois River region. His younger brother Waubansee (Foggy Day) also established a village in what would become Illinois.[22]

JOHN KINZIE'S RETREAT

The defeat of the western Indian confederacy at Fallen Timbers in 1794 affected non-Natives in Indian Country as well. John Kinzie, his partner John Clark, and their families, along with the other British traders who had been doing business in the region, scurried back to Detroit in the wake of American success at Fallen Timbers. The U.S. victory there was coupled with the

Jay Treaty, which negotiated the removal of British troops from the western forts, including Detroit and Michilimackinac.

The 1795 Treaty of Greenville signaled the real beginning of American colonial control in this region. In his early thirties, Kinzie had aligned himself for many years with the British. He had developed a business partnership, started a family, and built two homes. Now all that seemed in jeopardy. What lay ahead was unclear. Kinzie and his family returned to Detroit, where the large Forsyth clan provided comfort and advice.

The upheaval in Kinzie's life took an even more dramatic turn at Detroit. Margaret McKenzie's father, Moredock McKenzie, journeyed there in 1794 in search of his daughters, lost twenty years before in an Indian raid. One can only imagine the reunion between the father, his two now-grown daughters, and his five grandchildren. Incredibly, the two sisters and their children returned to Virginia without their husbands. It is impossible to know why Margaret and Elizabeth willingly broke up their families. Possibly Margaret McKenzie had simply grown weary of living in a war zone, especially after losing two houses to attacks by the American military. Perhaps their father convinced the young women of the error of living with Kinzie and Clark in common-law marriages (or with British partners).

Most harshly, John Kinzie might not have encouraged Margaret McKenzie to stay in Detroit, since her connections to the Shawnees were no longer as useful to him. Marriage alliances were of crucial importance in a world buffeted by so many wars and conflicts. Kinzie's marriage to Margaret McKenzie connected Kinzie closely into a network of Shawnee leaders and British traders. With the ascendancy of the Americans in the western Indian Country, these ties meant less economically and politically to Kinzie.

After the departure of Margaret McKenzie and their children, Kinzie retreated into his birth family, and "he found refuge and occupation at Detroit."[23] His mother and stepfather were dead, but his stepbrothers and half-brother—William, Robert, and Thomas Forsyth—were either at the tavern near the fort or at a farm east of Detroit at Grosse Point purchased by the Forsyth patriarch before his death. Their neighbors at Grosse Point were the same British traders with whom Kinzie had worked at Kekionga and Au Glaize.

At about the same time that Kinzie returned to Detroit, its citizens faced a dramatic choice. As well as shifting the forts at Detroit and Michilimackinac to American control, the Jay Treaty required regional residents to decide whether they wanted to remain British subjects. Those who did not publicly declare their continued British loyalty would, by default, become American citizens. Two of Kinzie's brothers, William and Robert Forsyth, pledged their ongoing fealty to Great Britain, as did Kinzie's trading partner, John Clark. Like many of those who remained British subjects, they moved across the river into Canada. John Kinzie and his youngest brother, Thomas Forsyth, were less deliberate in their choices. Neither pledged loyalty to Great Britain, nor did they publicly state allegiance to the United States. After a year, the U.S. government simply assigned them U.S. citizenship.

Regardless of their national allegiance, Kinzie and his brothers were looking for ways to make money in this transformed world. Interestingly, they turned not to trade but to real estate. In 1795 Kinzie, in partnership with Thomas Forsyth, received grants of land along (and islands in) the Miami River from the Odawas at Detroit. Robert Forsyth and Jonathan Shiffelin, both British subjects, witnessed these grants. Two years later, Kinzie and his younger brother sold these land grants, one for "one thousand pound currency of New York" and the other for "the sum of two thousand pounds Halifax currency." Robert and William Forsyth served as witnesses to these transactions. The brothers were not united in their national allegiances but worked closely together in business. The monies made here would become a base for Kinzie to begin anew.[24]

Kinzie and his brothers also sought stability and economic advantage through marriage. Kinzie's oldest stepbrother, William Forsyth Jr., married Margaret Lytle, whose family lived in western Pennsylvania during the Revolution. Margaret, her sister Eleanor, their mother, and a brother were taken captive by a Seneca war party. John Lytle, husband and father to these captives, quickly negotiated the release of his wife, son, and daughter Margaret. However, his daughter Eleanor remained captive until 1783. After a period of sorrow, Eleanor entered into her new life and "at length grew contented and happy." She "so completely learned their language and customs as almost to have forgotten her own." Eleanor was given the name "The Ship Under Full Sail" by her adopted mother, marking "her activity and the energy of her character."[25]

Despite Eleanor's contentment, her father did not stop negotiations to secure her release. Finally, in 1783 the Lytles were reunited and moved to

Detroit. Eleanor Lytle married a British militia officer, Daniel McKillip, and had at least one child, a daughter named Margaret. Her husband died fighting against American forces at Fallen Timbers. With the transition from British to American control at Detroit, Mrs. McKillip moved near her sister across the river in British territory.[26]

Through her sister and brother-in-law, the widowed McKillip met John Kinzie. They married at the home of William and Margaret Forsyth in January 1798. British sympathizers dominated the ceremony. Eleanor and John were both the children of British army officers. Eleanor's father, John Lytle, as well as Robert and William Forsyth, had indicated their intention to remain British subjects after the American takeover of Detroit. Their marriage certificate was registered with British authorities in Upper Canada.[27]

JOHN KINZIE MOVES WEST

John Kinzie decided to stay in the fur trade and entered into an active trading partnership with his younger brother, Thomas Forsyth. They turned westward, trading with Gomo, Shabbona, Main Poc, Mad Sturgeon, and Black Partridge. Kinzie worked for William Burnett, who with his wife, Kakima, operated a successful outpost at St. Joseph. Kinzie supplied Burnett with silver items and other trade goods as well as carrying letters for him to Detroit. He also placed orders in Detroit for goods that included blue stroud (plain cloth), blankets, cord, calico, ribbon, green cloth, metal buttons, silver brooches, cotton, nails, tea, and salt. While Burnett certainly valued Kinzie's skills as a silversmith, trader, and purveyor of information, a wariness remained between them. Part of this uneasiness might have stemmed from Burnett's staunch pro-American position and Kinzie's alliance with pro-British traders in Detroit.[28]

Burnett also worked closely with Jean Lalime. Jean Lalime was born in 1759 in the closing years of the French colonial era in North America. French remained a mainstay of the fur trade, but Lalime was also fluent in English and several Algonquian dialects. His extant letters show clear, firm handwriting and provide evidence that he had received some education.[29] In a world where many were illiterate, Lalime and Kinzie could read accounts and letters as well as formulate descriptions of events for those far from the scene.

Lalime began trading for Burnett in the mid-1780s and had a closer

working relationship with Burnett than did Kinzie. Burnett trusted Lalime
to check on Detroit accounts for him and gave Lalime permission to charge
anything he should want to Burnett's accounts with local merchants.
Though a Frenchman, Lalime clearly had the requisite skills to work with
the British traders at Detroit. Burnett also sent him west to Chicago, where
he supervised a warehouse. Lalime married Nokenoqua, a local Potawatomi woman, sometime during these years, and they had at least one
son, John.[30]

William Burnett also worked closely with Jean Baptiste Point de Sable
at Chicago. Burnett acted not only as a supplier to Point de Sable, but also
as his bank, accepting payments and extending credit. By the late 1790s,
Kinzie, Lalime, and Point de Sable were all regular visitors at the Burnett
house in St. Joseph.[31]

GREENVILLE COMES TO CHICAGO

With strong ties to Chicago, William Burnett waited for the U.S. government
to build a fort there on land ceded in the Greenville Treaty. Burnett saw that
the U.S. Army had established Fort Wayne immediately after Fallen Timbers. In 1798 William Burnett received information that caused him "to expect, that there will be one [a fort] built within a few months at Chicago."[32]

By 1798 Point de Sable was working for the U.S. government as an interpreter. He certainly knew that his Chicago outpost stood on land transferred to the U.S. government as part of the Greenville Treaty. Given the
anti-American sentiment among many Potawatomis in the region, Chicago
could easily become a volatile place. This was quite different from the late
1780s when Point de Sable established a presence at Chicago. It was then
an unexceptional site, appropriate as one of many métis trading outposts
in the western Great Lakes. After the Greenville Treaty, it became a symbol
of an imposed colonial presence.

In the spring of 1800, the governor of the Northwest Territory, General
Arthur St. Clair, visited Chicago. Since Point de Sable had the most substantial house there, it is reasonable to presume that the governor stayed with
him during his visit. St. Clair certainly knew Point de Sable from his work
for the U.S. government. Perhaps St. Clair's presence reminded Point de
Sable that change was certain to come. In any event, Point de Sable made
the decision to leave Chicago. By then unrest by area Potawatomis, Odawas,

and Sauks, as well as the machinations of the English and Spanish, added to his unease. Also, Point de Sable's wife and daughter had died sometime before 1800 (perhaps from the typhoid that raged through the area). Without them, operating the extensive outpost would have been difficult, if not impossible.

Point de Sable's decision to leave Chicago was also affected by Burnett's willingness to purchase his property there. This was no small thing, in a world where cash was scarce and credit limited. The sale of Point de Sable's establishment at Chicago was a complicated one. Point de Sable owed Burnett money from long years of trade. In exchange for clearing this debt, as well as outfitting Point de Sable as he left the region, Burnett was able to arrange the sale with little or no exchange of money. Complicating this transaction was the fact that Jean Lalime was the formal purchaser of the properties. While Burnett funded the sale, it remains unclear why he chose this convoluted arrangement.

John Kinzie had an interesting role here as well. In May 1800 Burnett and Kinzie made a formal inventory of Point de Sable's holdings at Chicago. A few months later, Kinzie served as a witness to the property sale. In the fall of 1800, Point de Sable packed up his belongings, Kinzie took the bill of sale to Detroit to be recorded, and a new chapter in Chicago's history began—a chapter where John Kinzie and the U.S. government would play central roles.[33]

PART TWO

Fort Dearborn and
Tippecanoe,
1803–1811

3 President Jefferson and the Founding of Fort Dearborn, 1803–1804

When Jean Baptiste Point de Sable sold his holdings at Chicago in 1800, he knew that the United States planned to take up the six-square-mile cession made by western Indians at the Greenville Treaty.[1] The reach of the U.S. government was growing, as Chicago became part of the newly created Indiana Territory under Governor William Henry Harrison. In March 1801 Thomas Jefferson was inaugurated as the third U.S. president. He would take a keen interest in the American West throughout his presidency (1801–1809).

In his first message to Congress, President Jefferson reiterated the language of the Greenville Treaty, stressing the importance of the peace that existed between the United States and its Indian neighbors and a hope that this would continue. At the same time, Jefferson outlined a program to integrate Indians into American society. He wanted western Indians to learn farming so they would become "more and more sensible to the superiority" of agriculture over their traditional "hunting and fishing."[2] Jefferson expected Indians to integrate themselves into the American agricultural economy so that they would more easily relinquish their territory to the United States for white settlement.

President Jefferson held an ambiguous, perhaps even duplicitous, view of Native Americans. On the one hand, he took a great interest in studying the languages, culture, and life of Native Americans. He very much wanted to preserve a record of their culture. While this was the approach of an Enlightenment scholar, it masked Jefferson's ruthless commitment to the removal of Native Americans from the West. Jefferson was committed to an "empire for liberty" made up of citizen-farmers in small households across an expanding West. There was no room here for traditional Indian villages. President Jefferson sought as many cessions as possible from Indians.

To President Jefferson, the Greenville Treaty was just a start. He encour-

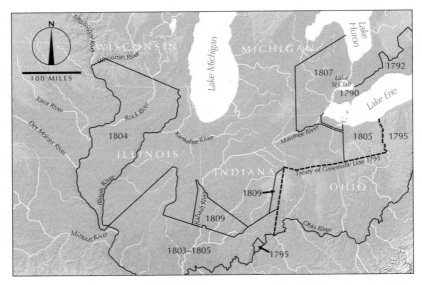

Map 7. 1795 Greenville Treaty and Further Cessions to 1809. Based on maps by Helen Hornbeck Tanner and Miklos Pinther. (Dennis McClendon, Chicago Cartographics)

aged William Henry Harrison, the powerful governor of the Indiana Territory, to negotiate further land cessions. Harrison's father had been a successful Virginia politician and friend of the president. Governor Harrison served in the U.S. Army until 1798, when he was appointed secretary and then congressional representative of the Northwest Territory. In 1800 he became the governor of the newly created Indiana Territory, most of which lay in the Indian Country west of the Greenville Treaty line. In addition, Governor Harrison served as superintendent of Indian Affairs in the Indiana Territory and the U.S. commissioner plenipotentiary for Indian treaties north of the Ohio River.[3]

Governor Harrison worked closely with President Jefferson and Secretary of War Henry Dearborn in demanding cessions in the Northwest Territory. Between 1803 and 1809, the Indians of the Northwest, Indiana, and Illinois Territories negotiated fifteen land treaties.[4]

President Jefferson also reached out to Little Turtle and William Wells. During the winter of 1801–2, Little Turtle and Wells journeyed eastward once again to meet with the new American president at Washington, D.C. Two Potawatomi chiefs, Five Medals from near Fort Wayne and Topinbee from St. Joseph, accompanied them. When they met with President Jefferson, he affirmed the Greenville Treaty and "the intention of both parties, to live together in future as friends and Brothers." The president reminded them: "Peace, brothers, is better than war, in a long and bloody war, we lose many friends and gain nothing."[5]

The Indian chiefs placed "great confidence" in Wells, who served as their interpreter. It was through him that they had "the means of communicating with, and perfectly understanding each other."[6] Jefferson agreed and appointed Wells as Indian agent as well as resident interpreter at Fort Wayne. In this capacity, Wells distributed annuity payments, regulated the Indian trade, and handled relations between the U.S. government and area tribes. Wells was one of the most highly paid U.S. officials in the Northwest Territory, receiving $750 as an annual salary, which, as Wells confirmed, "is sufficient to in able [sic] me to live comfortable and contented."[7]

Alongside cessions and annuities, President Jefferson promoted a "civilization" program to teach farming to western Indians. Of course, Little Turtle and William Wells knew that the women in their villages—including Sweet Breeze, Turtle's daughter and Wells's wife—were expert agriculturalists who raised pumpkins, squash, and melons, as well as tending extensive cornfields. One American observer noted that the rich bottomlands around Turtletown and Kekionga were filled with thousands and thousands of bushels of corn.[8]

Little Turtle and Wells recognized that the key transition would not be from hunting to farming, but from women as agriculturalists to men as farmers. Jefferson wanted Miami warriors to become farmers engaged in the grueling, often backbreaking work of farming that tied them closely to one place, instead of the free range of hunting. Little Turtle and Wells also acknowledged that this transition from warriors to farmers necessitated a revolution in gender roles. It was "evident that the President intended making women of the Indians."[9] The Quaker missionaries hired by the Department of War to effect these changes made little headway among the Miamis and Potawatomis.[10]

Just months after the delegation of Potawatomis and Miamis returned west, President Jefferson pressed for additional lands in and around Vincennes. He appointed Harrison as the treaty negotiator, with William Wells as his interpreter. The secretary of war encouraged Harrison to invite "Little Turtle and two or three other Chiefs" to "be present and be consulted." Jefferson wanted Harrison to take as much land as possible: "include as large a share of the most valuable lands for cultivation as circumstances will admit."[11]

Little Turtle, who had supported the Greenville Treaty, felt betrayed. The U.S. government was negotiating hard for additional land not included in the 1795 treaty. After all the assurances that the president had made to Little Turtle and others during their recent visit to Washington, D.C., Little Turtle could hardly believe that this was "the intention of our father the president." In Little Turtle's view, the Americans had "more lands already than they can settle." William Wells concurred and worked closely with Little Turtle. Despite their opposition, Potawatomi leaders like Topinbee and Five Medals signed the final treaty at Fort Wayne in June 1803.[12]

FOUNDING FORT DEARBORN

Soon after the 1803 Fort Wayne Treaty, the Jefferson administration made the much-anticipated decision to build a fort at Chicago on land that the United States gained at the Greenville Treaty in 1795. Before building the installation, the Jefferson administration needed someone to mark out a path between Fort Wayne and the proposed fort and reconnoiter about the general conditions around Chicago. William Wells seemed the ideal man for the job. Jefferson had met him the year before and had appointed him as the U.S. Indian agent at Fort Wayne. Wells's disposition was to listen and negotiate, and he was a keen observer. He knew the Algonquian language spoken by the Potawatomis. Wells had many friends in the region and might have convinced Topinbee or Five Medals to accompany him on his journey.

There was, however, a risk in sending Wells to Chicago. Alongside Little Turtle, he had objected to the land cessions just demanded by Harrison at Fort Wayne as an erosion of the Greenville Treaty. However, this was not a mission linked to Harrison's cessions. Instead, the outpost at Chicago would provide area Potawatomis with ready access to annuity payments and a U.S. trading post. The military at Chicago would protect the local Potawatomis and their allies from the incursions of American settlers. These were activities that Wells supported.

Wells journeyed to Chicago in the summer of 1803, taking notes on routes and distances. Since reconciling with his Wells relations, he rode the fine horses raised by his family in Kentucky. As well as marking a path,

Secretary of War Henry Dearborn directed Wells to ascertain the "disposition of area Indians to this intrusion through their territory." Dearborn saw that his army was small and no match against Potawatomi warriors if they chose to fight the establishment of a U.S. fort at Chicago. The secretary of war also instructed Wells to consult with William Burnett about "white inhabitants" who were "in the habit of cultivating the earth and raising stock on the St. Josephs or at or near Chikago."[13]

In consultation with Burnett, Wells recommended Jean Lalime as the first U.S. interpreter. Lalime had long ties to Burnett's trading world and was fluent in English, Potawatomis, and French. He was also at ease in the Potawatomi world, with a Potawatomi wife and child. Dearborn appointed Lalime as interpreter at Chicago after receiving sufficient assurances that he was "strongly attached to the government of the United States."[14]

Wells was not the only person whom Dearborn sent to Chicago in 1803. Dearborn appointed Captain John Whistler, a "discrete, judicious captain," to build a fort at the mouth of the Chicago River. The forty-eight-year-old

Figure 11. Captain John Whistler, who arrived at Chicago in 1803, supervised construction of the first Fort Dearborn. (A. T. Andreas, *History of Chicago* [1884])

Whistler had fought in the battles that led to the Greenville Treaty and then helped to build Fort Wayne in 1795.[15]

Whistler led a survey party from Detroit in April 1803, crossing terrain that was "generally level and wet," with oak forests, prairies, and swamps along the way. They met "Kenzey" (John Kinzie) at his trading outpost near St. Joseph but did not encounter any Potawatomis along the way—either at St. Joseph or at the "Calamac" (Calumet)—despite long-established Potawatomi villages at both places. At Chicago they found a sand bar at the entrance of the Chicago River into Lake Michigan that made it impossible for a ship larger than a canoe to pass. Point de Sable, Ouilmette, and others had built houses on the north side of the river, where the bank was about two feet and the land relatively firm and open. Across the river from the Point de Sable house, Whistler planned his fort on an embankment that was about eight feet high, on the highest ground in the area. The river between them was thirty yards wide and "from 18 feet and upwards, deep, dead water."[16]

Captain Whistler returned to Chicago with most of his troops on August 17, 1803. A few days later, a lake schooner carrying supplies—including two small cannons, more soldiers, and Whistler's family—arrived at Chicago. Some two thousand Potawatomis descended on Chicago to see the "big canoe with wings."[17] Drawn from the area, the Potawatomis could reasonably have included Shabbona, from the Fox River, and Naunongee, from the Calumet region (whose granddaughter Archange Ouilmette lived along the Chicago River). While only one extant account suggests that the Potawatomis threatened the American contingent, the numbers visibly reminded Whistler that they were indeed an outpost in Indian Country.

Captain John Whistler directed the construction of Fort Dearborn in the fall of 1803. His first official report from Fort Dearborn came December 31, 1803, and listed sixty-nine soldiers and officers. The 1803 transfer of the Louisiana Territory from France to the United States overshadowed Whistler's efforts. As well, Governor Harrison negotiated a cession of nearly eight million acres from the Kaskaskias that included much of what is today south-central Illinois. A second substantial cession the following year transferred much of what is now northern and western Illinois from the Sauks and the Fox, bringing land cessions to just west of Chicago at the Fox River and south of Chicago at the Kankakee River. The United States increasingly hemmed in the Potawatomis. Fort Dearborn would become a lightning rod for U.S. and Potawatomi relations.[18]

Fort Dearborn joined a network of U.S. forts in the Northwest Territory, including Detroit, Mackinac, and Fort Wayne. The officers and soldiers at these forts were part of a small professional military, wary of inevitable congressional budget cuts. The commanders at these forts knew one another and corresponded regularly. They shared world news as well as personal updates. In one 1804 letter exchange, Captain Whistler announced his daughter's marriage and learned that Aaron Burr had killed Alexander Hamilton in a duel. When a fellow officer was ordered to establish a fort on a western bank of the Mississippi after the Louisiana Purchase, Whistler provided intelligence and advice.[19]

Whistler and his fellow commanders also had to contend with a continuing British presence in the region. When the British relinquished control of their forts in 1796, they founded new forts in close proximity to the old ones—at St. Joseph Island to the southeast of Mackinac in Lake Huron and at Malden east of Detroit. On a day-to-day basis, there appeared to be cooperation between the United States and Great Britain. For instance, in April 1805 a dozen men deserted the British army at St. Joseph. The British captain wrote the American captain at Michilimackinac to be on the lookout for the deserters. The American commander replied that the deserters had not appeared but commented, "I think it a reciprocal benefit to both nations to assist each other in apprehending deserters."[20]

BUILDING FORT DEARBORN

Two Mrs. Whistlers accompanied the U.S. troops to Chicago in 1803 (although neither was the model for James McNeil Whistler's portrait of his mother; they were his grandmother, Ann, and an aunt, Julia). Ann Whistler was the daughter of a British nobleman and had eloped with John Whistler, who had served with the British during the Revolution. They fled to America, and John Whistler joined the U.S. Army. Until moving to Detroit in 1796, Ann and their many children (one account suggests fifteen) remained at Hagerstown, Maryland, while John Whistler served west of the Appalachian Mountains.

Five Whistler children came to Chicago in 1803: William, serving under his father in the Army; John Jr., a teenager; Catherine, married to Thomas Hamilton, who also served under her father; Sarah, who would marry in 1804; and George Washington, just three on his arrival at Chicago.[21] More than a dozen Whistler family members came to live at Fort Dearborn, and two grandchildren were born there—Meriwether Lewis Whistler in 1805 and John Harrison Whistler in 1807.[22]

Captain Whistler's attention during the first years after coming to Chicago was devoted to finishing the fort, including a two-story house for the commanding officer within the stockade.[23] Whistler's work was hampered by often-inhospitable weather, illness among his troops, and a lack of tools and supplies. While Whistler had his troops fell lumber from nearby woods, they lacked proper saws and files. His unit did not have enough warm clothing, hospital supplies, or cooking equipment. Whistler's commanding officer noted, "You deserve great credit for the work you have done, considering you have no clothing for your men, nor even the necessary tools to work with." By 1809 a visitor reported that Fort Dearborn was "the neatest and best wooden garrison in the country," one that "reflects great honor to Captain John Whistler, who planned and built it." Another observer noted that Whistler "worked so economically that the fort did not cost the government over fifty dollars."[24]

In addition to building the fort itself, Captain Whistler spent considerable time and energy finding enough food for his family and his men. For his family, Whistler oversaw a garden "of melons and other small fruits and vegetables" just south of the fort. Learning from his Potawatomi neighbors, Whistler tapped a stand of maple trees north of the fort every spring to provide sugar for his family and the garrison. Captain Whistler also took advantage of the good hunting and had a pair of hounds. One officer remembered, "Grouse and game birds were abundant, as were fish in the adjacent waters, so that in the hunting season much time was spent by the officers of the garrison with gun and rod." However, only officers could carry a gun when off-duty.[25]

Whistler found it difficult to acquire enough meat for his soldiers. At one point he traveled as far as Ohio to find salted pork. Eventually, Whistler decided it was easier to raise cattle and hogs at Chicago. To feed this livestock, Whistler and his family began to plant more and more corn. This seemed an elegant solution to the fort's inadequate food supply as well as providing needed employment for Whistler's extended family. However,

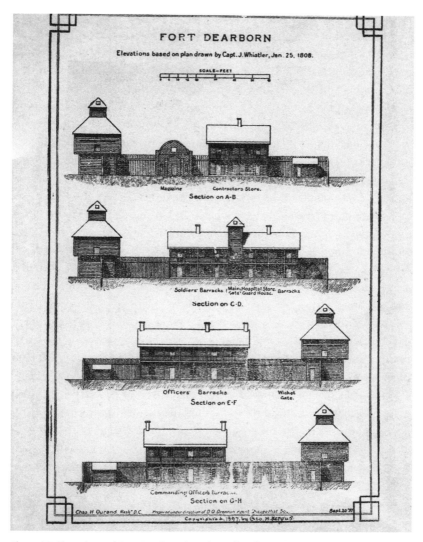

Figure 12. Elevations of Fort Dearborn based on plan drawn by Captain John Whistler in January 1808. (Chicago History Museum, ICHi-03047)

there were concerns about Whistler's assigning soldiers (whether off-duty or not) to work in these family enterprises. Charges of Whistler family profit at public expense followed and became a source of internal tension at the fort.[26]

In addition, John Whistler Jr. entered into a partnership with John Kinzie and became the military contractor providing these supplies to the fort. This made sense to Whistler, who operated Fort Dearborn as an extended family business because he could not count on the U.S. government to supply his post. From Whistler's vantage point, the U.S. Army literally forced him into this entrepreneurial position. However, the arrangement caused a deep tangle of public and private finances.[27]

Four sergeants, two corporals, four fifer and drum, and forty-one privates lived at Fort Dearborn alongside Whistler, his family, and his officers. Whistler's soldiers appreciated his efforts to keep them supplied, and most remained personally loyal to him. They endured the garrison's "dull uniformity" and reenlisted despite the isolation and hardships.[28] These soldiers were poorly paid. Privates received $7 per month, sergeants $10 per month, and officers (including the interpreter Jean Lalime) between $20 and $40 per month.[29] As well as salary, all of the U.S. soldiers, officers, and officials received daily rations, basic housing, and clothing. The standard army ration included beef, flour, rum (or other liquor), vinegar, salt, soap, and candles.[30]

These soldiers were responsible for building, maintaining, and protecting Fort Dearborn. Captain Whistler was responsible for keeping "the garrison clean and in good order," and he made sure that "the company perform their exercise well, their clothing, arms &C in good order."[31] Some soldiers also received special assignments and even earned extra wages by doing carpentry, blacksmithing, and butchering meat. A few were detailed to officers as servants or as messengers traveling to Fort Wayne or Detroit.[32]

Little is known beyond names and nationality of most enlisted men at Fort Dearborn. While most were born in the United States, a minority were of English, Irish, German, or French birth. James Corbin was typical of soldiers at Chicago. He came to Chicago with Captain Whistler in 1803 and spent much of his time there "constructing that fortress." He also honed his skills as a blacksmith while serving at Fort Dearborn until 1812.[33]

Recruiting and holding soldiers was a major concern for Captain Whistler. He turned over much of this work to Sergeant James Leigh, who came with the original contingent in 1803. Leigh not only convinced soldiers like James Corbin to reenlist (often more than once), but he also recruited new enlistees from Ohio and other points east. Leigh was literate and, unlike most soldiers, he was married. His wife, Martha, may have accompanied him to Chicago in 1803, but she might have come initially with her birth family. Her father, William Russell, was also a soldier at Fort Dearborn. In any event, the Leighs eventually had six children in their household.[34]

Alongside Sergeant Leigh's duties at Fort Dearborn, his family took care of cows and horses of officers and sold provisions to the garrison. While most discharged soldiers left the vicinity immediately, when Leigh resigned from the U.S. Army in 1810, he decided to stay in Chicago (as did William Russell, his father-in-law). American civilians were not encouraged to live at Chicago. There was no provision for local government, nor could settlers purchase land, so Leigh was a special case. As he wrote, "On my retiring . . . I got liberty from Capt. Whistler to reside in the reserves." Leigh built a house just to the south of the fort and had a cabin about three miles farther south along the Chicago River. There he tended "a large stock of cattle" that he butchered and sold to the garrison. By 1812 Leigh had "upwards of one hundred head of horn cattle," as well as horses and hogs.[35]

U.S. INDIAN AGENT AT CHICAGO

When Captain Whistler came to Chicago in 1803 to build Fort Dearborn, William Wells was the U.S. Indian agent responsible for all of the territory from Fort Wayne west to the Mississippi River. This meant that Wells was the civilian face of the U.S. government and was responsible for distributing annuities and gathering intelligence.

Two years after the founding of Fort Dearborn, the Jefferson administration decided to create an agency at Chicago to handle "relations with the Potawatomis, Sauk, Fox, Chippewa, Ottawa, and Miami who inhabited the region, extending from the St. Joseph River, south and west to the Mississippi, including northern Illinois."[36] The Department of War built an Agency House in 1805 just west of Fort Dearborn: "an old-fashioned log-building, with a hall running through the center and one large room on each side. Piazzas extended the whole length of the building, front and rear." The Potawatomis who came to do business with the Indian agent often camped west of the Agency House along the south bank of the Chicago River.[37]

Charles Jouett was the first Indian agent at Chicago. Born in Charlottesville, Virginia, in 1772 and trained as a lawyer, Jouett was a neighbor of Thomas Jefferson. As Indian agent at Detroit between 1802 and 1805, Jouett investigated competing land claims, settled two treaties, and gathered information about area Indians. In 1805 the Jefferson administration

Figure 13. Looking south across the Chicago River with Fort Dearborn in the center and the U.S. Agency House in the foreground. Lake Michigan is off to the left in the image. (A. T. Andreas, *History of Chicago* [1884])

transferred him to Chicago. He was accompanied by his wife, Elizabeth Dodemead, who was from a prominent Detroit family of merchants. Their daughter, Jane Harris Dodemead, was born in 1804 and traveled with her parents to Chicago as a toddler. They moved into the newly built Agency House that served as both as workplace and home. While Potawatomis were not welcomed into the fort, they were encouraged to visit the agent.

This made the Agency House a center for Indian affairs at Chicago. Helping Jouett to manage his dealings with Potawatomis and other Indians were his "commanding presence and physical strength." The Potawatomis came to call Jouett "White Otter." He stood six feet three inches tall, well above the average height. His family remembered that he was not easily intimidated. Once, when Main Poc, the stridently anti-American warrior, approached the Agency House "brandishing his scalping knife with furious menace," Jouett "sternly ordered him to give up his knife."[38]

Along with his wife and daughter, Jouett's household included at least one enslaved person, called Blackmeat by the Potawatomis. Blackmeat worked closely with Jouett in his agency work. As well, Jean Lalime and his wife became an integral part of this household. Lalime was the interpreter at Fort Dearborn when Jouett arrived in 1805. By then he lived just across the river just west of Antoine and Archange Ouilmette. His wife, Nokeno-qua, worked for the Jouett family as a housekeeper.

Lalime was critical to Jouett's success as Indian agent, as he had a deep knowledge of the people, villages, and relationships among area Potawato-mis. The two made an improbable pair, the tall imposing Jouett alongside the much shorter Lalime, who was "considerably advanced in life" and "a cripple" due to an improperly set leg fracture However, with Lalime's help, Jouett "secured the confidence of the Indians by kind and honorable treatment."[39]

Throughout Jouett's tenure at Chicago, Governor Harrison negotiated land cessions in the western Great Lakes. These cessions often put Jouett, his family, and the entire U.S. contingent at Chicago at risk of Indian attack. Jouett worked hard to maintain a fragile peace at Chicago. He sought con-trol of as much of the Potawatomi annuities as he could. This increased his power and influence across Indian Country by cementing good relations with Potawatomis around Chicago.[40]

Jouett also monitored the actions of the British in the region. Robert Dickson, the British Indian agent in the western Great Lakes, operated in the area, despite U.S. claims to the territory. In June 1807, when the Brit-ish warship *Leopard* fired on an American frigate, tensions rose across the region. More than a thousand Indians crowded around Chicago, and Jouett worried about the possibility of a "hostile" action. He blamed Dickson for encouraging the Potawatomis and their allies "to war against America."[41]

In Jouett's opinion, Captain Whistler did little to mitigate danger in 1807. While Jouett held a "good opinion of Capt. Whistler as a man," he worried about the captain's abilities to protect the U.S. outpost at Chicago. To the secretary of war, he offered a frank assessment of Whistler: "The present commanding officer of Chicago is incompetent."[42]

All the while this crisis was unfolding around Chicago, Jouett was deal-ing with personal tragedy. His wife, Elizabeth, died, leaving him solely re-sponsible for his three-year-old daughter. The help of Jean Lalime and No-kenoqua must have been of immeasurable importance during this difficult time. In August 1807, Jouett requested permission from the secretary of war "to convey my daughter and only child to Kentucky." While visiting his daughter the following year, Jouett married Susan Randolph Allen of Clark County, Kentucky. The newlyweds returned to Chicago in early 1809 "on horseback in the month of January . . . in the face of driving storms, and the frozen breath of the winds of the north." Later that year the couple welcomed a son, Charles Lalime Jouett, honoring Jean Lalime, who had helped them weather both professional and personal crises. Tragically, the infant died a few months later, and when Susan Jouett became pregnant again in 1810, the couple left for Kentucky. Jouett's absence would be keenly felt in the months and years ahead.[43]

THE U.S. TRADING HOUSE (FACTORY) AT CHICAGO

The United States set up a trading house (factory) at Chicago in 1805, adjacent to the Agency House. At the time of the Greenville Treaty (1795), Congress established the first trading houses. While Thomas Jefferson often argued for a limited federal government, he was an advocate of the trading houses. In order to be "kind and useful to all our red children," Jefferson proposed "to establish factories among them to supply them with the necessaries they want."[44] Essentially, the factories were government stores, which had several advantages over private traders: "No one who bought his goods in this country could sell them as cheaply as the factories, and this was possible because of their extensive credit, and the superior quality of their goods."[45]

Over time there were factories at Detroit, Fort Wayne, Chicago, Mackinac, Fort Madison (Iowa), and Sandusky (Ohio) in the Northwest Territory. In 1808 the secretary of war appointed Matthew Irwin as the third factor (government trader) at Chicago. Irwin was a young man with no western experience, but excellent political connections. His uncle was the governor of Pennsylvania, and his father was the state's quartermaster during the Revolutionary War.[46]

Irwin was a privileged young man in the early years of the Republic: "of medium height—perhaps a little more—well proportioned, of pleasing deportment, and quite interesting and popular in his address."[47] Despite his youth and inexperience, Irwin's appointment as Chicago factor came with a yearly salary of $1,000 (more than double that of Captain Whistler).[48]

The U.S. government placed a great deal of responsibility in the hands of young men like Matthew Irwin. His mission was to go "obtain and preserve" the friendship of Northwest Indians, as well as to represent the United States with "honor, integrity and good faith." It was an amazing charge for a young man who had no experience with Indians or the fur trade. Irwin supervised the arrival of goods chosen by eastern bureaucrats for sale: blankets, kettles, traps, silver trinkets, and tobacco. Then it was up to Irwin to set a price for these goods that would "cover the cost of transportation & to yield such profit only as will indemnify the establishments for the expenses at your Trading House." Irwin had been instructed to set prices that did not give Indians dissatisfaction, leaving much to his "discretion & prudence." He was also told to work in cash, although credit could be extended "to Principal chiefs of good character."[49] Despite his lack of knowledge and skills, Irwin operated successfully at Chicago. In 1811–12 alone, the Chicago Factory made a profit of $1,773.94, with almost $12,500 in stock on hand and furs and other assets valued at nearly $14,000.[50]

This success would have been a near-impossible task for the inexperienced Irwin, except for the ready skills of Jean Lalime. Already working for both Captain John Whistler at Fort Dearborn and Charles Jouett at the Agency House, Lalime also became an integral part of the Chicago trading house. Lalime helped to negotiate "the vast crowd of Indians which resort this post on account of the Agency and the Indian trading house."[51] Lalime's facility with English, French, and Potawatomi, as well as his extensive knowledge of the fur trade, made him an invaluable adviser to all the U.S. officials at Chicago. Lalime could "ascertain & examine the quality of Furs and Peltries . . . [and] send them off in good order carefully & safely packed."[52] Jean Lalime was essential to this American outpost in Indian Country.

Lalime knew as well as anyone that there was no monolithic U.S. presence at Chicago. The garrison was an insult to many local Potawatomis and their neighbors, who rejected the Greenville Treaty and subsequent land cessions. With a force well under a hundred, Captain Whistler's outpost remained ever vulnerable to attack. The work of Indian Agent Charles Jouett provided a counterpoint to military action. He cultivated good relations with area Potawatomis through the distribution of annuities and other gifts. At the same time, the U.S. factor, Matthew Irwin, offered goods at the government trading house at competitive prices to Potawatomis willing to come to Fort Dearborn to trade. The United States sent out mixed signals at Chicago to area Indians: offering friendship and building a fort; promoting peace and threatening war; offering gifts and taking land. These contradictions were inherent in the official policies of the Jefferson administration and made Chicago a place of opportunity and danger.

4 Kinzie & Forsyth, at Chicago and Peoria, 1803–1812

The small métis settlement at Chicago recognized the danger and opportunity that Fort Dearborn offered. The ongoing treaties negotiated by Governor Harrison to take as much land as possible from the Potawatomis and their allies left Chicago vulnerable to angry attacks. On the other hand, there were opportunities there. For instance, Jean Lalime worked for the various U.S. officials at Chicago. Others, like Antoine Ouilmette, transported goods and people across the river and through the portage.

The métis community continued to expand. Among those who came were Louis Buisson, a French Canadian trader born in 1758 with strong interests at Peoria who, like Louis Pettell, maintained houses and business at both places. He was not only operating as a fur trader, but also raising a herd of thirty-five to forty head of cattle at Peoria. Buisson married Archange Ouilmette's sister, Sheshi Chevalier, and lived to the north of the Chicago River along Lake Michigan. Louis and Sheshi Buisson raised at least five children. Later in life, Louis Buisson was described as "a large, portly, gray-headed man," and his wife as a "Pottawatomie Indian, enormous in size."[1]

Archange Chevalier Ouilmette, Angelique Pettell, Marie Therese Roy Le Mai, and Nokenoqua farmed land in and around Chicago. Their household work included caring for cows, horses, and sheep. These women were able to sell whatever surplus they raised, while their husbands worked in the fur trade. Together they created a stability that weathered upheavals that included the construction of Fort Dearborn in 1803. They "learned to deal with the chaotic world around them by retreating to their village and maintaining the integrity of their homes, farms, families, and customs."[2]

A number of other métis families settled at Chicago had close ties to Milwaukee. Jean Baptiste Mirandeau had been at Milwaukee from the 1790s. A contemporary described him as a good blacksmith who made "hoes, axes, knives, gigs, and spears for fishing, and shoe horses for the French traders." Through local traders, Mirandeau was able to acquire the iron he needed, and his household made "their own charcoal." Because Mirandeau was "very ingenious" with gun repairs, the garrison officers offered him employment as blacksmith for Fort Dearborn.[3] Mirandeau brought his wife, an Odawa woman, and some of their ten children to Chicago. Their fifth child, Victoire, recollected her father as "a religious man, [who] had prayers in his house every evening." Despite the many books owned by her father, Victoire never learned to read or write. Over time several of Mirandeau's children worked for the Ouilmette and the Kinzie families.[4]

As well as the Mirandeaus, members of the LaFramboise family also moved back and forth between Milwaukee and Chicago after the foundation of Fort Dearborn. François LaFramboise was part of an extended family of French traders around Lake Michigan.[5] He married Shaw-we-no-qua, a Potawatomi woman, and they raised five children: Claude, Joseph, Alexis, LaFortune, and Josette. After 1803 François moved his family to Chicago and lived along the east side of the south branch of the Chicago River.

While Joseph Bailly did not settle at Chicago, he sent two young men there to look after his interests. Bailly, who was staunchly pro-British, moved his trading operations from the Grand River on Lake Michigan's eastern shore to the Calumet region south of Chicago. In 1795, while Bailly and his Odawa wife, Marie, were still at Grand River, they took in eight-year-old Jean Baptiste Beaubien as an apprentice, a trader's assistant in their household. Beaubien was a younger son of an established French family in Detroit. From Bailly, Beaubien gained a basic education, an introduction to the Odawa and Potawatomi languages, as well as valuable lessons and contacts in the fur trade.[6]

In 1804 Beaubien had married an Odawa woman and came to Chicago, perhaps to represent Bailly's interests there. His wife died soon after given birth to a daughter, Marie.[7] The following year, 1807, Beaubien married his second wife, Mah-naw-bun-no-quah. She was the sister or daughter of Shabbona, an Odawa who had married a Potawatomi woman in a village to the southwest of Chicago. Their son Charles was born at Chicago in 1807, while their second son, Madore, was born at Grand River. Mah-naw-bun-no-quah died five years later, and Beaubien then married Josette La-Framboise, whose family had moved to Chicago from Milwaukee.[8]

Alexander Robinson was born in Mackinac in 1789, the son of a Scottish trader and a Odawa (or métis) mother. He was fluent in Odawa, Pota-watomi, Ojibwa, French, and English. In 1800, when Alexander Robinson was eleven years old, he was working for Joseph Bailly at his outpost on the eastern shore of Lake Michigan. Robinson learned the fur trade under Bailly and alongside Jean Baptiste Beaubien. However, in contrast to Beau-bien, who learned to read and write, Robinson remained illiterate. Robin-son overcame this disability by developing his own system of accounting so that he could work in the fur trade.[9]

Robinson continued to work for Bailly for many years, first at St. Joseph and then at Chicago. At St. Joseph he met John Kinzie, with whom he would maintain a close relationship for years to come. In one account, Robinson first came to Chicago in 1809 while still working for Bailly, to buy a canoe filled with corn. Sometime before 1812, Alexander Robinson built a house on the east side of the south branch, south of the LaFramboise family. He would eventually marry Catherine Chevalier, sister of Archange Ouilmette and Sheshi Buisson.

THE KINZIE FAMILY AT CHICAGO

When John Kinzie and his wife arrived at Chicago in 1804, they joined the métis settlement located on the north bank of the Chicago River. Kinzie had purchased the house, outbuildings, and other improvements made by Jean Baptiste Point de Sable from Jean Lalime. Juliette Kinzie described the house in later years as "a long, low building, with a piazza extending along its front, a range of four or five rooms. A broad green space was enclosed between it and the river, and shaded by a row of Lombardy poplars." As well as the main building, the Kinzie homestead included a "fine, well-cultivated garden extended to the north of the dwelling, and surrounding it were various buildings appertaining to the establishment—dairy, bake-house, lodging-house for the Frenchmen, and stables."[10]

While they shared much with their métis neighbors, they also stood apart from them. For instance, Archange Ouilmette and Eleanor Kinzie lived next door to one another from 1804 into the 1820s (although Kinzie was in Detroit from late in 1812 until 1816). Archange was a local, born just to the south at a Potawatomi village in the Calumet region. After moving with her family to western Pennsylvania, Eleanor spent several years as a Seneca captive, before a reunion with her family at Detroit. Archange grew

Figure 14. This image of the Kinzie House was based on drawings made by Mrs. John H. (Juliette) Kinzie. (A. T. Andreas, *History of Chicago* [1884])

up in a household speaking French and Potawatomi, while Eleanor learned English and then Seneca as a child. However, both became the matriarchs of successful households in Chicago. Together with their husbands, children, and extended families, these households crossed cultural and national boundaries, raising and manufacturing food and supplies for local trade, as well as trading for furs headed to Europe and China in exchange for tea, cloth, guns, and other products.

Over the years the Kinzie household at Chicago included John, Eleanor, their three children, one or two of John's brothers, and Eleanor's daughter from her first marriage. In addition, the Kinzies owned several enslaved people: Black Jim, Athena, Henry, and Pepper. Slavery was very much a part of this world, despite its nominal prohibition in the Northwest Territory. The Kinzies brought Athena and Black Jim with them from Detroit in 1804. Athena served the family as a cook and housemaid and was married to Henry. Black Jim, Pepper, and Henry were employed in the trading operations of Kinzie and in raising livestock and crops on nearby property.[11]

Athena, Henry, Black Jim, and Pepper were not the only bound laborers in the Kinzie household. John Kinzie also employed several engagés (contract workers), "who would cut and haul wood and assist in trading, as well as work in the truck patches [fields]."[12] They received rations, clothing, and equipment in exchange for modest annual wages. In addition, there were often one or two young women from métis households who performed all sorts of work, from farm chores to housekeeping. Sisters Victoire and Madaline Mirandeau came from Milwaukee with their métis family. Victoire joined the Kinzie household, while her sister worked for the Ouilmettes.

In total, there were often seventeen or eighteen people living in this household. They occupied the largest house at Chicago, but even still, it would have been crowded, especially with regular visitors. The engagés lived in one of the outbuildings described as "a lodging house for the Frenchmen." The rest fit into the house, with four rooms on the first floor and four cramped chambers on the second.

Household members not only slept there, but also labored at a variety of daily tasks. Their work is indicated by the buildings—the smokehouse, the bake house, the stables, the barns—and the garden fields. The women—whether family members, slaves, or "bound girls"—were responsible for baking bread, taking care of chickens, milking cows, making butter, and much more.

Women were busy cooking and washing over an open fireplace in the kitchen. They probably also maintained the fireplaces in the kitchen, dining room, and living room. There is no evidence that anyone had a loom at Chicago, but various kinds of cloth—stroud, jane (jean), and calico—were regular trade goods. The women used it to make the clothing needed by their household, including the shirts and coats worn by engagés.[13] Kinzie & Forsyth could also sell this clothing to other traders.[14]

The men in the Kinzie household, like the officers at the fort, were regular hunters. One frequent visitor remembered that there was "a variety of game, such as venison, raccoon, panther, bear, and turkey, varied as spring approached with swan, geese, and crane, besides almost every variety of duck."[15] Some men also tended cattle and hogs as well as horses. Other tasks included felling and chopping wood for the fireplaces, slaughtering and smoking meat, and building and maintaining structures and equipment. There is no evidence that Kinzie himself was a farmer. However, the Kinzie household grew wheat, corn, beans, and squash. They harvested maple syrup from groves around Chicago in late winter and early spring, as did Captain Whistler and their métis neighbors.[16]

KINZIE & FORSYTH

John Kinzie ran his business operations out of the house from a designated workroom on the southwest corner of the building. Here he worked his silver, making ornaments and trinkets, including crosses and armbands.[17] From this workroom, Kinzie also operated a trade network in partnership with his half-brother, Thomas Forsyth. Kinzie sold goods to most of the inhabitants at Chicago—both the métis on the north bank of the Chicago River and the U.S. officials and soldiers on the south bank. Canoes regularly passed back and forth in front of his window, and there were often people on his front porch.

On a table somewhere in the workroom, Kinzie had his ledger books. The ledger's first entry, dated May 12, 1804, is from soon after he arrived at Chicago. The account books quickly came to include most residents of, and visitors to, Chicago. Each family (and sometimes individuals within families) had a folio page. Every transaction was listed (whether a sale or a purchase) for a number of years. Local families sold items like bread, sugar, whiskey, clothing, and corn. In return, they purchased those items they could not produce in their own households. From time to time, accounts were settled. Kinzie also had another ledger in which he recorded all transactions on a daily basis. His partner, Thomas Forsyth, held yet another ledger in Peoria. Customers could hold accounts at both places, and from time to time, Kinzie and Forsyth brought the books together for reconciliation.[18]

Between 1805 and 1809, John Kinzie served as sutler to Fort Dearborn in partnership with Captain John Whistler's son. Soldiers had to trade with Kinzie & Whistler. They sold the soldiers at Fort Dearborn small luxury items that made their lives more pleasant: whiskey, bread, sugar, tea, and chocolate. While the bread and sugar (and perhaps whiskey) was produced in the Kinzie household, the green tea and chocolate were part of an international trade.

The Fort Dearborn trade offered Kinzie & Whistler, as well as Kinzie & Forsyth, ready money in a world of credit. The regular stream of money from the U.S. government helped to offset the complicated credit arrangements of the fur trade. There was little money in circulation and no banks. Business was done through a complex series of transactions recorded in trader account books. Traders had to rely on the honestly and reliability of other traders. They also had to extend regular credit to one another to maintain the trade network. Cash or credit from the U.S. government offered an attractive alternative. When the partnership of Kinzie & Whistler broke up in 1809, Kinzie lost his hold on suttling for a time, but he would regain this trade in early 1812.

While the names of soldiers as well as métis residents were listed in the Kinzie & Forsyth ledger books, there were virtually no Indian names. Seldom did Potawatomis walk up to the Kinzie veranda and enter his workroom to do business. Instead, Kinzie & Forsyth established a network of trading posts (stations) to the north at Milwaukee and along the Rock River and to the south on the Illinois and Kankakee Rivers into what is now Sangamon County. At each place John Kinzie or Thomas Forsyth sent a head trader, a group of engagés and voyageurs who paddled canoes and carried packs.[19]

In late summer and fall, Kinzie & Forsyth hired traders and engagés, and outfitted them with the goods needed for trade (called an adventure). The traders brought a group of engagés to one of the trading posts controlled by Kinzie & Forsyth. Then the engagés sought out groups of Potawatomis, distributed goods to them on credit in the fall, and waited on payment in furs after the winter hunt. Most engagés wintered at Potawatomi camps and often married Potawatomi women, furthering their close connections to their trading partners. Some were illiterate and innumerate, but all had to track complicated trade accounts (or have complete trust in their partners).Without literacy and numeracy, engagés had little hope, though, of becoming traders on their own.[20]

Kinzie & Forsyth came to rely heavily on three men who worked closely with them as traders and clerks. Antoine LeClair was "somewhat less than six feet in height, well built and a successful trader." He was a native of Montreal, born around 1766, who began trading around St. Joseph, Michigan, sometime around 1790. LeClair married into a prominent Potawatomi family at St. Joseph, and two sons were born there in 1795 and 1797. In 1800 LeClair and his family set up a trading outpost at Milwaukee, where they worked closely with John Kinzie, Thomas Forsyth, Robert Forsyth, and William Burnett. Sometime in 1809, LeClair and his family relocated to Peoria, where he worked closely with Thomas Forsyth.[21]

Billy Caldwell was the son of a Mohawk woman and William Caldwell Sr., a British officer at Fort Malden. Caldwell went to school in Detroit but was not recognized as his father's legitimate son. He began working for Thomas and Robert Forsyth in the late 1790s at St. Joseph and on the Wabash River. After 1803 Caldwell worked for Kinzie & Forsyth as a clerk at Chicago. During these years he married twice, first to La Nanette, daughter of the Potawatomi chief Wabinewa (White Sturgeon) and niece of Nuscotomeg (Mad Sturgeon) from along the Illinois River. After La Nanette's death, Caldwell married the daughter of Robert Forsyth and an Ojibwa woman.

Jean Baptiste Chandonnai, the métis nephew of Potawatomi chief Topinbee of St. Joseph, came to Chicago to work for Kinzie. By 1812 he was working as Kinzie's chief clerk and living in a house just north of their trading operation along Lake Michigan.[22]

Besides these men, Kinzie & Forsyth relied on several enslaved men to help with the time-consuming work related to the fur trade. Kinzie & Forsyth purchased Jeffrey Nash, who worked with Forsyth at Peoria.[23]

While Chicago was the center for the trading network built by Kinzie & Forsyth, over time much work was done at Peoria. Thomas Forsyth and his wife, Keziah, moved to Peoria from Detroit in 1804. Their first sons, John Kinzie Forsyth and Robert Allen Forsyth, were born at Peoria in 1806 and 1808. Their substantial house was larger than that of John and Eleanor Kinzie at Chicago. They furnished the house with two bedsteads and a mattress, three tables, seven chairs, and two cupboards. They had a well-stocked kitchen with forks, knives, teakettles, a butter churn, and a grindstone. The Forsyth family also maintained a bake house and barns for horses, a pair of oxen, a bull, and cows. They had over an acre of land planted with corn and potatoes.[24]

Keziah Malott Forsyth, like Eleanor Kinzie, had been an Indian captive as a child. In 1778 a group of Shawnees attacked Malott's family on the Ohio River as they traveled by flat boat to Kentucky. Keziah was either a newborn or not yet born when this attack took place. While Keziah's father escaped, the Shawnees held her mother and several brothers and sisters for more than four years. Through the intervention of British authorities, the Malott captives were freed and made their way to Detroit. There, Keziah's sister Catherine married the British trader and Indian agent Simon Girty, despite his advanced age. Thomas Forsyth lived intermittently at Malden and married Keziah Malott there in 1804.[25]

Thomas and Keziah Forsyth's move to Peoria strengthened the connections of Kinzie & Forsyth to the villages of Potawatomis, Miamis, and Kickapoos in central Illinois. Information, people, and goods traveled easily from north to south, from Chicago to St. Louis along the Illinois River. Travel was also easy eastward along the Kankakee River to the Wabash and Tippecanoe Rivers in what is now Indiana.

The rhythms of the fur trade meant that the population at Chicago and Peoria ebbed and flowed, as those involved in the fur trade traveled in and around the western Great Lakes. Engagés and voyageurs often wintered with their Potawatomi trading partners. The late spring and late summer brought a flurry of activity as the engagés settled their accounts with Kinzie & Forsyth. Kinzie and Caldwell (and later Chandonnai) counted, examined, and sorted the skins, before pressing and packing them. The process of valuing furs required great skill and knowledge. Kinzie would then create an invoice for a square pack, which generally weighed around one hundred pounds. The invoice included not only the number, but also the quality and kind of skins.[26]

Like the grading of furs, the trade itself had a real hierarchy—traders like Kinzie and Forsyth were known as bourgeois. They were indeed of the middle class. With the engagés, they shared a deep knowledge of the trading world, but they also had access to capital, or more accurately the ability to borrow. Bourgeois like Kinzie were at the local end of a trade network that extended upward through a business chain to merchants in Montreal, New York, and London. Men like Kinzie and Forsyth negotiated with merchants at Mackinac or Detroit, who in turn served as intermediaries for trade in Montreal. At Montreal the trading firms shipped furs to London for sale in the European market. London prices "determined the profits for everyone along the chain from the traders in the interior to wholesalers at Mackinac and Detroit to the merchants in Montreal."[27]

The whole cycle of the fur trade took place over a two- to three-year period. At each step along the way, goods were advanced with the hopes that profits would return. The fur trade was a high-risk operation, "little more than a huge gamble for most of those directly engaged in it." Most bourgeois, merchants, and trading firms wound up in debt that could become insurmountable. Montreal merchants had to advance credit to traders like Kinzie (often through an intermediary in Detroit). Kinzie's engagés traded directly with the Potawatomis, who received their goods on credit and sometimes were not able to repay their debt if the winter's hunt was

Figure 15. The beaver was a key resource in the fur trade in the western Great Lakes. Indians trapped the beavers and traded with engagés who came to their villages. These engagés brought the skins to outfits like Kinzie & Forsyth, who graded and packed the skins for shipping out of the region. (Joseph Kirkland, *The Chicago Massacre of 1812* [1893])

not good enough. At any step in the process, the ability to repay debts could disappear.[28]

William Burnett outfitted Kinzie & Forsyth when they set up a trading outpost at Fort Dearborn. However, their relationship deteriorated, as Kinzie & Forsyth cultivated other trade connections, especially with Richard and Hugh Pattinson. Richard Pattinson had established a trade outpost near Burnett on the St. Joseph River in 1803. Burnett, a strong American partisan, had differences with Pattinson, who held openly pro-British sentiments. In 1805 Kinzie & Forsyth held packs for a trader who owed money to both Burnett and Pattinson. Rather than splitting the packs between them, Kinzie sent them all to Pattinson. Burnett felt the sting of betrayal: "I have been very much duped. The confidence I had in Mr. Forsyth, induced me to think that he certainly would have done for me equally as what he has done for himself, but in this I have been very much disappointed."[29] Burnett became less and less important to Kinzie & Forsyth, while Hugh and Richard Pattinson became important sources for Detroit trade goods and credit.

LALIME AND KINZIE

The lives of Jean Lalime and John Kinzie afford contrasting views of Chicago after the establishment of Fort Dearborn. Both Kinzie and Lalime worked for William Burnett and traveled to Chicago during the years that Catherine and Jean Baptiste Point de Sable lived at Chicago. Both came to own the Point de Sable house and built careers that centered on trade and good relations in Indian Country. Their prosperity was based in "acute readings of market drifts and consumer tastes." They spent years honing the skills necessary to operate in several cultures.[30]

Jean Lalime worked closely with the Americans. William Wells first appointed him as the interpreter for the fort. Then Lalime began to work as well for Charles Jouett, the Indian agent, and Matthew Irwin, the U.S. factor. Lalime became invaluable to the outpost. He was vital to good relations between the U.S. officials at Chicago and the surrounding Potawatomi villages. This was particularly important as hundreds of Potawatomis and their allies regularly came to Chicago to receive annuities and trade directly at the factory. Lalime, as interpreter, facilitated payments, transactions, and communication.

Across the Chicago River, Kinzie & Forsyth established a private trading empire, with customers at Fort Dearborn, in the métis community at Chicago, and in Potawatomi villages across the region. Kinzie outfitted traders at Chicago, and then they traveled out into the villages of Potawatomis, Ojibwas, Odawas, Ho-Chunks, Kickapoos, and other groups. In contrast, those same Indians came to Chicago to trade directly with the factor (aided by Jean Lalime) at the U.S. trading post.

Both Lalime and Kinzie had to scrutinize their market and determine prices for their goods. However, the factor's (and so Lalime's) first concern was to maintain good relations with area Indians, while Kinzie was intent on making profits both over the short and long term. Matthew Irwin, as the factor, and Jean Lalime, as interpreter, received set salaries, and their tenure in office did not rest solely on the amount of goods bought and sold. Kinzie & Forsyth, in contrast, looked for ways to make money at every turn.

While Kinzie & Forsyth generally maintained good relations with the

U.S. garrison and officials, because both the factor and the sutler could sell goods to soldiers, disagreements seemed inevitable. Both could extend credit to the garrison. While the U.S. Factor Matthew Irwin was not concerned about the undue influence he might have on the officers and soldiers, he worried about the power that the sutler could have over officers and soldiers when he arrived at Chicago in 1809.

Liquor was also a contentious issue. Congress outlawed the sale of liquor by any U.S. trading house. In contrast, the sale of liquor—primarily whiskey—was an integral part of Kinzie's operation. While the official U.S. trading house sold goods more cheaply that Kinzie & Forsyth, the factor could not sell liquor to Indians. Here, Kinzie & Forsyth made money by selling to their traders, who brought liquor to Indian villages. Most Potawatomis like Black Partridge shrewdly understood that they got goods cheaply at the Chicago factory, but they could only buy liquor from private traders.

Fundamentally, Jean Lalime cast his allegiances unambiguously with the United States. He drew his salary from the federal government and worked to implement U.S. policies at Chicago. In contrast, John Kinzie's national allegiance was uncertain. He and his half-brother, Thomas Forsyth, had married into families with deep British roots, and at least one of their brothers lived in the British community across the river from Detroit. While Kinzie and Forsyth were both American citizens, at times it appeared that they were working against, or at least not for, the United States. During the embargo of 1807, Kinzie & Forsyth continued to trade with British traders at Detroit, despite the prohibitions against this. Their national allegiance was tempered by a search for profits that crossed territorial borders.[31]

5 President Jefferson, Main Poc, and the Founding of Tippecanoe, 1808–1811

One hundred miles to the southeast of Chicago, Tippecanoe was like Chicago in that it offered easy access to the western Great Lakes and the Ohio and Mississippi Rivers. Located on a branch of the Wabash River, it was two days from the Ohio River. Traveling upstream and then across a seven-mile portage, travelers could reach Fort Wayne in less than three days. As well, Tippecanoe was about equal distance from the Potawatomi villages at St. Joseph in western Michigan and those along the Illinois River.

Tippecanoe was also as much a result of the 1795 Greenville Treaty as the U.S. garrison at the mouth of the Chicago River. Located near the abandoned French Fort Ouiatenon, the site was one of the six-square-mile reservations, including Chicago, that the United States acquired at Greenville.[1] However, the federal government had not taken up this claim, as they had at Chicago. Instead, the Potawatomi chief Main Poc, an opponent of American expansion into Indian Country, invited the nativist prophet Tenskwatawa and his brother Tecumseh to relocate their growing multi-ethnic village from Greenville, Ohio, to the site.[2] Planting a nativist village there was a provocative act—in keeping with many of the actions of Main Poc and Tecumseh toward the United States.

Tippecanoe stood as a defiant alternative to the integration of Indian Country into the United States. It was unsettling not just to Americans, but to U.S.-allied Indians in the region—like Little Turtle, Black Partridge, and Topinbee. Tenskwatawa and his brother Tecumseh rejected the cession of any more lands to the United States and looked to the British to support their independence. Main Poc, while not an ardent supporter of Tenskwatawa's nativism, looked for every opportunity to halt U.S. expansionism.

Tippecanoe was readily accessible by Indian tribes from both the East and the West, but it was also within range of both U.S. and British outposts in the western Great Lakes. While William Wells saw Tippecanoe within

Figure 16. Tecumseh (*pictured here*) and his brother Tenskwatawa (the Shawnee Prophet) moved their multi-ethnic village from Greenville, Ohio, to Tippecanoe on the invitation of the Potawatomi leader Main Poc. (Joseph Kirkland, *The Chicago Massacre of 1812* [1893])

the purview of his Indian Agency at Fort Wayne, Charles Jouett at Chicago and William Henry Harrison at Vincennes carefully watched events unfold there as well. The Shawnee Prophet Tenskwatawa and his followers could quickly arrive at Fort Dearborn, Vincennes, Fort Wayne, Detroit, or Malden. Its location fostered jurisdictional jockeying between U.S. outposts, as well as with Britain.

THE NATIVISM OF THE SHAWNEE PROPHET

When Tenskwatawa moved Prophetstown from Greenville to Tippecanoe in 1808, he preached a nativist spirituality that denounced all Euro-American people, customs, and goods. A series of visions in 1804 moved Tenskwatawa to denounce "the consumption of alcohol," to condemn intertribal violence, and to "return to the communal life of the past." He instructed his followers to return to the "food, implements and dress of their ancestors," and end their participation in the fur trade.[3] Indian women living with white men were to leave their families and return to their birth villages. These were crucial conditions for the nativist call of Tenskwatawa.

Tenskwatawa's dictates struck at the heart of long-standing relationships between Indians and white traders. According to nativist tenets, Little Turtle was to have no connection to his grandchildren whose father was William Wells. Sweet Breeze, his daughter, would have to leave her husband and children. Kakima, long married to William Burnett, was expected to leave him and their children and return to her brother Topinbee. Archange Ouilmette and Sheshi Buisson were to return to their birth village in the Calumet region, leaving their husbands and children at Chicago. These demands were untenable for the many Miamis and Potawatomis who had long lived alongside Euro-Americans.

Tenskwatawa also advocated the end to land cessions with the United States that he saw simply as conquest. The Shawnee Prophet suggested that Governor Harrison and others pursuing land cessions were "cheating the Indians." His message fell on fertile ears, as Governor Harrison pressed ahead with further treaty negotiations aimed to take millions of acres in Indian Country.[4]

Tenskwatawa rejected the cultural conquest within the "civilization" programs of the Jefferson administration that funded Quaker and Moravian missionaries to teach Indian men to farm. Despite President Jefferson's strong general stand on the separation of church and state, Jefferson supported this sectarian effort to convert Indians to Protestantism as well as to teach men Euro-American farming. Tenskwatawa and his supporters refused to accept the efforts at religious and agricultural conversion.[5]

Tecumseh and the Shawnee Prophet rejected Jefferson's views of "civilization" in favor of the older nativist traditions of women farmers and warrior men. They understood the central role of food in the conflict with Americans in the region. Emphasis was placed on rooting out the Euro-American customs, like raising stock: "To them [Americans] I have given cattle, sheep, swine and poultry for themselves only. You are not to keep any of these animals, nor to eat their meat." Instead, nativists called for the Miamis and Potawatomis to hunt and fish for their own use only: "You must kill no more animals than are necessary to feed and cloth[e] you."[6]

Nativist leaders saw bread as another symbol of conquest. They instructed their followers on no "account to eat bread. It is the food of the

Whites." Instead, nativist leaders exhorted followers to plant corn: "But plant no more than is necessary for your own use. You must not sell it to the Whites."[7]

They abstained from drinking alcohol because it drew Indians away from their own culture. Alcohol sold by private traders, and distributed at treaty negotiations by Governor Harrison, eroded traditional Indian life and made it easier for the United States to gain more territory. While it was illegal for the government factories to sell liquor, private traders more than made up for it in the western Great Lakes. One observer noted that in some villages western Indians drank "til they are absolutely senseless." Tenskwatawa called for a renunciation of all liquor and drunkenness.[8]

MAIN POC AND TIPPECANOE

Main Poc was drawn to Tenskwatawa, whose powerful speeches drew hundreds of Indians to his village at Greenville between 1804 and 1807. Main Poc traveled from Illinois to Greenville in October 1807. Tenskwatawa welcomed Main Poc as a warrior who had opposed the 1795 Greenville Treaty. While Main Poc did not accept all of the Prophet's teachings—he continued to consume alcohol and to plan raids on the Osages—he was drawn to its anti-American rhetoric. After a two-month visit, Main Poc invited Tenskwatawa to move closer to his village on the Illinois River, to a site along a tributary of the Wabash River—the Tippecanoe.

Tenskwatawa accepted the invitation of Main Poc, recognized by many as the "greatest warrior in the west" who had "more influence than any other Indian." He made plans to move his village to Tippecanoe.[9] After issuing his invitation to Tenskwatawa, Main Poc traveled home by way of Fort Wayne. William Wells welcomed the opportunity to "take good care of him and if possible prevent his ever listening to the prophet again."[10] Wells supplied Main Poc with food, drink, and other supplies to keep him from becoming "a very troublesome Enemy." Main Poc told Wells: "My friend[,] you have caught me: like a wild Horse is caught with a Lick of Salt, you have hobbled me."[11]

Unfortunately for Wells, Secretary Dearborn did not see things in the same way. He admonished Wells for spending too much money on Indians who "have been so inattentive to themselves and their families as not to have provided the necessary provisions." Dearborn suggested that "they ought to suffer—it will not do to indulge them in such idleness." He seemed not to discern the importance of maintaining good relations with Main Poc and was more concerned that distributing food would discourage area Potawatomis and Miamis from full participation in civilization programs.[12]

MAIN POC VISITS PRESIDENT THOMAS JEFFERSON

In the fall of 1808, William Wells invited a group of western Indians to travel with him to Washington, D.C., to visit President Jefferson. Wells hoped that the trip would impress western warriors enough to make them solid U.S. allies. He convinced the Potawatomi warriors Main Poc and Siggenauk (Blackbird) to make the trip. It also gave the Indian agent, accompanied by Little Turtle, an opportunity to better explain the challenges that Tenskwatawa and his militant nativism presented to the United States in Indian Country.[13]

Main Poc spent "two or three hours daily, in the duties of the toilet, painting his face, dressing his hair, and arranging his appearance by a small mirror held up before him by his wife who stood near him for the purpose, pronouncing occasionally on the effect produced and giving instructions." Adhering to doctrines of the Shawnee Prophet, Main Poc dressed in clothing "entirely made up of the skins of wild animals, which had been killed by his own hands." He refused "to wear any article of clothing manufactured by white people and was by no means reserved in his expressions of hatred toward the whole nation, who he maintained, had violently wrested from them all their most valuable possessions."[14]

Little Turtle, like most of those with whom he traveled, "dressed in a costume usually worn by . . . citizens of the time: coats of blue cloth, gilt buttons, pantaloons of the same color; and buff waistcoats." He also "wore a long red military sash around the waist and his hat was ornamented by a red feather," as well as donning traditional leggings and moccasins. Like Main Poc, the Miami warrior understood the value of making a striking impression.[15]

Little Turtle enjoyed meeting people and attending dinners and receptions en route and in Washington, D.C., Philadelphia, and Baltimore. In contrast, Main Poc turned down invitations to meet with many who sought his acquaintance. In one instance, Main Poc and his wife picked fruit and nuts instead of attending a formal function. The rest of the delegation sat down to the dinner given in their honor and "drew a comparison between savage and civilized life, and in favor of civilization."[16] Main Poc made his points not in conversation, but in action.

Main Poc had been persuaded to make the trip in hopes that he would gain "favorable impressions of the power of the Federal government and relieve his mind of the idea of taking up arms against it." None of this took place. Instead, Main Poc "refused every civility tendered him alike in Washington, remaining shut up with his wife, in his apartments, while all the rest of his companions partook of every enjoyment offered them." Little Turtle chided Main Poc that he "would return home in the same state of ignorance in which he had left it."[17]

The delegation had a private meeting with President Jefferson, who addressed Main Poc directly as "My Son Manchot, the Great War Chief of my Children the Poutewatamies." Jefferson was pleased to meet the "distinguished men of the Potawatomies and to give them the same assurances of friendship and good will which I have given to all my other red children." He explained that his civilization program would allow the Potawatomis to "live in plenty and prosperity, beginning to cultivate the earth and raise domestic animals for their comfortable subsistence."[18]

There is no record of Main Poc's reply to President Jefferson. It may be supposed that he listened as he did to Little Turtle over the course of the trip "with apparent good humor, but remained unmoved."[19] In a missive to William Wells earlier in 1808 on the same subject, Main Poc noted that it was "evident that the President intended making women of the Indians" since farming was women's work. Main Poc intended to resist this by remaining a warrior and by working in concert with warriors in other tribes. Main Poc felt that "when the Indians were all united they would be respected by the President as men."[20]

President Jefferson also spoke to Main Poc about the Potawatomi raids against the Osages across the Mississippi River. The Potawatomi warriors traveled south through territory claimed by the United States and increasingly settled by American farmers. Main Poc, along with other Potawatomis, was not party to the treaties that ceded the land to the U.S. government. The president noted: "Your war parties cannot pass from your towns to the country of the Osages, nor can the Osages come to revenge themselves on your towns without traversing extensively a country which is ours." He hoped that the Potawatomi warriors would put down their weapons and take up farming: "My desire to keep you in peace arises from my sincere wish to see you happy and prosperous."[21]

Jefferson's words did not sway Main Poc, who returned west in early 1809 unconvinced of the need to become a farmer. He remained very much influenced by Tenskwatawa and his nativist vision. President Jefferson saw these Native leaders as "interested and crafty individuals," who "inculcate a sanctimonious reverence for the customs of their ancestors."[22] Main Poc saw otherwise. He understood that Jefferson sought the end of his way of life.

1809 TREATY OF FORT WAYNE

While Main Poc, William Wells, and Little Turtle were on their journey to Washington, D.C., Governor Harrison began planning a final round of land cessions before the end of Jefferson's administration. This seemed ill advised. Tenskwatawa and Tecumseh were solidly entrenched in the region and very hostile to further land cessions. The British at Malden offered friendship and supplies to disaffected Potawatomis and their allies.

William Wells worried very much about these treaty plans, concerned about the effect that further cessions would likely have on the already-deteriorating U.S. relations with the Potawatomis and their allies. Wells was particularly concerned with discontent among the Potawatomis, describing them as a large nation that also had great "influence among the other nations of this country." He argued that Main Poc and other Potawatomis already felt a "general dissatisfaction among this nation towards our government."[23]

The cessions of 1803, 1804, and 1805 remained open wounds in U.S. relations with the Potawatomis. While the Potawatomis had not been party to these treaties, other groups had ceded territory that Potawatomi villages used and claimed.[24] By the summer of 1809, Governor Harrison completed negotiations for further cessions with Miami and Potawatomi delegations. By then, President James Madison expressed some concern that these new land cessions might incite violence among western Indians. Still, Harrison pressed on with further negotiations.

It is interesting that Governor Harrison chose to negotiate the final treaty at Fort Wayne. The small garrison under Captain Nathan Heald offered Harrison a small military presence. He also needed the Miamis and

Potawatomis in northwest Indiana and southwest Michigan to sign on to this treaty. In order to assure their presence, Harrison came to them.

William Wells had returned to Fort Wayne from Washington, D.C., with a new bride from Kentucky, Polly Geiger, as well as his four teenage children (the grandchildren of Little Turtle). On arriving at Fort Wayne, Wells learned that he had been removed as Indian agent, despite personal meetings just months before with President Jefferson and Secretary of War Dearborn. Wells suffered a real loss of income and status, remaining at Fort Wayne only as a U.S. interpreter employed directly by Governor Harrison.[25]

Wells, who in previous treaties had cajoled Indian leaders to attend, now did not have the power to do so. When Harrison arrived at Fort Wayne, he did not find the Potawatomi and Miami leaders he needed for negotiations. Many had in fact sent word that they were not coming. Some, like Topinbee and Five Medals, had gone to Detroit to avoid Harrison. Even Little Turtle was not at Fort Wayne. He was stricken by gout and angry with the U.S. government's treatment of William Wells. Governor Harrison had to draw warriors to Fort Wayne on his own. He did so with bribes of food and alcohol and the promise of more annuities.

Harrison sought two tracts of land that would open up central Indiana to American settlers. Both were territories that the Miami Confederacy had long claimed. In recognition of the power of Tecumseh and Tenskwatawa, Governor Harrison recommended the return of the small tract of land near Tippecanoe taken by the United States at Greenville in 1795.[26]

These cessions were a sharp blow to the Miami Confederacy. Neither Little Turtle, who was too ill to actively participate, or William Wells wielded much power at these negotiations. Harrison was able to play on "the jealousy and resentment that the civil chiefs harbored against Little Turtle."[27] In addition, food shortages and regional unrest meant that many area Indians were more dependent on annuity payments than usual. Harrison simply held annuity payments until he got what he wanted.

In the end, 1,400 Potawatomis and Miamis came to Fort Wayne for the negotiations. Still missing were western Potawatomis like Main Poc and Siggenauk, as well as most of the followers of Tenskwatawa. Essentially, the assembled St. Joseph Potawatomis signed this treaty that involved lands they did not claim themselves because it provided them with more annuity payments. One Potawatomi leader, Winamac, addressed the council and signaled consent for Harrison's proposals: "Your proposition is right and just." Many Miami chiefs stood and left the Council House on hearing this speech.[28]

While Harrison was ready to press on for more land cessions, the Madison administration was fearful of an Indian war. The enmity that many Potawatomis felt for the Miamis (and vice versa) over the 1809 treaty did not portend a peaceful future. Despite these differences, western Indians shared a fundamental distrust and hostility toward the U.S. government, which kept demanding more land. An alliance with Great Britain seemed more attractive than ever. Even more Indians were drawn to the militant nativism of Tecumseh and his brother. Wells explained that "the purchases made by the United States immediately became unpopular among them and as no effort was made to keep down the spirit of discontent among them, they threw themselves into the arms of the Shawnese prophet."[29]

The 1809 treaty—signed by older leaders of the Miamis, Delawares, and Potawatomis like Little Turtle, Topinbee, Five Medals, and Winamac—also brought a sharp generational divide within these tribes. Younger leaders like Main Poc, Siggenauk, and Chebanse were not part of the process and looked increasingly to the Shawnee Prophet. As historian David Edmunds explains, "After the Treaty of Fort Wayne, the nature of the Indian movement changed." Increasing numbers of western warriors turned to the "pragmatic leadership of Tecumseh." Main Poc also gained support in the wake of the 1809 treaty. He became a "dangerous man . . . the pivot on which the minds of all the Western Indians turned."[30] Main Poc, as much as the Shawnee Prophet, would be crucial to the fate of the region.

6 Battle of Tippecanoe, November 1811

In May 1810 Captain Nathan Heald rode his horse from Fort Wayne to Chicago, following a path blazed by William Wells seven years before. Heald had been the commander at Fort Wayne for less than three years, and now he had been transferred to Chicago. He had joined the army in 1799 as a twenty-five-year-old from New Hampshire. Fort Wayne was his second command, following Fort Massac in southern Illinois. At Fort Wayne, he had watched the comings and goings of key leaders from across Indian Country: Main Poc, Tecumseh, Tenskwatawa, Little Turtle, Topinbee, and Five Medals. He witnessed the September 1809 negotiations that had led to the Fort Wayne treaty.[1]

Heald came to know William Wells and Little Turtle quite well. He had seen Little Turtle make the arduous journey to Washington, D.C., in the fall of 1808 and watched as his health began to fail. When Heald came to Fort Wayne, William Wells had been the Indian agent. Heald observed that even after he lost the agency, Wells managed to support a large household that included his niece Rebekah, with whom Heald was quite taken.[2]

Rebekah's father, Samuel, operated a substantial farm and raised horses in Kentucky.[3] Her childhood was very much shaped by the frontier. Rebekah grew up knowing that her young uncle had been an Indian captive. Her father participated in many battles, including Fallen Timbers as an officer in the Kentucky militia. Her cousins, the mixed-race children of Sweet Breeze and William Wells, spent several years in Kentucky after the death of their mother.[4] In 1809 Rebekah traveled with her cousins to Fort Wayne after her own mother died.

Captain Heald and Rebekah Wells were soon regularly riding together. As well, the couple frequently took rifle practice together. Rebekah Wells became "extremely expert in that soldierly exercise." As one account described, Heald was "a candidate for the favor of the fair markswoman."[5]

However, Captain Heald's transfer from Fort Wayne to Chicago halted their budding romance.

Heald replaced Captain John Whistler, Fort Dearborn's first commander. In 1810 Whistler and his family left Fort Dearborn, after Factor Matthew Irwin had waged a successful campaign against their administration. Whistler had run Fort Dearborn like an extended household. He had taken care of everyone, but profits had flowed back to his family. The fastidious Irwin expected clear lines between the personal and public finances, and was outraged that "no check exists in their dealings, against extortion."[6]

Irwin charged Whistler and several of his officers with misconduct. In the end, the Department of War chose not to proceed with any formal charges against these officers. While Whistler and his officers had clearly breached military rules, the U.S. Army could not afford to lose three men willing to serve at a remote outpost in Indian Country. Instead, the Secretary of War reassigned Captain Whistler to Detroit, moved Captain Heald to Chicago, and transferred an officer from Detroit to Fort Wayne.

Upon arrival at Chicago, Heald found fifty-one soldiers and two officers under his command. Most had been recruited by Captain John Whistler. The two officers were the same men who had been accused of wrongdoing by Matthew Irwin. Even though neither officer had been prosecuted, both were professionally wounded. The surgeon's mate, Dr. John Cooper, left the army in early 1811. Lieutenant Seth Thompson, the other officer, took sick and died in March 1811.

Factor Matthew Irwin, who had forced Heald into a game of musical chairs that led to his reassignment to Chicago, remained in place. There was little hope for an amicable relationship between Heald and Irwin. Irwin had no problem sending off letters to superiors in Washington, D.C., that ended careers. He was a very tough companion at an isolated fort, where trust was of the utmost importance.

Charles Jouett, the Indian agent, was getting ready to leave Chicago for Kentucky with his pregnant wife. The couple had lost a child at Chicago just the previous year. During Jouett's extended absence, no replacement was sent. Captain Heald and the interpreter Jean Lalime were expected to carry on and shoulder the extra work.

Because there was no civil authority at Chicago, Heald was also responsible for residents around Fort Dearborn, including John and Eleanor Kinzie and other trading families. From 1803–9, Chicago had been part of Indiana

Territory, under the purview of Governor William Henry Harrison at Vincennes. Then it became part of the newly created Illinois Territory. Ninian Edwards, a scion of the prominent Pope family from Kentucky, was appointed the first governor of the Illinois Territory. Chicagoans understood that they remained in a backwater, perhaps never clearer than in 1811 when the secretary of the treasury admitted that he did "not know in what territory Chicago" was located.[7]

Heald was not happy with Chicago from the start. He wrote his commanding officer in June 1810: "I am sorry to inform you I am not pleased with my situation." Heald found Chicago a good place only "for a man who has a family & can content himself to live so remote from the civilized part of the world." Heald sought a transfer, and when it was not forthcoming, took a nine-month furlough to New England.[8]

Mulling over his options, Heald took his own advice about Fort Dearborn being a good place for a married man. On his way back to Chicago in the spring of 1811, he stopped at Fort Wayne and rekindled his relationship with Rebekah Wells. They were married shortly and began their wedding trip to Chicago. Heald pragmatically decided that to "prevent my being troublesome in my applications for furlough in future I am taking on a wife with me."[9]

As befitted a young bride from a leading Kentucky family, Rebekah and her husband rode on fine horses and carried a wedding trunk filled with items to begin housekeeping. Rebekah wore a distinctive set of hair combs that may have belonged to her mother. In addition, an enslaved woman named Cicely accompanied the Healds. Enslaved people were part of the

Figure 17. Rebekah Wells Heald brought this trunk to Chicago as a young bride in 1811. (Chicago History Museum, ICHi-64677)

substantial household and farm operated by Samuel Wells in Kentucky. Cicely might have accompanied Rebekah Wells from Kentucky in 1809 or been given as a wedding gift by her father or her uncle.

So it was that Captain Heald journeyed again by horseback to Chicago in June 1811, but this time accompanied by his wife and servant. While Charles Jouett and his family were gone, three new officers had arrived at Chicago over the preceding year. George Ronan was a young ensign only recently graduated from West Point. Fort Dearborn was his first posting. Lieutenant Linai T. Helm, of German heritage, came to Fort Dearborn from Detroit on the death of Lieutenant Thompson. Helm was married to Margaret McKillip, the daughter of Eleanor Kinzie and the stepdaughter of John Kinzie. Helm found living in Detroit expensive and sought the transfer to Chicago to save money as well as to bring his wife closer to her mother.

In addition, the surgeon's mate at Fort Dearborn was new to Chicago. In his early twenties, Isaac Van Voorhis had recently graduated from medical school and had just joined the army. He replaced Dr. John Cooper, who left Chicago in the spring of 1811. Van Voorhis and Cooper were both from Fishkill, in Duchess County, New York, and classmates at the College of Physicians and Surgeons in New York City. Cooper was born in 1786 and Van Voorhis a few years later, making Van Voorhis in his early twenties in 1812. Alongside these new arrivals, Captain Heald and his wife, Rebekah, settled into life at Chicago.

RETAKING INDIAN COUNTRY

While the Healds had an uneventful trip from Fort Wayne to Chicago, it must have been fraught with the knowledge of recent raiding by Potawatomis and their allies. Main Poc, undeterred by President Jefferson's personal admonitions, responded to the 1809 Treaty of Fort Wayne by escalating the raids and attacks on both American settlers and Osage villages in southern Illinois.

Main Poc's brothers-in-law, Nuscotomeg (Mad Sturgeon) and Wabinewa (White Sturgeon), launched raids on settlements near Kaskaskia, stealing forty horses and killing livestock. In assaults on American settlers at Shoal Creek and at Price farm, they killed several people and took one captive. The Potawatomi warriors brought the captive, a young woman named

Rebecca Cox, back to Main Poc's village on the Illinois River north of Peoria. Then a white militia attacked the village, and the wounded Rebecca escaped. Warriors from Main Poc's village launched two more attacks on southern Illinois in June 1811, including one on a ferry across the Mississippi River.[10]

White settlers launched retaliatory raids. In July 1811 Illinois governor Ninian Edwards told local Potawatomis that he "found it almost impossible to prevent the white people from rushing to your towns to destroy your corn, burn your property, take your women, and children prisoners, and murder your warriors." The governor called on leaders like Gomo and Black Partridge to turn over "bad men" who "had done the mischief." The governor saw the raiders as "enemies both to you and to your white brethren."[11] This may have been the case, but Gomo and Black Partridge had little control over the action of warriors like Main Poc, Siggenauk, and Mad Sturgeon.

While some American settlers continued to fight Main Poc and his warriors, others built defensive blockhouses to protect themselves against his raids. Still others simply gave "up their crops and moved into the thicker parts of the settlements." This was exactly as Main Poc had hoped.[12] It was much the same strategy employed by the Senecas, Miamis, Shawnees, and others during the 1770s and 1780s in western Pennsylvania and along the Ohio River.

While Main Poc and other warriors were creating havoc across Indian Country, Tecumseh was busy trying to harness the unrest that followed the 1809 Fort Wayne Treaty into support for his nativist cause. By 1811 Tecumseh and Tenskwatawa had been at their village along the Tippecanoe River for almost three years. Tecumseh opined, "We must not leave this place [Tippecanoe], we must remain steadfast here, to keep those people who wear hats in check."[13] Tecumseh hoped to unite as many of the western Indians as he could, sending some to Tippecanoe and resettling others onto the lands ceded to the United States since the 1795 Greenville Treaty.

In order to put this wider plan of expansion into action, Tecumseh visited Potawatomi, Winnebago, Shawnee, and Sauk villages on both sides of the Mississippi in the fall of 1810. Tecumseh made these visits quietly and urged his followers not to share information with whites. He recruited individuals, or whole villages in some instances, to stand with him against further U.S. incursions in Indian Country.[14] Billy Caldwell, who had served as

John Kinzie's clerk at Chicago, visited Tecumseh at Prophetstown and grew close to the nativist cause. Caldwell traveled with Tecumseh and Shabbona across the West in 1810.[15]

One of the village chiefs swayed by Tecumseh was Shabbona, the Odawa leading a Potawatomi village on the Fox River just southwest of Chicago. As a young man, Shabbona had traveled with two Odawa prophets. When Tecumseh came to his village in 1810, Shabbona welcomed him and then accompanied him as he traveled to Odawa, Potawatomi, Sauk, and Ho-Chunk villages.

While traditional leaders like Gomo and Black Partridge remained unmoved, Tecumseh drew support among the Sauk and Ho-Chunk villages along the Rock River and north to Lake Winnebago. The Sauk warrior Black Hawk remembered that the Shawnee Prophet invited his village to Prophetstown. Black Hawk, who was attracted to nativism his whole life, listened carefully to Tecumseh's call to join his movement, threatening that "the Americans will take this very village from you."[16] Tecumseh also had some success with the Kickapoos south of Peoria, but very little with the western Shawnees across the Mississippi River. After long months in the West, Tecumseh turned eastward and visited the British at Malden, accepting their presents and counsel.[17]

WILLIAM HENRY HARRISON AND THE BATTLE OF TIPPECANOE

While Tecumseh traveled quietly across the region in 1810, his plans to journey south in the summer of 1811 were quite public. He hoped to counsel with the Creeks and their allies in what today is Alabama and south Georgia. There leaders like Red Eagle and Manewa faced similar challenges from the United States: demands for ongoing land cessions and assimilation. Their nativist response, known as the Red Sticks, called for a rejection of Euro-American culture and goods similar to what Tenskwatawa preached from Prophetstown. Tecumseh hoped that cooperation would bring a better chance of resisting further American incursions.

Tecumseh traveled south from Tippecanoe with a contingent of more than three hundred warriors and stopped at Vincennes. William Henry Harrison had lived at Vincennes since 1800 with his growing family. Grouseland, his substantial estate, served as the seat of power for the Indiana

Territory. Harrison was the American face of the string of cessions that had culminated in the 1809 Fort Wayne Treaty. He wanted white settlers to move into his territory as quickly as possible, so that Indiana would quickly have a sufficient white population to become a state.

Harrison met Tecumseh's warriors on their arrival at Vincennes on July 27, 1811, with a militia of eight hundred, drawn from among Kentucky and Indiana settlers. It was not simply a meeting between two leaders, but a show of force. Tecumseh told Harrison that he had successfully united the villages in the region around Vincennes and was heading south to recruit among the Creeks and Cherokees. Then they were going to move into the territory ceded to the United States in the 1809 treaty, directly challenging Governor Harrison's plans to encourage rapid white settlement and speedy Indiana statehood. Tecumseh's plans were in fact the mirror image of Harrison's strategy to encourage quick American settlement on ceded lands. Tecumseh threatened to turn the treaty process on its head by encouraging the expansion of Indian villages into the path of white settlement. Full-out war would likely be the result.[18]

In his desire to impress Harrison, Tecumseh very much overstated his support among the western Indians, but Harrison did not know this. Better intelligence might have kept Harrison in Vincennes. Instead, as soon as Tecumseh and his force had moved south, the governor made plans to attack Prophetstown, where Tenskwatawa remained with the families of warriors who accompanied Tecumseh.

Despite little direct knowledge, Governor Harrison felt threatened by Tippecanoe. Harrison had met at length with Tecumseh and described him as "a bold adventurer," who through the "intrigues and advice of foreign agents, and other disaffected persons" had filled the minds of western Indians "with suspicions of the justice and integrity of our views towards them."[19] Harrison saw an attack on Tippecanoe as a way to counteract the influence of Tecumseh and Tenskwatawa.

Soon after Tecumseh departed for the South, Harrison moved his family to Cincinnati. Across Ohio, Indiana, and Kentucky, he raised a military force of more than a thousand soldiers. Samuel Wells, father of Rebekah Wells Heald, was among the officers of the Kentucky militia who heeded Harrison's call for troops. In mid-October Harrison marched these forces up the Wabash River from Vincennes to present-day Terre Haute, where he threw "Fort Harrison up on the high banks of the stream." On October 29 Harrison left the newly constructed fort with his troops and camped about a mile northwest of Prophetstown.[20]

Harrison worked with limited information about Tippecanoe as few Americans had visited there. Jean Lalime, the interpreter at Chicago, shared what he collected from trusted sources with Harrison and other U.S. officials. In late October 1811, Harrison knew that Tecumseh was not present at Tippecanoe but that there were still hundreds of warriors at Prophetstown, along with many more family members. Harrison raised enough troops to meet this force.[21]

Tippecanoe had only a meager supply of powder and shot. Shortages of ammunition were an ongoing problem for Tecumseh and his allies. While the most radical nativists renounced firearms, Tecumseh and Tenskwatawa saw them as vital to holding off further American incursions into their territory. The Americans tried to limit ammunition available to western warriors, but firearms were a necessary component of the fur trade and could not be halted entirely.

When Tenskwatawa learned of Harrison's advancing troops, the warriors moved their families to other villages, abandoning Prophetstown. Instead of waiting for Harrison's assault, Winnebago and Kickapoo warriors led a nighttime surprise attack on his camp. At least fifty Indian warriors and sixty-eight soldiers under Harrison were killed. In the end, Harrison's forces prevailed, but it was not much of a victory. After the battle, Harrison plundered the deserted Tippecanoe, seized corn stores, and torched the village. While Harrison did not kill any civilians, by destroying food supplies in late fall, he sentenced many to great hardship and even death. In addition, by burning villages and supplies, Harrison created "a feeling of revenge in the hearts" of Tenskwatawa and his followers.[22]

Weeks after the Battle of Tippecanoe, some of the strongest earthquakes ever recorded rocked the region. Occurring between December 11, 1811, and February 3, 1812, they centered on New Madrid, a community in the Louisiana territory about 160 miles south of St. Louis. At St. Louis, there were toppled chimneys, broken china, and rattled nerves. The tremors were felt for hundreds of miles, well into the area around southern Lake Michigan. Residents around Tippecanoe and Chicago felt the quakes but were far from the epicenter. John Kinzie recorded an earthquake occurring on December 16, 1811, from his home at Chicago but noted no damage.[23]

News of the Battle of Tippecanoe and the New Madrid earthquakes slowly rippled through the region and beyond. Individuals quickly shared these events with villages across Indian Country, as well as with Fort Wayne, Detroit, Chicago, and St. Louis. Letters and newspapers were soon full of details and speculation. Some of the earliest reports suggested that William Henry Harrison had been killed in battle, but those were soon refuted.[24]

Harrison gave a full accounting of his actions at Tippecanoe after his return to Vincennes. By early January, Secretary of War William Eustis acknowledged the receipt of his official reports. His response was less than the high praise that Harrison expected, because the secretary of war was preoccupied with the wider threat of war with Great Britain. Rather than congratulations, Secretary Eustis instructed Harrison to extend a hand of friendship to Tenskwatawa and his brother Tecumseh. He further wrote, "It is peculiarly desirable at the present crisis, that measures should be adopted to reestablish the relations of peace and friendship."[25] In public, the secretary stood behind Harrison, but the private rebuke no doubt stung him.

Tecumseh returned to Prophetstown during January 1812. He had been in Missouri at the time of the battle at Tippecanoe and the earthquakes. He was saddened by destruction that he found. Tecumseh professed no interest in retribution and willingly met with Governor Harrison, on orders from the secretary of war. By February Harrison reported that he had "made peace with the Indians . . . and the Hatchet is buried." However, these conciliatory words covered growing unrest in the region.[26]

CHICAGO AFTER TIPPECANOE

Chicago residents received their first news from Tippecanoe in late December 1811. A party of Winnebagos (Ho-Chunks) stopped in Chicago and shared their accounts. The Ho-Chunks accepted "the pipe of peace" and pledged to "discontinue hostilities against the United States." In early February 1812, the officials at Fort Dearborn still had not received any official written accounts. Instead, as Jean Lalime noted, "We have had but very indifferent news of the battle that took place on the Wabash . . . from the Indians."[27]

From these Indian visits, Lalime was able to piece together an account that he shared through letters: "My duty calls me to inform every officer of government of the news in this critical time." Lalime felt that the attack on Tippecanoe put Fort Dearborn at great risk, as it gave the Potawatomis confidence to go to war against the Americans: "I have been informed that war is the common talk of the Potawatomis, and that whenever they get together they are forming plans to attack this garrison." Lalime was not certain of the strength of support for the Prophet, but he was sure that area Indians were "inclined to War and will commit some depredations this spring." The interpreter at Fort Dearborn understood that many Potawatomis were fueled by "the fire of revenge" for the attack of William Henry Harrison on Prophetstown. Still, Lalime also cautioned that many tribes and villages were divided over their support of Tecumseh or Main Poc. The trick would be to discern friend from foe.[28]

Thomas Forsyth traveled to Chicago from Peoria in early January 1812. While he had not been at Tippecanoe, he shared what he had learned from his Indian sources. Forsyth suggested that Harrison's attack on Prophetstown had only dispersed the settlement "for a moment" and that Tecumseh's supporters were quickly regrouping. Like Lalime, Forsyth wrote U.S. officials with this intelligence and warned of upcoming reprisals for the attack on Tippecanoe.[29]

Kinzie & Forsyth were busy during these winter months. They received several deliveries of supplies that included stroud, blankets, powder, and lead to Kinzie's warehouses across the Chicago River from Fort Dearborn. The partners also managed to stockpile liquor during these uncertain times. They had negotiated with the Pattinson brothers, avowed British traders at Detroit, for goods they would need for the coming season. Despite the dangers after Tippecanoe, Kinzie & Forsyth saw an opportunity for profit.[30]

Factor Matthew Irwin watched the goods arrive at Kinzie's establishment in violation of a non-importation law that prohibited British trade goods from entering the United States. Irwin, who had already complained about similar violations over the previous year, felt compelled again to write to the secretary of war. He accused John Kinzie and Thomas Forsyth of being disloyal to the United States. Irwin found this particularly troublesome because in January 1812, in the wake of the news about Tippecanoe, Captain Heald had made a curious decision: he had issued a garrison order making Kinzie & Forsyth the exclusive sutler at Fort Dearborn.

Captain Heald's reasons for ordering his soldiers and officers to trade only with Kinzie & Forsyth are not clear, but he certainly strengthened his ties to the most influential traders at Chicago. In uncertain times, Kinzie & Forsyth offered a steady supply of goods. As well, Kinzie & Forsyth's network of information and influence could be of great use to the garrison. Captain Heald had been in Chicago for a total of ten months, and he did not have the advice of the U.S. Indian agent, who had been absent for over a year. John Kinzie's counsel was of immeasurable value. Besides Kinzie, only Jean Lalime could offer Heald the intelligence he needed to keep his troops from harm's way. Closer to home, Rebekah Heald was five months pregnant, so Heald had even more reason to make Chicago as stable a place as possible.

Regardless of what Captain Heald hoped to accomplish with the exclusive suttling arrangement, he faced the strong opposition of Factor Matthew Irwin. Irwin had railed against an exclusive suttling order made by Captain Whistler in 1809, and he remained adamantly opposed to such arrangements. Irwin worried that the debts U.S. Army officers would incur with Kinzie would create a "subserviency of the Officers to the Suttler." He was also concerned that this order increased the dependence of the outpost on Kinzie and other "British traders," undermining Chicago's defense in time of war.

Matthew Irwin also relayed other concerns about Captain Heald in his January letter to the secretary of war, because of "a regard for the safety of this place." Irwin worried about the readiness of Chicago in case of attack. Irwin identified deficiencies in Captain Heald's war-readiness efforts. Irwin recommended that instead of maintaining a supply of wood sufficient only for one day's consumption that "the Commanding Officer, be ordered to use every effort to have a Supply sufficient for two or three months." Irwin also suggested that the U.S. Factory and U.S. Agency buildings adjacent to the fort be fortified to "render them capable of being defended and afford, in case of accident happening [at] the fort, an asylum to the troops & others."[31]

Several months later the secretary of war ordered Captain Heald to make these improvements. Heald responded angrily to Irwin's actions and accusations: "Your [Irwin's] secret underhanded representations to the Sec of War respecting my conduct here when we were, as I thought, on terms of friendship shall never be forgotten." Irwin's letter may have made Fort Dearborn safer from Indian attack, but it did not improve relations between the two top U.S. officials stationed there. As well, Irwin understood his complaints about smuggling and suttling "might render [his] situation very unpleasant—perhaps dangerous."[32]

Chicagoans began to hear of revenge attacks for the Battle of Tippecanoe along the Mississippi and near Vincennes. Nearly fifty Americans lost their lives in Louisiana, Illinois, Indiana, and Ohio during the first six months of 1812, more than five times the number killed in all of 1810 and 1811. The Kickapoos murdered a white family at St. Charles, Missouri. Mad Sturgeon led a group of Potawatomi warriors who burned a house north of Vincennes and killed two families of white settlers. Winnebago warriors attacked lead mines on the Mississippi River. At least three hundred white settlers, along with their families, fled the Illinois Territory in early 1812.[33]

Illinois governor Edwards assembled a group of Kickapoos, Potawatomis, Ojibwas, and Odawas at Cahokia to stem the tide of violence. White settlers fired on the group as they made their way south along the Illinois River, under the "protection" of Lieutenant Linai Helm from Fort Dearborn. Edwards told the assembled Indians of "the strong and sincere desire of our government to maintain peace and harmony," despite the fact that the envoy had been attacked by white settlers. Edwards could not control his allies, nor could the Indians who met with him. Gomo, one of the Potawatomis who traveled to Cahokia, admitted that neither he nor any other chief possessed the power to keep the peace.[34]

On March 10, 1812, Matthew Irwin reported that a party of Ho-Chunks from the Fox River visited Fort Dearborn. The party showed no hostile intentions, though it was not clear whether they had come from Prophetstown or had sympathies with Tecumseh. Nervous about the situation, Irwin sought to employ a spy to gain "such information as might lead to forming more accurate conclusions."[35] Irwin was right to be concerned. At the very same time of the Ho-Chunk visit, an informant in Indiana reported, "Chicago is the first place the Indians contemplate to attack."[36]

LEIGH FARM

April 6, 1812, began without much notice at Chicago. Eleanor Kinzie went a few houses to the west along the north bank of the Chicago River to visit a neighbor, Mary Burns, who had just given birth to a little girl. Mary Burns was a widow with four small children who had married a discharged soldier from Fort Dearborn.[37] While most of the soldiers at Fort Dearborn tended to regular duties that day, a party of seven soldiers took canoes up the south branch of the Chicago River to go fishing sometime after noon. They passed a farm about three miles south of Fort Dearborn, where three men and a teenage boy planted crops and tended to cattle. The boy, John Leigh, was the son of James Leigh and the grandson of William Russell, the retired soldiers who operated the farm and sold their stock and crops to the garrison.[38]

Sometime after the soldiers in canoes had passed, eleven Winnebago warriors, from the same group that had professed no hostile intent toward Fort Dearborn less than a month before, approached the Leigh farm. They were "all young men—armed with guns, tomahawks, & knives." John Leigh and John Kelso, an army private working the farm in his free time, fled north to the fort. The remaining two men were "not only shot, but scalped, and stabbed in various places." Captain Heald later wrote that the men were "shockingly butchered."[39]

Eleanor Kinzie was still at the Burns House when young John Leigh and Private John Kelso came running away from the Winnebago attack. Eleanor quickly alerted her family, and they all took shelter in the fort. Once there, they realized that the Burns family was still at their home. Several volunteers crossed the river in a scow and "took the mother, with her infant scarcely a day old, upon her bed to the boat, in which they carefully conveyed her and the other members of the family to the fort."[40]

In the meantime, Captain Heald fired one of the cannons, to warn the soldiers fishing up the south branch. It was dark when they heard the gun, so they silently made their way back to the fort. As they passed the Leigh farm, they stopped to check on the men there. In the dark, one soldier "placed his hand upon the dead body of a man. By the sense of touch he soon ascertained that the head was without a scalp and otherwise mutilated." The soldiers retreated to their canoes and hastily made their way back to the fort.[41]

In the wake of this attack, the residents of and around Fort Dearborn were on high alert. Captain Heald suspended all interaction with Indians, including the "friendly" tribes who lived nearby, until he could "find out to what nation the murderers belong." A group of Potawatomis from the Calumet region were forced to wave a white flag when approaching the fort to avoid an armed confrontation.[42]

With this order, Heald effectively shut down the U.S. Factory, so Matthew Irwin could no longer trade. With the trading house closed, area Pota-watomis, Ojibwas, Odawas, and Ho-Chunks were forced into the hands of private traders, many of whom worked for or with Kinzie. Incensed, Irwin opined that the main beneficiary of this policy was John Kinzie. He wrote that shutting the factory worked for "pretended Americans" like Kinzie who convinced Heald "that the Indians are generally unfriendly" and then supplied those same Indians through his private trading network.[43]

After the attack at the Leigh farm, Kinzie and his family moved into the garrison, while Lalime and the other civilians living around the fort (about fifteen men, described by Captain Heald as the "Chicago militia") moved into the house of the Indian agent, vacant since Charles Jouett had left the previous year. They included Leigh and Russell, as well as many of the French traders and engagés who lived around the Chicago River. Heald furnished the militia with arms and ammunition.

Other civilians departed Chicago. Samuel and Emmaline Clark, who had sold their crops and stock to the garrison, disappeared from Chicago as silently as they had arrived. Several families from Milwaukee returned there in the weeks after the Leigh farm attack. Jean Baptiste Mirandeau, who had been working as the blacksmith for the garrison, returned to Milwaukee (although he left his two daughters, Victoire and Madaline, in the Kinzie and Ouilmette households). François Laframboise and his two sons initially joined the militia, but then decided it was wiser to return to Milwaukee. They left Chicago, taking more than a dozen horses that did not belong to them. Jean Baptiste Beaubien married Laframboise's daughter Josette and followed her family to Milwaukee, well away from Fort Dearborn.[44]

Antoine and Archange Ouilmette stayed at Chicago, despite the threats made openly by soldiers to kill any Indians or mixed-race people. Archange Ouilmette's parents and siblings from the Calumet region were not allowed to enter the settlement in which she lived. Individual soldiers and members of the militia threatened the Ouilmettes, who had been at Chicago longer than anyone else. Irwin felt that Kinzie was behind this intimidation, as he "embraced all opportunities to inflame the minds" of soldiers "against a reconciliation with the Indians." Specific threats were also made against Jean Lalime and Matthew Irwin, who cautioned against branding all Indians as the enemy. Irwin felt that Kinzie, who masked his conduct "under the most Clamorous & ardent professions of patriotism to our government," was a most "dangerous character."[45]

PART THREE

In the Wake of the
Battle of Tippecanoe,
Late Spring 1812

7   Planning for War, Spring 1812

Sometime in the weeks after the attack on the Leigh farm, two young women, the wives of officers at Fort Dearborn, played a game called battledore, then a fashionable diversion in both Europe and the United States. Their play could have taken place in a Jane Austen novel as easily as at Chicago. Battledore was essentially an early form of badminton, with two players hitting a shuttlecock as many times as they could without allowing it to hit the ground. The battledore itself was a simple racket, used to hit the lightweight shuttlecock, often made by poking feathers into a small piece of cork. It was a frivolous game, with little purpose except to pass the time.

One could argue that the young women who played battledore were themselves frivolous. Both had arrived at Fort Dearborn the previous spring as recent brides of army officers and did not run their own households since they lived in quarters within the fort. While one of them was expecting her first child, neither woman yet had children in their care. Neither had kitchens to run, gardens to tend, cows to milk, or fires to keep. The operation of the fort did not require their presence. Instead, a pregnant Rebekah Wells Heald and Margaret McKillip Helm were at Fort Dearborn to be good company to their husbands, Captain Nathan Heald and Lieutenant Linai Helm.

During one of their games that spring, Naunongee, a Potawatomi leader from the Calumet region, came to visit Captain Heald. Jean Lalime accompanied him to interpret the Potawatomi words for Captain Heald. Naunongee was the grandfather of Archange Ouilmette and Sheshi Buisson, two residents at Chicago who supervised substantial households and had little time for games like battledore. As Naunongee passed the young women, he remarked, "The white chiefs' wives are amusing themselves very much; it will not be long before they are hoeing in our cornfields!"[1]

Figure 18. Painting of Fort Dearborn and the Kinzie House by Edgar S. Cameron, 1911. (Chicago History Museum, DN-0009351)

While Naunongee's words were "considered at the time an idle threat," they were a reminder of the fragility of the world that Americans inhabited at Fort Dearborn. Around them swirled the winds of war that would eventually sweep them up. By the spring of 1812, Rebekah Wells Heald and Margaret Helm might well have recognized the incongruity of their play. Following the Leigh farm murders, these women, like the other residents at Chicago, wrestled with the brutal violence that had taken place in their midst. Still, the game took them away from their troubled world.

The violence at the Leigh farm and other revenge attacks for Tippecanoe were in many ways a diversion from planning under way for interrelated wars that would affect the region around Chicago. Tecumseh was planning a pan-Indian war against the United States from his base at a rebuilt Tippecanoe, while President James Madison was planning a war against Great Britain from Washington, D.C. Tecumseh hoped that the moment was right to expect British aid in efforts to hold Indian Country against U.S. aggression.

Tecumseh certainly saw revenge attacks like that at the Leigh farm as working against a successfully orchestrated Indian war. His professed peace with General Harrison in late January 1812 provided him time to organize his response to Tippecanoe. Tecumseh denounced the revenge attacks by Ho-Chunk, Potawatomi, and Kickapoo warriors, and blamed "the bad acts" on "our brothers, the Potawatomies."[2] Tecumseh knew that his war plans rested on a ready supply of ammunition. By distancing himself from these attacks, Tecumseh hoped to get food and ammunition from both the Americans and the British.

While Tecumseh renounced the revenge attacks, they did provide him with cover during the first half of 1812. Some U.S. officials continued to believe that the main threat came from these unorganized raids. Illinois territorial governor Ninian Edwards thought "that the war will be carried on by the Indians for some time to come in small parties." Edwards acknowledged that a "general attack upon some of our towns and villages may possibly happen." However, the Illinois governor did "not consider it a probable event at the present time."[3]

TECUMSEH'S WAR PLANS

Before Harrison's November 1811 attack, Tecumseh planned a large expansion of Tippecanoe and the settlement of his supporters onto lands ceded in the 1809 Treaty of Fort Wayne. After Tippecanoe, many of Tenskwatawa's staunchest supporters among the Potawatomis, Kickapoos, and Winnebagos questioned his power and standing. Nevertheless, Tecumseh still hoped to garner their support for a pan-Indian confederacy that could take advantage of a U.S. war with Great Britain.[4]

Tecumseh attended an intertribal council in May at Mississinewa, about midway between Tippecanoe and Fort Wayne along the Wabash River, to enlist support for his plans. The Mississinewa council lasted about twelve days with representatives from the Wyandots, Ojibwas, Odawas, Potawatomis, Delawares, Miamis, Eel Rivers Weas, Piankashaws, Shawnees, Kickapoos, and Ho-Chunks. They came from as far east as the Appalachian Mountains and from west of the Mississippi River, as well as from south of the Ohio River. Among these representatives were familiar figures like Little Turtle and Five Medals. Also invited were British and American observers, including William Wells and Billy Caldwell, who had served as Kinzie's clerk at Chicago but more recently had worked closely with Tecumseh.[5]

Tecumseh made several speeches to the Mississinewa council, arguing for a united pan-Indian military force. He had been calling for a confederacy for several years. Now it was even more important, as war between the United States and Great Britain loomed. Tecumseh described this union as an "island" amidst the turmoil fomented by the United States. Such a confederacy would provide protection against any future American aggression. Tecumseh said that if "any of our people [have] been killed we will immediately send to all the nations on or towards the Mississippi, and all this island will rise like one man."[6]

Besides making speeches, Tecumseh had private talks with British representatives as well as with his allies assembled at Mississinewa. Tecumseh built on the relationships he had honed in his travels across the region. He organized "the Indians from Detroit and on the lakes . . . with all the other Indians to the westward as far as the river St. Peter on the Mississippi." This alliance was divided into "four grand divisions" that were "to aid one another" in "cases of necessity." The westernmost divisions consisted of the Sioux and Fox. A second division, headed up by Main Poc, included the Sauks, Ho-Chunks, Ojibwas, Odawas, Kickapoos, and Potawatomis in the area that is now Illinois and Wisconsin. Tecumseh would head the third division, which included the Potawatomis of the Kankakee, St. Joseph, Yellow, Wabash, and White Rivers, while a final division included the Miamis and Potawatomis in Michigan and northeast Indiana.[7]

To the assembled representatives at Mississinewa, Tecumseh announced that he was going to return to Tippecanoe so his women kin could plant corn. He encouraged his followers to do so as well. While waiting for the corn to ripen, Tecumseh planned to send a "party to Fort Malden for powder and lead." In so many words, Tecumseh set out a timetable for events in the region. His supporters would harvest a corn crop, while he accumulated the ammunition needed to fight a war. In the meantime, Tecumseh cautioned his supporters—especially Potawatomi leaders like Mad Sturgeon, White Sturgeon, and Main Poc—to refrain from further attacks against American settlers, in order to keep a fragile peace while preparations were under way.[8]

To further solidify plans, Tecumseh encouraged warriors to meet in June at Peoria, Milwaukee, and Saukenauk, the largest Sauk town at the juncture of the Rock River with the Mississippi. Tecumseh did not attend these councils but sent "black wampum with carrots of tobacco painted red," which was a "recognized invitation to war." At Saukenauk on June 26, 1812, at least twenty-five representatives met, including Shawnees, Winnebagos, Kickapoos, Potawatomis, and Sauks. While some accepted Tecumseh's invitation to war, others, including Black Hawk, were more responsive to the call of the British Indian Agent Robert Dickson, who was also raising troops.[9]

A June council at Peoria accepted Tecumseh's call to war after the corn harvest. Among the twelve hundred warriors in attendance were Black Partridge and Gomo, who had long supported the United States. Tecumseh's ally Main Poc was still in Detroit, but his brothers-in-law, White Sturgeon and Mad Sturgeon, were present. Naunongee and other Calumet warriors might have journeyed to Peoria as well. While Thomas Forsyth did not attend the council, he received regular reports about it and passed along selected information to the Illinois governor. Forsyth assured Governor Edwards that war would not come until after harvesttime.[10]

There was little overt support or sympathy for Americans in the Peoria villages. Thomas Forsyth found that even Gomo, one of the strongest allies of the United States in the region, was unwilling to appear pro-American. Gomo related to Forsyth after the June council at Peoria that the Indians needed arms and ammunition but were not able to get any at Chicago, where they had done so in the past. While Gomo would not cast his lot with the United States, he was discouraged by the actions and words of his fellow villagers. He went so far as to consider abandoning the Potawatomis to "live and die among the White people."[11]

Representatives from still more Potawatomi, Ojibwa, and Winnebago villages held a third council in late June at Milwaukee. Among them was Siggenauk (Blackbird), who had accompanied Main Poc on many southern raids as well as to Washington, D.C., in late 1808. Warriors at Milwaukee also considered messages from Robert Dickson, who encouraged them to join him at Fort St. Joseph, the British outpost near Mackinac.

From the Milwaukee council, more detailed war plans emerged. Warriors there had matters arranged so that "the Americans would be attacked at different places at one and the same time."[12] They intended to lay siege at Chicago in August, "as corn gets its roasting ears," followed by similar actions at Fort Madison, Fort Wayne, and Fort Harrison.

The representatives at Milwaukee were confident of an easy victory at

Chicago and laughed "at the idea of its holding out against the force with which they [could] attack it."[13] From Fort Dearborn, they planned first to take as many horses as possible and drive away the cattle from the garrison. Then they could begin a siege, eating the garrison cattle as they waited for the soldiers to surrender the fort and the ammunition held within its palisades.[14]

SECURING AMMUNITION

The Potawatomis, Miamis, Kickapoo, and Winnebago warriors who counseled for war still lacked supplies, especially ammunition.[15] Captain Heald's decision to shut down trading operations at Chicago had a devastating effect on the warriors' ability to wage war. They hoped that British-allied traders, including Louis Buisson and Joseph Bailly, could obtain ammunition from the British at Fort St. Joseph. Thomas Forsyth, at Peoria, worried that "should the traders who are gone to Mackinaw bring any gunpowder the Indians will take it [Chicago] by force."[16]

Main Poc was already in Detroit waiting on supplies through the spring and early summer of 1812. Illinois governor Ninian Edwards sought information about Main Poc and "what his disposition may be towards the U.S." Edwards worried about "what forces he [was] likely to raise."[17] At the same time, Potawatomi warriors along the Illinois River waited "his arrival with impatience," sure that Main Poc would "bring the truth and good news of War from their British fathers." They also expected Main Poc to bring "a large supply of powder."[18]

However, the British were hesitant about releasing guns and ammunition, and Main Poc remained at Detroit. They preferred to hold Main Poc for the anticipated fighting around Detroit. One historian has suggested that Main Poc, after spending the winter at Fort Malden, "had developed a considerable taste for creature comforts" and wanted to remain "next to the source of British largess." Whatever the motivation, Main Poc stayed on the British side and "could not get across the river to return home."[19]

Main Poc was not the only Indian caught by hardening international lines. By June 1812 "the whole of Detroit River from one end to the other was lined with troops to stop the communication of the Indians." It became impossible for anyone—Indian, American, or British—to move easily across this usually porous international border.[20] Rather than returning to fight in the West, Main Poc could only send messages to his supporters in western Michigan, Indiana, Illinois, and Wisconsin to keep to their war plans.

While Main Poc hoped to bring British ammunition into the western Great Lakes, Tecumseh also saw a real opportunity at Fort Wayne to get supplies from the Americans. The garrison and environs were deeply unsettled by a series of events. Little Turtle died in early June 1812, after returning home from Mississinewa. He had been a steadfast ally of the United States since 1795 and counseled many in the region against joining Tecumseh's confederacy. The loss of his influence and insight compromised U.S. interests in the region.

Little Turtle's death further diminished the authority of William Wells. For more than fifteen years, Wells had worked closely with the powerful Miami warrior. Coupled with the fact that Wells was no longer a U.S. Indian agent, he could not keep order at Fort Wayne. Governor Harrison, recognizing Wells's importance at Fort Wayne, had tried unsuccessfully to have him reinstated as the Indian agent.[21]

Instead, President James Madison had appointed the son of a close friend as the new U.S. Indian agent at Fort Wayne. Benjamin Franklin Stickney arrived in Fort Wayne on April 11, 1812, with little or no experience in Indian Country. He was pompous, vain, and inexperienced. Stickney immediately became embroiled in a conflict with Governor Harrison, arguing that Harrison had no authority over him. Harrison pointed out the threat this posed: "a jarring and discord more fatal to the public interests than even the intrigues of the enemy."[22]

Tecumseh took advantage of this unsettled situation. After Little Turtle's death, he came to Fort Wayne with Tenskwatawa. They flattered the new U.S. Indian agent, suggesting that they would negotiate with him but no one else. William Wells, who watched Tecumseh ingratiate himself with Stickney, complained that he had "completely duped the agent" and kept him "blind to his movements."[23] More troublesome, Stickney gave them "powder and lead," ostensibly to keep the delegation from starving, but in reality supplying Tecumseh with badly needed ammunition.[24]

After dispensing the powder and lead from Fort Wayne to his supporters, Tecumseh continued on his way to Fort Malden. He hoped to "to receive from the British government 12 horse loads of ammunition for the use of his people at Tippecanoe." Instead, Tecumseh arrived at Malden just as the United States and Great Britain went to war. Tecumseh immediately "declared that he would join the British against the United States."[25] As was the case for Main Poc, Tecumseh did not return westward, but instead stood and fought with the British against the Americans at Detroit.

THE BRITISH PREPARE FOR WAR
WITH THE UNITED STATES

All the while Tecumseh and his allies across the West were laying out war plans, the British were also making preparations for war with the United States. While the plans began separately, once hostilities ensued, they melded in the West into a military action that quickly entangled Main Poc, Tecumseh, and other warriors. While the war was initiated by the United States, at least in the western Great Lakes the British made better preparations for war. This was in no small part because of Robert Dickson.

Dickson was the most important British-allied trader based along the Mississippi River northwest of Chicago. After the Battle of Tippecanoe, he understood that war between the United States and Tecumseh's forces as well as war between Great Britain and the United States were increasingly likely. During the winter of 1811–12, Dickson distributed "his entire stock of goods, which had cost him at Montreal about $10,000," among his contacts from Green Bay to Saukenauk, thus cementing the loyalty of many villages to him. His intention was to keep his trading partners loyal to him, not to Tecumseh's confederacy or to American traders.

Dickson had traded for more than two decades in the upper Great Lakes, especially in the territory between Michilimackinac, Green Bay, and Prairie du Chien. An unusually tall, red-haired man, he emigrated from Scotland and embarked on a career in the fur trade.[26] Nominally a U.S. citizen after 1796, Dickson sought appointment as the U.S. Indian agent for the upper Mississippi in 1808. However, Americans there felt that Dickson's ties to British fur traders were too strong, as was his loyalty to the crown. These were reason enough for "refusing to appoint him to an office of so much trust and responsibility."[27] Instead, Dickson developed even closer ties with British agents and traders. As well, he married the sister of the Sioux leader Red Thunder, and this helped "him to achieve a unique position of trust" among western Indians. By 1812 he was described as "perhaps the most influential [white] man in the Indian Country."[28]

In the spring of 1812, while Dickson was at Green Bay, he received messages from the British commander in the West soliciting his help in raising a force of Indian warriors to fight against the United States, weeks before a formal war declaration. He was able to raise a force of three hundred to five hundred warriors "of all sorts of different languages." This force exhibited the depth and range of Dickson's influence, as well as his ability to raise a pan-Indian force that was not wedded strictly to the nativist vision of Tecumseh. These warriors arrived at St. Joseph Island, the British fort near to Mackinac, at the beginning of July, just before word of the declaration of war between Great Britain and the United States reached them. Dickson's Indians "were eager for the attack. . . . [T]he decided stand they took determined the course of other tribes."[29]

8 John Kinzie's Ambiguous Loyalties and a Forgotten Murder, May–June 1812

While Robert Dickson's allegiances were quite clear in 1812, John Kinzie's were ambiguous. He and his partner, Thomas Forsyth, had accepted a large supply of trade goods (and concomitant debt) from British-allied merchants at the beginning of the year. While their goods were British in origin, they traded them in U.S. circles and served as the exclusive sutler for the garrison. John Kinzie sold British goods to U.S. soldiers and officials at Chicago, even though this was in direct violation of non-importation laws.[1]

Kinzie was less troubled by any apparent inconsistency in his trading practices. He sought profit, not strict allegiance to a national government. For Kinzie, "country" was not the United States or Great Britain, but the Indian Country in which he lived.[2] The best outcome of the unsettled times would be for the United States or Great Britain to prevent settlers from moving into the region, in order to maintain a territory where "the citizens of the United States are kept at such a distance from those tribes."[3]

While Captain Heald and John Kinzie reached some sort of accommodation (perhaps Heald even agreed with his vision for the region), the U.S. factor at Chicago remained rigid in his condemnation of Kinzie. For years Matthew Irwin had been complaining to officials in Washington, D.C., that Kinzie was getting his trade goods from the British, thus breaking non-importation laws. In Irwin's view, Kinzie was a British sympathizer, one of the "enemies of the Country." Irwin's allegiance to the United States was unambiguous; for him, there was no Indian Country to protect, just British and American territory to be defended.

In early 1812 Irwin complained to Secretary of War William Eustis about Heald and Kinzie. These perilous missives undermined any cooperation at Chicago.[4] Captain Heald knew that Irwin had succeeded in removing his predecessor from the command of Fort Dearborn. He acknowledged that Irwin wielded real power with the secretary of war, but that would not induce him to "adopt your opinions in preference to my own in military affairs . . . for fear of offending you."[5]

Captain Heald also had to contend with the troublesome officers under his command: Surgeon's Mate Isaac Van Voorhis, Lieutenant Linai Helm, and Ensign George Ronan. Ronan had graduated from West Point and Van Voorhis from the College of Physicians and Surgeons in New York City, but both were inexperienced and new to the West. Fort Dearborn was their very first posting in the army. The more experienced Lieutenant Helm was John Kinzie's son-in-law. All three became embroiled in the disputes between Heald and Irwin.

Irwin cultivated Surgeon's Mate Isaac Van Voorhis as his ally. Following Irwin's lead, Van Voorhis wrote directly to the secretary of war several times during the first half of 1812. Van Voorhis understood that this was a serious breach of military etiquette but felt it was necessary under the conditions he faced at Fort Dearborn.

Van Voorhis did not attack Heald directly but complained instead about Lieutenant Helm and Ensign Ronan and their "unofficer-like and extravagant conduct." Van Voorhis noted the most striking part in Lieutenant Helm was his "ignorance." While Captain Heald was trying to "ensure the friendship of the well-disposed savages about this post," Helm and Ronan subverted his intentions at every opportunity. Helm "opposed every part of his [Heald's] policy in a most daring manner, taking the soldiers . . . and inflaming them against every peaceable Indian of the place." Van Voorhis claimed that Ronan was under the influence of Helm and did his bidding.[6]

Together, Irwin and Van Voorhis painted a picture of an ineffective commander with two rogue officers. According to Irwin and Van Voorhis, John Kinzie controlled Lieutenant Helm and held great influence over Captain Heald. Van Voorhis wrote that Kinzie "labours daily to inflame the minds of the subalterns against the Indians with probably interested motives." In this view, Kinzie was two-faced: condemning the "peaceable Indians" who came to Fort Dearborn as "damned rascals," all the while supplying belligerent Indians "in their own country." For Irwin and Van Voorhis, Kinzie was a traitor who threatened to undermine any U.S. control at Chicago.[7]

All of this must have been distressing to Captain Heald, a man at home with the order fostered by the military. Additionally, Heald was waiting on an overdue promotion to major that would bring not only a higher rank, but also more pay. As a captain, Heald received $480 a year in salary, less than half what Matthew Irwin earned as the factor. Heald kept a small notebook with him that served as a diary and held other important information. In it, Heald maintained two sets of statistics: the progression of his salary and his relative rank against other U.S. Army officers. The captain was very aware that his salary fell far short of that of his nemesis Matthew Irwin.

Heald's diary entries were intermittent and short, and of a personal nature. He made only one entry in the first six months of 1812; on May 4 he noted that "we had a son born dead for the want of a skillful Midwife." Rebekah Wells Heald, the young woman who had so cheerfully played battledore outside the officers' quarters just weeks before, now mourned the loss of her first child. The delivery was too difficult for her neighbors Martha Leigh, Mary Burns, Archange Ouilmette, and Eleanor Kinzie, who assisted one another through pregnancies and illnesses. Moreover, the trained physician at Chicago, Dr. Isaac Van Voorhis, was aligned against Heald in the officers' feud. The commander at Fort Dearborn was preoccupied with this personal tragedy as well as the political machinations among his officers, but events beyond the fort also pressed in.[8]

BRITISH MESSENGERS FOR ROBERT DICKSON

In late April 1812, three visitors to Chicago seemed to confirm Irwin's and Voorhees's worst fears about Kinzie's allegiance to Great Britain and Captain Heald's incompetence. The British, in anticipation of a declaration of war, sent out instructions to their agents across Indian Country "for the purpose of exciting the Savages to take up the tomahawk against the United States."[9] The three men who arrived at Fort Dearborn were messengers sent from Fort Malden in search of Robert Dickson.

The party consisted of two Ojibwa warriors and a French trader familiar with the western Great Lakes. In the eyes of U.S. officials like Matthew Irwin, the two Ojibwas were accompanying the French messenger, Francis Reheaum. In reality, the Ojibwas were the messengers, while the French trader was a foil to confuse U.S. officials. Indeed, Captain Heald arrested the French trader on suspicion that he was a British emissary but instructed the two Ojibwas to remain at a distance from the outpost (as all Indians had to since the Leigh farm murders).[10]

At the same time that this party arrived at Chicago, Captain Heald was dealing with the birth and death of his son. His distrust of Factor Irwin and

Surgeon's Mate Voorhis, as well as the now long-term absence of Agent Charles Jouett, left Heald with few people he could rely on, but he needed help in interviewing Reheaum. Jean Lalime, the garrison interpreter, seems not to have been present at Chicago, and Heald certainly missed his counsel. Instead, Heald turned to John Kinzie, as a U.S. justice of the peace, for help.[11]

Kinzie formally questioned Reheaum for an official deposition. In his testimony, Reheaum stated that he was "a subject of Great Britain" and a "resident of the Town of Malden in upper Canada."[12] In the course of the deposition, Reheaum confessed that he had been employed by the Indian agent at Malden to find Robert Dickson, who was expected at Green Bay. The Ojibwa messengers carried letters that asked Dickson to recruit Indian warriors and proceed immediately to the British St. Joseph Island, on an island near Mackinac. After giving his statement, Reheaum was allowed to return to British Fort Malden.[13]

Even before this interview, the Ojibwa messengers had fled in the night, carrying their messages to Dickson. Irwin complained to the secretary of war that no effort was made to hold the Ojibwa travelers. Instead, they remained "at a distance from the garrison, & as might have been expected, made their escape." Irwin surmised that "whatever object is in view in sending those persons to Green Bay that the most secret part is confided to the guides."[14]

The actions of John Kinzie and Captain Heald, as well as the harping criticisms of Matthew Irwin, had a real effect on war preparations. Because of Kinzie's deposition of Reheaum, Captain Heald was able to let U.S. officials know that Dickson had been asked to recruit warriors and head to Mackinac. However, this information did not reach authorities in time for it to be useful. Instead, because the Ojibwa messengers were allowed to pass through Chicago unmolested, Robert Dickson received his instructions in time. He arrived at Mackinac with a force of up to five hundred warriors at the start of the war.[15]

Robert Dickson, like Kinzie, had straddled the American and British worlds for over two decades. However, in 1812 he clearly cast his support to the British in anticipation of war. John Kinzie's position was not so clear. One could conclude, as Irwin and Van Voorhis did, that the incident confirmed Kinzie's British loyalties, "despite his most Clamorous & ardent professions of patriotism to our government."[16] Kinzie allowed the Ojibwa messengers to pass safely through Chicago and so left the British far better prepared for the beginning of the war in the West.

However, Kinzie stepped in and helped Captain Heald at a moment of great personal crisis. He did not let the feuding junior officers at Fort Dearborn miss an opportunity to gain information from a deposition that might be useful to the Americans. Perhaps it would be best to understand Kinzie's loyalties as personal, to Captain Heald, rather than a monolithic national allegiance.

THE DEATH OF JEAN LALIME

Alongside the puzzle of Kinzie's motivations, there remains the question of where the U.S. interpreter at Fort Dearborn, Jean Lalime, was during these days. There is no record of Jean Lalime's presence at Chicago during the Reheaum visit. His absence was unfortunate since Jean Lalime was the longest serving U.S. employee at Fort Dearborn. He provided stability, deep memory, and broad knowledge of the region to the Americans stationed there. Lalime also regularly corresponded with U.S. officials at Fort Wayne, St. Louis, and Kaskaskia about local conditions and information he had gleaned. This was well beyond his duties as the interpreter at Chicago. It is quite possible that Lalime was traveling within the region in late April and early May, collecting intelligence to share with U.S officials.

It had not been an easy spring for Jean Lalime at Fort Dearborn. The infighting among the officers at the garrison, as well as the growing conflict between Factor Irwin and John Kinzie (and Captain Heald), had inevitably entangled Lalime. Lalime worked most closely with Matthew Irwin at the U.S. Factory and with Captain Heald in distributing annuities and managing Indian affairs in the absence of the U.S. Agent Charles Jouett. When Captain Heald shut down the factory in the wake of the Leigh farm attack, Lalime was cut loose from the work that had consumed so much of his time.

Lalime also found himself threatened by Lieutenant Helm and Ensign Ronan. Helm got into a strong argument with Jean Lalime and made "some harsh expressions . . . against the U.S. Factor and Factory." Helm told Lalime that he hoped "the Factory would be done away." Lalime "defended the pure motives and just dealings of the institution." Also, Ensign Ronan "threatened to shoot the Interpreter." As spring turned to summer, the threats continued.[17]

However, it was not Lieutenant Helm or Ensign Ronan who attacked Jean Lalime. Instead, John Kinzie fought Lalime on the evening of June 17, 1812, just outside Fort Dearborn. Their conflict may have been related to the earlier threats of Ronan and Helm. It certainly was premeditated, as both men were armed and ready. Lalime—the older, slighter of the two—carried a pistol. Kinzie had sharpened a large butcher's knife on the grindstone behind his house and hidden it under his coat. Both men came out from the fort together, but it is not altogether clear whether they had agreed to a fight or not. According to one source, Lieutenant Helm shouted a warning to Kinzie that Lalime had a pistol.[18]

Several people witnessed the fight, including two young métis women, one of whom was then working for the Kinzie family. The young women—sisters—were just outside Fort Dearborn, while Matthew Irwin, the third witness, stood about thirty feet from the fight. One of the sisters later remembered, "We saw the men come out together; we heard the pistol go off, and saw the smoke. Then they fell down together. I don't know as Lalime got up at all but Kinzie got home pretty quick. Blood was running from his shoulder where Lalime shot him."[19] Captain Heald, who did not witness the attack, described it as one citizen stabbing another citizen.[20]

Eleanor Kinzie and Nokenoqua rushed to the aid of their injured husbands, although neither witnessed the fight. Nokenoqua "screamed aloud when she saw her little old husband bodily lifted off the ground by the red bearded gigantic Kinzie."[21] Lalime died immediately. Kinzie, having received a gunshot to his shoulder, returned to his family's quarters, where his wife cleaned and dressed his wounds.[22]

When Kinzie realized there were eyewitnesses to the attack, he decided to leave the fort. Both Matthew Irwin and Isaac Van Voorhis saw Lieutenant Helm escort Kinzie out of the garrison around ten o'clock at night. Helm walked Kinzie to the river, shook his hand, and watched Kinzie slip across the water. John Kinzie fled into the woods north of the river, where he stayed for several days. Captain Heald put out an arrest warrant for Kinzie. However, the officers and soldiers at Fort Dearborn were not able to capture Kinzie, even though he was "within gun shot of the garrison." Van Voorhis wrote to the secretary of war: "This much appears but too plain, the Officers seem not to wish to apprehend him, or at least the measures taken are not calculated to prove effectual." Given that one of the other officers was Lieutenant Helm, Kinzie's son-in-law, this may well have been true.[23]

REASONS FOR THE MURDER

Eleanor Kinzie long argued that her husband killed Lalime in self-defense. She portrayed two men, well known to each other, who had a violent falling-out. Eleanor Kinzie remembered that Jean Lalime and her husband "had for several years been on unfriendly terms, and had had frequent altercations."[24] Kinzie and Lalime certainly had a long and contentious relationship going back to the 1790s at St. Joseph when they both worked for William Burnett. Certainly, the tangled transactions surrounding the sale of Point de Sable's holdings to Lalime and then in short order to Kinzie between 1800 and 1803 may have been an ongoing cause of conflict.

As well, the competition between the U.S. Factory, the sutler at Fort Dearborn, and private fur trading in the region involved Kinzie and Lalime and might have set off their deadly fight. In fact, sometime before Lalime's death, James Leigh, the discharged soldier who was selling beef and other food to the garrison (and whose farm had been attacked), went into partnership with John Burnett, the son of the longtime trader at St. Joseph, William Burnett. Leigh & Burnett hoped to capture some of the suttling trade at Fort Dearborn but were rebuffed when Captain Heald granted Kinzie & Forsyth the exclusive suttling rights in January 1812.

It is possible that Lalime tried to help Leigh & Burnett, based on his long friendship with the Burnett family. Soon after Lalime's murder, Matthew Irwin recommended that suttling remain "open to every one" in order to reduce conflict at Chicago.[25] That Irwin saw this as a way of reducing conflict in the future suggests that it might have fed the conflict between Kinzie and Lalime as well as between Heald and Irwin.

The conflict between Lalime and Kinzie might also have stemmed from Lalime's work as interpreter. In fact, before Lalime's death, "Kinzie and others had been intriguing to get Mr. Lalime dismissed" and one of their employees hired in his place. Lalime had served as the interpreter for all of the U.S. operations at Chicago. His position was a powerful one as he could slant the meanings of words and gestures to affect the outcome of any negotiation.[26]

For Matthew Irwin, Jean Lalime's death was an inestimable loss. It was almost impossible for him to trade in furs without an expert like Lalime. There was little chance that the U.S. Factory could reopen in the near future without an interpreter. Soon after Lalime's death, Captain Heald advised

Matthew Irwin to hire John Kinzie's employee, probably Pierre LeClair, as the new interpreter. Not surprisingly, Irwin refused to hire the "intemperate Frenchman," whom Irwin thought was a British subject under Kinzie's control.[27]

Finding a replacement for Lalime as interpreter at Fort Dearborn was hard enough, but Lalime had also provided the U.S. officials with information about Indian Country. Here, too, Kinzie competed with Lalime. In fact, Lalime's death cleared the way for Kinzie's partner and half-brother, Thomas Forsyth, to control information going to American officials in Illinois and Missouri. Forsyth would benefit from an appointment to a U.S. post that provided a steady income to augment irregular fur trade earnings.

Alongside all of these possibilities, it is important to remember that John Kinzie was a volatile and violent character. He was nearly fifty years old and had several small children. Along with Thomas Forsyth, he carried enormous debt and held a considerable store of trade goods. The strong likelihood of war in the region could interrupt regular trade for years, which could destroy Kinzie & Forsyth (or make their fortunes). The half-brothers had strong ties to Great Britain and upper Canada, but they had cultivated connections to American officials at St. Louis and Kaskaskia. All of this uncertainty may have led Kinzie to kill Lalime for one, many, or no clear reason.

Lalime became "the skeleton in Kinzie's closet." There was no inquest concerning Lalime's death, and by legend he was buried near the Kinzie house. In 1891 the remains of a man were unearthed on the north bank of the Chicago River near the spot where the Kinzie house had once stood. These remains were identified as Jean Lalime and were donated to the Chicago Historical Society. A newspaper account at the time explained the murder simply: Lalime "was on the side of the state in the conflict of economic and alcoholic policies," while Kinzie was "on the other side."[28]

IN THE AFTERMATH OF LALIME'S DEATH

Tensions were very high at Chicago in the wake of Lalime's murder. As witnesses to Lalime's death, Matthew Irwin and Dr. Isaac Van Voorhis feared for their lives.[29] Soon after Kinzie fled, Irwin moved into the quarters of Isaac Van Voorhis within Fort Dearborn for better protection. However, just a few days after Lalime's murder, a messenger arrived with letters from

Washington, D.C. Captain Heald received a reprimand from the secretary of war, based on Irwin's complaints about the management of Fort Dearborn. An enraged Captain Heald, with Helm and Ronan at his side, confronted Irwin.

While the words spoken are lost, Heald laid out his points in a letter posted to Irwin. Heald, generally careful with his emotions as well as his words, wrote: "Your secret underhanded representations to the Sec of War respecting my conduct here when we were, as I thought, on terms of friendship shall never be forgotten." Heald felt there was no "doubt [of] your intentions to injure me as a military commandant in every way in your power." Heald forbade Irwin from staying with the surgeon's mate, he took away the military servant that had been assigned to help Irwin in his house, and he had Irwin's "chief amusement," his garden, destroyed. In short, Heald tried to make Irwin as miserable as he could.[30]

These actions came on top of the fact that Irwin could do little of his work as factor without an interpreter and assistant like Jean Lalime, and so Irwin chose to leave Chicago. He feared for his life from many quarters, both inside the garrison and in a region on the brink of war. However, Irwin explained to the secretary of war that he was leaving because he could not find "a suitable waiter" or a place to board. He admitted that his situation was "very unpleasant" and he had chosen "to quit this place."[31]

Irwin closed up the factory and placed the government keys and account books in the care of Surgeon Mate's Van Voorhis. Irwin, afraid of "certain intemperate persons whose principals I had reason to think were too lo[o]se for my personal safety," left Chicago on July 5, 1812, in an open boat headed for Michilimackinac. Irwin stated quite plainly: "The murder of John Lalime, Indian Interpreter for the U.S. Trading house at Chicago by John Kinzie, made it necessary for me to leave that place."[32] He might have mentioned, but he did not, that his habit of writing letters filled with complaints to the secretary of war also made him a persona non grata at Fort Dearborn.[33]

Van Voorhis also feared for his life. Like Irwin and Lalime, he had faced threats by Ronan and Helm in the preceding months. In May 1812 he had written the secretary of war about his "extremely unpleasant, if not truly hazardous" position at Fort Dearborn. He would "prefer the regions of Zembie to Fort Dearborn." Again, in early June he wrote the secretary of war with concerns about his person: "I have not only been threatened by Lt. L.T. Helm, who is son-in-law to Mr. Kenzie [sic], in the presence of his father-in-law and others, but from him have been handed a challenge from Mr. Kenzie himself." Van Voorhis considered his "present Situation as really unpleasant at least." Van Voorhis asked again to be removed from Fort Dearborn. Because Van Voorhis was a U.S. Army officer, he was less able (or willing) to abandon his post. Instead, he wrote the secretary of war yet again, as Irwin made his preparations to leave Chicago, pleading to also leave because of "imminent danger."[34]

John Burnett afforded Nokenoqua and her son support and protection in the days after Jean Lalime's murder. Nokenoqua would eventually marry Burnett, who was at Chicago working with his partner, James Leigh. When Captain Heald issued an arrest warrant for Kinzie, Leigh & Burnett saw an opportunity to take over the suttling (or at least part of it) from the fugitive Kinzie. They approached Captain Heald with an application to supply the garrison as sutler.[35]

However, Heald was not interested in changing the suttling arrangement at Fort Dearborn, despite the fugitive status of John Kinzie. Leigh & Burnett "were told if the brother of Mr. Kinzie would continue his business, they could not be encouraged."[36] This despite the fact that Leigh & Burnett offered "to supply the Troops at a much more reasonable rate." After Heald turned down their proposal, James Leigh headed to Mackinac, perhaps on the same ship as Matthew Irwin. He left behind his wife and children.[37]

By June 1812 Thomas Forsyth had been John Kinzie's trading partner at Peoria for more than eight years. During that time he honed trade and personal relationships with Potawatomis, Sauks, and Kickapoos in the area west from Peoria to the Mississippi River. Black Hawk, the famous Sauk leader who lived along the Mississippi, described Forsyth as "my old friend."[38]

Forsyth traveled regularly to Chicago and made his way there with the packs of furs collected at Peoria that spring. He no doubt heard the account of Lalime's murder from Eleanor Kinzie and took time to reassure Captain Heald that Kinzie & Forsyth would continue to suttle at Fort Dearborn despite Kinzie's absence. Forsyth stayed at Chicago long enough to see the firm's fur packs loaded on a ship headed for Mackinac (probably the same vessel that carried Matthew Irwin and James Leigh). Unfortunately for Forsyth and his brother, the ship ladened with their furs fell "into the hands of the enemy" at Mackinac, and they never recovered them.[39]

In the weeks preceding Lalime's death, Forsyth had been in negotiations with William Clark and Ninian Edwards to become a salaried employee of the United States who would provide information to officials in Illinois and Missouri. Lalime's death made it even more important that the American government employ Forsyth. But Forsyth wanted a more substantial post and salary than that of an interpreter, the position held by Jean Lalime at his death. An agreement on terms stalled because of Forsyth's demands for more money as well as Clark's concerns about his loyalties.[40]

While Forsyth was clearly knowledgeable about the western Indian Country, Clark was worried about his allegiance to the United States. As with Kinzie, Forsyth's background suggested British sympathies rather than American loyalties. Through his marriage to Keziah Mallot, Forsyth was related to British Indian Agent Simon Girty. This served Kinzie & Forsyth well as they sought financing for their trading ventures in Illinois. However, these connections were liabilities when trying to convince American officials of their loyalty.[41]

Forsyth had the support of Governor Edwards. Since coming to Illinois as territorial governor in 1809, Edwards had stayed close to Cahokia and Kaskaskia, within the orbit of St. Louis. Forsyth presented Edwards with information about parts of Illinois he did not know, especially Peoria and Chicago. Edwards was delighted with Forsyth and found him to be "a very intelligent, gentlemanly man [who] has a perfect knowledge of the Indians, and would make a first rate agent." Edwards encouraged William Clark and the secretary of war to offer Forsyth the salary he requested. Edwards emphasized that Forsyth's knowledge of Peoria and environs was critical as it was "now a most important point to collect information" as well as to "command and [have] control over the Indians."[42]

Edwards and Clark agreed about the value of Thomas Forsyth and his intelligence gathering.[43] Lalime's assassination made it even more important for them to hire Forsyth, despite lingering concerns about his loyalties to the United States.[44] They agreed to hire him secretly as a subagent of Indian Affairs out of St. Louis. Forsyth embarked on a long and distinguished career with the United States Indian Agency, just as Lalime departed the scene.

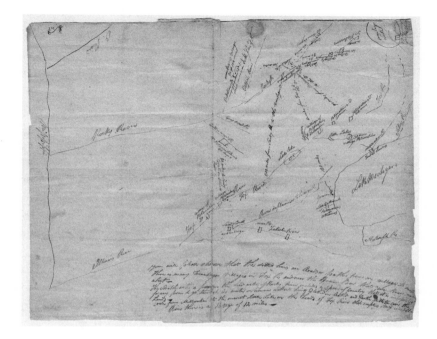

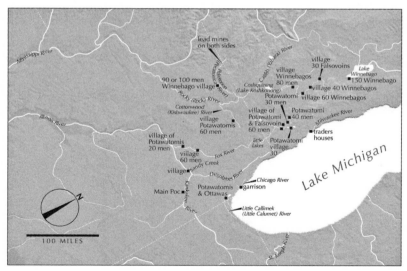

Map 8. a. Indian Country around Chicago in May 1812, drawn by John Hay, U.S. postmaster at Cahokia. (Chicago History Museum, ICHi-51821) *b.* Interpretation of the 1812 Hay Map. (Dennis McClendon, Chicago Cartographics)

Chicago until the attack on the Leigh farm. In fact, Jean Baptiste Mirandeau, whose daughters were living still with the Kinzies and Ouilmettes,
may have guided the wounded Kinzie to Milwaukee.[2]

Kinzie arrived at Milwaukee on June 21, 1812, in the midst of one of the
war councils called by Tecumseh just weeks before. Potawatomi, Winnebago, and Ojibwa warriors gathered to discuss messages from Tecumseh as
well as from British emissaries. Tecumseh urged them to join a pan-Indian
war, while the British sought their allegiance against the United States.
Kinzie was not immediately welcomed at Milwaukee, despite his long ties
there. At first, the Indians gathered at Milwaukee took Kinzie for "a person
sent to spy [on] their country." While he had strong ties to British traders
at Detroit, Kinzie was also the sutler at Fort Dearborn. The Indians at Milwaukee were as suspicious of Kinzie's loyalties as had been Matthew Irwin
back in Chicago.

Fortunately, Kinzie had the help of Jean Baptiste Mirandeau and Antoine
LeClair in convincing the assembled warriors of his anti-American stance.
LeClair was a familiar figure at Milwaukee, where he lived with his family
as a successful trader before going to work for Kinzie & Forsyth at Peoria. Antoine LeClair arrived in Chicago the day after Kinzie fled to Milwaukee. He was gathering intelligence across Potawatomi country for Thomas
Forsyth, who secretly shared this information with American officials at
Kaskaskia and St. Louis (so, in fact, the Indians at Milwaukee were right
to be suspicious of spies). LeClair followed Kinzie to Milwaukee, where he
eased Kinzie's acceptance into the assembled group. Following this, Kinzie
was shown "every act of friendship."[3]

Now welcome at the Milwaukee council, Kinzie met the two mysterious
Ojibwas who had evaded U.S. officials at Chicago just weeks before. Kinzie
confirmed that they had delivered messages to British trader Robert Dickson at Green Bay. Now they brought Dickson's call to stand with Great Britain against the United States. They "presented four pipes" from the Sioux,
who embraced Robert Dickson's call for war against the Americans. Kinzie
learned that a contingent of western Indians under Dickson's direction was
already on its way to the British outpost near Mackinac.[4]

Kinzie found the Potawatomis at Milwaukee among the most militant.
They were anxious to join Dickson in the "English War." The Winnebago
representatives were the "quietest." Kinzie felt their reticence was due to
a reprimand they had received for the attack at the Leigh farm at Chicago

some months before. Their attack had made it more difficult for the gathered Indians and their villages to get the supplies they needed. But most of the Indians at Milwaukee advocated war against the United States.

After staying a few days at Milwaukee, Kinzie headed south but did not return to Chicago. Instead, Kinzie remained in Indian Country and skirted west of Chicago along the Fox River. He stopped near the mouth of the Fox River at what is now Ottawa, adjacent to Starved Rock. From area Potawatomis, Kinzie learned that his half-brother, Thomas Forsyth, had passed through just two days before on his way to Chicago. Kinzie was able to send Forsyth a letter at Chicago (probably delivered either by or through Mirandeau). Kinzie wrote that he would travel to Peoria, where he would await his brother's return home. Kinzie arrived at Peoria around July 10, 1812, and no doubt stayed at Forsyth's house.[5]

PEORIA

Thomas Forsyth and his wife, Keziah, had lived at Peoria for eight years with their two young sons. Like Chicago, Peoria was a métis community, where several families lived and traded with neighboring villages of Potawatomis, Miamis, and Kickapoos. Information, people, and goods traveled easily from north to south, from Chicago to St. Louis along the Illinois River. Travel was also easy eastward along the Kankakee River to the Wabash and Tippecanoe Rivers in Indiana. Thomas Forsyth arrived home by July 13, 1812, to find his half-brother awaiting his arrival.

Kinzie and Forsyth were soon joined by at least two other men: Antoine LeClair finished his intelligence gathering at Milwaukee and returned to Peoria, while Billy Caldwell made his way to Peoria from Indiana. Caldwell—known as Sakonosh, or "English-speaking Canadian"—was a British subject. He had served as clerk for Kinzie & Forsyth when they first established an outpost at Chicago.[6]

These four men came together in Peoria in mid-July 1812, just as the war in the West was getting under way. Perhaps they met in the ample trading room in Forsyth's house, where Forsyth kept the ledger book for the accounts of Kinzie & Forsyth. On July 15, 1812, Antoine LeClair purchased three bottles of whiskey, and Billy Caldwell bought a pipe (of tobacco). None of the four likely envisioned that these would be the closing entries in the ledger book of Kinzie & Forsyth at Peoria.[7] However, they all understood the real danger in the region. They strategized about the months ahead, perhaps moving from the trading room to Forsyth's porch to drink whiskey and smoke in the July heat of central Illinois.

They were an enigmatic group. LeClair had access to councils like that at Milwaukee, because he presented himself as a British sympathizer, not an American partisan. The information that he gathered made its way into reports that Thomas Forsyth was sending off to Illinois territorial governor Ninian Edwards.[8] Billy Caldwell had been with Tecumseh in the spring but also shared information with Edwards. John Kinzie was the U.S. sutler at Fort Dearborn but allowed British messengers to pass unharmed through Chicago. Thomas Forsyth was a paid subagent of the United States, but many of his Potawatomi and Sauk friends expected him to heed Robert Dickson's call to aid the British cause.

There is no direct record of their discussions. In fact, Forsyth went to some lengths to disguise the fact that Kinzie and Caldwell ever came to Peoria. Kinzie and Caldwell wrote letters that Forsyth could share with American officials, leaving the impression they had not been in Peoria. Each of these men had allegiances to groups that would soon be at war with each other. Therefore, their meetings remained secretive, if not secret.[9]

Certainly, they must have discussed Kinzie's culpability in Jean Lalime's death. All four men had known and worked with Lalime over their decades at St. Joseph, Chicago, and Peoria. This gathering gave Kinzie an opportunity to explain what had happened. Kinzie may have defiantly claimed self-defense, but perhaps in the company of these old friends he expressed remorse concerning his "unfortunate affair." In the end, they agreed that Thomas Forsyth would go to Vincennes to plead his brother's case before Governor Harrison.

The decision to go to Harrison was a curious one, especially since Forsyth was in regular correspondence with Governor Edwards of Illinois. Forsyth did not even know Harrison and had to ask Edwards for an introduction. However, in 1804 Harrison had appointed Kinzie as a magistrate for the Indiana Territory. Perhaps the foursome hoped that this would provide some aid in Kinzie's case. The fact that Billy Caldwell agreed to travel with Forsyth to Vincennes added another layer of mystery to this decision. Caldwell had accompanied Tecumseh to British Detroit just weeks before. Now he traveled to a powerful U.S. official in the region. There remains a possibility that Lalime's murder provided cover for Forsyth and Caldwell to consult with Governor Harrison at a very sensitive moment.[10]

In fact, the four men together had intelligence about the planned wars in the West that Harrison might have valued enough to aid Kinzie. Arguably, they knew more than almost any other group in the West about war preparations. Billy Caldwell, from his long months with Tecumseh, reported that his pan-Indian allies on the Wabash were "anxious for war" but sought more supplies before hostilities. Antoine LeClair and John Kinzie, from their time among the Potawatomis and Ho-Chunks, saw that they were planning "war with the Americans." Kinzie knew that hundreds of warriors had already joined Robert Dickson in an attack on Mackinac, while other Potawatomis at Milwaukee waited with plans to attack the garrison at Chicago.[11] Forsyth found many of his Potawatomi and Miami neighbors awaiting the arrival of Main Poc "with impatience," so that an Indian war could begin.[12] Kinzie could also report on the internecine feuding among the officers at Fort Dearborn and a general lack of preparedness at Chicago for war.

By sharing this information with one another—and then with American officials—Kinzie, LeClair, Forsyth, and Caldwell betrayed many trusts. They all understood the dangerous positions they held. Forsyth worried about leaving his "property to merciless savages" and whether he would "get off with [his] life." While Forsyth shared information provided by these men, he pleaded with Governor Edwards "to keep the names of the writers a profound secret." Forsyth explained that there were rumors of his cooperation with U.S. officials that made his situation "very critical." Forsyth overtly denied collaboration with the Americans, leaving open the possibility that he was a British sympathizer.[13] Kinzie had done much the same at the Milwaukee council in June, assuring the Indians assembled there of his loyalty and then providing information to U.S. officials.

Why did these men risk their lives and property to come together at Peoria? Perhaps most importantly, they must have trusted one another completely. They wanted to support each on the cusp of hostilities, as well as to aid John Kinzie in any way they could. All four men were part of a trading world that knit together Indian, European, and American settlements into an Indian Country. Kinzie, LeClair, Caldwell, and Forsyth, like many other traders over time, crossed cultures. They made their living by making connections among groups. Their prosperity was based on "relying on friends and kin, and by positioning themselves as upstanding members of their milieus."[14]

War would upset these valuable connections and would lead these traders to be charged as traitors. Their ability to cross cultures, so valued in peacetime trade, left them with ambiguous allegiances. More than anything, these four men were allies in protecting their lives, families, and livelihoods during difficult times. They came closest to aligning themselves with those Potawatomis who were trying to stay out of the head-on clash between these two colonial powers and militant Potawatomis like Main Poc, Mad Sturgeon, and Blackbird.

After meeting for a few days, the men separated. Antoine LeClair stayed at Peoria and continued to collect information from area Potawatomis, Kickapoos, Sauks, and Ho-Chunks. Forsyth and Caldwell headed to Vincennes to plead Kinzie's case with Governor Harrison as well as to share their concerns about an imminent Potawatomi attack on Fort Dearborn.[15]

From Vincennes, Caldwell may have traveled back to Tippecanoe and ultimately on to Detroit to rejoin Tecumseh. Just a few months later, he would join the British Indian forces.[16] Forsyth headed to Chicago to manage the interests of Kinzie & Forsyth. Soon he accepted appointment as a U.S. subagent and provided American officials with regular information throughout the war.

Even before Forsyth made it to Chicago, Captain Heald decided to recall Kinzie. He understood that, regardless of the facts of the case, he needed Kinzie's knowledge of languages and personal connections. Heald posted a garrison order that permitted Kinzie to return and "live unmolested with his family until the civil authority takes him up." The Lalime murder was swept up in the tide of war.[17]

AUGUST 1812: CHICAGO

Kinzie returned to Chicago soon after he learned of Captain Heald's order. Kinzie knew that the Indians around Chicago, mainly Potawatomis, were increasingly hostile to the United States, only waiting for the word "to commence hostilities." Their resentment was compounded by the fact that the U.S. Factory (trading post) at Chicago was closed, and there were no plans to make annuity payments in the near term despite the large stock of sup-

plies held at Chicago. Hoping that some of these goods would be distributed, a growing number of Potawatomi warriors and their families were
"collecting at this post."[18]

In addition to managing affairs at Fort Dearborn, Captain Heald had
been ordered to send a contingent of Indian leaders to a council beginning
August 15 at Picqua, in northwest Ohio. Captain Heald pressed Kinzie to
take up this duty in the absence of an agent at Chicago. The intention of
the U.S. government was to draw away the leadership among Indians in
order to postpone any hostile actions. Local Potawatomi leaders hoped that
by attending the conference they would receive deferred annuities due or
other gifts from the United States. However, they were concerned that the
U.S. government might take the opportunity of their absence to launch
their own attacks (not unlike Harrison's attack on Tippecanoe the previous November). Kinzie was able to assemble a group of seventeen Potawatomi, Odawa, Ojibwa, and Ho-Chunk leaders only by offering his family
as "a pledge that no treachery would be made use of by our Government."
He accompanied the chiefs on their way to Picqua, leaving his family and
goods as ransom that the U.S. government would do them no harm. Eleanor Kinzie, by agreeing to this arrangement, also worked to maintain peace
at Chicago.[19]

The assembled group left Chicago in early August, traveling along the
southern shore of Lake Michigan.[20] According to Kinzie, they were near
St. Joseph when they met a messenger sent by General Hull, the U.S. commander at Detroit. The messenger, a Potawatomi named Winamac (Cat-
fish), told the group that Mackinac had fallen to the British. He also let
them know that he carried orders for Captain Heald to evacuate Chicago.
Captain William Wells and a party of Miamis either traveled with Winamac
from Fort Wayne or met him near St. Joseph as well. Kinzie and his group
halted their trip to Picqua and returned home. Kinzie sent word ahead to
Captain Heald "not to evacuate until they arrived" at Chicago.[21] Captain
Wells also agreed to come to Fort Dearborn, perhaps staying for a time
in the St. Joseph area in consultation with Topinbee and members of the
Burnett family.

Winamac arrived at Fort Dearborn on August 9, 1812. By then Captain
Heald and the contingent at Fort Dearborn knew that British-allied Indians
and traders had taken the U.S. fort at Michilimackinac without firing a shot.
From Winamac, they learned that after initial successes at Sandwich and

Amhertsburg just east of Detroit into Canada, British forces, aided by Tecumseh and Main Poc, were pressing hard against General Hull's army. On the day that Hull learned that Mackinac had fallen, he sent Captain Heald his evacuation order. Chicago was on the outer reaches of his threatened territory—Hull did not have the resources to send reinforcements.[22]

In a letter to the secretary of war, General Hull explained that the retreat was to take place "provided it can be effected with a greater prospect of safety than to remain." Hull noted, "Captn Heald is a judicious officer" and expressed confidence in "his discretion."[23] Heald interpreted this order to mean: "evacuate the post and proceed with my command to Detroit, by land, leaving it at my discretion to dispose of the public property as I thought fit."[24]

Hull's orders contradicted the learned experience of the U.S. Army over two decades of Indian war. Among the hard-earned rules for engagement that had evolved was the instruction to stay close to a "strong fortified base." Abandoning Fort Dearborn flew in the face of this tested tactic.[25] However, Fort Dearborn was on the periphery of General Hull's operations. Nor was it central to the operations of Indiana governor William Henry Harrison, Illinois governor Ninian Edwards, or Louisiana governor Benjamin Howard. Not one of these leaders saw Chicago as vital to the area that they governed. No one sent further instructions or aid to Heald.

Instead, the only outside assistance that came to Fort Dearborn was from William Wells, a disgraced former Indian agent who was seen as a traitor by many Indians. The death of his longtime ally, the Miami chief Little Turtle, further diminished Wells's influence. However, Rebekah Wells Heald was his niece, and he felt an obligation to help. Without Wells's sense of personal responsibility, no one would have come to the aid of Fort Dearborn.

Both Wells and Kinzie pressed Captain Heald to evacuate quickly or to prepare to stay at Chicago. Kinzie felt that the fort had sufficient supplies to withstand an attack from Indians even with British assistance. However, Captain Heald remained firm in following Hull's order to evacuate.[26] He felt there was no choice. The captain could not expect any help. If he had to surrender, it would not be to the British (as was the case for his counterparts at Mackinac and Detroit) but to a loose confederation of Potawatomis and their allies. According to his son, Captain Nathan Heald did not face much of a decision: "My father was a soldier and knew his duty. His commanding officer, Hull, had ordered him to withdraw, and withdraw he did."[27]

The news of Hull's order traveled quickly across Indian Country. Many hurried to Chicago with the expectation that the goods and ammunition at the factory would be distributed to area Indians as a goodwill gesture. Hundreds of warriors, as well as women and children, already camped at Chicago. They hoped to receive a share of the stockpiled goods and ammunition. They did not necessarily mean to attack. However, their presence threatened the small group of U.S. soldiers and settlers at Chicago. Kinzie family members remembered feeling that the start of every day seemed to "bring them nearer that most appalling fate."[28]

While the vast majority of the Indians surrounding Fort Dearborn did not exhibit active hostility, there were incidents that suggested an undercurrent of danger. In the days before Heald led the contingent from Fort Dearborn, an Indian shot and wounded an ox "that was very near the captain." There was also fear about the Indians that the contingent might encounter on their way to Fort Wayne, especially with the proximity of Tippecanoe and the "prophet's Indians" along that route.[29]

DISTRIBUTION AND DESTRUCTION

Captain Wells, accompanied by a group of Miami warriors and one U.S. soldier from Fort Wayne, arrived at Fort Dearborn on August 13, 1812. They came to escort the contingent to Fort Wayne.[30] Because Wells and Kinzie could not convince Captain Heald to remain at Fort Dearborn, they advised the destruction of the liquor that "would only inflame them [the warriors]" and the ammunition that "would undoubtedly be used in acts of hostility."[31] Captain Wells had been writing all spring about the danger of providing area Indians with ammunition. He excoriated the U.S. agent at Fort Wayne for doing just that. Wells understood that to distribute these goods was to fan the fires of war.[32]

On August 14 Heald complied and held back the liquor and ammunition when he "delivered the Indians all the goods in the factory store, and a considerable quantity of provisions." He then ordered the destruction of all surplus arms, ammunition, and liquor.[33] While Heald decided to destroy the ammunition and liquor that the United States held at Chicago, there were also large stores held privately, particularly by Kinzie & Forsyth. Since Tippecanoe, Kinzie & Forsyth had provided no ammunition to the Indians, leaving 850 pounds of gunpowder in their warehouses. The partners also held 1,200 gallons (150 kegs) of whiskey.[34]

Heald knew that the large stores held by Kinzie & Forsyth presented as much danger as the public goods. In Indian hands, the ammunition could help to fuel a war. Heald expected that the Indians surrounding the fort would "take immediate possession of the place" and gain access to any remaining goods at Chicago. According to claims later made by Kinzie & Forsyth, "Major Heald advised the petitioners to permit their property to be also destroyed, in order to prevent it from falling into the hands of the enemy, which was accordingly done."[35]

Destroying 850 pounds of gunpowder and 1,200 gallons of whiskey was not an easy task. Kinzie wrote that once Heald issued the order, "the business of destruction was immediately commenced." They planned to dump the gunpowder and the liquor into the river through a protected door (the sally port) on the north side of the fort, just yards from the Chicago River. The men broke open the heads of the whiskey kegs and poured the contents into the river. While the work was done under cover of darkness, it did not remain a secret for long. The Indians outside the fort heard the hammering and wanted to know what was going on. Kinzie assured the Indians that they were only "opening barrels of pork and flour" in preparation to leave the fort the following day; he did not try to dump his gunpowder into the river, but instead threw it into the well within the stockade. All the liquor and ammunition was either dumped into the well or the river. So great a quantity of whiskey had been dumped in the river that by the next morning it was described as "strong grog."[36]

Heald counted on the continued friendship of most of the Indians surrounding the fort and liberally distributed food to the crowds. Indeed, Heald and his officers ate with Potawatomi leaders at the fort since they "had a superabundance of provisions to make away with." However, the destruction of the alcohol and ammunition severely challenged good relations.[37] Some among the Potawatomis made it clear to Captain Heald that they were unhappy about this, and these Potawatomis informed Heald that "there was serious trouble ahead."[38]

The officers at Fort Dearborn, along with Kinzie and Wells, continued to discuss the best course to follow as late as the night before the retreat.

Despite his direct orders from Hull, it is unlikely that Captain Heald would have evacuated if he had felt that an attack was inevitable. Kinzie and Wells knew that some of the warriors outside Fort Dearborn were hostile to the United States, but they needed only some Potawatomis to accompany them to safety. They met with Indian leaders and arranged for six to seven hundred to escort them to Fort Wayne.[39]

10 The Potawatomi Attack, August 15, 1812

In the twenty-four hours before the garrison evacuated on August 15, 1812, the small settlement at Chicago swelled to nearly a thousand people. Captain Nathan Heald, in his characteristic low-key manner, described the gathering as "unusually large." From around the neighborhood of Chicago, at least five hundred warriors came to camp within range of Fort Dearborn. Most were no doubt from the twelve hundred Potawatomis living in villages within ten to sixty miles of the mouth of the Chicago River, but others had come from farther afield and from other tribes. There were Ho-Chunks, Odawas, Ojibwas, and Sauks among the temporary camps set up south, west, and north of the fort. This was not simply an attack force, as there were nearly two hundred women and children in the temporary camps surrounding Fort Dearborn.[1]

Many of the people around Fort Dearborn spoke Potawatomi and related Algonquian languages, but others spoke the Siouan language of the Ho-Chunks. A significant number must have known multiple Indian languages, as well as French and English. However, the commander at Fort Dearborn and his soldiers needed interpreters to explain what was on the minds of the sea of people surrounding them. Much could be lost in translation.[2]

Why did hundreds of warriors and their families gather at Chicago in sight of Fort Dearborn? Many had a natural break in their work, having just harvested their crops. Others had experienced privations after Tippecanoe and sought extra supplies to head off starvation in the coming winter season. Still others hoped, as the Shawnee Prophet had during his long stay at Fort Wayne earlier that summer, to receive the gunpowder needed both for hunting and for warring. All gathered in anticipation of obtaining goods from the U.S. Factory that had been closed since April.

They also gathered because of plans made at Milwaukee, Peoria, Mississinewa, and Saukenauk to attack western forts "as soon as corn gets its roasting ears." The Potawatomis outside Fort Dearborn knew that it was vulnerable and "laugh[ed] at the idea of its holding out against the force with which they can attack it."[3] Tecumseh encouraged these actions by sending runners from Detroit through the summer and "offering the warriors large rewards to fight."[4] The warriors also awaited the return of Main Poc, who was still fighting outside Detroit with Tecumseh alongside the British.

Many of those surrounding Fort Dearborn understood more about events in the wider region than those inside the stockade. Regular messengers linked Chicago with Main Poc and Tecumseh. The Indians at Chicago knew that Mackinac had fallen easily in the previous month. Some might even have been a part of that battle. After the British takeover of Mackinac, Robert Dickson sent five hundred warriors to Detroit by way of Chicago. The Indians surrounding Fort Dearborn knew of Hull's evacuation order before Captain Heald received it. Young Louis Ouilmette, son of Antoine and Archange, learned the news from Potawatomis north of Chicago and quickly shared it with family and then the garrison across the river.[5]

In sum, they gathered for hundreds of individual reasons: following family members or friends; taken with the vision of Tecumseh and his brother or the anger of Main Poc; frustrated with the U.S. land policy, settlers, and the closed factory; or simply to see what would happen. Once there, they waited. Their very presence unnerved the small U.S. force at Chicago: "At night they scarcely dared yield to slumber, lest they should be aroused by the war-whoop."[6]

While most of those who came to Chicago before August 15, 1812, remain nameless, the actions of a few individuals carried more weight and are remembered in history. Nuscotomeg (Mad Sturgeon), Black Partridge, Blackbird, Naunongee, and Topinbee were among the Potawatomi warriors who shaped events as they unfolded.

Blackbird traveled to Chicago in mid-August 1812 from Milwaukee. Since his 1808 trip to Washington, D.C., with Main Poc, William Wells, and Little Turtle, he had continued his raiding in southern Illinois. He was part of the June council at Milwaukee that sought war with the United States. The warrior was most concerned with the encroachment of American claims and settlement on Indian lands. He opined that Americans were "the White Devil with his mouth wide open," ready to take the lands of Potawatomis and their allies. Blackbird looked to the British for support in stanching this

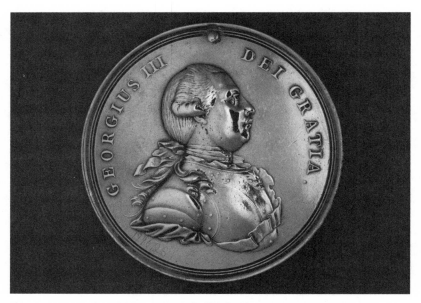

Figure 19. In 1815 the British presented Blackbird with a loyalty medal for his service during the War of 1812, which included leading the attack against the U.S. contingent leaving Fort Dearborn. (Chicago History Museum, ICHi-64721)

American onslaught.[7] While he had been allied with Main Poc for many years, Blackbird did not develop a public relationship with Tecumseh or the Shawnee Prophet, although they shared an active resistance to American encroachment in Indian Country.

During his previous trips to Chicago and Fort Wayne to collect annuity payments from the U.S. government, Blackbird undoubtedly came to know Captain Heald as well as John Kinzie. One can only imagine the bitter surprise Blackbird felt when he found that Kinzie, who had worked so hard to gain the confidence of those meeting at Milwaukee in June, had proved a turncoat, supporting Captain Heald and the Americans.

Blackbird also had a long acquaintance with William Wells. They had spent three months in 1808 traveling together to Washington, D.C., with Main Poc and Little Turtle. Blackbird rejected the accommodationism advocated by William Wells and his late father-in-law, Little Turtle. He certainly regarded Wells as a traitor who "was fed and cared for by the Indians. He was adopted by a great chief, he fought side by side with the braves against the white men, and then he turned against them."[8]

Blackbird was joined at Chicago by Main Poc's brother-in-law Nusco-tomeg (Mad Sturgeon). He came to Chicago from his village almost directly south of Fort Dearborn at the intersection of the Kankakee and Iroquois Rivers. Mad Sturgeon's Potawatomi village was less than ninety miles west of Prophetstown. While he was not an open supporter of Tecumseh, this proximity provided many opportunities for information to flow between villages.

Mad Sturgeon's brothers, Wabinewa (White Sturgeon) and Wasachek (Clear Day), were also at Chicago in August 1812. They lived near Mad Sturgeon in villages along the rivers south of Chicago. They had regularly joined their brother and Main Poc in raids against the Osages and American settlers throughout southern Illinois. Together these warriors were the subject of many, many complaints to American officials from Vincennes to Kaskaskia to Chicago and St. Louis. They fought a low-grade guerrilla war for more than a decade. President Jefferson had described Main Poc, Mad Sturgeon, and his brothers as "unruly young men going to War."[9]

Not all of the Potawatomi warriors assembled outside Chicago were young men. Naunongee, a Potawatomi chief with a village at Lake Calumet, camped south of Fort Dearborn in the days before August 15 and was the grandfather of Archange Ouilmette and Sheshi Buisson, who lived at Chicago with their French trader husbands. While his great-grandchildren lived in the shadow of Fort Dearborn, Naunongee allied with Mad Sturgeon and his brothers against the Americans. Naunongee, Mad Sturgeon, Wild Sturgeon, and Wasachek were related; the brothers may have been Naunongee's grandsons.[10]

Nor were all of the Potawatomi leaders assembled at Chicago ready to do battle. Black Partridge (Mucktypoke) arrived in Chicago in mid-August. He had likely been part of the contingent of leaders who had agreed to travel with John Kinzie to a U.S. council at Picqua but returned soon after their departure upon learning of Hull's order to evacuate Fort Dearborn. Black Partridge was a powerful village leader from the Illinois River and had been a consistent ally of the United States since the 1795 Greenville Treaty. He chose negotiation and accommodation with the Americans after seeing the total destruction wrought by American troops on the Indian villages along the Maumee and Au Glaize Rivers in the early 1790s.[11]

Black Partridge continued to support the United States. However, as the Americans sought more and more land cessions, his own young warriors became increasingly restless. Some, including his younger brother Waubansee (Foggy Day), chose to fight alongside Tecumseh. Waubansee's village was at the intersection of the Des Plaines and Fox Rivers about forty miles to the southwest of Chicago. Waubansee had been at the Battle of Tippecanoe in November 1811, where he "seized an opportunity to ambush a supply party moving up the Wabash River, killing one of the boatmen single-handed."[12] Waubansee was not at Chicago in August 1812, only because he was part of Tecumseh's forces outside Detroit.

Black Partridge probably also felt the loss of one of his neighbors, Gomo, who absented himself from Chicago in August 1812. While Gomo had for several years met with American representatives to explain the behavior of his militant Potawatomi neighbors, he had become dissatisfied with the role. The previous year Gomo had betrayed his increasing impatience: "You Americans think that all the mischiefs that are committed are known to the chiefs, and immediately call on them for the surrender of the offenders. We know nothing of them; our business is to hunt, in order to feed our women and children."[13] Gomo's exasperation was clear—he was tired of taking responsibility for the actions of men like Main Poc, Mad Sturgeon, and Blackbird.

By August 1812 Gomo understood that the Potawatomis would be the losers in any conflict between Great Britain and the United States. Gomo was sure that the Americans, who built forts and garrisons "wherever they go," intended to drive out the Potawatomis from their villages.[14] At the same time, he had little confidence that the British would support the Potawatomis in maintaining Indian Country. Nevertheless, many still courted his support, including Main Poc, who sent messages with tobacco, encouraging Gomo to come join the fight.[15] Gomo demurred, preferring to watch from the sidelines at Peoria.[16]

Even among this small sample of Potawatomi warriors massed outside Fort Dearborn in mid-August 1812, there was a wide range of postures. Native Americans, like their American and British counterparts, responded to the crisis created by the U.S. declaration of war against Great Britain as individuals, as well as members of villages and ethnic groups. There was no uniform "Native" response or action. Instead, individuals made decisions mediated by personal networks, beliefs, and aspirations. Blackbird, Mad Sturgeon, and Naunongee took strident anti-American stands. At the same time, Black Partridge and others urged caution. There was no consensus among the Potawatomis massing outside Fort Dearborn, as there was little unanimity among Indians across the western Great Lakes.

MAIN POC'S CALL TO WAR

On August 14, 1812, a little before sundown, an Indian arrived from Fort Malden with a message from Main Poc. The messenger likely went to Mad Sturgeon, who was Main Poc's closest ally among the Indians outside Chicago. The message was contained in a belt of wampum, "all painted red with vermillion," a traditional call to war. With it, Main Poc instructed his allies to "immediately take up the tomahawk and strike the Americans."[17]

Following custom, Mad Sturgeon displayed the red wampum belt sent by Main Poc in front of his wigwam. Inside, Mad Sturgeon, Blackbird, and their supporters made war plans. Outside, warriors who wanted to join with Mad Sturgeon and Blackbird gathered around the wampum belt that represented the pact made by warriors to do battle together. They laid out plans for a surprise attack the following day on the evacuating American garrison.[18]

Blackbird, Mad Sturgeon, and his brothers had organized war parties for years, launching attacks on American settlers in southern Illinois and against the Osages. In some ways, this was no different. They hoped to attack an unsuspecting enemy as they had in their southern raids. Blackbird and Mad Sturgeon looked to cause great casualties among their enemy, as well as to take prisoners and booty.[19]

JOHN KINZIE'S ALLIES

While hundreds of warriors assented to this plan, there were those who questioned its wisdom. Among them were trading partners and friends of John Kinzie who took pains to warn him of the danger. Black Partridge went to Kinzie and Captain Heald the night before the planned evacuation and warned them to be very careful after leaving the fort the following morning. He "stated that he no longer could be responsible for his warriors." In a dramatic gesture, Black Partridge returned the friendship medal that U.S. officials had given him at the 1809 Treaty of Fort Wayne. This must have given Heald and Kinzie pause, as they "personally knew the old chief as an honest, truthful man."[20]

John Kinzie's allies at St. Joseph also moved to warn him, as they had

Figure 20. Black Partridge returned the peace medal he received from the Americans at the 1809 Treaty of Fort Wayne on the eve of the attack on the U.S. contingent. (Joseph Kirkland, *The Chicago Massacre of 1812* [1893])

seen the messenger who brought the red wampum belt on his way to Chicago. This set off an alarm among Potawatomi leaders, who were generally sympathetic to the Americans, but in particular friends of the Kinzie families. They knew there was great danger at Chicago. Topinbee, long a Kinzie friend, also knew that his young nephew Jean Baptiste Chandonnai was Kinzie's clerk and in danger as well.

Therefore, Topinbee, with two other Potawatomis from St. Joseph, Leopold Pokagan and Keepotah, "started in great haste on horseback around the head of Lake Michigan." They traveled all night and arrived at Chicago early on Saturday morning, August 15, just before Captain Heald's contingent left the fort. They were unable to dissuade John Kinzie from marching with the retreating U.S. contingent but persuaded him to place his family out of immediate danger.

The extended Kinzie household was also not safe remaining at home, where there were still "large amounts of goods" accompanying the troops.[21] Kinzie arranged for the members of his household to leave Chicago in a bateau. In the large, open boat were Eleanor Kinzie, her four younger children, Josette LaFramboise (who was married to, or soon to marry, Jean Baptiste Beaubien), Jean Baptiste Chandonnai (Topinbee's nephew and Kinzie's clerk), two enslaved men (including Black Jim), the boatman, and "two Indians who acted as their protectors." The bateau also held trade goods and personal belongings of the Kinzie family.[22]

The boat full of the Kinzie household members sat anchored near the mouth of the Chicago River as the U.S. force began their evacuation. Their plan was to paddle across Lake Michigan to St. Joseph, where they would join the troops if all went well. On the morning of the evacuation, Topinbee strongly encouraged Kinzie to accompany his wife and family in the boat. He told Kinzie "that mischief was intended" by the Potawatomis who were to escort the U.S. contingent. Kinzie demurred but willingly accepted the aid of Topinbee's nephew Jean Baptiste Chandonnai and two Potawatomi warriors who accompanied the boat with the Kinzie family.[23]

After getting in the boat, the Kinzie family anchored just offshore at the mouth of the Chicago River. The mouth of the river was almost a mile south of where it is today (the river takes a turn because of a sandbar and meanders south parallel with the lakeshore). Kinzie's family would be visible to him during the crucial first miles of the retreat, and, with luck, they could join the retreating troops at St. Joseph. With his family safely offshore, Kinzie was ready to join the Fort Dearborn contingent.

THE ATTACK

On the morning of Saturday, August 15, 1812, a ring of temporary Indian camps encircled Fort Dearborn. The Indians carefully guarded all the trails in and out of Chicago. Indeed, in some ways, the fort was already under siege when Captain Heald led his troops out from the fort. Despite this, Captain Heald expected that Miami and Potawatomi warriors would escort them to Fort Wayne.

After feeding close to seven hundred Potawatomis on the morning of August 15, 1812, Captain Heald hoped that his contingent and their families could march to Fort Wayne safely. Consequently, at nine o'clock, the U.S. contingent at Fort Dearborn made their way out of the fort and began to march southward along the lakefront. Captain Heald was in the front of a column of fifty-six regular troops and twelve men composing the Chicago militia.[24] John Kinzie rode alongside Captain Heald and Captain Wells at the front of the contingent. He "believed that his presence might operate as a restraint upon the fury of the savages."[25]

Also accompanying Captain Heald were William Wells and his contingent of Miami warriors. Wells, mounted on a Kentucky thoroughbred, "had blackened his face before leaving the garrison" in preparation for a possible

Map 9. August 15, 1812, at Chicago. (A. T. Andreas, *History of Chicago* [1884])

battle.[26] No longer carefree young women at play, Rebekah Wells Heald and Margaret Helm left Fort Dearborn on horseback accompanied by their officer husbands.[27]

At the rear of the column were wagons with the children, supplies, and baggage. There were eighteen children in two wagons with their mothers either with them or alongside them, including Cicely (enslaved by Rebekah Wells), Suzanne Corbin, Mrs. Isaac Holt, Mary (Cooper) Burns, Martha Leigh, Sarah Needs, and Susan Simmons.[28]

As Heald's contingent slowly left Fort Dearborn, the expected Potawatomi escort did not materialize. The soldiers first passed a group of Potawatomis from the Calumet region camped at the edges of an oak forest south from the fort that likely included Naunongee. Potawatomi warriors from St. Joseph had also established a camp along the route south from Chicago, but the retreating soldiers found it empty.[29]

It was too late to turn back, and Captain Heald led the contingent slowly southward. In 1812 the mouth of the Chicago River had not yet been straightened, so that the group headed south for more than a mile along the south bank, as it became the west bank of the Chicago River paralleling Lake Michigan. Months later Captain Heald described the contingent's march along a narrow corridor (about one hundred yards) "between the sand beach of Lake Michigan on the east and a high sand dune to the west with a part of the Miamies . . . detached in front, and the remainder in our rear, as guards, under the direction of Captain Wells."[30]

A young soldier in the retreating force remembered that they had proceeded about a mile and a half between the lake and the sand dune when "it was discovered the Indians were preparing an attack on us."[31] The Potawatomis, who had promised to provide an escort, instead turned on the contingent. One Miami warrior, accompanying the U.S. contingent, chastised the Potawatomi warriors for their treachery: "You have deceived them and are about to murder them in cold blood."[32]

The attack followed a simple pattern that the Potawatomis had long used in surprise attacks against their enemies.[33] Mad Sturgeon and Blackbird used familiar tactics they had honed in small-party raids, "employing stealth, ruse, and ambush." Their weakness was a lack of unity and discipline, making it nearly impossible "to take a fortified position by force of arms." If Captain Heald had remained at Fort Dearborn, his soldiers might have resisted. Once he led his troops out of the fort, he lost a key advantage.[34]

The contingent leaving Chicago was quickly encircled. At around present-day Twelfth Street, Potawatomi warriors armed with muskets appeared along the ridge of the sand dune to the west of the retreating contingent. Heald's troops followed traditional Euro-American military maneuvers. Traveling in organized columns, units fell back into defensive positions or lines, ready to meet an attack. In Euro-American fighting, there was an expectation that their opponent would fall into similar lines about eighty yards away, the effective range of the flintlock or smoothbore musket.[35]

Captain Heald formed his men into the traditional line facing the Potawatomi warriors up the sandbank. He then marched his company up the bank, and as he did so, the action commenced.[36] John Kinzie remembered that the men advanced up the bank, and "as they rose the Indians fired their first volley."[37] This first volley was an innovation for Potawatomi warriors, who had traditionally employed bows and arrows in the initial surprise attack. The muskets proved far superior to bows and arrows in disrupting and demoralizing "an unsuspecting, unprepared enemy unit." Warriors then killed and mortally wounded many of their stunned opponents.[38]

After the initial attack with muskets, the Potawatomis turned to weap-

Figure 21. Warriors used weapons like this wooden war club with brass studs after an initial musket attack. (Chicago History Museum, ICHi-64722)

ons useful in close combat, including ball-headed war clubs, tomahawks, flat war clubs, knives, spears, and lances. This hand-to-hand combat was particularly fierce in the battle south of Chicago on that August Saturday morning. The fighting targeted not only the soldiers and militia, but also the women and children. One of the mule-drawn wagons at the rear of the column was filled with supplies, guns, and ammunition, while children traveled in the other. Placing the women and children near the supplies was a terrible mistake, as it put them directly in harm's way. The Potawatomi warriors sought the booty held in the supply wagon, and many children wound up in their path. One young Indian, filled with drink and fury against his fallen comrades, "killed several children with his tomahawk."[39]

The two officers who accompanied the wagons, Ensign George Ronan and Surgeon's Mate Isaac Van Voorhis, were killed early in the battle. Three women and twelve children died in "shocking scene[s] of butchery." Warriors used tomahawks, clubs, and knives to cut down anyone surrounding the wagons. The battle was over quickly.[40] Among the women and children killed were Rebekah Heald's enslaved servant, Cicely, and Cicely's infant son.

Potawatomi warriors also engaged the soldiers and militia in hand-to-hand combat in the second phase of the battle. Every man who marched as part of the Chicago militia was mortally wounded either by musket shot or with knives, clubs, or tomahawks. Several of the soldiers' wives who traveled alongside their husbands found swords and fought until their deaths against Potawatomi warriors.[41] Sergeant Otho Hayes engaged in hand-to-hand combat with the Potawatomi warrior Naunongee, the grandfather of Archange Ouilmette. Naunongee mortally wounded Hayes, but before Hayes died, he killed his attacker with his own tomahawk.[42]

Most of the violence was over in very short order. Captain Heald remembered that all of their horses, provisions, and baggage had been taken within fifteen minutes of the attack and that the battle itself was over within an hour.[43] He later reported that about fifteen Potawatomi warriors lost their lives in this fighting, alongside thirty-eight of his own men.[44] Almost all of the remaining soldiers were injured, including Captain Heald, who suffered gunshot wounds in his thigh and right forearm.

The Potawatomi warriors targeted William Wells early in the fighting in part because his Miami escort had scattered. There was considerable animosity between the Miamis and Potawatomis over the 1809 Treaty of Fort Wayne, and Potawatomi warriors likely targeted Miamis as well as American forces. Wells was on horseback and was shot during the last volley of musket fire. According to family accounts, the wounded Wells found his niece, bid her good-bye, and asked her to "tell my wife that I died at my post doing the best I could."[45] After William Wells fell to the ground, a group of Potawatomi warriors approached him. Rebekah Wells Heald later remembered that her uncle pointed to his heart and one of the warriors shot him dead. The Potawatomis took his heart to eat later as a testament to his bravery. They took his scalp as a trophy.[46]

KINZIE'S PROTECTION

John Kinzie's family just offshore remained unharmed during the battle. Eleanor Kinzie remembered seeing smoke, "then the blaze—and immediately after the report of the first discharge sounded in their ears. Then all was confusion."[47] They were lucky, but John Kinzie also recounted that near the end of the battle "an order was given out among the Indians that they should neither hurt me or my family." It may have come from Blackbird, who showed Kinzie's family "kindness" during the battle and aftermath.[48] In any event, Kinzie and all those under his care also received special defense from Black Partridge, Topinbee, and Topinbee's nephew Jean Baptiste Chandonnai.[49]

In order to guard the family as the battle wound down, Black Partridge claimed them all as his prisoners—both those at the battle site and those in the bateau.[50] Black Partridge disarmed Kinzie and took him, as well as his daughter-in-law Margaret Helm, under his protection. Margaret misunderstood this kindness, thinking Black Partridge's actions were hostile. She ran from Black Partridge into Lake Michigan and had to be dragged back to safety. Later Margaret told a more colorful version of this basic story, insisting that "a young Indian raised his tomahawk on me" and that Black Partridge saved her.[51]

The other officer's wife, Rebekah Wells Heald, also found shelter with the Kinzies. As he lay dying, William Wells urged his niece to stay with John Kinzie. Wells understood that Kinzie was the one man who could protect her. It would be hard to overstate the danger that Mrs. Heald faced, as the niece of William Wells and the wife of the American commander at Fort Dearborn. She had sustained a number of wounds to her arms, breast, and side. In addition, her left arm was broken. Despite these serious injuries, she remained on her horse.[52]

As the hostilities were winding down, Rebekah and her horse became an important prize for a Potawatomi warrior. Despite the fact that John Kinzie claimed she was under his protection, a young Potawatomi chief, Kawbenaw (the Carrier), captured her.[53] Kawbenaw led Rebekah Heald off to his wife, who tried to pull out the blanket that lay under her saddle. Heald, in defiance of the danger she was in, used her riding whip on Kawbenaw's wife. Fortunately for her, Kawbenaw was amused and not angered by her actions.[54]

Eleanor Kinzie saw the wounded Rebekah Heald, now prisoner of Kawbenaw, from her boat just off the shore in Lake Michigan. She asked Jean Baptiste Chandonnai to negotiate for Mrs. Heald's release.[55] He successfully ransomed Mrs. Heald but not her horse. Rebekah Heald was brought on board the bateau, where she lay in pain from her many wounds.[56] Years later while Rebekah Heald mourned the death of her slave, "poor black Cicely" who lost her life in the battle, she worried about what became of her horse. She feared that "among its new owners its fate was hard and its life short."[57]

Because Black Partridge had already claimed them as prisoners, John

Figure 22. Rebecca Wells Heald, the niece of William Wells and wife of Captain Nathan Heald, was in special danger during the August 15, 1812, attack. John and Eleanor Kinzie offered her assistance. (Joseph Kirkland, *The Chicago Massacre of 1812* [1893])

Kinzie and Margaret Helm were not part of the negotiations between Captain Heald and Blackbird. They walked northward as the battle ended, with an eye on the open boat that held Rebekah Wells Heald as well as Eleanor Kinzie, Chandonnai, and other members of the Kinzie family. Their friends had successfully shielded them all from harm.[58]

SURRENDER

According to John Kinzie, "Nescotnemeg [Mad Sturgeon] was the author of the massacre. The Black Bird commanded."[59] Both were certainly central figures in planning and executing the attack, but they did not control events as a Euro-American commander might have. Instead, war parties were very much decentralized, relying on a loose confederation that rested in "individual initiative." In contrast to Euro-American military traditions where a battle ended with a clear surrender and cessation of hostile activities, Indian warriors often pursued the remnants of a defeated enemy.[60] After the initial concerted effort, the action would break into smaller attacks in order to kill more enemy warriors, take more prisoners, and obtain more booty.

The business of surrender was a tricky one, especially as the Americans and the Potawatomis differed so fundamentally on the means and aims of warfare. Captain Heald, seriously wounded, still had vital work ahead of him. He had twenty-eight men still alive, some of them badly wounded. Heald had to negotiate quickly or even more of his men would perish. Heald led his remaining men to an elevated spot that was "out of shot of the bank." Near him, Blackbird and a group of Potawatomi warriors assembled. Blackbird—accompanied by Pierre LeClair, who served as his interpreter—motioned to Heald to step forward.[61] Through LeClair, Blackbird demanded that Heald surrender, "promising to spare the lives of all the prisoners." Captain Heald acquiesced, although he was not entirely confident that Blackbird would be able to protect all of the prisoners.[62]

Other accounts of the surrender suggest that the interpreter, Pierre LeClair, played a more active role in the negotiations, not only translating but also advising Heald not to surrender "unless they would give pledges for the lives of the prisoners."[63] LeClair was in an interesting position. He was a single métis man who served in Kinzie's household and as a member of the militia. However, at the first sign of fighting, LeClair deserted the soldiers and made his way back to Chicago. He later asserted that he fled because "it was the only way to save his life."[64]

In any event, LeClair, a member of Kinzie's household, reappeared at the end of the battle in a central role as the interpreter or messenger between Blackbird and Captain Heald. Both the Potawatomi warriors and Captain Heald placed some confidence in Kinzie and his employee. His son-in-law Lieutenant Helm later noted that Kinzie "stood higher than any man in that country among the Indians" and that he was "the means of saving us from utter destruction."[65]

PART FOUR

In the Aftermath of

August 15, 1812

11 John and Eleanor Kinzie's Neighbors, August 1812

For many years, accounts of the Chicago Massacre stated straightforwardly that the "entire population" of Chicago evacuated on the morning of August 15, 1812. However, this was clearly not the case and reflects a long-standing tendency to ignore women and people of mixed race in the historical record. While all of the soldiers and their families were part of the retreat, some of the Kinzie family's métis neighbors stayed in their homes. Indeed, all through the morning of the massacre, Archange Ouilmette was at home north across the Chicago River from Fort Dearborn. Her husband, Antoine Ouilmette, left Chicago as tensions mounted and "stayed in hiding" until the hostilities had ended.[1] However, Archange Ouilmette—granddaughter of Naunongee, one of the Potawatomi warriors—was not fearful for her life or that of her children. She and her sister Sheshi (Chevalier) Buisson stayed at home throughout the attack and after the surrender.[2]

The sisters watched the soldiers and militia march out, with some of the officers and their wives on horseback. They saw that the expected Potawatomi escort did not materialize. Instead, only a small group of Miamis accompanied the troops. As well as soldiers, the contingent included several of the families that had been their neighbors for many years, including Martha Leigh and Mary Burns, both married to discharged soldiers.

Mary's husband was part of the Chicago militia that also marched with the troops. Mary shepherded five children, including an infant born on the day of the April attack on the Leigh farm. Martha's oldest son was also in the militia. Her husband had gone to Mackinac in July, so Martha loaded some of their belongings and her children into one of the wagons that brought up the rear of the retreating force.

It is not difficult to imagine Archange Ouilmette's emotions when she and her sister heard gunshots just after the contingent was out of view. While they were not able to see what was going on, they could see smoke

Figure 23. Archange Ouilmette and her sister offered assistance to several fleeing the attack on August 15, 1812. This portrait of Archange Ouilmette was done almost a century
after her death. (Wilmette Historical Society)

and "smell the powder."[3] What sadness, perhaps fear, they must have felt
when they "recognized the screams of Mrs. Leigh." While Martha and Mary
survived the attack, both witnessed the death of several of their children.[4]

Despite the danger, Mary and Martha had little choice but to join the retreat. They could not stay in their homes like Archange Ouilmette because
they were so clearly associated with the U.S. Army. Sukey Corbin, another
woman married to a U.S. soldier, hid in an abandoned house with her two

children when her husband marched off on the morning of August 15. For a time, it might have seemed a good choice, as the nightmarish screams of Martha Leigh and others were heard in the distance. However, as the Potawatomi warriors returned to Chicago, they were discovered and the warriors killed Sukey Corbin and her children, who found "no sanctuary, no rest, no mercy, no hope."[5]

Archange and her sister were not able to help Martha, Mary, or Sukey, but others received their aid. Alexander Robinson, a trader who had a house on the south branch of the Chicago River, had left the trading post of Joseph Bailly (near what is today Chesterton, Indiana) in his canoe bound for Chicago, where he hoped to buy corn. He got as far as the mouth of the Calumet River by canoe and, realizing the danger, came stealthily into Chicago and sought refuge with Archange. Robinson remembered hearing the "shots of the combatants" and the "shrieks of the victims" as he sat hidden in her house during the battle.[6]

Despite the fact that Archange's grandfather and other relatives were fighting against the U.S. Army, she also provided refuge to an American soldier. As the U.S. contingent set off, Sergeant William Griffith was sent back to retrieve the medical supplies and horses. When he tried to rejoin the retreating column of soldiers, he realized that a battle was under way. As Griffith fled, Topinbee took him prisoner and told him to hide himself across the river beyond the Ouilmette and Kinzie houses. Griffith cautiously made his way to the Ouilmette garden, where he screened himself behind some currant bushes. Eventually he climbed into their house through a window. When Archange Ouilmette found Griffith in her house, she took it in stride. She had Griffith change out of his U.S. army uniform and into "a suit of deer skin with belt, moccasins and pipe, like a French engagé." She let him stay along with Robinson until it was safe to move on.[7]

PRISONERS OF WAR

As the morning progressed, Archange Ouilmette and Sheshi Buisson realized that the battle had ended. At some point, they learned that their grandfather had been killed in the fighting. Slowly, "the noise of the firing grew gradually less and the stragglers from the victorious party" came back to Chicago with their prisoners.[8] Blackbird had pledged to protect the lives of those taken prisoner, but only those who were not mortally wounded.

Potawatomi warriors customarily killed prisoners who could not travel back to their villages. In the end, the fate of the captive rested with the warrior who had captured him or her, not with Blackbird. For many of the "badly wounded" captives, the violence was not over.[9]

As the prisoners were marched past the battle site, they recoiled at the sight of the dozens of dead men, women, and children strewn near the wagons. The warriors took them back to their camps around the fort, where the prisoners were "distributed among the different tribes."[10] Once they arrived at the camps, another "horrible scene ensued." Six soldiers, perhaps those already wounded, were stripped of their clothing and tortured. Potawatomi women, "infuriated at the loss of friends" in the attack, were among those who assaulted the prisoners with whatever utensil they had available. Seriously wounded in battle, Mary Burns's husband, Thomas, was one of six men who were tortured and tomahawked that evening. Mary and two of their children watched in horror as he was stabbed with a stable fork and so "inhumanly murdered."[11]

From her house just across the river, Archange Ouilmette had a clear view of the prisoners' arrival and their mistreatment. Describing the encampment that night as a "torture ground," she witnessed Indian women subjecting soldiers to "the most fearful torture and indignities."[12] As well as torturing some of the prisoners, the victorious warriors and their families had a "general frolic" the evening after the massacre. They feasted on the cattle and the remaining food at Fort Dearborn, as they celebrated their victory over the American forces. Before long, the body of Captain Wells was brought to the encampment. Following Potawatomi custom, the warriors ate his heart to increase their own power and bravery.[13]

DEPARTURES AND ARRIVALS

Because Black Partridge claimed the Kinzie family as his prisoners, they enjoyed considerable freedom in the wake of the Potawatomi victory. Late in the day on August 15, Mrs. Kinzie, her children, and other household members were "allowed" to leave their boat and return home, where they were later joined by John Kinzie. Huddled together in their house with their four children and Margaret Helm, the Kinzies could hear the cries of terror and celebration outside their door. Chicago was now controlled not by the U.S. Army, but by a loose confederation of Potawatomis, Odawas, and their allies. In addition to Black Partridge, the Kinzies owed their safety to Topinbee, who had arrived after the battle itself and who remained a presence on the outskirts of the unfolding events. Together with Keepotah and Leopold Pokagan, Topinbee closely guarded the Kinzies and posted guards to keep other warriors away from their prisoners.[14]

The next morning most of the Potawatomis left Chicago with their captives and booty. From their house, the Kinzie family watched them set fire to the fort, parading around in the "finery" they had taken in battle: shawls, ribbons, and feathers. One young warrior was dressed in a muslin gown and wore a bonnet that "under other circumstances" would have afforded amusement.[15] The Kinzies, Ouilmettes, and other remaining families must have breathed a sigh a relief with the departure of these groups. Many warriors, their wives, and children headed toward their villages along the Illinois River, accompanying horses loaded with goods and "several soldiers of the garrison of Fort Dearborn as prisoners."[16]

Before the victorious parties left Chicago, John Kinzie successfully negotiated for the release of Captain Heald, an intervention that spared Heald from torture and death. Some warriors wanted to take Heald's life because they were still quite angry about the destruction of the whiskey and ammunition held at the fort. Kinzie argued for leniency, explaining that Heald was simply following orders to destroy all the goods at the garrison. A Potawatomi warrior from the Kankakee claimed Captain Heald as his prisoner and made ready to take him back to his village. Fortunately for Captain Heald, this chief, perhaps Mad Sturgeon, had a "strong personal regard for him."[17]

Heald's release involved a substantial bribe. Captain Heald had hidden a considerable amount of money in his undergarments before the battle. While a prisoner, Heald placed some of it in a pocket of Kinzie's overcoat. In addition to offering Heald's captor $500, Kinzie promised the Potawatomi chief two valuable and longtime members of his own household, the enslaved Black Jim and Henry. These men had done much of the hard physical work for his family as well as for Kinzie & Forsyth. The Potawatomis accepted the payment, and Heald was able to return home with Kinzie.[18]

Captain Heald and his wife were reunited at the Kinzie house soon after his release on the morning of August 16, 1812. John Kinzie had been warned about the danger so long as they remained at Chicago and hoped to have them moved away in short order.[19] Topinbee took charge of the Healds, and

Figure 24. While the Odawa warrior Shabbona was strongly anti-American, he came to the aid of John Kinzie and his family after the August 15, 1812, battle. (Joseph Kirkland, *The Chicago Massacre of 1812* [1893])

they became his prisoners. Topinbee's nephew Jean Baptiste Chandonnai, who had ransomed Rebekah Wells Heald the day before, transported Captain Heald and his wife to St. Joseph in his canoe. Sergeant Griffith, who had hidden in Antoine Ouilmette's house during the battle, was sent with the Healds. Topinbee and the others who had come from St. Joseph returned on horseback to their village.[20]

As news of the battle filtered outward, several individuals headed to Chicago. When the Odawa leader Shabbona realized how many warriors had gathered near the fort, he left his village near the Fox River. Upon his arrival, he became one of the village leaders who protected the Kinzie family.[21] Far from being an ally of the United States, Shabbona remained strongly anti-American and would leave shortly for Detroit to fight alongside Tecumseh. Only his strong loyalty to Kinzie drew him to Chicago.

Thomas Forsyth, John Kinzie's half-brother and business partner, traveled north from Peoria when he realized that the garrison was set to leave.

Forsyth arrived at Chicago the day following the attack. Along his route, he met Potawatomi warriors and recognized some of the soldiers they had taken prisoner. When he got to Chicago, Forsyth headed to his half-brother's house, where he helped to assess the damage and make plans for the future.[22]

Indeed, even in the uneasy days after the destruction of Fort Dearborn, John Kinzie and Thomas Forsyth actually managed to do some trading. Charles Chandonnai, the Mackinac trader, appeared in their account book, as did the St. Joseph trader John Burnett.[23] It is not clear what trade goods Kinzie & Forsyth had left, but something remained of their stores.

A CODA TO THE BATTLE

The relative calm that descended after the warriors, their families, and their prisoners left Chicago was disrupted by the arrival of more warriors about three days after the battle. John Kinzie remembered that about a dozen Indians "painted black and armed" came menacingly to his house. Some of them sought revenge for John Kinzie's role in the release of Captain Heald and his wife. Others were simply angry that they had missed the battle.[24] The hostile Indians who showed up were identified as "Wabash Indians" who may have been Potawatomis, Ho-Chunks, or Kickapoos. They were probably nativists aligned with Tecumseh. Thomas Forsyth wrote to Captain Nathan Heald that the "murdering dogs from the Wabash, [were] very much displeased when they found you were gone." Forsyth had told them that it was useless to follow the Healds, as they had traveled quickly by boat away from Chicago.[25]

While Topinbee, Keepotah, and Leopold Pokagan had returned to St. Joseph, Black Partridge and Shabbona helped protect the Kinzies from this latest threat. Black Partridge was particularly concerned about the safety of Margaret Helm because she was married to a U.S. officer. He advised that Margaret Helm dress in the ordinary clothes of a métis woman: a short gown and petticoat, with a blue cotton handkerchief around her head. Dressed in this way, Black Partridge took her next door to the Ouilmette house. Once again Archange provided assistance by taking Margaret Helm into her home.[26]

The hostile Indians soon approached the Ouilmette house. Archange and her sister Sheshi were fearful that despite the métis clothing, Margaret

Helm's "fair complexion and general appearance" would betray that she was an American. Therefore, the two sisters "raised a large feather bed and placed her under the edge of it, upon the bedstead, with her face to the wall." Sheshi then seated herself at the front of the bed and commenced sewing. It was a stifling hot August day, and Margaret Helm was sweltering under the feathers and coverings. Nevertheless, Sheshi remained calmly working on a patchwork quilt she had laid out. In doing so, she gave the "appearance of the utmost tranquility." She remained calm, despite the danger.[27] Though the Indians searched the Ouilmette house, they did not find Margaret Helm. The two sisters had once again prevailed in saving a neighbor from a devastating fate.

From the Ouilmette house, the hostile Indians proceeded next door to the Kinzies'. On the porch stood Black Partridge, Alexander Robinson, Shabonna, and several other warriors protecting the family within. The hostile Indians forced their way into the parlor still armed and ready for battle. Black Partridge despaired at being able to save his friends and told Mrs. Kinzie, "We have done everything in our power to save you, but all is now lost."[28] Black Partridge felt tremendous responsibility for the Kinzies, as they remained his prisoners.

At this point in Kinzie family lore, Billy Caldwell and Waubansee arrived at the Kinzie house.[29] Caldwell told the hostile Indians that Kinzie was "the Indian's friend" and always supplied them with what they needed. Caldwell had Kinzie offer them presents from his remaining stores. The Indians left Chicago, but not before warning the Ouilmettes away from Chicago.[30]

The appearance of Waubansee and Billy Caldwell exemplified the wide-ranging and deep relationships that the Kinzie family had developed over the decades they lived and traded in this region. Billy Caldwell, Waubansee, and Shabbona were all decidedly on the side of Tecumseh and the British.[31] Despite this, they all looked to protect John Kinzie and his family.

Black Partridge feared for his prisoners, the Kinzie family, in this escalating violence.[32] He put the Kinzies in a boat that went first to the Little Calumet River and then on to St. Joseph. Alexander Robinson, who had hidden in the Ouilmette house and then stood to protect the Kinzie family from the Wabash Indians, took them to St. Joseph, where they came under the protection (or were prisoners of) Topinbee.[33] They would not return to Chicago for four long years. The Ouilmettes returned by the beginning of September and remained there for the duration of the war.

The battle on the morning of Saturday August 15, 1812, was a brutal attack in which dozens of unarmed children lost their lives. For many, it was a catastrophe that brought death and destruction. However, this violence should be set alongside the "many individual acts of mercy and kindness" recorded and recalled by participants from Black Partridge, Billy Caldwell, Waubansee, Blackbird, Archange Ouilmette, Sheshi Buisson, John Kinzie, and Eleanor Kinzie.[34] While the attack had opened up a deep wound in the fabric of local society, these acts of mercy would provide a base for slowly reweaving the settlement at Chicago.[35]

12 Captors and Captives, Fall 1812

On the morning of August 15, 1812, Rebekah Wells Heald left Chicago wearing considerable jewelry that included rings, a breast pin, earrings, and a hair comb. Many of the pieces were distinctive Wells family heirlooms. When Heald first was taken prisoner, her captors took the jewelry as part of the spoils of war. The morning following the battle, a young warrior rode around Chicago wearing Heald's comb, even though he had hardly enough hair to hold it. His comical appearance added a moment of levity as the fort burned.[1]

Shortly after this performance, Rebekah was reunited with her husband. Their captors, Black Partridge and Topinbee, took them to St. Joseph, Michigan, along with Sergeant William Griffith, who had been protected by Archange Ouilmette. In contrast, Rebekah's jewelry and other items journeyed westward with other Potawatomi warriors leaving Chicago for their home villages. The story of what happened to Rebekah Heald, on the one hand, and to her jewelry, on the other, highlights the fractured nature of Potawatomi control and the wider war just under way.

Rebekah Wells Heald last saw her comb at Chicago as part of the costume worn by a victorious young warrior. When that warrior returned to his village in Peoria, he sold the comb and other items for whiskey. The new owner thought it worth taking them to St. Louis for sale. There, an old friend of the Wells family recognized the treasures as belonging to Rebekah Wells Heald and wrongfully—but reasonably—concluded that she and her husband had been killed at Chicago.

The family friend quickly purchased the shell comb and other items and sent them to Samuel Wells "as a memento of his daughter and her husband, both supposed to be dead." The items reached Louisville just a few weeks later, and the whole of the Wells clan assumed that their family members had indeed perished. Not for several weeks more would they

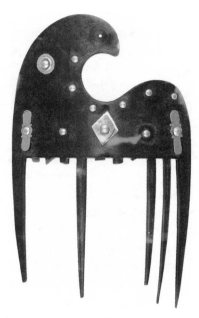

Figure 25. After the battle, Rebekah Wells Heald's distinctive tortoiseshell comb landed for sale in St. Louis. A family member recognized the comb and mistakenly assumed that its owner had perished during the attack at Chicago. (Chicago History Museum, ICHi-65720)

find out that these dire assumptions were not true and that there was a "brighter side to this story of death."[2]

While they survived the attack, the couple suffered serious wounds. Rebekah sustained several knife and gunshot wounds, while her husband received gunshots to his hip and his right arm a little below the elbow. The ball shot into his hip was not removed and would cause Captain Heald numbness for the rest of his life. He never saw active military service again, and he was forced to walk with a crutch or a cane.[3]

While recuperating from their injuries, the couple was allowed to stay at the Burnett home at St. Joseph, where a Potawatomi healer treated their injuries. Kakima Burnett was a recent widow, but she welcomed the Healds, even though it was dangerous to do so. No sooner had they settled in than Topinbee received word that the Potawatomi warrior who had released Captain Heald was under pressure to reclaim him. Topinbee decided to send the couple to Mackinac, where he could "deliver them up to the British."[4]

For $100, Alexander Robinson accepted the perilous task of paddling Captain Heald and his wife, as well as Sergeant Griffith, to Mackinac. They left at the end of August, while many Potawatomi warriors were busy at Fort Wayne. Their journey took over two weeks.[5]

Upon reaching Mackinac, they surrendered to the British commanding officer, who made them as comfortable as he could. As was customary, Captain Heald and Sergeant Griffith signed paroles pledging not to fight against Great Britain until properly exchanged. They then traveled to Detroit and reported to the British commander, who gave them passage to Buffalo. On January 18, 1813, Heald was part of an officer exchange that included William Hull, Lewis Cass, Winfield Scott, and John Whistler.[6] Finally free, the Healds traveled from Buffalo to Pittsburgh and then on to Samuel Wells's farm near Louisville, Kentucky, where delighted family members joyfully returned Rebekah's comb and other treasures.

The distinctive travels of Rebekah Wells Heald's belongings and her person provide insight into the complicated connections that made up Indian Country in 1812. If this had been just an Indian war, the Healds might not have survived. Both seriously wounded, they might have been killed soon after the battle, as was the Algonquian custom. However, because this was a wider war, more moderate Potawatomi warriors had the option of sending prisoners to the British, who used them in exchanges with the United States. Their fortunes improved because the British and Americans subscribed to the parole system for officers and did not consider Rebekah Heald a prisoner at all.

POTAWATOMI CAPTIVES

Just under half of the original U.S. party survived the battle south of Fort Dearborn on August 15, 1812. Traditional accounts confirm that twenty-nine soldiers, seven women, and six children were taken prisoner by the Potawatomis and their allies. The women and children fared better than the men. Five of the children taken captive eventually were ransomed, and six of the women survived. Seven soldiers, most of them badly wounded, were tortured and killed at Chicago after the battle. Four more died during their captivity. Through diplomacy, British ransoms, and personal negotiations, at least eighteen soldiers taken captive later returned to the United States.[7]

The warriors divided the survivors among villages in Illinois and Wisconsin. For the victorious warriors and their families, participation in the attack brought prisoners, supplies, and ammunition. When the warriors brought captives home, they shared the decision about the fate of prisoners, according to well-established Indian traditions. Some captives became servants, while others became replacements for deceased family members.[8]

A permanent captivity for prisoners of war was not a traditional part of Euro-American warfare. Instead, prisoners were held only until they could be exchanged. In the Euro-American system, individual soldiers did not claim prisoners; armies took prisoners and cared for them. Despite this broad responsibility, prisoners of war suffered privations of many sorts, often from want of food and medical attention.[9]

At least a dozen soldiers who survived the battle and its initial aftermath were seized as captives by Potawatomi warriors along the Fox River west of Chicago. Among the villages they were taken to were those of Main Poc, Shabbona, and Mad Sturgeon. Lieutenant Linai Helm had been taken captive by Mittatass, an Odawa warrior from along the Illinois River. Despite the efforts of John Kinzie, his father-in-law, Helm was taken away from Chicago. However, before leaving Chicago, Eleanor Kinzie pleaded for kind treatment of her son-in-law, promising a substantial reward if he remained safe. A few weeks later, Thomas Forsyth successfully negotiated Helm's release by offering Mittatass two horses and a keg of whiskey. Lieutenant Helm returned with Forsyth to his home in Peoria. Eventually, Helm made his way to St. Louis and took a ship back to the East Coast from there.[10]

Corporal Walter Jordan had accompanied William Wells to Chicago. During the battle, he fought alongside the soldiers from Fort Dearborn. In a lighthearted version of his experiences, Jordan recounted that the Indians first shot the feather off his cap, then the epaulet off his shoulder, then the handle off his sword. At that point, the Potawatomi warrior White Raccoon claimed him, having recognized him as the soldier at Fort Wayne who had given him tobacco. Once at White Raccoon's village outside Fort Wayne, Jordan was put to work parching corn during the day but was tied up at night. Before long, his hard work in the cornfields had gained Jordan more freedom. One night, no longer restrained, he stole a horse and returned to Fort Wayne.[11]

Several soldiers endured longer times as captives. While James Corbin's wife and children were killed in the aftermath of the battle at Chicago, he survived even though he was badly wounded. Corbin had been shot in the right heel and the left thigh, and suffered a tomahawk wound to his right shoulder. He was not killed because he convinced his captors that his skills as a blacksmith would be useful to them.[12]

The prisoners were put to work at whatever tasks needed to be done, and most had the freedom to move about their villages. After recovering from his wounds, James Corbin was put to work finding sugar kettles that had been left out beyond the village. Another captive was sent out to find horses that were allowed to wander freely around the village.[13]

While they sometimes experienced kindness at the hands of their captors, captives were also subject to threats, intimidation, and torture. One captive was brought back to the battle site to see his mutilated dead comrades. When several captives first arrived at one village on the Fox River, inhabitants brandishing war clubs and tomahawks greeted them. More terror followed as one of the warriors roasted the hearts of two Americans. Other prisoners recalled the threatening signs of visiting Winnebago warriors, leaving them fearful again for their lives.[14]

Many captives later recalled their hunger. James Corbin noted that the other prisoners in his village gleaned the fields for missed corn husks. However, because of his injuries, he could not do this, and he often went days without food. James Van Horne complained of working all day making sugar "without anything to eat." During the winter of 1812, many warriors left the Fox River to fight at Detroit, leaving captives behind without enough food for sustenance.[15] One soldier froze to death, another was tomahawked because of "excessive fatigue," and a third lost his mind during the winter and was killed by his captors.[16]

Potawatomi warriors from a village along the Fox River claimed Sarah and John Neads and their infant son. John Neads had been a private stationed at Fort Dearborn and had sustained serious injuries during the battle. There was little for anyone to eat in the village during the winter of 1812–13. In early December 1812, their Potawatomi captors could no longer endure the cries of hunger from their baby. They tied the infant to a tree, where it froze to death.[17] John Neads succumbed in January 1813 from battle injuries as well as his weakened state. Sometime that same month, Sarah Neads was tied to a tree, and she also died from hunger and cold.[18] While these brutal acts still shock centuries later, they reflected not so much Potawatomi callousness regarding their captives, so much as the precarious nature of village life during this extremely harsh winter.

In contrast, an older Potawatomi woman with three daughters claimed a wounded U.S. soldier as her prisoner. The widow and the soldier knew each other because the soldier had often shared his food with the struggling family. The widow took the wounded man back to her camp along a small lake about forty miles north of Chicago. After recovering from his injuries, the soldier and the widow married and formed a family. The soldier showed no interest in returning "to civilization" as he was by then an integral member of an Indian family.[19]

Black Partridge, the Potawatomi chief who helped both the Heald and Kinzie families, also claimed Martha Leigh and her two surviving daughters, twelve-year-old Mary and baby Sally. He knew Martha and her family from his many visits to Chicago. Young Mary was severely wounded and in great pain. Following tradition, Black Partridge killed her because she could not travel back to his village. Black Partridge later said that it was the hardest thing he ever had to do. He brought Martha and her baby back to his village, where they were treated as family members.[20]

Mary Burns, a neighbor of Martha Leigh, lost her husband and three of her children during the battle. A young warrior scalped her twelve-year-old daughter Isabella, but an older Potawatomi woman who had regularly visited the Burns family saved her from death. This woman claimed the three Burns women and took them back to her village, where she nursed Isabella back to health.[21]

Susan Simmons came to Fort Dearborn as the young bride of U.S. Army corporal John Simmons. Both had grown up along the frontier near Picqua, Ohio. During the battle, warriors killed her husband and three-year-old son. Simmons and her infant daughter (also named Susan) survived the attack. Susan Simmons remained stoic as she was led away from the battle site, even as she passed a row of slain children that included her son.[22]

Warriors who lived at Green Bay claimed Simmons and her baby as their captives. Arriving there, Simmons did not find a warm welcome. Instead, she was forced to run a gauntlet formed by the women and children of the village. Those who had lost loved ones in the fighting took out their anger on the captives, hitting them with sticks and clubs. Still, after this beating, an older Indian woman washed her wounds, gave her food, and adopted Simmons into her family. Simmons came to regard her as her "Indian mother."[23]

BRITISH RANSOMS

Many of these captives hoped that they would be ransomed through the intervention of the American government or by local traders. However, several factors worked against quick rescues. For one, there was considerable misinformation about the fate of the Fort Dearborn garrison. Four days after the battle, the commander at Fort Wayne provided the first news of the attack to Americans, describing "the destruction" of the company.[24]

At the end of August, Governor Harrison confirmed "the massacre of the garrison," again holding out little hope for any survivors as he lamented the death of his old nemesis William Wells.[25] Far from taking action on behalf of the forty-two left alive after the attack—nearly half of the retreating force—Harrison did not search for any survivors. Instead, he and Governor Ninian Edwards of Illinois launched retaliatory actions against the Potawatomis and their allies that made it even more dangerous for any American, whether captive or not, to be in Indian Country.[26]

Another factor working against the quick ransom of captives was the American surrender of Detroit to the British at almost the same time that Fort Dearborn was abandoned. When word of the attack on the retreating garrison reached Fort Malden, the British quickly denied any involvement in the attack or "any influence over the Indians."[27] The British wanted to make clear that they were not party to the attack at Chicago. British general Henry A. Proctor expressed regret over the attack, and like Harrison erroneously believed that only a very few, if any, Americans had survived.

Not until October 1812, when Captain Heald and Sergeant Griffith arrived in Detroit after their parole by the British commander at Mackinac, did the news of the many survivors finally surface. Heald and Griffith reported that "nearly half the garrison" and "a number of women and children" had survived the battle and been taken captive. Captain Heald, despite the fact that he was a British prisoner and badly injured, sought British aid to ransom his troops.

Most importantly, Heald appealed to Judge Augustus Woodward, a prominent Detroit resident, who had standing with the British. Heald provided

Woodward with a list of more than thirty soldiers and civilians he thought to be still in captivity.[28] Woodward applied to British general Proctor for help in ransoming these captives from Chicago.[29]

General Proctor could not simply send British troops in to collect the American soldiers and their families who were captives. Neither the British nor the Americans had that kind of control over Indian Country. Instead, Proctor appealed to the Potawatomis as his allies. Two weeks after receiving Woodward's letter, Proctor informed the chiefs involved in the attack "of his desire that the captives be brought to him." Not until the early spring of 1813, however, did Proctor lay out a specific plan for the recovery of these American captives.[30]

In the end, Proctor turned to Robert Dickson, the influential Indian trader who had convinced so many warriors to fight alongside the British at Mackinac. In March 1813 Dickson stopped at Chicago and shared with local traders and Indians a proclamation from General Proctor, calling for the survivors of the garrison at Fort Dearborn to be handed over to the British, with a reward offered for each captive.

The bounties proffered enticed several area traders to devote considerable time and effort to ransoming captives. Louis Buisson, the brother-in-law of Archange Ouilmette, and François Des Pins, quickly realized the profit to be made by trading in Indian villages for the captives and transporting them to Mackinac. Both traders had houses at Chicago and probably knew most of the Fort Dearborn captives by sight. Over the late spring of 1813, Buisson and Des Pins traveled from village to village. They purchased captives with the British goods left for them by Dickson.

Among the first captives they ransomed were Martha Leigh and her infant daughter from Black Partridge. Sometime afterward, Martha married Des Pins and lived out her life as a trader's wife. As well, Des Pins and Buisson ransomed Mary Burns and her two daughters, who ultimately made their way to Detroit.[31] Susan Simmons and her daughter were captives near Green Bay, beyond the area that Buisson and Des Pins worked. But Simmons was taken to Mackinac by warriors in her village, where she was ransomed by the British. The British let her go, but she had to travel on foot back to her parents' home near Picqua, Ohio. She had left three years before as a young bride and returned a widow.[32]

While the British did not hold these women and children as prisoners, the U.S. soldiers ransomed from their Indian captors became British prisoners of war. As they were not officers, they were not offered parole. Instead, they were sent as a group to Detroit and held for a time on a prison ship along with members of the Kentucky militia. As one soldier captive remembered, "The Indians were constantly endeavoring to come on board the prison ship and massacre us." Not until May 1814 were they exchanged and returned to the United States.[33]

While the ransom efforts were generally successful, they did put other traders, especially those identified with the Americans, at greater risk. Thomas Forsyth had worked for the release of captives, including Lieutenant Helm, from the days immediately following the battle at Chicago. In the spring of 1813, Forsyth asked his neighbor Gomo, generally sympathetic to Americans, for aid in ransoming some of the remaining captive soldiers. Gomo told him that he could not help him because of General Proctor's order. Forsyth himself was in danger of being rounded up along with the Fort Dearborn captives and taken to Mackinac as a British prisoner of war.[34]

JOHN KINZIE, INDIAN CAPTIVE

While John and Eleanor Kinzie came to the aid of many captives after the battle at Chicago, they were prisoners of war themselves. As the violence was winding down on the morning of August 15, 1812, Black Partridge and Topinbee claimed the various members of the Kinzie household as their captives. They protected the Kinzie family a few days later when hostile Indians threatened them again. Eventually, the Kinzie family was moved to St. Joseph, still as prisoners of Topinbee.

They arrived at St. Joseph, joining Captain Heald and his wife at the Burnett trading post. John Kinzie wrote that he and his brother Thomas Forsyth were "totally ruined."[35] After a few weeks, Topinbee let Eleanor and the children go to Detroit, but he wanted John Kinzie to remain at St. Joseph. Kinzie had little choice but to comply and remained at St. Joseph for several months. He traveled across the region with Topinbee, dressed in Potawatomi clothing "in order to escape capture and perhaps death at the hands of those who were still thirsting for blood." Eventually, he was allowed to travel to Detroit, where General Proctor paroled him. Topinbee may have received a bounty for turning Kinzie over to the British. In any case, Kinzie was treated as an enemy combatant, as a part of the American militia at Fort Dearborn. On his parole, Kinzie pledged not to reenter the war, a promise he would find hard to keep.[36]

John Kinzie joined his family at Detroit before the end of 1812. Detroit had been in the hands of the British for more than three months after U.S. general William Hull surrendered Detroit.[37] The British placed a small garrison at the fort in Detroit, but there was little interference in everyday life from them. The town then contained about 150 houses and 700 inhabitants.

While Detroit had only very recently become an occupied city, it had for many years been a divided city. Since the 1794 Jay Treaty, some residents professed their continued allegiance to Great Britain, while others had identified themselves as Americans. To some degree, this division was physical—with many of the British subjects moving across the river to Sandwich. For families and neighbors, the war in 1812 was something of a civil war.[38]

This was certainly true for Eleanor and John Kinzie, who had deep roots in Detroit. Many of their Lytle and Forsyth relatives had declared loyalty to Great Britain following the Jay Treaty and remained loyal in 1812. They lived near one another at Sandwich, across the river from Detroit, in Canada. James Forsyth, one of Kinzie's stepbrothers, was "an active participant on the British side."[39] At the same time, Robert, another of the Forsyth brothers, had sworn his allegiance to the United States and worked for the United States. After the British takeover of Detroit, General Proctor arrested Robert on charges of spying for the Americans.[40]

Eleanor and John Kinzie's choice of residence was an important clue to their allegiances. When she fled to Detroit in September 1812, Eleanor had three small children in her charge: John Harris was nine, Ellen was eight, and Robert was two. She may have gone first to her sister's house in Sandwich. However, when her husband finally joined her, they moved into the Forsyth house adjacent to the fort in occupied Detroit. The house, where Kinzie had lived as a young man with his stepfather, William Forsyth, was unoccupied in the fall of 1812. As Kinzie's nephew and British partisan James R. Forsyth later angrily argued, the Kinzie family "made my grandfather's house their home." They chose to live in occupied, but American, Detroit, rather than in Canadian Sandwich with most of their family.[41]

Soon after the Kinzie family settled at Detroit, the war again came to their doorstep. In January 1813 William Henry Harrison launched an unsuccessful attack south of Detroit at the River Raisin. Having just lived through the fighting at Chicago, the Kinzie family was once again engulfed by the war. Just outside their door streamed dozens of U.S. soldiers, taken captive at River Raisin by British-allied Indians. It would have been understandable if they had kept their doors closed to the American captives, many severely injured and suffering from the cold. Instead, the Kinzies, along with other Detroit families, ransomed as many of these captives as possible. They set up one room in the house on Jefferson Street for these soldiers, nursing them back to health. The Kinzie family once again came to the aid of individuals caught in the same maelstrom of war.[42]

13 A Savage Fall: 1812 in the West

While Kinzie and other captives from the August battle at Chicago negotiated their way in Indian Country, the war expanded on several fronts. In the unsettled days of early September 1812, Thomas Forsyth warned, "The die is cast and the United States may expect nothing but war." He advised U.S. officials across the West that what lay ahead was "a war of extermination."[1] There was a bellicose outlook in every direction.

Emboldened by their success against the retreating garrison from Fort Dearborn, the Potawatomis and their allies moved forward with their plans to attack other western U.S. installations despite the absence of Main Poc and Tecumseh. They hoped that the British would come to their assistance as their plans unfolded.

However, the British had a different strategy: to keep the fighting tightly focused in and around Detroit. To that end, they encouraged their Indian allies to come to Detroit and fight alongside them. In 1812 and 1813, this winning strategy stanched an American invasion into Canada.

The U.S. government, focused on the eastern theater of the war, had few regular troops to spare for the West, leaving the response to Fort Dearborn and other Indian attacks to local militia units. The militias, drawn from Kentucky and across the Northwest, targeted the destruction of Indian villages they saw as culpable for the attacks on U.S. installations. Their savagery only inflamed more anti-American sentiment across western Indian Country.

INDIAN ATTACKS ON U.S. FORTS IN THE NORTHWEST

The Potawatomis who attacked the retreating garrison at Chicago were not operating in isolation. A series of offensives after the harvest and during the full moon (August 25) had been planned since the spring of 1812. The

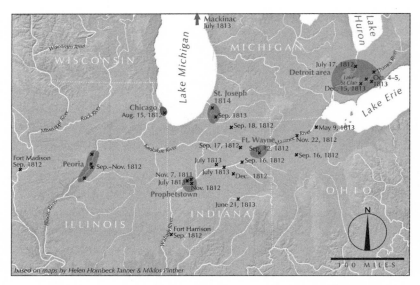

Map 10. Western War, 1811–15. Based on maps by Helen Hornbeck Tanner and Miklos Pinther. (Dennis McClendon, Chicago Cartographics)

assault on the retreating garrison at Chicago before the full moon took advantage of circumstances. After the battle, the Potawatomis and their allies planned their next step. They had ammunition and a renewed sense of purpose.[2]

A week after the full moon, September 3, Shawnee, Winnebago, Kickapoo, and Miami warriors from Prophetstown led an attack on Fort Harrison on the Wabash River. Captain Zachary Taylor, who commanded fifty-five regulars at Fort Harrison, was aware of the general plan to attack his garrison.[3] As at Chicago, a small group of women and children took refuge at the fort. However, Captain Taylor had no orders to evacuate and instead prepared for a siege. He refused entry to any warriors camped outside Fort Harrison, even when a few waved a white flag. For ten days, Taylor and his small company of soldiers held the fort. Then Governor Harrison sent a thousand U.S. troops, mostly militia units, to end the siege. In contrast to Captain Heald at Fort Dearborn, Captain Taylor stayed in his outpost and was able to maintain the advantage over the loosely organized warriors.[4]

Two days after the start of the siege at Fort Harrison, a party of Ho-Chunks and Sauks attacked Fort Madison on the Mississippi. The warriors destroyed the U.S. Factory, filled with trade goods. Unable to set the fort on fire, they soon retreated. In contrast to Fort Dearborn, where Potawatomi warriors successfully destroyed Fort Dearborn, Fort Madison remained standing as a symbol of the U.S. presence along the Mississippi River.[5]

Flush from victory at Fort Dearborn, Potawatomi warriors, including Blackbird, organized an attack on Fort Wayne. Warriors from several Potawatomi villages in northern Indiana and southern Michigan, including St. Joseph, joined the war party. Among them were Five Medals and Metea, who had long supported the United States. Five Medals had accompanied Little Turtle and William Wells on several of their official trips to Washington, D.C. Now there was enormous pressure on warriors like him to fight against the U.S. presence in the region.[6]

By late August a considerable force of warriors had surrounded Fort Wayne. Unable to breach the stockade, they destroyed livestock, crops, and dwellings outside the fort. One of the houses they destroyed was that of Captain William Wells, killed just a few days before at Chicago. The officers and soldiers sorely missed Wells and his deep understanding of Indian ways. The warriors outside hoped to trick his unseasoned replacement into opening the fort gates to a wider attack, much as Tecumseh had swindled Benjamin Stickney into supplying him with ammunition earlier in the year. However, this time Captain Rhea, a competent army officer who had replaced Nathan Heald at Fort Wayne, maintained control.[7]

Captain Rhea and his soldiers, like Captain Taylor at Fort Harrison, successfully endured the siege. Perhaps the perspective of Walter Jordan helped them to understand the challenge they faced. Jordan was a Potawatomi captive during the battle at Chicago and had just escaped back to Fort Wayne. His stories of death and destruction on the path away from Fort Dearborn certainly helped convince the U.S. soldiers that retreat was not a viable option.[8]

On the evening of September 6, a force of six hundred warriors attacked the fort, but the troops held their ground, expecting that reinforcements would be on the way. While Captain Heald at Chicago had held no hope for reinforcements, Captain Rhea expected General Harrison to send them. Outside, the Potawatomis also waited for reinforcements from the British and the arrival of Tecumseh and Main Poc.[9] Blackbird and other warriors tried in vain to burn the stockade surrounding the fort. Then they attacked the fort but were unable to pierce its walls. Finally, without needed reinforcements, they withdrew from Fort Wayne, just before the arrival of General William Henry Harrison with force of more than two thousand men.[10]

The quick victories at Mackinac, Detroit, and Chicago in the opening weeks of the war were countered in the early fall with stalemates at Forts Madison, Harrison, and Wayne. Potawatomi warriors and their allies failed to receive needed assistance from the British or from their own leaders like Tecumseh and Main Poc, who remained at Detroit.

RETRIBUTION OF THE "LONG KNIVES"

The U.S. Army companies assigned to the string of forts in the Northwest were a small fighting force, no match for the thousands of Indian warriors in the region. Instead, Governor Harrison turned to local militias to create a western army. He traveled to Kentucky and Ohio to raise troops following U.S. defeats in July and August. More than two thousand men volunteered to serve in militia units under him, and a grateful governor appointed Harrison as major general in the Kentucky militia. General Harrison, though not from Kentucky, was immensely popular among these troops. Western settlers were well pleased with his great success in gaining Indian land cessions while territorial governor of Indiana. His attack against Tenskwatawa at Tippecanoe the preceding year was widely supported by western citizens, who applauded direct military action against recalcitrant Indians.

By September 1812 General Harrison had the troops to support U.S. outposts from Indian offensives. He also had a force eager to retaliate for the Indian attack at Fort Dearborn. The force went first to Fort Wayne, where their impending arrival ended the siege. The warriors dispersed before their arrival. Harrison then moved to "to punish" the Potawatomis and their allies.[11]

General Harrison planned attacks against Indian villages in Indiana, southwestern Michigan, and Illinois "suspected of harboring anti-American warriors."[12] Units of his militia raided and burned Miami settlements along the Wabash River as well as Potawatomi villages along the Elkhart River. They destroyed cornfields of Potawatomi villages near St. Joseph, where the Heald and Kinzie families had been afforded refuge after the attack south of Chicago. Another village destroyed was that of Little Turtle, one of the most loyal supporters of the United States, who had died a few months before. Harrison seemed to make little distinction between friend and foe in his path of devastation.[13]

Samuel Wells led a detachment of Kentucky militia troops in several of these early fall actions. He went with General Harrison to end the siege at Fort Wayne. For Wells, these military actions provided an opportunity for personal revenge. By then, Samuel Wells knew of the brutal death of his brother, who had come to the aid of his daughter at Chicago. He still believed that his daughter had also been killed there.

In his defense, Samuel Wells did not yet know of the compassionate actions of many Potawatomis, including Black Partridge and Topinbee, in keeping his daughter alive and safe from harm. He did not know that Captain Nathan Heald and his wife were treated for their wounds at St. Joseph, just weeks before Wells and his militia burned some of these same Potawatomi villages and destroyed crops waiting for harvest. However, it was a difficult reality for Potawatomi leaders like Topinbee to wrestle with—their kindness was returned with violent reprisals.[14]

Another village destroyed by Wells and his militia was that of Five Medals, another longtime friend to the United States. However, Five Medals participated in the siege at Fort Wayne. Harrison specially charged Wells with destroying his village, located on the Elkhart River, a tributary of the St. Joseph River. What Harrison saw as a betrayal of American friendship, Five Medals saw as necessary for survival in an increasingly anti-American environment. Harrison saw only black-and-white in an increasingly gray world.[15]

Over the course of the next three months, Harrison's militia burned twenty-one Indian towns in northern Indiana and southern Michigan. They destroyed crops in the field as well as any stored food. In addition, they burned villages and seized any movable property.[16] These raids turned many American allies to the British, who provided some food relief.[17]

For the most part, the Indians were aware of the American troop movements and stayed away from them. Occasionally, the militiamen encountered villagers who fought against destruction. At one village at Mississinewa in December 1812, Americans killed or captured fifty Miamis, including many women and children. One of the officers at the battle reported: "The troops rushed into town[,] killed eight warriors and took forty-two prisoners[,] eight of whom are warriors, the residue women and children. I ordered the town to be immediately burnt." The troops also burned and pillaged "three considerable villages" nearby, killing "a great many cattle." The following day warriors from these villages attacked the U.S. camp, but "the enemy paid dearly for their temerity. From the trails through the snow and those found dead, we could not have killed less than thirty. . . . The enemy did not take a scalp." The numbers involved were about the same as at Chicago and no less brutal.[18]

After weeks devoted to the destruction of the villages of Potawatomis and their allies, Harrison turned to an attack against the British at Fort Malden across the frozen Detroit River in early 1813. During the closing weeks of 1812, while officials in Washington, D.C., were distracted with the presidential elections, Harrison began to build a "huge army" that would cost far more than the U.S. government intended to spend in the West.[19]

WAR PARTIES AND MILITIAS IN ILLINOIS

The attacks at Forts Dearborn, Madison, and Harrison evidenced the threat of violence in Illinois. However, because of territorial boundaries, Harrison focused his attention on the Potawatomis and Miamis in Indiana, Ohio, and Michigan. The Potawatomis living across the border into Illinois Territory concerned him less, and his Kentucky militia were disinterested in fighting beyond Indiana.[20]

By early September three hundred Potawatomi warriors, including long-time American ally Gomo, had organized loosely as a war party. They intended to attack the United States but did not have a specific target in mind. They met at Peoria on September 7 but dispersed before launching any large-scale offensive.[21] There was also a danger of war from warriors organized by Robert Dickson. Some among them had hoped to attack American settlements around St. Louis, but Dickson convinced them to go to Detroit to serve alongside the British.[22]

Illinois governor Edwards took notice of this unrest. He sent his family to Kentucky, secured his papers, and collected forces to defend Illinois.[23] The American settlers in southern Illinois quickly organized militia units. However, these militiamen were difficult to control, and Edwards scrambled to find the funds to pay them. Using these militia units, Edwards moved up the Illinois River with the intention of attacking the Potawatomi, Kickapoo, and Miami villages in and around Peoria. There was a concentration of about eight hundred warriors there. Many had relocated to the area in 1811, through the encouragement of Main Poc and over the objections of more moderate leaders like Gomo.[24]

In October 1812 Edwards and his militia destroyed five Potawatomi, Kickapoo, and Miami villages in and around Peoria, in much the same way as Harrison's forces had ranged across northern Indiana. Just as Harrison's troops had found, the Indians were well aware of most of the American moves. They left their villages in advance of the arrival of the Illinois militia, so only a few Indians were killed in these raids.[25]

There were some exceptions. At one village, at the head of Peoria Lake (a widening in the Illinois River), Edwards and his soldiers encountered Kickapoos and Miamis fleeing from them. Edwards's troops killed as many of these villagers as they could as they fled their homes. At another village, they burnt a "great quantity of provisions, and other valuable Indian property." All told, Edwards estimated that they had killed twenty-four to thirty Indians and taken about eighty horses, all without "the loss of a single man."[26]

Governor Edwards and his militia seemed unable to distinguish between friend and foe. They especially targeted Black Partridge's village to the north of Peoria, in order to "to avenge the massacre of the troops at Fort Dearborn."[27] Governor Harrison and his militias ignored (or did not understand) that Black Partridge had done all he could to mitigate the violence and brutality at Chicago.[28] Perhaps they had heard that Black Partridge had returned his medal of friendship with the United States on the eve of the battle outside Fort Dearborn, but they must also have heard that he protected Captain Heald and his wife, as well as members of the Kinzie family. For whatever reason, and much like General Harrison to the East, Governor Edwards and his militias refused to take a nuanced view, where Black Partridge was a true friend of many Americans, both at Chicago and across the region.

Edwards and his militia wanted to take Black Partridge's village by surprise, in order to capture or kill its inhabitants, as well as destroy property. When the militia arrived, there were few warriors at the village; Black Partridge was not present. Instead, women, children, and elderly adults inhabited most of the houses. The villagers were unaware of the approaching danger, until shots were fired. Many were badly wounded in the initial volley, and the militia killed many women and children "in cold blood." After the battle, the militia burned the village to the ground. They took around a hundred horses, a thousand bushels of corn, as well as beans, dried meat, and pumpkins. The American militia carried off (or destroyed) the food necessary to support this (and many other) villages in the winter ahead.[29]

A toll of the lives taken at Peoria, like those lost at Tippecanoe in 1811 or in Indiana during the fall of 1812, must include those who starved during the following winter or died from exposure because the American militia had burned their "strong and well built" houses. At Black Partridge's village, where few warriors were present, the American attack can be seen as "a one sided massacre of innocents—old men, women, and children; as unnecessary and ruthless and indefensible as the massacre at Fort Dearborn, a short time before."[30]

FORSYTH'S MÉTIS PEORIA

While the militias in Illinois and Indiana mainly attacked empty Indian villages during the fall of 1812, they also threatened métis trading villages. For the militiamen, the French and métis traders were as much a part of the Indian Country that they sought to destroy as the Indians themselves. As well, many suspected that the traders were in league with Great Britain.

For instance, at Peoria, Thomas Forsyth, Antoine LeClair, François Des Pins, Louis Buisson, and others operated a trading village. Kinzie & Forsyth had operated there because it was "the most important place in all of Indian Country." Indians crossing from Detroit to points across the West stopped "to rest themselves and get a little tobacco." As well, information about events and plans from Mackinac, Detroit, the St. Joseph River, Chicago, Milwaukee, and Green Bay all quickly made their way to Peoria's traders.[31]

The trading village at Peoria held mixed loyalties. Forsyth had hosted a quiet meeting with LeClair, Billy Caldwell, and John Kinzie at his house in Peoria during the previous summer. By then, LeClair and Forsyth were providing information to the United States. However, Forsyth's ties to the United States were not well known, and many in the region assumed that he had British allegiances. Louis Buisson and François Des Pins, Forsyth's neighbors, openly allied with the British and worked closely with Robert Dickson, both in raising troops among the western Indians and in ransoming Indian captives.

Forsyth found Peoria an increasingly dangerous place. When writing to American officials, Forsyth cautioned them not to "mention my name to any person, for if the French get hold of it my life is gone." "The French" might here refer to his neighbors Louis Buisson and François Des Pins. Forsyth also feared area Indians might uncover his contact with American officials like Governor Edwards.[32]

Forsyth worried about attacks from both within and from outside his village, including an assault from pro-British Potawatomis, Kickapoos, Ho-Chunks, and Miamis. There were hundreds of Indians with anti-American feelings in and around Peoria, so his concerns were well founded. At the same time, Forsyth had personal friendships with Gomo as well as Black Hawk, a leading Sauk warrior. He hoped that these long relationships would help to protect the trading village at Peoria from attack.

Forsyth and the other traders at Peoria watched with trepidation as Governor Edwards and his militia units swept through the area in early October 1812, burning neighboring Indian villages, taking horses, and destroying farm fields. Even though Forsyth worked for Edwards, this was not common knowledge, certainly not to members of the militia units marauding around Peoria. After the American forces had left the region, Forsyth thought it "prudent" to take his "most valuable effects" to St. Louis. If his family had not already left Peoria, Forsyth got them out of harm's way.

While Forsyth was away, Miami and Kickapoo warriors descended on the traders' town in retaliation for Edwards's militia raids. The warriors attacked the trading village and took "every article they could carry away." The warriors forced residents to board canoes and abandon their homes. Only through the intervention of Gomo were the métis wives and children of the Peoria traders able to flee.[33]

Soon after the Miami and Kickapoo warriors left, Captain Thomas Craig arrived with a renegade Illinois militia. To their disappointment, they had missed the militia attacks on the Indian villages in and around Peoria. Craig encountered only women and children at the Peoria trading village, as many of the men had fled in the wake of the earlier Kickapoo and Miami attack. Craig and his men emptied the houses and outhouses of the town "of every kind of property that was portable." The militia loaded their booty onto boats.[34]

Thomas Forsyth and other men of the village confronted them about the theft of their property. Craig accused Forsyth of being a "friend of Indians," not of the Americans.[35] However, Craig agreed to return some of their property and prepared to leave Peoria, but before he could leave, area Indians fired on his men. Craig blamed the attack on the residents of Peoria, whom he described as "dam'd rascals."[36] He took them all as prisoners of war and burned their houses and barns filled with wheat. Craig brought forty-two people to Kaskaskia as prisoners of war, including Thomas Forsyth, despite the fact that most were American citizens.[37] Governor Edwards recognized the group once they reached Kaskaskia and released them all. However, their community had been twice ransacked and little remained of their settlement. The destruction of their trading outpost was simply collateral damage in the ongoing war.

MAIN POC AND TECUMSEH RETURN

Longtime American allies like Black Partridge and Gomo saw their own villages, and those around them at Peoria, destroyed with no special consideration given by the Illinois militia. In the same way, American allies in Indiana like Five Medals experienced the wholesale retribution of Harrison's army. It became increasingly difficult for these leaders to maintain anything but hostile relations with the United States.

By December 1812 Main Poc and Tecumseh, who had fought alongside the British around Detroit in the opening months of the war with the United States, returned home. They found that militant anti-American sentiment had grown dramatically since the opening of the war. The West was radicalizing with little room for moderates.

Tecumseh went to his village, still near Tippecanoe. He was ill, and his wife and sister cared for him at home on the Wabash River. While he recuperated, his warriors skirmished with U.S. militia units throughout the winter. Tecumseh remained near Tippecanoe until April 1813.[38]

When Main Poc returned to Illinois, he moved north of the fighting around Peoria, setting up a village at the juncture of the Fox and Illinois Rivers, to the southwest of Chicago. Over the course of the winter of 1812–13, parties of Sauks, Ho-Chunks, and Potawatomis visited him and made plans. Main Poc became convinced that Captain Craig's raid on Peoria was just the start of an American invasion up the Illinois River. He rallied support among the Potawatomis and Sauks to meet this anticipated attack. As well, Main Poc encouraged warriors to continue raids against Kaskaskia, Vincennes, and other American settlements to the south. However, in the late spring of 1813, Main Poc, like Tecumseh, returned to Detroit to fight alongside the British. If they had stayed, this story might have been very different.[39] Instead, both were swept up into the British war centered around Detroit. They took many warriors with them, leaving only women and children in villages across Indian Country, lessening the Indian threat in Illinois and Indiana.[40]

14 1813: Shifting Allegiances

In 1812 many Indians in the western Great Lakes saw an opportunity to push Americans back east and south out of their region to achieve the pan-Indian vision imagined by Tecumseh and his allies. To this end, Indians attacked U.S. forts in the Northwest in July, August, and September of 1812. The Potawatomis and their allies destroyed Fort Dearborn and helped the British to take Detroit and Mackinac. However, they were unable to take and hold U.S. installations at Fort Harrison and Fort Wayne, not because the U.S. Army sent needed reinforcements, but because western militias rose up to fight against the Indian attacks. Once organized, they inflicted a heavy toll of destruction on Indian villages. Even moderate Potawatomi warriors turned against the United States in the face of this indiscriminate violence.

Neither the United States nor Great Britain was interested, or able, to support an escalation of war west of Detroit. Both countries wanted to avoid the cost and uncertainty of this heightened conflict that both Indian warriors and western militias embraced. General Hull's order to evacuate Fort Dearborn in the summer of 1812 recognized the unwillingness of the U.S. Army to protect its far-flung installations in the West.[1]

At the same time, both powers encouraged western Indians and militias to join the war at Detroit. British Indian Agent Robert Dickson recruited warriors to fight alongside British regular troops at Mackinac and Detroit. Tecumseh and Main Poc came to Detroit, hoping that a British victory would send the United States out of the region entirely.

On the U.S. side, William Henry Harrison saw the possibility of national glory in moving his militias into action against the British. During the fall of 1812 these militias had brutally attacked Indian villages in Indiana, Michigan, and Illinois. In late 1812 Harrison planned a campaign using his western militiamen to retake Detroit. The British and their Indian allies would stand against Harrison's troops.

John Kinzie and his family had retreated to Detroit, while Thomas Forsyth took his wife and sons to St. Louis. The two brothers, who had been in close and regular contact for more than a dozen years, seem not to have seen each other after they parted at Chicago in September 1812. As 1813 began, both the British and U.S. governments saw the two men as useful to their causes and sought out their loyal service. Both men wrestled with their choices, without the benefit of regular conversation.

DETROIT

In January 1813, with Tecumseh and Main Poc spending the winter at their home villages in the west, General William Harrison began to assemble his militias and U.S. Army troops south of Detroit. Unfortunately, his offensive began prematurely at the River Raisin just outside Detroit.[2] The British attacked the American troops, killed one-third of them, and took the rest prisoners. Indian warriors tortured twenty of these prisoners to death. Like the violence at Fort Dearborn, these depredations were the subject of considerable discussion in American newspapers over the succeeding weeks and months. The British were roundly condemned for not protecting the American prisoners at River Raisin, who had reason to believe that they were surrendering to British troops, not their Indian allies. "Remember the Raisin" became a rallying cry for American militia during the rest of the western war.

The British, realizing the tenuous hold they had over their Indian allies, scrambled to find individuals who had influence in Indian Country. British officials approached three men at Detroit in January 1813, all of whom had deep connections in Indian Country: Robert Dickson, John Kinzie, and Billy Caldwell. All knew each other well, for they traded in the western Great Lakes for many years. The British appointed Dickson as Indian agent west of the Mississippi River and hoped to appoint Caldwell and Kinzie to work with western Indians as well.

Billy Caldwell had deep ties in British Detroit. After spending his earliest years with his mother's Mohawk family near Niagara, Caldwell came to Detroit to live with his father, William Caldwell, a British officer. For more than a decade, the younger Caldwell had worked for and with John Kinzie. Since 1810 he had been closely associated with Tecumseh, traveling with him across the West. Caldwell made his way to Detroit in late 1812 and found his father organizing Caldwell's Rangers out of Fort Malden. The senior Caldwell secured commissions for two of his legitimate sons, but not for his oldest (and illegitimate) son. Instead, Billy Caldwell secured a captaincy in the British Indian Department in January 1813. In that capacity, he fought alongside Indian warriors engaged on the British side. Caldwell was seriously injured in his first battle at River Raisin but recovered to fight around Detroit over the next two years.[3]

Robert Dickson, a longtime trader in Indian Country, had spent the summer and early fall of 1812 recruiting western Indians for the British. He returned to Detroit in January 1813 and, like Caldwell, accepted an appointment in the British Indian Department.[4] At the same time, the British offered John Kinzie a position in the British Indian Department, on Dickson's recommendation. Kinzie neither accepted the position nor turned it down. In March the British renewed their offer. While Kinzie later stated he "would sooner have been a private in the U.S. Service than a captain in the Indian Department," his response at the time must have been more ambiguous. The British, in fact, thought he had accepted their position.[5]

The trouble was that Kinzie was also working to draw Indian support away from the British for U.S. general William Henry Harrison. Kinzie's connection to Harrison came through his half-brother, Thomas Forsyth. Neither of the brothers had met the governor of Indiana before the late summer of 1812, when Forsyth met Harrison to plead leniency for Kinzie in the murder of Jean Lalime. Whatever discussion took place, Kinzie was never prosecuted for the crime but soon thereafter began providing information and aid to Harrison. In fact, Kinzie employed two men, including his young métis clerk, Jean Baptiste Chandonnai, in this recognizance work for the United States. Kinzie later claimed that through their efforts, many Potawatomis chose not to fight alongside the British at Detroit.[6]

In contrast, Robert Dickson very deliberately took up his post as the British Indian agent in the West. He left Detroit soon after his trade goods arrived in March 1813. At St. Joseph, Dickson promised the Potawatomi warriors enough ammunition and goods to carry out war "against the Long Knives." The Potawatomis, recovering from William Henry Harrison's strikes against their villages the previous fall, listened carefully. Dickson must have been persuasive, because Topinbee, a longtime supporter of the United States and a special friend of John Kinzie, agreed to travel to Malden to fight alongside the British.[7]

Six days later, within sight of the shell of Fort Dearborn, Dickson met with more Potawatomi leaders, including Gomo from Peoria. He distributed food and supplies to the Potawatomis, Miamis, and Kickapoos whose villages had been destroyed by the Illinois militias the previous fall. While Gomo demurred, other Potawatomis accepted Dickson's call to arms and traveled to Malden to fight with Main Poc and Topinbee.[8]

While at Chicago, Dickson found two small brass cannons that had been left behind by the U.S. Army. He arranged to have these cannons sent to Mackinac and called area Potawatomis to turn over their captives from Fort Dearborn to the British.[9]

Dickson returned to Detroit after three months of recruiting in the West with over a thousand warriors, including Black Hawk, who left his Sauk village on the Mississippi River. The warriors fought in several battles in and around Detroit, including attacks on two U.S. forts in Ohio (Meigs and Stephenson). Tecumseh had pushed hard for the latter, as part of his goal to wipe out U.S. posts across the Northwest. These wound up being the final British offensives in the region. The British also exhausted their food supplies and were no longer able to issue rations to their Indian allies.

The war around Detroit was at a turning point. In late August 1813, Commander Oliver Perry won a significant naval victory that resulted in American control of Lake Erie. Coupled with the British retreat from Ohio and food shortages, many of the warriors assembled by Dickson and by Tecumseh returned westward. One British general complained that an Indian force was "never to be relied on in time of need." However, their Indian allies correctly surmised that the British were not fighting the war they wanted.[10]

John Kinzie's role in the steady stream of Potawatomis returning home is not entirely clear. However, Kinzie and Jean Chandonnai negotiated with retreating warriors to make peace with the United States. All the while, the British employed both men: Chandonnai as an interpreter and Kinzie working directly for Robert Dickson. Enraged when he realized this duplicity, Robert Dickson pressed for their arrest on charges of high treason.[11]

In September 1813 the British took Kinzie into their custody and moved him across the river to Fort Malden. When his friends among the Potawatomis learned about his detention, they crossed the river and brought him back home to Detroit. These warriors told British general Proctor that Kinzie was "their friend and prisoner." Kinzie was able to remain at home until the arrival of Robert Dickson, who personally arrested Kinzie for advising U.S. general Harrison and giving Indians information "detrimental to the views" of the British.[12]

Tecumseh also complained of Kinzie's duplicity. He told the British that if they did not hang Kinzie, "the Indians themselves would put him to death." Tecumseh found Kinzie to be "acting a treacherous part with the Indians," by sharing information with the Americans.[13]

Kinzie was held for seven weeks at Fort Malden, during which time he was kept in a dungeon and in irons. His confinement corresponded with the victory of American commodore Perry on Lake Erie. Soon after, the British decided to withdraw from Detroit. Kinzie, however, was not to be part of the retreating force. Instead, he was taken overland to Quebec, where he was loaded onto a ship headed for England. The British did not parole Kinzie like other Americans. He was without question perceived as a very dangerous, unprincipled man, too treacherous to let go.

But the British plans to imprison Kinzie in England went awry. When Kinzie arrived in Quebec, the ship he was put on was "chased by an American frigate" and returned to Canada. Then the ship set sail a second time, only to be forced back when it "sprung a leak." After this Kinzie was returned to Quebec, where, after some months of confinement, he was released with other prisoners "to return to their friends and families, although the war had not yet ended." A man too dangerous to parole had found his way to freedom.[14]

While Kinzie was away, the British retreated across the Detroit River into Canada. Tecumseh and hundreds more warriors accompanied the British eastward. Governor Harrison and his troops followed and confronted them on October 5, 1813, at the Thames River. With Tecumseh was a key group of his supporters, including Blackbird, Shabbona, and Billy Caldwell. Caldwell served as their liaison with the British Indian Department. Tecumseh was killed early in the battle, which went badly for the British and their Indian allies. Harrison's victory at the Battle of the Thames solidified American control over much of what became Ontario, but Indian resistance to the Americans did not end.[15]

1813–14: PEORIA

While General Harrison focused his attention at Detroit, he left the rest of the Northwest on its own, in part because the federal government called for severe restrictions on military spending in the West. These economies limited Harrison's ability to call out more militias, draw supplies, or go on the offensive.[16] This was particularly worrisome for Illinois, which faced retaliation for the fall 1812 attacks in and around Peoria. Potawatomi and Kickapoo warriors undertook a series of raids in the early spring of 1813 on American settlements in southern Illinois. Warriors from Mad Sturgeon's village killed two men along the Saline River in southern Illinois, and Gomo led a war party that killed another pair on the Little Wabash River. Kickapoo warriors attacked travelers and took horses across southern Illinois. Raiding continued into the summer of 1813, fueled by a "thirst for revenge" among the many warriors whose villages had been burned out the previous fall.[17]

There were few American allies across northern Illinois. Thomas Forsyth was working at St. Louis as a U.S. Indian subagent under William Clark. Desperate for information from Indian Country, Illinois governor Ninian Edwards had the temerity to write Thomas Forsyth for help. Edwards understood that Forsyth was probably still "offended at circumstances which I regret as much as he does [the destruction of his Peoria house in November 1812 by an Illinois militia]." Still he asked Forsyth to travel into northern Illinois to gather information. Forsyth was not immediately willing to make the dangerous trip.[18]

Ultimately, Forsyth made two trips up the Illinois River on behalf of the United States in late spring 1813. Antoine LeClair traveled with him as his interpreter. They stopped at Peoria, where they viewed their burned-out homes. Ironically, they found the only two houses not destroyed by the American militia were those of British-allied traders, Louis Buisson and François Des Pins. Still, Forsyth felt that the former residents of Peoria should be "encouraged to return back and build up their village." Forsyth thought this would aid the Americans immensely by providing trading opportunities for area Indians that were not controlled by the British.[19]

In May 1813 Forsyth made a second trip up the Illinois River. There he met one of the Fort Dearborn captives, who reported that his village had received a letter and a "belt of Wampum" from Robert Dickson. Dickson asked for as many warriors as possible to "repair to Detroit as quickly as possible." Dickson reminded the Indians that the British offered to help "drive the Americans out of the Island (America)."[20]

Forsyth and LeClair met with Gomo and other Potawatomis near Peoria. Gomo welcomed them, saying that their villages were "open to all their friends at all times." From Gomo, Forsyth learned that Tecumseh had returned to Detroit with many warriors.[21] Forsyth also met with Main Poc, who was making plans to return to Detroit to help defeat "General Harrison's army" and "drive the Americans over the Ohio." Main Poc promised to return to finish the fighting in the West as soon as the British and their Indian allies had defeated Harrison's army.[22]

Forsyth's importance to the Americans can be gauged by the intense interest that Robert Dickson took in him. Although Forsyth had worked for U.S. officials in Illinois and Missouri even before the beginning of the war, his allegiance to the United States was not well known. Even if Dickson believed that Forsyth had allied with the Americans, he hoped to convince him to change sides. He sent "express after express to him, and had offered . . . large sums of money" to Forsyth to join the British. Instead Forsyth sent word that "your British father had not money enough to induce him" to join Dickson and his warriors. Unlike his half-brother, John Kinzie, Forsyth showed no tendency to equivocate.[23]

Unable to convince Forsyth to join the British, Dickson then offered Potawatomi warriors a substantial reward to capture him. Dickson particularly sought the help of Gomo, who was unwilling to turn on his longtime friend. Instead, Gomo and other Potawatomi warriors tipped off Forsyth so he could avoid capture, and they continued to supply Forsyth with regular intelligence.[24]

Armed with information from Thomas Forsyth and Antoine LeClair, American officials in Illinois and Missouri decided to establish a U.S. fort at Peoria.[25] In September 1813, in preparation for construction of the fort, American forces burned three Indian villages near Peoria, including that of Gomo (this despite the welcome he offered to Thomas Forsyth in his spring trips).[26] Completed by November 1813, the fort signaled the intention of the United States to fight for control of the Illinois River Valley from a position of military strength.[27]

With the death of Tecumseh at the Battle of the Thames and the return of U.S. control at Detroit, some Potawatomis decided to make peace with the Americans. In December 1813 a group including Black Partridge approached Fort Clark waving a white flag. They shared a pipe and talked with the commander at Peoria. They "proposed that they should send a delegation of their chiefs and warriors to St. Louis," including Gomo and Black Partridge, to pledge their allegiance to the United States. Their loyalty was maintained by the liberal distribution of food from Fort Clark during the remainder of the war. By March 1814 Forsyth wrote that Gomo, Black Partridge, and others "are very friendly to the garrison at Fort Clark." Still, U.S. officials worried that Dickson or Main Poc would lead a unified attack down the Illinois River toward St. Louis.[28]

ST. JOSEPH

While Detroit and Peoria were more and more firmly in American hands by the end of 1813, the trading outposts and villages around St. Joseph remained contested space. Potawatomi warriors shifted their allegiances in response to the course of the war and changing support from local traders. Early in the war, Robert Dickson had provided a steady supply of goods to area villages and traders like Joseph Bailly, Jean Baptiste Beaubien, and Alexander Robinson. This continued into 1813.[29]

In January 1814 Robert Forsyth, brother of Thomas Forsyth and John Kinzie, led a party of American-allied Indian traders and interpreters to capture Joseph Bailly and three other traders at St. Joseph.[30] Accompanying Robert Forsyth was Jean Baptiste Chandonnai (Kinzie's clerk) and Isaac Burnett (son of William Burnett, longtime American-allied trader at St. Joseph). Chandonnai held Bailly at gunpoint, while Burnett informed him that he was a U.S. prisoner.[31] By arresting traders like Bailly, the Americans sought to cut Indian supply lines from the British, making it more difficult for them to continue waging war.

Sometime after Bailly's arrest, John Kinzie returned to the area. Now unambiguously allied with the United States, Kinzie began working directly for the governor of Michigan.[32] He reconnected with his family and close associates. Kinzie and Chandonnai traveled to St. Joseph to persuade Potawatomi leaders to attend an American conference at Greenville. Topinbee, Five Medals, and Metea agreed to make the trip to Ohio, while Main Poc, Mad Sturgeon, and Chebanse remained loyal to the British.[33]

Kinzie and Chandonnai encountered more than words of resistance at St. Joseph. Chandonnai's uncle Charles Chandonnai was present at St. Joseph when they arrived in July 1814. The older Chandonnai had raised Jean as his own son in the fur trade at Mackinac and had worked closely with Robert Dickson. During the war Charles Chandonnai was one of Dickson's most loyal agents, working hard to maintain Potawatomi loyalties to the British. When uncle and nephew met at St. Joseph, their opposing allegiances led to a gunfight. Jean Chandonnai used the pistols he had pointed earlier that year at Joseph Bailly and killed his uncle.[34]

When U.S. forces launched an unsuccessful attempt to retake Mackinac in August 1814, Potawatomi warriors and local traders from St. Joseph split in their allegiance. Mad Sturgeon and Chebanse traveled to Mackinac to help the British repel the American attack.[35]

The unsuccessful attack on Mackinac did not end the deep divisions around St. Joseph between pro-American and pro-British Potawatomis. The U.S. secretary of war ordered the destruction of Potawatomi villages along the St. Joseph and Kankakee Rivers, but this did not happen. Potawatomi warriors at Topinbee's village wanted peace but feared they "would be forced to fight alongside the Americans once again."[36]

By the fall of 1814, Kinzie and his brothers Robert and Thomas were playing similar roles—as information gatherers and scouts for the United States. They used their knowledge and connections from years in the fur trade to further the American war effort. Arriving at St. Joseph in the midst of an anti-American council in September 1814, Kinzie presented himself as a "trader of an old standing among the Potawatomi," as well as a U.S. representative. Kinzie told the anti-American Potawatomis that he expected peace between the British and Americans at any time and that he hoped to return to trade. Kinzie and Jean Chandonnai served Americans so well that the British had offered $500 for their scalps. Kinzie was only able to escape injury because of his high regard among area Potawatomis.[37]

PART FIVE

After the War of 1812

15 The End of Indian Country in the Neighborhood of Chicago, 1816–1829

When word of the end of the war between Great Britain and the United States reached Main Poc in March 1815, he refused to believe it. He traveled from his village on a tributary of the Kankakee River north to Mackinac, hoping to find that the rumors of peace were not true. He was bitterly disappointed when British officials there confirmed the end of hostilities. Main Poc did not return home. Instead, he set up a solitary camp along Lake Michigan. For him, the end of the war came only with his death in the spring of 1816.[1]

Peace did not come all at once for the Potawatomis, though most other warriors were less resolute than Main Poc in their resistance to the end of the war. Some made their peace with the Americans in a negotiated settlement with General Harrison after Tecumseh's death. By the end of 1813, a number of Potawatomi leaders from the Illinois River—including Gomo, Senachewine, and Black Partridge—journeyed to St. Louis to profess their allegiance the United States. Slowly but surely, most of the Potawatomis and their allies ended their warring with the Americans.[2]

This was the state of affairs when the United States and Great Britain entered into formal peace negotiations in December 1814. The two countries ratified the Treaty of Ghent in February 1815. The Americans returned Fort Malden to the British, who returned Mackinac to the United States. The boundaries lines between Canada and the United States remained the same as those negotiated in the Jay Treaty of 1794. As well, the British agreed to terminate their support of Indian allies in the Northwest. At a leave-taking in 1816, a thousand warriors traveled to the British outpost east of Mackinac to mark the end of British involvement. Despite these ceremonies, the British would remain a force in the western Great Lakes for several more decades.[3]

As the Potawatomi leaders journeyed back to their villages from outside Detroit and St. Louis, they expected to pick up their lives as before the war. Many of the villages had sustained heavy losses. American forces had killed many warriors, while hunger had decimated the very old and the very young. Messengers with wampum belts and pleas for aid had interrupted regular seasonal rhythms. Now spring fishing and maple sugaring, summer planting and festivals, fall harvests and winter hunts would again mark the seasons of the years. Most hoped that they could take up their village life in an Indian region. However, the end of the war brought fundamental changes to their world.

Once peace had been established, U.S. secretary of state James Monroe invited tribal delegations to negotiations along the Missouri River west of St. Louis at Portage des Sioux and at Springwells near Detroit. The Portage des Sioux treaty was the first with the Illinois River Potawatomis since 1795 that did not include Gomo. He died just as word of the Treaty of Ghent was making its way into the Illinois Country. His brother Senachewine replaced him as village chief and accompanied Black Partridge to the negotiations. Main Poc would not travel to Springwells, but other warriors who had opposed the United States—including Chebanse, Topinbee, Five Medals, Metea, and Mad Sturgeon—attended.[4]

At these councils, the United States set out its terms for long-term peace. The United States appeared magnanimous in their victory, agreeing to forgive all attacks and injuries. While the United States made it clear that it would not demand new cessions of land as punishment for Potawatomi hostilities during the war, all parties reaffirmed existing treaties. That meant the Potawatomis were forced to acknowledge the validity of treaties like those with the Sauks and Fox in 1804 that ceded more than half of Illinois to the United States.[5]

In late 1815 the U.S. government informed the Potawatomis along the Illinois River that government surveyors would be coming through the area to survey the Sauk and Fox cession. Not surprisingly, many Potawatomis who had long lived with war responded aggressively to the arrival of U.S. surveyors in the spring of 1816. However, the United States addressed this belligerent response with negotiations, gifts, and annuities. Over time this approach curtailed the power of warriors, as the influence of civilian leaders and métis traders increased.

THE UNITED STATES AFTER 1815

The changes in the trajectory of treaty negotiations with the Potawatomis stemmed from factors besides the victory in the War of 1812. Most critically, after the war the United States rejected an expansion of the military to cover its expanding borders and territory. In 1815 Congress reduced the number of officers and men in the regular military from 62,000 to 10,000. The U.S. Army was so small that it could not even hire all of its graduates from West Point. Despite these cuts, several forts were constructed in the West, including Fort Dearborn, Fort Armstrong (Rock Island), Fort Crawford (Prairie du Chien), and Fort Howard (Green Bay). However, the garrisons at each remained quite small.[6]

While reducing the size of the military, Congress encouraged westward expansion of the population and national economy. Internal improvements were a critical part of federal plans for westward expansion. By the early 1820s, steamboats were a growing presence on the Mississippi River and the Great Lakes, and in 1825 the Erie Canal opened a 364-mile waterway that linked New York City with the Great Lakes.[7] The time it took to travel from New York City to Chicago dropped from six weeks to two, drawing the region into closer reach of eastern businesses and population.

James Monroe, who was secretary of state during the war and president from 1817 to 1825, certainly saw an important link between the economic development of the United States and Indian relations. Over time President Monroe came to see that eastern tribes, including the Potawatomis, "were to be strongly encouraged to sell out." Settlers and speculators could then purchase their lands, and any surplus generated from sales could be used to fund roads, canals, and harbor improvements.[8] Chicago would come to fit into the United States in a very different way, no longer part of Indian Country but within the American Northwest Territory and then after 1818 in the northeast part of the new state of Illinois.

This vision stood in stark contrast to that held by John Kinzie and many of his Potawatomi neighbors. At the end of the war, Kinzie hoped that the Potawatomis and other western tribes would continue to exert sovereignty over the western Great Lakes. Kinzie wanted the U.S. government to prevent its citizens from settling in Indian Country.[9] Most of all, Kinzie wanted a territory where "the citizens of the United States were kept at such a distance from those tribes" and where the United States banished British traders.[10] In essence, Kinzie sought a permanent Indian Country.

By 1817 John Kinzie's hope of keeping American settlers out of the region seemed increasingly unrealistic. President Monroe insisted that the permanent Indian Country that Kinzie envisioned in and around Chicago be moved west of the Mississippi River. Kinzie's brother and trading partner, Thomas Forsyth, chose to follow this path. After the war, he did not return to Peoria but instead remained in St. Louis with his family. He continued to work as a subagent for Indian Affairs and eventually was promoted to U.S. agent to the Sauks and Fox. He worked closely with William Clark, Missouri territorial governor and then superintendent of Indian Affairs at St. Louis, the architect of many of the treaties negotiated from St. Louis. Forsyth became a trusted part of this treaty process.[11]

Treaty after treaty increasingly made an ongoing Indian Country around Chicago a fleeting dream. William Clark worked with Lewis Cass, governor of the Michigan Territory from 1813 to 1831, on the negotiations. While Thomas Forsyth worked with Clark, John Kinzie, as interpreter and subagent at Chicago, worked with Cass.[12]

Kinzie, who hoped for a permanent Indian Country, instead became a critical force in moving the treaty process forward, a process that would ultimately divest the Potawatomis of their claims to territory in the region of Chicago. Like the Potawatomis, Kinzie became dependent on federal dollars. This dependence made both Kinzie and the Potawatomis who lived around him susceptible to federal land policies.[13]

TREATIES AT ST. LOUIS AND CHICAGO

Between 1816 and 1833, the Potawatomis ceded virtually all of the eighteen million acres of land they claimed east of the Mississippi. This was an almost bloodless conquest of monumental proportions. The Potawatomi lands cut a wide swath from Detroit to the Mississippi, moving hundreds of miles on either side of what would become the southern boundaries of Michigan and Wisconsin. This territory was taken through a series of land treaty negotiations instead of on a battlefield.

The process began almost immediately after the War of 1812. In 1816 Illinois governor Ninian Edwards and Missouri governor William Clark began negotiations with Potawatomis already assembled at St. Louis to negotiate

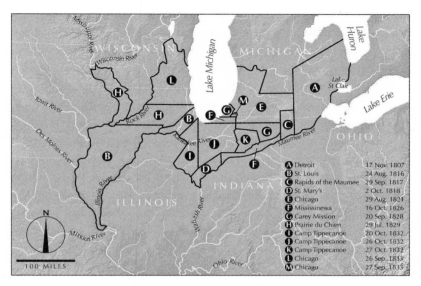

Map 11. Native Land Cessions in Illinois, 1816–33. (Dennis McClendon, Chicago Cartographics)

for the safe passage of U.S. surveyors along the Illinois River. Thomas Forsyth served as a liaison and interpreter. As well, the U.S. officials negotiated for a twenty-mile-wide cession, running from Chicago southwest to the Illinois River. The federal government intended this land for a canal that would link the Great Lakes to the Mississippi, part of the grand plan for internal improvements across the United States.

For the first time, the reservation at the mouth of the Chicago River was a contiguous part of lands claimed by the United States. Chicago was no longer in the heart of Indian Country, but part of a U.S. transportation corridor. The Potawatomis, who had just sued for peace with the United States, were in no position to object. In return for this crucial cession along the Illinois River where so many of their villages stood, the Potawatomis received annuities that included $1,000 in trade goods for twelve years.[14]

After this first postwar land cession, treaties were negotiated regularly with the Potawatomis, including Maumee Rapids (1817), St. Mary's (1818), Chicago (1821), Mississinewa (1826), Carey Mission (1828), Prairie du Chien (1829), Tippecanoe (1832), and Chicago again (1833). In all, twenty-eight treaties were negotiated between 1816 and 1833.

Quickly, a standard process for treaties and their negotiation evolved.

American officials—pressured by settlers, politicians, or speculators—announced a preliminary proposal for a specific land cession. Potawatomi leaders would meet with U.S. officials like Thomas Forsyth, Lewis Cass, and William Clark, who helped village leaders build support for negotiations. Then the U.S. president appointed treaty commissioners and gave them specific instructions. A place and time were set for the treaty talks, and preparations were made to accommodate thousands of participants. Treaty negotiations took place over weeks, requiring substantial stores of food, liquor, and gifts.[15]

The treaties themselves also developed a regular structure with four parts. The first part consisted of a declaration of peace between parties. The second part specifically described the cession of land. The third section dealt with the monies and annuities to be paid in exchange for the ceded lands, while a final section included any special conditions.[16]

After negotiating for a wide corridor across northern Illinois that included Chicago, U.S. officials next targeted residual Potawatomi lands in Ohio and Indiana in 1817 and 1818. Buoyed by these successes, the American government moved to acquire all of the remaining Potawatomi lands in Michigan, primarily around the St. Joseph River and including the villages of Topinbee, Chebanse, Five Medals, and Metea.

John Kinzie had deep ties to these Potawatomis. When Kinzie envisioned a permanent Indian Country, it was among Topinbee, his family, and his kinsmen. He also had deep ties with the Burnett family, who were related to Topinbee through William Burnett's widow, Kakima. During the War of 1812, Topinbee and Kakima had provided special support to John Kinzie, his family, and his friends.

Realizing the great attachment that St. Joseph Potawatomis had toward their home, Governor Cass set the treaty negotiations across Lake Michigan at Chicago, where John Kinzie worked as U.S. interpreter at the second Fort Dearborn. The newly appointed Indian agent at Chicago, Alexander Wolcott, worked behind the scenes for a year in preparation for the negotiations. He supervised construction of an open "bower" that provided seating for the chiefs and headmen on the north bank of the Chicago River, adjacent to the Kinzie and Ouilmette houses. The site was "directly under the command of the guns of the fort" and "ensured both safety and order for the occasion."[17]

On August 17, 1821, more than three thousand Potawatomis came to

Chicago, almost three times the number that had assembled nine years before on the eve of the destruction of the first Fort Dearborn. John Kinzie was there greeting his old friends, while knowing that the United States wanted to reduce their lands to small reservations, to end the Indian Country that he, too, had come to know and love. While Kinzie did not record his feelings, they must have been bittersweet.

From the start, Governor Cass made his intentions clear. He opened the conference by observing that the Potawatomis claimed "an extensive country about the river St. Joseph" that they did "not cultivate nor appear to want." Cass encouraged the Potawatomis to cede this land to the United States. He suggested that it would "probably be many years before the country will be settled by the Americans." In the meantime, the Potawatomis could continue to live on the lands "at the same time that you are drawing annuities for them." Cass assured those assembled at Chicago that they would not have to leave their homes. However, his proposal also meant that the Potawatomis around St. Joseph would no longer have a large-enough territory for traditional hunting and fishing.[18]

Governor Cass and the other U.S. commissioners were surprised to find that the Potawatomis were resistant to the proposed cessions. Metea, one of the warriors who had successfully destroyed the U.S. outpost at Chicago just nine years before, voiced strong opposition to the loss of his homeland without a fight. Metea spoke eloquently about the plight of the Potawatomis and his astonishment that the United States needed his land. He noted that their country had once been very large, "but it has dwindled away to a small spot; and you wish to purchase that!"

Metea tried to explain that his home had been "given to us by the Great Spirit, who gave it to us to hunt upon, and to make our corn-fields upon, to live upon, and to make down our beds upon, when we die." Metea referred to recent cessions where "we said we had a little and agreed to sell you a piece of it; but we told you we could spare no more. Now you ask us again. You are never satisfied!"[19]

Topinbee, a longtime friend of John Kinzie, also rose to speak against the cession very near to the site where he had protected Kinzie's family from Indians bent on destruction. Now Topinbee saw that his home was threatened, but Kinzie did not step forward to protect it. Topinbee plainly stated his position: "We are averse to selling any more of our lands." Cass responded to this recalcitrance by pointing out that the Potawatomis "are

Figure 26. Metea was a Potawatomi warrior who initially spoke against ceding land to the United States at the 1821 Treaty of Chicago but finally signed the accord. (Joseph Kirkland, *The Chicago Massacre of 1812* [1893])

thinly scattered over a very great extent of country—[a] great part of which they cannot occupy, and do not want." He reminded the assembled Potawatomis that they would receive increased annuities and extra funds for their cooperation.[20]

By then a tired old man who drank too much, Topinbee did not have the energy to continue his fight, especially because Cass refused to distribute any whiskey until the Potawatomis relented. Twelve days into the negotiations, the Potawatomis capitulated. In the end, Metea, Topinbee, Chebanse, and many others signed the treaty.

Under the articles of the 1821 Treaty of Chicago, the Potawatomis ceded much of what is today southwest Michigan. In an inverse of the 1795 Greenville Treaty, where the United States gained "islands" within Indian Country, the St. Joseph Potawatomis negotiated five tracts of thirty-six square miles within U.S. territory for their own villages. The Potawatomis had no intention or desire to move away, and probably hoped that it would be many years before the U.S. government surveyed and sold the lands that they had ceded around their reservations. In return for this cession, the United States gave an additional annuity of $5,000 in specie for twenty years and funding for a blacksmith, a teacher, and a Baptist missionary from Kentucky who received money to build a mission school (later the Carey Mission).[21]

In addition to these reservations, the treaty also granted tracts of land (one-half of a section to three sections) to specific individuals, "all Indians by descent," in and around St. Joseph. These men and women were métis, all the children of Potawatomi mothers and Euro-American traders.

The children of Kakima and William Burnett each received grants. Burnett had been a crucial trading partner of Jean Baptiste Point de Sable and John Kinzie, as well as a staunch American supporter. Burnett's son John had married Nokenoqua, the widow of Jean Baptiste Lalime, who had been killed by John Kinzie. Their son, Jean (John) Baptiste Lalime, also received a land grant in Michigan. Jean Baptiste Chandonnai, the son of another Potawatomi woman at St. Joseph (Chippewauqua) and close associate of John Kinzie, also received a grant at St. Joseph. As a group, they were people to whom Kinzie was greatly indebted.[22]

THE ASCENDANCE OF MÉTIS CULTURE AND LEADERSHIP

After the 1816 and 1821 treaties, life in Potawatomi villages began to change. Annuity payments from the federal government meant that individuals could afford to purchase many more goods. The Potawatomis purchased hats, buttons, and ribbons, as well as more tobacco, salt, and powder. This shift was evident in dress, as Potawatomi men and women discarded deerskin clothing for "garments of brightly colored calico or flannel."[23]

In many ways, their models were the métis households of the trading outposts in Indian Country. For years these households had mixed traditional Potawatomi culture with French and Anglo customs. In Chicago Catherine Point de Sable, Archange Ouilmette, and Sheshi Buisson all married Euro-American traders and created métis families. Their clothing, language, food, farming, and child rearing reflected not one culture, but several interwoven into something new. Increasingly, Potawatomi families adopted this métis culture, sending their children to mission schools and dressing them in clothing purchased from Euro-American traders.

Leadership also changed in the face of the growing influence of métis culture. The long war had thinned the ranks of warriors, and the postwar peace left fewer opportunities for fighting. The older generation of leaders, many of whom had served their villages since the 1795 Greenville Treaty, was fading out. Topinbee died in the summer of 1826, while Metea died the following year. There remained "few chiefs of tribal stature."[24]

The Potawatomis increasingly supported métis men as tribal leaders. The children of traders, agents, and government officials, these métis had often grown up not in Potawatomi villages, but in trading outposts or Euro-American towns like Detroit or St. Louis. Their families, neighborhoods, and livelihoods were related to, but not of, the Potawatomi villages of the region. Over time many who had been part of a distinctive métis culture came to identify themselves as Potawatomis. Because of substantial federal payments to Potawatomis during these years, there was a "sharp rise in the marginal value of being identified as Indian, at least in the short-term."[25]

Four métis men were particularly important to the Potawatomis living in the neighborhood of Chicago: Billy Caldwell, Shabbona, Alexander Robinson, and Joseph LaFramboise. None of them fought for the United States during the War of 1812. Shabbona was a supporter of Tecumseh, who fought alongside the British at Detroit. Joseph LaFramboise fled Chicago with his father and brothers to avoid enrollment in the Chicago militia. Billy Caldwell, the son of a British officer, was a captain in the British Indian Department and fought alongside Tecumseh. Alexander Robinson worked for Joseph Bailly, a noted British partisan, although he did transport Captain Heald and his wife to Mackinac after the destruction of Fort Dearborn. At the same time, all had good relations with John Kinzie both before and during the war.

Of the four, only Shabbona was a traditional village leader. He was an Odawa who had married into a Potawatomi village and was drawn to the nativism of men like Tenskwatawa. After the War of 1812, he returned to his village near Ottawa, Illinois, and professed a friendship for the United States. Over time the Americans and the Potawatomis relied on him to negotiate their differences.[26]

Joseph LaFramboise was descended from an illustrious French trad-

Figure 27. Alexander Robinson worked for a British trader during the War of 1812 but rose to a leadership position among Potawatomis in the Chicago area after the war. (Joseph Kirkland, *The Chicago Massacre of 1812* [1893])

ing family in the Great Lakes. After spending the war years at Milwaukee, his family returned to Chicago and purchased the Leigh farm. Joseph La-Framboise married a Potawatomi woman and traded for the American Fur Company at Chicago. By the late 1820s, Joseph LaFramboise was identified as a Potawatomi leader, despite his residence at Chicago and involvement in the fur trade.[27]

Alexander Robinson settled at Chicago after the destruction of the first Fort Dearborn. He farmed with Antoine Ouilmette, selling produce to the U.S. Army after their return to Chicago, and then worked in the fur trade. He married Catherine Chevalier, sister of Archange Ouilmette and Sheshi Buisson. She had been raised at a Potawatomi village at Lake Calumet. Robinson, known as Che-Che-Pin-Qua, was identified as a Potawatomi chief and served in that capacity in treaty negotiations.[28]

Billy Caldwell acquired the designation as Potawatomi chief, despite the fact that he was the son of a Mohawk woman and a British soldier.

Sometime around 1820, Caldwell came to Chicago, no doubt with the encouragement of his good friend John Kinzie. Caldwell married the métis daughter of Kinzie's brother Robert Forsyth and slowly became a representative for area Potawatomis. The Americans sponsored him as an "officially recognized chief of the Prairie band of the Potawatomi."[29] Like Shabbona, Robinson, and LaFramboise, Caldwell became an important figure in treaty negotiations between the Potawatomis and the U.S. government.

THE 1829 TREATY OF PRAIRIE DU CHIEN

The calm that followed the 1821 Chicago Treaty was broken in 1827. During the annual annuity distribution at Chicago, word came that Red Bird, a Ho-Chunk warrior, had killed several white settlers along the Mississippi River near Prairie du Chien. After Red Bird's attack, residents in and around Chicago raised a militia unit. To assuage local fears, Billy Caldwell, Shabbona, and Alexander Robinson traveled to Big Foot's village at Lake Geneva in Wisconsin. Big Foot's village was multi-tribal, with Ho-Chunk as well as Potawatomi families. There they received assurances that the Potawatomis were not part of an orchestrated uprising.[30] Nevertheless, Red Bird's attack led Congress to send a garrison to reopen Fort Dearborn, which had been shuttered in 1823. As well, Governor Cass came to Chicago in August 1828, laying the groundwork for a conference with Potawatomis and Ho-Chunks.[31]

By 1829 the state of Illinois was set to survey the twenty-mile-wide corridor between Lake Michigan and the Illinois River relinquished by the Potawatomis in 1816 to finance the construction of the Illinois and Michigan Canal. Steamboats traveled up and down the Mississippi, and the recent opening of the Erie Canal had greatly reduced travel times from the East Coast to northern Illinois. It is little wonder that the Ho-Chunks and the Potawatomis were unsettled. Major changes were under way across the region.

Within Indian Country, the real shift from traditional warrior leadership to métis mediators became evident at Prairie du Chien in 1829. Black Partridge's brother Senachewine and other older leaders refused to attend the 1829 conference altogether, so the Potawatomi contingent was led by Billy Caldwell and Alexander Robinson. Thomas Forsyth and his nephew John Harris Kinzie were official U.S. representatives. At this 1829 council, the

Potawatomis relinquished two large tracts of land in northern Illinois and southwestern Wisconsin. The Potawatomis received $20,000 in immediate gifts, with $16,000 as an annual annuity payment. The U.S. government also agreed to pay more than $10,000 in debts that the Potawatomis had accrued with local traders.

The Treaty of Prairie du Chien reflected a growing pressure from American settlers for more land in the region. The tract along the Mississippi River extended cessions northward into Wisconsin. The second tract of land followed the Rock River as its western boundary and ran east to a point twelve miles north of Chicago along Lake Michigan that marked the northeast land claimed by Antoine Ouilmette and just above the Indian boundary line set in the 1816 treaty.[32]

Alongside the two large cessions made by the Potawatomis and their allies at Prairie du Chien, the treaty also included fourteen tracts of land assigned to individuals along Lake Michigan, the Chicago River, the Des Plaines River, or the Fox River, above or below the 1816 Indian boundary lines. Most were one-mile-square grants (640 acres).[33]

Archange Ouilmette received a land grant along Lake Michigan. Billy Caldwell accepted land north of the Indian boundary line at the Chicago River, while Victoire Porthier and Jane Mirandeau (the sisters who had witnessed Jean Lalime's murder in June 1812) each had grants near Caldwell's on the Chicago River. Above the Indian boundary line along the Des Plaines River, Claude LaFramboise (a brother of Joseph LaFramboise) and Alexander Robinson had land grants.

The Treaty of Prairie du Chien also included provisions to pay debts owed by the Potawatomis, Odawas, and Ojibwas. The American Fur Company received $3,000 from the total $11,601 paid out in this manner for trading debts since 1815. The treaty also dealt with older debts. Joseph LaFramboise's father received $2,000 for merchandise taken by the Ojibwas and Odawas in 1799. Interestingly, the treaty also made restitution to John Kinzie and Antoine Ouilmette for "depredations" committed against them "at the time of the massacre at Chicago." John Kinzie's children received $2,000, while his stepdaughter Margaret Helm received $800, as did Antoine Ouilmette.[34]

A similar treaty, signed three years later at Tippecanoe, involved lands to the south of the 1816 Indian boundary land that included much of northwestern Indiana. The treaty was negotiated with the Potawatomis and other Indians with villages along the Wabash and Kankakee Rivers. Again, specific individuals received tracts of land, including the daughters of Monee, the French-Ottawa wife of Joseph Bailly, as well as members of the LaFramboise, Bourbonnais, and Beaubien families.[35] By 1832 the Potawatomis claimed lands only in the very northeast section of Illinois and southwestern Wisconsin. Within a few years, this land would also be ceded away, and the Indian Country controlled by the Potawatomis would pass into history.

16 Kinzie's Retreat to Chicago, 1816–1828

John and Eleanor Kinzie returned to Chicago in the autumn of 1816. They had been gone for more than four years, and their children—John Harris (13), Ellen Marion (12), Maria Indiana (9), and Robert Allen (6)—had gotten used to living in Detroit, a town with hundreds of inhabitants. They had many relatives in and around Detroit, and the older children attended school.[1] Of course, these were not idyllic years in Detroit. The Kinzie family arrived during the British occupation of Detroit, and even after the Americans regained Detroit in 1813, it was never too far from the war itself. John Kinzie was arrested and imprisoned for treason, and his family had to endure many privations.

In 1816 John Kinzie was fifty-three years old and his wife, Eleanor, was forty-seven. They had been married for eighteen years. Both had lived the whole of their lives with war. In August 1812 they had gathered up their young family and fled first to St. Joseph and then Detroit. When the war ended, the decision to return to Chicago was not an easy one. There were no schools or extended family. They returned to an empty shell of a house that had once been home. Very few of their household items remained—the quilts and blankets, the chairs and crockery—all destroyed or taken as the spoils of war. The Kinzie family would have to start over again to build a life at Chicago.[2]

They did not have much choice. John Kinzie and Thomas Forsyth together carried debts of between $12,000 and $15,000. The pair had bought goods on credit at Detroit in late 1811 from the British traders Hugh and Richard Pattinson, despite the prohibitions on international trade. Kinzie & Forsyth lost their fur packs in the first western action of the war at Mackinac in June 1812. Two months later the partners lost a great deal more property when Fort Dearborn was destroyed. Finally, in October and November

1812, all of the firm's property at Peoria was destroyed "first by the Indians and secondly by a party of militia commanded by Capt. Craig."[3]

After the war the Pattinson brothers sought the money that Kinzie & Forsyth owed them (as their creditors pushed hard on them for their own debts). Kinzie & Forsyth had to post a special bail in order to avoid imprisonment for their debts. John and Eleanor Kinzie sold all their property, including a lot they received for losses in an 1805 fire in Detroit. They also sold a farm at Grosse Point that Eleanor Kinzie may have brought to their marriage (either from the estate of her first husband or from her father). There is also a good possibility that the couple sold any enslaved people still in their possession.[4]

In addition, Kinzie sold the house in Detroit where his family lived during the war. It had belonged to his stepfather, and Kinzie likely shared ownership with his brothers, but the proceeds went directly to Kinzie & Forsyth's creditors. This created considerable enmity between Kinzie and his other Forsyth relatives, especially the heirs of Robert Forsyth.

After more than a year of trying to get repaid, the Pattinson brothers ended their legal actions against Kinzie & Forsyth.[5] John and Eleanor Kinzie had sold almost everything of value to them in order to keep John out of prison. They may have even sold their house or other building at Chicago. This crushing debt, and the lengths that John and Eleanor Kinzie went to get out from under it, certainly affected their return to Chicago. Their children were not yet old enough to contribute to the household income. They had used all of the property that Eleanor had brought into their marriage to pay off the debt. Kinzie's only income in 1816 was that of interpreter for Michigan governor Lewis Cass. The several hundred dollars a year he earned at that job was not enough to support a family in Detroit. Chicago, in contrast, was a place where they might eke out a subsistence living with farming and some trading. It was a retreat to Chicago, not a choice.

While John and Eleanor Kinzie worked to meet their debts in Detroit, Thomas Forsyth worked indefatigably to recoup some of what Kinzie & Forsyth had lost during the war from the federal government. He sought compensation for the losses of Kinzie & Forsyth from August 1812 at Chicago, as well as from Captain Craig's raid at Peoria in November 1812. Thomas Forsyth thought "it but just that we should try and recover as much of the losses as possible." Forsyth first submitted petitions for damages at Chicago in December 1812. He wrote that he and his brother had destroyed all their gunpowder and whiskey "in order to prevent it from falling into the hands of the enemy." As well, Kinzie & Forsyth provided "a number of horses and mules" to Captain Heald and his contingent. Forsyth sought compensation for his loss of horses and mules, as well as the destroyed liquor and ammunition.[6]

The congressional committee ruled, "The horses and mules should be paid for by the government, inasmuch as they were in the service of the US and were captured by the enemy." However, the committee refused to compensate for the whiskey and gunpowder. They argued that Kinzie & Forsyth would have lost the liquor and ammunition, whether or not Heald had advised them to destroy these stores. Forsyth then began the painstaking task of documenting the number of horses and mules lost, in order to submit a new petition to Congress.[7]

This was a difficult task, as the eyewitnesses were scattered across the country. In particular, Captain Nathan Heald was unwilling to testify regarding the losses of Kinzie & Forsyth at Chicago. Perhaps he was afraid that he would perjure himself if his recollections did not line up with available documentation. His reluctance may also have reflected his fear that Congress would find him personally liable for the losses or that he would be held responsible in some other way. Heald had seen the court-martial that General William Hull endured over his surrender of Detroit in July 1812.

Finally, in December 1817 Heald provided Forsyth with a confirmation that he rented horses and mules from Kinzie & Forsyth and that their stores of whiskey and gunpowder were destroyed on his decision. Still, no congressional reimbursement to Kinzie & Forsyth was forthcoming.[8] Forsyth went to Washington, D.C., in early 1818, hoping to receive some compensation from Congress. Despite Heald's testimony, Congress again rejected their petition, and Forsyth let the matter drop.

Kinzie & Forsyth also sought reimbursement for losses of $1,184 at Peoria in November 1812 at the hands of the rogue militia unit under Captain Craig. The claim included compensation for livestock, trade goods, furniture, food, and the house and outbuildings destroyed in the raids. Other Peoria residents also submitted claims for damages, but again Congress ruled against any compensation for losses.[9]

Ultimately, the Kinzie and Forsyth families received compensation for losses at Chicago and Peoria through treaties at Prairie du Chien (1829) and

Chicago (1833). However, that did not solve their problems in the immediate aftermath of the war. Without capital, it was almost impossible for Kinzie & Forsyth to return to the fur trade at the end of the war. Instead, both men sought positions with the U.S. government as a way to gain a steady income for their families.

While Thomas Forsyth was in Washington, D.C., in early 1818, trying to get congressional reimbursement for losses at Chicago, he met with Secretary of War John C. Calhoun. Calhoun was sympathetic, and he appointed Forsyth as U.S. Indian agent for the Sauks and Fox, at a salary of over $1,000 a year. This appointment afforded Forsyth a comfortable living.[10]

The Sauks welcomed Forsyth, their "old friend, the trader of Peoria," as their agent.[11] He traveled north to the Sauk and Fox villages along the Mississippi during the summer months, while his family stayed in St. Louis. This was possible because Antoine LeClair served as Forsyth's interpreter. LeClair had worked closely with Forsyth at Peoria, and he moved close to the Sauks, providing Forsyth with regular information.[12]

John Kinzie also sought employment with the U.S. government. Kinzie had helped Michigan governor Cass in the closing months of the War of 1812, and he recommended Kinzie for the post of U.S. Indian agent at Chicago.[13] In his recommendation, Cass noted, "Mr. Kinzie is an old Indian trader, a man of good judgment and of great personal influence among the Indians." He further described that Kinzie had "more personal influence among the Potawatamies than any other man in the country."[14]

However, Cass's recommendation did not carry the day. Charles Jouett, who had been U.S. Indian agent at Chicago before the War of 1812, was reappointed to the post. Instead, Kinzie received an appointment as interpreter at Fort Dearborn with a salary of $250 per year. It is somewhat ironic that Kinzie took up the post that Jean Lalime (the man Kinzie had killed) had held at the first Fort Dearborn.

CHICAGO, 1816–1821

The Kinzie and Jouett families both returned to Chicago in 1816, shortly after two companies of soldiers had arrived to rebuild Fort Dearborn. The soldiers set up a temporary camp, and workers came from Detroit to build a new fort on the site of the old one. The fort was smaller than the original, with only one blockhouse and a single palisade. By the end of 1816, Major

Figure 28. The second Fort Dearborn was constructed in 1816 on the site of the original outpost. (A. T. Andreas, *History of Chicago* [1884])

Daniel Baker had arrived to command the troops at Fort Dearborn. Baker had participated in the western war, faced Tecumseh outside Detroit, and been a prisoner near there. He lived at Chicago with his wife and daughter until 1821.[15]

Charles Jouett found that his former home in Chicago, the U.S. Agency House, had been burned to the ground along with the first Fort Dearborn. He supervised construction of a new Agency House and successfully lobbied to have a portion of the Potawatomi annuities distributed at Chicago. However, Jouett and his family decided to return to Kentucky in 1817.

Kinzie again tried to secure the post of U.S. Indian agent at Chicago. Kinzie wrote to the new president, James Monroe, pleading for the post. Charles Jouett, who knew Monroe personally, wrote a recommendation that described Kinzie as "a man of strong mind, firm integrity, and invincible courage." While Jouett admitted that "no man earthly has a stronger claim on the favour of his country than Mr. Kinzie," he did not recommend Kinzie as his replacement. Instead, Jouett suggested that Kinzie would make an excellent subagent. In Washington, President Monroe followed Jouett's advice directly. Kinzie was appointed as subagent at Chicago in 1817 at $750 a year. Kinzie and his family would live on his subagent and interpreter salaries as well as some trading.[16]

After Charles Jouett left Chicago, Dr. Alexander Wolcott was appointed to replace him. Wolcott was a Yale graduate who trained as a medical doctor. He served with the U.S. Army at Vincennes as a surgeon's mate from 1812 to 1817 before his appointment as Indian agent at Chicago. Wolcott admitted that he was "but little acquainted with Indians and Indian Affairs," but accepted the much larger salary that came with his new appointment.[17]

As U.S. Indian agent at Chicago, Wolcott came to rely on the experiences and insights of the Kinzie family, much as Charles Jouett and Matthew Irwin had leaned on Jean Lalime before the War of 1812. The Kinzies, Dr. Wolcott, and the officers of the fort created a small social circle. Wolcott married Kinzie's daughter Ellen Marion in 1823, and John Harris Kinzie would marry Wolcott's niece Juliette Magill in 1830.[18] These marriages offered economic and political connections not unlike those made by French traders with Indian women in earlier days.[19]

The United States also reestablished a factory (trading post) at Chicago after the war. The U.S. factor was Jacob B. Varnum, who had served in the same post at Sandusky, Ohio, before the war. He was the son of a U.S. senator from Massachusetts and his older brother, Joseph, had been the U.S. factor briefly at Chicago before the War of 1812. Waiting at Mackinac to accompany the army units assigned to reestablish Fort Dearborn, Varnum met and married a young woman who came to Chicago as his bride. She died in childbirth the following year, and Varnum quickly got remarried to the daughter of a Detroit innkeeper.

Varnum remembered that when he arrived at Chicago in 1816, it "presented a desolate appearance." He quickly developed a good working relationship with John Kinzie, who acted as his interpreter. Varnum loved to hunt and enjoyed the winters in Chicago when he often returned home "with a good supply of game." He caught many ducks and pigeons "in a net of [his] own devices."[20] Varnum had considerable time to devote to hunting, as there was little activity at his factory, despite his $1,000 annual salary.[21]

Throughout these years, Kinzie still felt the aftereffects of his heavy war debts. He cobbled together a living from several appointed posts as well as from trading and farming. Some sources suggest that he successfully raised and sold corn and was able to purchase thousands of dollars in trade goods from the American Fur Company.[22] This is backed up by the tax assessment done in Chicago in 1825 that found Kinzie to be one of the wealthiest men at Chicago, with $500 of assessed property.[23] Still, when Kinzie lost his interpreter post in August 1821, he complained, "I have been reduced in wages. . . . It does work me hard to . . . maintain my family in a decent manner."[24]

While John and Eleanor moved back to their house in 1816, there is some evidence that Kinzie did not own the structure. They might have sold it to Detroit creditors in order to pay off their debts. In 1821 Kinzie and his family had "to change houses" while awaiting the arrival of "tenants" for the house. Perhaps until then, the actual owners of the Kinzie house had no tenant and allowed the Kinzie family to stay at the house.[25]

The Kinzie house, like several others—including the Chandonnai, Ouilmette, Pettell, and Le Mai houses—remained standing on the north bank of the Chicago River after the War of 1812. During the war Louis Buisson and François Des Pins lived at Chicago and worked closely with Robert Dickson, the British Indian agent. After the war they returned to Peoria with their families, where they continued in the fur trade. Des Pins had married Martha Leigh, ransomed from Black Partridge, while Louis Buisson was married to Sheshi Chevalier, sister of Archange Ouilmette. Martha Leigh's daughter later married Sheshi's son.[26]

The Ouilmette family was back to Chicago before the war was over. Their house had been ransacked, and they lost pigs, horses, and cattle.[27] For a time the Ouilmette family retreated to their fishing and maple sugar camp at Gross Point. In 1816 there were five children, including an infant daughter, in the family. Three more Ouilmette children were born before 1820. The Ouilmettes were well liked by their neighbors. Antoine Ouilmette was remembered from those years as "a kind, whole souled, generous man of remarkable energy and perseverance, who made friends with everybody, both Indians and whites, and he in turn was universally liked and respected."[28]

Jean Baptiste Chandonnai returned to Chicago after spending the war years working for John Kinzie in Michigan. Several métis families who had spent time in Chicago before 1812 also returned, including the LaFramboise, Mirandeau, Porthier, and Beaubien families, all from Milwaukee. Many took advantage of opportunities for work with U.S. officials at Chicago.

In some ways, Chicago in the years after 1816 very much resembled Chicago before 1812. The fort anchored the settlement, with the Kinzie and Ouilmette households across the river. As well as the U.S. Army, a factor, agent, subagent, and interpreter represented the United States. Other families took advantage of work opportunities presented by the American presence and lived along the main stem of the Chicago River.

Beyond the settlement at Chicago, Potawatomi villages continued to dot the landscape along the rivers to the east (St. Joseph), south (Wabash), and west (Fox, Kankakee, and Illinois). Waubansee—the younger brother of Black Partridge who while a British ally had protected the Kinzie family in August 1812—headed a village directly west from Chicago along the Fox River (near what today is Aurora). The women in his village continued to raise corn, beans, and squash, while the men hunted and fished.

About thirty miles farther west of Waubansee's village was that of Shabbona. From Shabbona's village there was easy access south to Peoria and northeast to Milwaukee. Senachewine, Gomo's brother, moved north about forty miles from Peoria along the Illinois River.[29]

To the north of Chicago, Mettawa and Aptakisic (Half-Day) had villages along the Des Plaines and Chicago Rivers, respectively. Mettawa was about fifty years old and headed a village with four or five wigwams and about ninety people. The village was "situated in a little grove of timber on the prairie." Like the women in Waubansee's village, those at Mettawa's raised "good corn."[30]

To the east at St. Joseph, Metea, Topinbee, and Leopold Pokagan continued to live in a dense cluster of Potawatomi villages. They had repaired the damage rendered by the War of 1812 and continued to farm and hunt as they had for several generations in this area. Village leaders could travel to Fort Wayne to meet with the U.S. Indian agent there or go west to Chicago.

THE FUR TRADE

Still, in important ways, the settlement after 1816 was dramatically different from the one at Chicago before August 1812. All around Chicago, the Potawatomis and their allies were ceding more and more of their territory to the United States. There was less and less land open to the fur trade. While Chicago was still ringed with Potawatomi villages, more and more American settlers were moving into the region, reducing hunting grounds more every year.

As well, the dynamic of the fur trade itself was changing, especially with the rise of John Jacob Astor and the American Fur Company. Astor was the same age as John Kinzie. Like Kinzie, he had entered the fur trade in the western Great Lakes during the long years of war. However, Astor worked on a much larger scale, initially through the Northwest and Southwest fur companies, and eventually through the American Fur Company. He created an integrated global enterprise on several continents from his headquarters in New York City.[31]

After the War of 1812, Congress excluded British traders from operating within the United States. Eventually, this prohibition was softened so that Canadian interpreters and engagés could be hired, so long as Americans headed the outfits.[32] Because only American citizens could run trading operations, the question of citizenship became a key concern to the American Fur Company. Until 1819 the U.S. government had simply accepted that anyone living in American territory who did not state allegiance to Britain was an American citizen. In 1819 the U.S. attorney general overturned this view of citizenship, looking for more stringent citizenship requirements that would weed out "British traders."[33]

Alongside the lively debate about national loyalty and the fur trade, Astor and his American Fur Company became embroiled in another argument over whether the fur trade should be under public or private control. Since the 1790s, the federal government had operated a system of factories or public trading houses. These factories were in direct competition with private traders. Some felt that the federal government should exert monopoly control over the fur trade, while others sought the complete abolition of the public trading houses. Astor put his considerable resources behind the latter and found a champion for their cause in Missouri senator Thomas Hart Benton. Benton successfully shepherded legislation through Congress that abolished the factory system in 1822.[34]

The American Fur Company changed the trading landscape at Chicago. Astor assigned Ramsey Crooks and Robert Stuart to direct operations for the western Great Lakes at Mackinac, and operations in the Chicago area came under their purview. They sought out established traders in the region, offering them goods and credit. For instance, Joseph Bailly was a longtime British trader at the south end of Lake Michigan who became a U.S. citizen and worked out an arrangement to sell his furs through the American Fur Company.[35] Repeatedly, Crooks and Stuart brought experienced traders into their organization, quickly expanding the reach of the American Fur Company in the region.

While the American Fur Company relied on former British traders, they also recruited young U.S. citizens to work with older traders (often French-speaking métis in the western Great Lakes). In 1818 the American Fur Company hired more than a hundred young men from around Lake Champlain on five-year contracts (indentures) "who had grown up around Canadians and knew French."[36] Among them was Gurdon S. Hubbard, who was sent out first as a clerk and then as the head of the Illinois outfit. He worked with older traders, including Louis Buisson at Peoria, who were not American citizens.[37]

At Mackinac, Hubbard met John Harris Kinzie, the fifteen-year-old son of John and Eleanor who was serving an apprenticeship with the American Fur Company. John Kinzie must have carefully weighed the value of this apprenticeship to his son's career. Interestingly, he consulted with Robert Dickson, who had arrested Kinzie on charges of treason, concerning this decision. Clearly, they had made amends after the war. Dickson encouraged Kinzie to enter into the arrangement, and Kinzie sent his son to Mackinac, with a personal assurance from Ramsey Crooks that he would become "a man of business."[38]

John Kinzie welcomed Gurdon Hubbard into his home whenever he traveled back and forth to Mackinac.[39] By 1818 Kinzie himself was working for the American Fur Company. Ramsey Crooks approached him to supervise the transfer of fur packs that the American Fur Company expected to be coming through Chicago from the trans-Mississippi. Kinzie was also employed by the American Fur Company to collect debts and manage bills of lading. His knowledge of the local fur trade made him useful to the company.[40] Kinzie had done this work before the War of 1812 in partnership with Thomas Forsyth. Now he was simply an employee of a growing company, where the profits went to John Jacob Astor in New York.[41]

The American Fur Company did not hold anything like a monopoly in Chicago trade in these years. John Crafts was a twenty-seven-year-old single man when he arrived at Chicago in 1816 as the agent for the Detroit firm of Conant & Mack. Born in New Hampshire, he established a very successful trading post along the south branch of the Chicago River. John Kinzie and his family welcomed Crafts to Chicago. As with Gurdon Hubbard, they included him in family meals and celebrations. By the early 1820s, Crafts was courting Maria Indiana Kinzie, the teenage daughter of John and Eleanor. This was entirely in keeping with the Kinzie approach to marriage—Crafts would be good for the family "business."[42]

However, the American Fur Company, faced with Crafts's successful operation, hired Jean Baptiste Beaubien to represent their interests at Chicago. Beaubien purchased the house just south of the fort along the lakeshore from Martha Leigh Des Pins for his expanding family and business operation.[43] He had success as a trader at the far eastern edge of Chicago River. Beaubien's arrival at Chicago was problematic for Kinzie, as Beaubien usurped his place with the American Fur Company. However, both men continued to cooperate on several business ventures.

During these same years, the son of John Kinzie and his first wife, Margaret McKenzie Hall, came to Chicago. James Kinzie had grown up in Virginia, and there is no evidence that he had seen his father in the intervening years. However, some kind of contact drew the young man west. In 1821 James Kinzie moved to Chicago and built a house on the east bank of the south branch of the Chicago River. His father arranged for him to work for the American Fur Company. James Kinzie operated outposts at Milwaukee and Racine, both of which were part of the Chicago trade that the older Kinzie knew so well.[44]

The American Fur Company bought out Crafts in 1822 and then appointed him to head the Chicago operation. In turn, Kinzie and Beaubien began working for Crafts.[45] About the same time, the United States ended the factory system, and Jacob Varnum shuttered his government trading post at Chicago and sold his stock to local independent traders. The American Fur Company purchased the factory building, and Jean Baptiste Beaubien set up his trading operation there. The Kinzie family may have moved into Beaubien's vacant house south of the fort along the lakeshore. Other independent traders continued to operate in and around Chicago, but the American Fur Company increasingly dominated the scene.

THE END OF THE FUR TRADE

Despite the expansion of the American Fur Company into the area around Chicago after the war, the fur trade itself was in decline. Ongoing land cessions reduced the scope of Indian Country. With this contraction came a slow reduction in hunting, although a brisk trade continued with annuity monies distributed to the Potawatomis and their allies. Many traders moved west rather than operate in this transition. Faced with the American prohibitions against non-citizen trading, as well as the contractions in

Indian Country, Robert Dickson moved west and encouraged other traders to join him, opining that "the Indian trade in this country is not in my opinion worth following; it is like walking in mud until you get soused over head and ears."[46]

Whiskey, not furs, became a mainstay of the Indian trade. While the federal government prohibited the sale of liquor within Indian Country, each passing year reduced the lands where the prohibition held sway. After 1816 private traders could sell liquor in the wide corridor along the Illinois River between Chicago and the Mississippi. The American Fur Company encouraged their employees to trade along the boundary between ceded land and Indian Country, so that they could sell liquor legally.[47] For instance, James Kinzie, as an American Fur Company trader, overstepped this boundary and was arrested for selling "large quantities of whisky" to the Indians around Milwaukee in what was still Indian Country.[48] He became a prime example of the unprincipled behavior of the American Fur Company in a national campaign against their growing presence in the region. While the company fired Kinzie in the immediate aftermath of the scandal, he was rehired as soon as congressional scrutiny had moved on to another target.[49]

Compounding local problems, in 1825 John Crafts contracted malaria and died. Eulogized for his "character and pleasing personality," Crafts's death cast the fur trade at Chicago into turmoil.[50] Robert Stuart asked John Kinzie to work with Jean Baptiste Beaubien to administer the Chicago outfit for the American Fur Company. Despite feuding between Beaubien and Kinzie, the Chicago trade made a considerable profit in 1826–27. It seemed that Chicago, and the Kinzies, had weathered yet another crisis.[51]

In anticipation of an even better year in the fur trade in 1827–28, Beaubien and Kinzie ordered more goods at Chicago. Instead, the fur trade in Illinois abruptly ended, with a precipitous decline in available game.[52] The end of the fur trade at Chicago, and in Illinois more generally, was part of wider patterns of change. The development of the lead mines in western Illinois, the invention of the steel trap in 1823, and the cutthroat tactics of the American Fur Company all led to the demise of the fur trade.[53] Coupled with the hurried cessions of Potawatomi lands, white settlers poured into the region, leading to rapid demographic and economic change.[54]

By 1828 Ramsey Crooks and the American Fur Company began closing down their operations in the Chicago region. As the Potawatomis and their

Figure 29. John Kinzie grave in Graceland Cemetery. (John J. Keating)

allies ceded their lands to the U.S. government, the American Fur Company gained thousands and thousands of dollars at treaty negotiations as the holders of Potawatomi trading debts. The American Fur Company was out of the fur trade in Illinois, and the fur trade itself was nearing a close in the region around Chicago.[55]

THE DEATH OF JOHN KINZIE

John Kinzie died of a cerebral stroke on January 6, 1828. His lifetime stretched across the American era of the fur trade in the region of Chicago. With his death, he left to his wife and children the complex transition to an American world. Kinzie had hoped that the region around Chicago would remain a permanent Indian Country, protected from outside encroachment by the U.S. government. Instead, in the last decade of his life, Kinzie saw his Indian Country become American territory.[56] A generation of people—including Shabbona, Billy Caldwell, Archange Ouilmette, and Eleanor Kinzie—who grew up and lived in this transnational world would grow old and die in an American world.

17 The 1833 Treaty of Chicago

For a time after John Kinzie died, his widow, Eleanor, and their younger children stayed at Chicago. She moved into the Agency House, where her daughter and son-in-law Alexander Wolcott resided.[1] However, on the death of her son-in-law in 1830, Eleanor moved to Portage, Wisconsin, where her son John Harris Kinzie was Indian agent.[2] Eventually they returned to Chicago, but they never again lived in the Kinzie "Mansion." The house that Catherine and Jean Baptiste Point de Sable had built in the 1780s served as a residence and business for a succession of Chicago migrants. Anson Taylor operated a store from the house, Jonathan Bailey ran the post office there, and Judge Richard Young presided over circuit court sessions, perhaps in the old trading room. By 1833 the house was unoccupied, and it was gone before 1835. Over the next two hundred years, many businesses would locate on the site, most prominently Cyrus McCormick's first reaper works before the Civil War and the Tribune Towers after the 1920 opening of the Michigan Avenue Bridge.

By the time Eleanor Kinzie left in 1830, Jean Baptiste Beaubien's house, located south of Fort Dearborn, was the largest in town. The substantial frame structure served as the center for meetings and political activities across the 1820s. By 1831 Jean Baptiste Beaubien's brother Mark had built the Sauganash Hotel near the forks of the Chicago River (Wolf Point). Juliette Kinzie described it as "a pretentious white two-story building with bright blue wooden shutters" when she arrived in Chicago in 1831. Mark Beaubien's hotel replaced his brother's house as the center for political gatherings, social events, and business meetings.[3]

Eleanor Kinzie was perhaps surprised to find that Chicago had also become a magnet for her husband's relatives from his first marriage to Margaret McKenzie. By 1829 at least twenty had journeyed from Virginia to make their homes at Chicago. They included John Kinzie Clark (Kinzie's nephew

and son of his trading partner at Kekionga), Jonas and Elizabeth Clark Cly-
bourne (Kinzie's niece and daughter of his trading partner at Kekionga),
Samuel and Elizabeth Kinzie Miller (Kinzie's daughter), and Archibald and
Emily Hall Caldwell (her brother was married to Margaret McKenzie).

After Kinzie's death, his former wife, Margaret, came to Chicago with
her husband, Benjamin Hall. The Caldwells, Halls, Clybournes, and Clarks
embraced the end of Indian Country and started new businesses aimed at
white settlers in the ceded territory: tanneries, slaughterhouses, taverns,
blacksmith shops, and whiskey distilleries.[4] They were part of a group that
transformed Chicago from a trading outpost in Indian Country to an industrial and commercial powerhouse, a place that John Kinzie himself did
not envision when he called for a permanent Indian Country at the close
of the war.

Kinzie's relations helped Chicago to grow during this crucial time. By
1830, looking at the whole of the Great Lakes region, the white population was 1.7 million (1.47 million in the United States), while the Indian

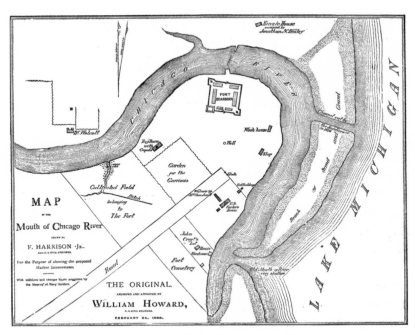

Map 12. Mouth of Chicago River, 1830. (A. T. Andreas, *History of Chicago* [1884])

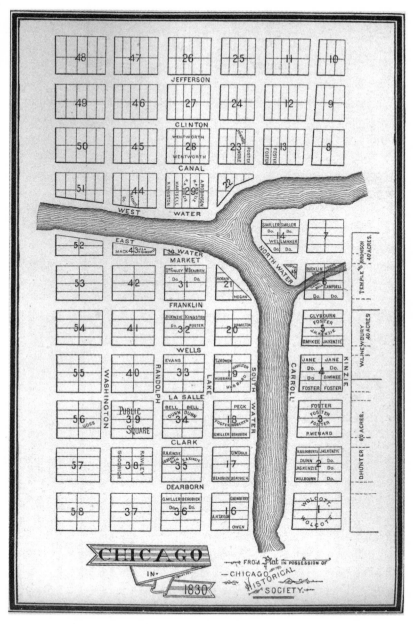

Map 13. 1830 Thompson Plat of Chicago. (A. T. Andreas, *History of Chicago* [1884])

population stood at about 72,000 (60,000 in the United States). In Illinois and the Wisconsin part of Michigan Territory, there were 3,635 Indians to 157,445 non-Indians.[5] While Indian villages still dotted the area around Chicago in 1830, the dramatic demographic shift was already under way as the region moved from an Indian world to one dominated by settlers purchasing ceded lands.[6] Indications of this transition abound—from the end of the fur trade in 1828 to the initial 1830 plat of Chicago to the organization of the first local government in 1830.

The transition was readily apparent as Chicago became part of the regular government of the United States. For many years, Chicago was technically a part of territories that exerted little authority over it. In fact, Chicago had been transferred from territory to territory, with little apparent effect on its residents. However, after Illinois became a state in 1818, with Chicago in its far northeast corner, local government came to life. The first tax rolls were created in 1825, with Jean Baptiste Beaubien identified as the wealthiest man in Chicago, with a tax valuation of $1,000. The first elections were held at Beaubien's house in 1825, with thirty-five men voting in the first general election in 1826. Over the next few years, voters elected U.S. presidents and congressional representatives, as well as justices of the peace, trustees for the school section, sheriffs, election judges, and constables.[7]

1832 BLACK HAWK WAR

The Black Hawk War was the start of the final chapter of Chicago in Indian Country. Black Hawk was the Sauk warrior who had fought alongside Tecumseh against the Americans in 1812–13. After the war, Black Hawk returned to his village along the Mississippi River due west from Chicago. Thomas Forsyth, John Kinzie's brother and business partner, was Indian agent for the Sauks and Fox, and together with his interpreter Antoine LeClair (father and then son) developed close relationships with the Sauks, including Black Hawk.

With the arrival of steam travel on the Mississippi in 1818 and the discovery of more lead mines, white settlers quickly settled on the ceded lands that the Sauks and Fox continued to inhabit. Forsyth and LeClair did their best to smooth relations between newly arrived Americans and the entrenched Sauks.[8]

In 1830 Forsyth was removed from his post, ostensibly for frequent absences, but actually as part of a wider shake-up within the Jackson administration (Forsyth had indeed been living most of the time at St. Louis for more than a decade). In any event, the Americans lost their most knowledgeable contact with the Sauks at a critical moment, as Black Hawk decided to fight rather than move west peacefully. Forsyth felt sure that he could have forestalled this war, claiming: "If I had remained at Rocky Island as Indian agent no trouble would ever have taken place."[9]

Black Hawk sought wide support for his war among the Potawatomis across northeast Illinois and southern Wisconsin. While many had sympathy for Black Hawk's cause, Potawatomi leaders in Illinois feared that an alliance with Black Hawk would lead to an "uncompensated removal." The 1830 Indian Removal Act made it clear that the U.S. government would not tolerate Indian lands east of the Mississippi. The Potawatomis understood this and hoped to make the best deal possible for themselves.[10]

By 1832 the Potawatomis supported leaders who worked well with the Americans. They were not interested in volatile warriors. Instead, métis like Billy Caldwell, Alexander Robinson, and Joseph LaFramboise, along with Shabbona, had negotiated for the Potawatomis since 1829.

When Black Hawk sent emissaries to Shabbona in the spring of 1832, he "rejected all offers of alliance made by Black Hawk." Instead, Shabbona and other Potawatomi leaders warned American settlers of the impending danger. Despite their best efforts, some young warriors joined in an attack on American settlers at Indian Creek, to the southwest of Chicago, where fifteen men, women, and children were killed.[11]

At this point, Caldwell, Robinson, Shabbona, as well as other Potawatomi leaders including Waubansee and Aptakisic (Half-Day), found themselves at "a critical crossroads."[12] After a conference at Chicago attended by the new Indian Agent Thomas J. V. Owen, the Potawatomi leadership decided to bring all of the warriors to a camp along the Des Plaines River near what is now Riverside. There the young men were kept until the end of the war. Aptakisic insisted that this enforced encampment was necessary because "the love of war was so strong, especially with the young warriors, that they could not be trusted to remain neutral if left upon their hunting grounds and villages." While the warriors were held in the camp, the women and children were allowed to remain in their villages unmolested, where they raised their usual crop of corn, beans, and squash.[13]

Figure 30. Black Hawk, the Sauk warrior. (Chicago History Museum, P&S 1920.557)

Black Hawk was defeated by September 1832 with very little Potawatomi participation. The Potawatomi leadership understood that he was fighting for a lost cause. Many had fought unsuccessfully against the Americans in the War of 1812 and understood the stakes involved. Removal was coming, whether compensated or uncompensated. Billy Caldwell, Shabbona, and others sought a compensated removal that smoothed a path for their people west of the Mississippi River.

TREATY OF 1833

The 1833 Treaty of Chicago was the last between the United States and the Potawatomis. Six thousand Potawatomis and their allies came to Chicago in September 1833 for the negotiations. While the American government got the cessions they sought, the Potawatomis successfully negotiated for their futures, within the constraints posed by American settlers and the U.S. government. They were not simply "hapless victims," but active participants.[14]

The 1833 treaty was one of the first negotiated after the 1830 Indian Removal Act. The Potawatomi experience stands in sharp contrast to the familiar Cherokee removal story. Under the leadership of Caldwell, Robinson, and Shabbona, the Potawatomis negotiated a settlement that allowed those from northern Wisconsin and southwest Michigan to return home. The Potawatomis from Illinois and southeast Wisconsin negotiated a removal westward (or relocation to Canada—the choice of Black Partridge, Blackbird, and others). They were among the first Native people subject to the Indian Removal Act, but their acquiescence to removal came with compensation to themselves and their creditors, as well as a negotiated destination. Their leaders proved to be "tough, capable, skilled negotiators" who took "the best advantage they could from an impossible situation."[15]

At its core, the treaty exchanged five million acres of land in northeast Illinois and southeast Wisconsin for five million acres of land west of the Mississippi River first in Missouri and then in Iowa. There was also a long list of Potawatomi debts to be covered, as well as payments to individuals. Finally, the treaty included a twenty-year annuity, so long as the Potawatomis emigrated as soon as possible. The Potawatomis negotiated close to $1 million in immediate payments, in addition to annuities. About one-third of that total was distributed to non-Potawatomi individuals in lieu of reservations or in payment of debts.[16]

As well as Potawatomi and U.S. negotiators, traders and their representatives were also at the table. Some of the traders, like Antoine Ouilmette or the Kinzie family, had worked with the Potawatomis for decades. Others, like Stephen Mack or James Kinzie, were recent arrivals. All hoped to collect on their debts (and more). In many ways, this treaty was "the last major operation of the fur traders in Chicago," as they sought one last round of profit.[17]

Over 225 individual, partnerships, or companies received reimburse-ments totaling $175,000. The American Fur Company was the largest single recipient of money to cover Potawatomi debts, receiving $17,000. Robert Stuart, as representative of the American Fur Company, also collected debts owed to the company from traders receiving compensation through the treaty. For instance, Jean Baptiste Chandonnai received $2,500, but the treaty explicitly stated that $1,000 was to be paid directly to the American Fur Company.[18] Jean Baptiste Beaubien received $3,000 from the treaty, but eventually Ramsey Crooks collected $2,000 of it for the American Fur Com-pany. Less typically, Gurdon Hubbard managed to keep at least part of his $6,000, despite company claims that he owed it all to them.[19]

In addition to traders' debts, the treaty included payments to indi-viduals who in previous treaties might have received reservation lands in the area. The U.S. government no longer allowed their Indian partners to grant parcels of their ceded land to individuals. Instead, the U.S. govern-ment paid cash, amounting to $100,000 in this treaty. Here the Potawatomi negotiators generally made provision for the prominent métis families in the region, including the Ouilmette, Chevalier, LaFramboise, Bourbonnais, Caldwell, Beaubien, Robinson, Porthier, and Bailly families.[20]

Some of these families had long been supporters of the United States in the region, but others had worked against the United States during the War of 1812. After the war, however, they became important allies of the Americans. Their allegiance was a practical one, born of years of conflict. Many, like John Kinzie, were reluctant Americans.[21]

This treaty was in important ways a closing chapter on the War of 1812 at Chicago. The Kinzie and Forsyth families received more than $50,000 from the treaty (far more than any other group outside the Potawatomis, including the American Fur Company). Eleanor Kinzie and her three chil-dren received $5,000 each, while Eleanor's daughter Margaret Helm re-ceived $2,000. Thomas Forsyth's children each received payments of $3,000. John Kinzie's first wife, Margaret McKenzie Hall, and her extended family received at least $10,000 in the settlement. Although a long time in com-ing, one could argue that these payments were generous compensation for the many losses suffered by the Kinzies and Forsyths during the War of 1812, as well as their ultimate loyalty to the United States and their Pota-watomi neighbors. John Kinzie was dead, and while Thomas Forsyth lived to sign the treaty in August 1833, he died two month later. However, the

Figure 31. An artistic rendering of a Potawatomi family forced to make their way westward across the Mississippi River by the U.S. government. (Joseph Kirkland, *The Chicago Massacre of 1812* [1893])

monies received in the 1833 treaty launched their families easily into the American era.[22]

In contrast, Potawatomi village leaders confronted the daunting task of organizing a move hundreds of miles westward, as well as ongoing uncertainty about their actual destinations. While the Potawatomis had signed an agreement for acreage in Missouri, Congress changed that to lands in Iowa. Billy Caldwell led a group 700 Potawatomis in 1835 across the Mississippi. Some went into Platte Country (not yet annexed to Missouri), while others went to Iowa near Council Bluffs.

Not until the fall of 1836 did Waubansee abandon his village on the Fox River directly west of Chicago to join Billy Caldwell and others in Missouri. He followed a large contingent of about 750 Potawatomis who had assembled at a camp on the Des Plaines River in late September and were accompanied by U.S. agents and other officials. Waubansee led a smaller group behind the larger party across Illinois through rain and then snow. In late October they all joined Caldwell's group in Missouri. There they faced not only an unfamiliar landscape, but also a Missouri militia that did not want them to stay, as well as thieves who coveted their horses.

The following year, under intense pressure from the U.S. government,

Caldwell and Waubansee were forced to move the group from Missouri (now numbering over a thousand) to Iowa. Most walked the distance, but the federal government was so anxious to have the group out of Missouri that they hired two steamboats to take those Potawatomis who could not travel overland to Council Bluffs. There they faced Sioux who were unhappy with their arrival. Many of the Potawatomis would relocate again to Kansas.[23]

For a time after the 1833 treaty, Shabbona and Billy Caldwell moved back and forth between Chicago, Missouri, and Iowa. They each had annuities and cash from the 1833 treaty and lands in the Chicago area from the 1829 treaty. Caldwell left in the late 1830s to serve as a Potawatomi representative with the Americans at their reservation near Council Bluffs, Iowa. He died there in 1841. Shabbona lived on his Chicago land for fifteen years but regularly traveled to Iowa (and then to Kansas when the Potawatomis relocated). On his return to northern Illinois from one of these extended trips in 1849, he found that "the old home he and his family had occupied for more than 40 years, was lost to him forever."[24] The U.S. government had sold his reservation lands away from him. Gurdon Hubbard later remembered: "It ought to be a matter of regret and mortification to us all, that our government so wronged this man, who so often periled his own life to save those of the whites."[25]

In the end, only Alexander Robinson lived out his life on the lands he received in the 1829 treaty along the Des Plaines River. He visited his Potawatomi friends several times in Kansas and entertained Potawatomis who came to Chicago. Robinson was able to leave his children "handsome competence in the valuable acres so long in his possession."[26] An 1872 newspaper article, written at his death, reminded the readers that over his lifetime, a succession of events "transformed the cherished wilderness fur region into the Great Interior of our own day."[27]

Like Caldwell, Shabbona, and Robinson, the Ouilmettes were well compensated in the 1829 and 1833 treaties. Archange and Antoine Ouilmette left their house at Chicago sometime in the 1820s and moved to their property at Gross Point (now Wilmette). Here the Ouilmettes raised their children and operated a substantial farm. They received two sections of land (1,280 acres) as part of the 1829 Treaty at Prairie du Chien, as well as monetary grants in both 1829 and 1833 (more than $1,400 in the 1833 treaty).[28] This allowed them to live quite comfortably and at a distance from the changing world at Chicago.[29] They continued to tap maple sugar and net whitefish in the spring.

However, by the 1830s the Ouilmettes began to have problems with trespassers who were cutting timber on their lands. Antoine Ouilmette tried to prosecute one of the trespassers, but the court ruled against him, and "the sheriff levied a pair of fine Indian ponies belonging to Ouilmette" as his fine. These horses were Ouilmette's "special pride," and soon after the incident, he and his wife, Archange, left for Iowa, "never to return." Both died near Council Bluffs in 1841.[30] Despite substantial lands at Chicago, Archange and Antoine Ouilmette no longer felt at home at Chicago.[31]

In contrast to her old neighbor Archange Ouilmette, Eleanor Kinzie returned to Chicago after her family received substantial settlements in the Chicago Treaty of 1833. She had been living with her son John Harris and his wife, Juliette Magill, at Fort Winnebago near Portage, Wisconsin. John Harris Kinzie had left the employ of the American Fur Company after his father's death in 1828 to work for Governor Lewis Cass, of the Michigan Territory. In that capacity, John Harris had traveled to Washington, D.C., compiled cultural information including grammars and dictionaries, and participated in treaty negotiations. He was particularly interested in the Winnebagos, and when Cass became secretary of war in 1829, he appointed Kinzie as Indian subagent at Fort Winnebago.

Turning his back on his years in Indian Country, John Harris Kinzie resigned his commission with the Department of War and returned to Chicago upon receiving monies in the 1833 treaty. He became a leading citizen in a new era at Chicago, serving as the second town president and subdividing the property north of the Chicago River that his family claimed. He established a forwarding and commissioning business with Major David Hunter, who married his sister Maria Indiana. In 1834 he began construction on a substantial brick residence in his new subdivision. Eleanor did not witness the completion of this home, as she died while in New York City visiting her eldest daughter.[32]

While John Harris Kinzie's story was tied to the rising star of a new Chicago, his younger brother Robert Allen Kinzie was drawn westward. After marrying Gwenthlean Whistler, the daughter of the commander at Fort Dearborn, William Whistler (and the granddaughter of Captain John Whistler, who had supervised construction of the first fort at Chicago) in 1834, he moved into the Indian Country west of the Mississippi River. He traded among the Potawatomis in Iowa and then in 1843 became the sutler at a U.S. fort at Des Moines. Together with his brother-in-law John H. Whistler, he traded with the area Potawatomis. They moved to Kansas with the Potawatomis in the late 1840s. Eventually Robert returned to Chicago, where he took an appointment as a paymaster in the U.S. Army until his death in 1873, when he was buried alongside his father at Graceland Cemetery.[33]

The 1833 treaty dramatically reshaped the lives of all those who had lived at Chicago in the first decades of the nineteenth century. These early inhabitants witnessed the transition from a first Chicago, set in an Indian Country, to a new one soon firmly in the hands of American settlers. The later period brought peace of a kind but made this region as inhospitable to the Potawatomis as it had once been their home. Even métis families like the Ouilmettes fled in the face of changing racial lines and societal norms. At the same time, the Kinzie family was able to operate in both the old and new worlds, a fact that no doubt would have made their father proud.

Epilogue
Why It Was Not a Massacre

> The kind of history that has the most influence upon the life of the com-
> munity and the course of events is the history that common men [and
> women] carry around in their heads.
>
> —*Carl Becker*[1]

On August 15, 2009, the Chicago Park District dedicated a new park at Calumet
Avenue and Eighteenth Street, a block away from where *The Fort Dear-*
born Massacre monument once stood and near the site of the 1812 battle.
The Battle of Fort Dearborn Park is a small play lot that contains a historic marker commemorating the significance of this site in early Chicago
history. Over several years of discussion, community residents banished
the word "massacre" from the story. John Low, a member of the Pokagan
Band of Potawatomis and executive director of the Mitchell Museum of the
American Indian, suggested that the park name reminds Chicagoans that
Natives and non-Natives were not simply "victims, villains, or heroes," but
"people first, often presented with difficult circumstances and choices."[2]

Despite the serious consideration given to the renaming, some Chicagoans dismissed Low's perspective as simply another round of "historical
revisionism," vowing to continue to use "massacre" in relation to the attack
on August 15, 1812. They were willing to stand tall with the alarmist and
propagandist writings of the fall of 1812 that sought to inflame American
sentiment against Indians, rather than reconsider the event in light of new
information and perspectives.[3]

This discussion over historical revisionism and the use of the word
"massacre" goes to the heart of what history is (or is not). History is not
simply a record of everything that has happened in the past. There is no
such record, and even if there were, historians could never access it all. No
one will ever know everything about Chicago on August 12, 1812. We can
only know what can be assembled from available accounts, but we continue to uncover more documentation and glean additional information

from the available historical record. Our understanding of the past and its intricacies is ever evolving.[4]

Today historians know more about the attack on that August morning in 1812 than many of the participants and those who first wrote about it. When a Detroit judge used the word "massacre" to describe these events in October 7, 1812, he did not know the fate of many of those under attack at Chicago. Nor did he know what the U.S. Army did in response to the Chicago battle. More information on the "massacre" is available to us in 2012 than existed in 1812 or even in 1912, when Milo Quaife completed the last full-scale review of these years. In *Chicago and the Old Northwest*, Quaife described the event as a "massacre" in his text but headed his chapter "The Battle and Defeat." Since 1912 Quaife and others have added to our store of records by uncovering materials from more survivors, including John Kinzie. In addition, a blossoming of Indian history and regional studies provides a richer context in which to consider Chicago in 1812.

Reconsideration has been going on for decades. In 1943 Harry A. Musham, a Chicagoan who devoted his retirement decades to studying Fort Dearborn and seeking public memorialization of it, could no longer describe the 1812 attack as a "massacre." He noted: "It was not a massacre as it was not an indiscriminate killing. Those who perished were killed in the fighting or soon afterwards in accordance with Indian customs." Musham suggested that the event be called the Battle of Chicago, as it "did not occur at Fort Dearborn."[5] Musham did not create his own definition of "massacre"; he used the established dictionary definition: "the unnecessary, indiscriminate killing of a large number of human beings."[6]

Certainly, the attack on the morning of August 15, 1812, led to the "killing of a large number of human beings." Sixty-eight of 110 people evacuating Fort Dearborn were killed. However, it was not indiscriminate. The Potawatomi warriors attacked an armed company of U.S. soldiers during a time of war.

From the Potawatomi perspective, it was a planned attack, part of a clear regional strategy in a war begun by the United States. The Potawatomi warriors who attacked the U.S. soldiers on their way to Fort Wayne saw an opportunity to avenge the savage actions of the U.S. military the previous November at Tippecanoe. They had ammunition for the attack from their success at Mackinac, as well as from the neophyte Indian agent at Fort Wayne.

They followed plans worked out at councils across the western Great Lakes in May and June, and were spurred into action by the war belt that Main Poc had sent from Detroit. The night before the attack, Black Partridge returned his medal of friendship to the U.S. officials at Fort Dearborn and warned them about the impending violence. In the same way, William Wells, who had come to Chicago to accompany his niece to safety, blackened his face as an Algonquian warrior headed into battle. Wells—although stripped of his influential position as U.S. Indian agent at Fort Wayne and without the protection of Little Turtle (who had died just weeks before)— understood the great danger he and the American contingent faced, despite the assurances of Potawatomi warriors of a safe passage.

On first glance, the killing of many children and women accompanying the U.S. soldiers and militia might seem indiscriminate. However, from the perspective of the Potawatomis, those women and children represented an advance guard of American settlers who challenged the bounds of Indian Country by placing their families in harm's way. Even here, the attack was not indiscriminate. The officers' wives were not killed as they were valuable for ransom. Nor were Kinzie's relatives attacked, showing the influence that the trader exerted within Potawatomi villages.

No longer a "massacre," blame for the event lies more squarely on the shoulders of the U.S. government. When declaring a war, they did not prepare to protect the isolated outpost at Chicago. Its commander received very little information or guidance. He had to rely heavily on Kinzie, because he did not have the advice and counsel of the U.S. Indian agent, factor, or interpreter assigned to Chicago. The first had left because of personal tragedies, the second because of fear and anger, and Kinzie had killed the third. The commander, Captain Nathan Heald, was grieving the loss of his newborn son. He was poorly informed, received perfunctory orders from an officer who was soon to be court-martialed, and made the imprudent decision to evacuate.

Beyond the dictionary definition, it is worth noting the unequal way that "massacre" has been applied across U.S. history. In 1899 Simon Pokagon, a Potawatomi whose father arrived at Chicago in the wake of the August attack, pointed out this disparity. He noted that "when whites are killed, it is a massacre, when Indians are killed[,] it is a fight." He contrasted the language used to describe the "Battle" of Tippecanoe in 1811, where Americans "slew many warriors, women and children, burned our villages and supplies, leaving us and our little ones naked and destitute," with the use of "massacre" to describe the attack at Chicago the following year. This was the immediate, but by no means the only, example of this disparity, ranging as far back in U.S. history to the Pequot War of the 1630s and the 1890 battle at Wounded Knee, where three hundred Lakotas were killed by U.S. soldiers in the final chapter of the Indian wars in America. In 1973 Indian activists, protesting the continued use of "massacre" to describe events at Chicago on August 15, 1812, asked, "Why don't they show our side of it? Why don't they show Wounded Knee as a massacre too?" "Massacre" is a word tainted through misuse by U.S. authorities in their decades-long war against Native Americans.[7]

Because it was called a "massacre" soon after the event, it is difficult to move away from this descriptor. However, it was not a "massacre," but part of a declared war that the United States waged against Great Britain and their Indian allies. As such, the Potawatomis and their allies won a military victory. Still, it was also an episode in the long war of conquest that shifted control of this region from Indians to the U.S. government.

WHAT TO DO ABOUT THE MONUMENT?

For over a decade, *The Fort Dearborn Massacre* has not been on public display. With a discredited title and a problematic representation can, or should, this monument be rescued from storage? One of the most important accomplishments of history is the ability to revise narratives about the past based on new information. Rather than hiding the monument, it should be used to explore what nineteenth-century civic leaders and twentieth-century historians thought about the events of 1812, as well as the forgotten story of conquest on which Chicago history rests. With careful reinterpretation, the monument can help reshape our collective memory of early Chicago, allowing us to see the effect of layers of earlier history.[8]

For starters, the monument could be returned to the area around Eighteenth Street and Prairie Avenue.[9] Reinstalling the sculpture at its original site would provide an opportunity for the public to reconsider how differently Chicagoans regarded the Fort Dearborn monument when it was first put on public display. At the dedication in 1893, Edward G. Mason, the director of the Chicago Historical Society, asserted that the bronze memo-

Figure 32. The Fort Dearborn Massacre stood at the entrance to the new wing of the Chicago Historical Society in 1972. (Chicago History Museum, ICHi-36552)

rial reflected the remarkable progress of the city over the preceding eighty years. Mason described the Potawatomis in the monument as "invaders" and "Barbarians," who had to be vanquished in order to bring "civilization" to Chicago. These vitriolic sentiments, regarded as "truth" in the nineteenth century, contrast sharply with our present-day understanding of the city's multi-ethnic origins.[10]

The Fort Dearborn Massacre was dedicated with much pomp and circumstance during the 1893 World's Fair. The Danish sculptor Carl Rohl-Smith, who created the monument, was in Chicago working on a statue of Benjamin Franklin for the Exposition's Electric Building. In the year of the World's Columbian Exposition, Chicagoans celebrated the events of August 1812 as a part of the continental expansion of the United States. Chicago was by then the "City of the Century," having recently surpassed one million in population. It was a significant urban place essential to the rise of the United States as a modern industrial nation.

The fair itself was part of a celebration of the four hundredth anniversary of Columbus's voyage to the Americas that began the long arc of a conquest narrative that ended for the United States in 1890 at Wounded

Figure 33. Since 1998 the monument has been out of the public eye. Seen here are the figures of Black Partridge and Mrs. Helm, in storage, June 2011. (Con Buckley)

Knee. At the Columbian Exposition, historian Frederick Jackson Turner proclaimed that the frontier era in U.S. history was over. It was a moment of great triumph at the conclusion of a long war of conquest.

A reinterpretation of the monument on Prairie Avenue could focus on its tangible link to Wounded Knee. Sculptor Rohl-Smith used Sioux prisoners, Kicking Bear and Short Bull, as his live models. The U.S. Army captured them at the Battle of Wounded Knee and held them at Fort Sheridan, in north suburban Chicago. Kicking Bear and Short Bull tightly link the 1812 battle to the wider war of conquest in which it rested.[11]

While the monument could be returned to Prairie Avenue, there is also a powerful argument to move it into, or adjacent to, the Administration Building of the Pullman Company, now the property of the state of Illinois at 111th Street and Cottage Grove Avenue on Chicago's South Side. George Pullman, whose mansion stood just steps away from the original Prairie Avenue site, commissioned the monument and paid $50,000 for its design, casting, and installation. For successful Chicago industrialists like George Pullman, the statue symbolized the United States' overwhelming success in transforming the continent and Chicago's dramatic rise to the nation's second city. For Pullman, the monument was a tribute to the success of American economic, military, and political power.[12]

ON AUGUST 15, 1812, INDIANS ATTACKED A SMALL GARRISON AND CITIZENS EVACUATING FORT DEARBORN, KILLING FIFTY-THREE SOLDIERS AND WOMEN AND CHILDREN. A MONUMENT COMMEMORATING THE TRAGIC EVENT, DONATED BY GEORGE M. PULLMAN, STOOD ON THIS SITE FROM 1894 TO 1931. THE MONUMENT IS NOW IN THE CHICAGO HISTORICAL SOCIETY.

CHICAGO HISTORICAL SOCIETY

Figure 34. The Chicago History Museum erected this plaque at the original monument site in the 1930s. Since 2009 a new plaque stands a block to the east at the recently dedicated Battle of Fort Dearborn Park. (Chicago History Museum, ICHi 38956)

Since 1893 the fortunes of the Pullman Palace Car Company have changed dramatically. Then, George Pullman and his company seemed indomitable, and thousands of people who came to the World's Columbian Exposition traveled to see the town he created on the shores of Lake Calumet. In 1982 the Pullman Car Works closed its operations, leaving thousands of unemployed workers and an abandoned industrial operation. Like the Potawatomis before them, the Pullman Company also was defeated, tumbling to oblivion in the post-industrial economy. The monument to the vanquished Indian can be set within a space now dedicated to preserving remnants of an industrial world that has also been vanquished—the conquered and the conquerors become one in the rich irony of history. Locating the monument at Pullman would set the conquest of the Potawatomis alongside the collapse of the industrial age in Chicago, and provide a visual reminder of the impermanence of any single group or era over the long sweep of history—and the hubris of thinking otherwise.

The monument could also be returned to the Chicago History Museum, to highlight the crucial importance of this moment in Chicago's multi-ethnic past. Too often, Chicago's history is told through broad-brush generalizations based in race, class, and ethnicity. The memorial reminds us that it was individuals, not groups, who made this history.

The monument portrays the moment when Black Partridge saved Margaret McKillip Helm from the attack of an unidentified Indian, with the wounded Surgeon's Mate Isaac Van Voorhis and an unidentified white child in the background. This was not a faceless attack on an unknown enemy. All three of the identified people depicted in the monument knew each other, and it is quite likely that the attacking Indian, as well as the small child, were also familiar to each other. For years the U.S. military, some settlers, the Potawatomis, and their allies had lived in uneasy coexistence. Juliette Kinzie told a story of great violence, but also one of neighborliness and courage.

The attacking Indian has remained unidentified in the monument scene. However, among the warriors outside Chicago by August 15, 1812, were many supporters of the Potawatomi warrior Main Poc, including his brothers-in-law Nuscotomeg (Mad Sturgeon), Wabinewa (White Sturgeon), and Wasachek (Clear Day). For years all three had joined Main Poc in raids against American settlers throughout southern Illinois. Any one of them could have been the young warrior in *The Fort Dearborn Massacre*.

Margaret Helm, the woman at the center of *The Fort Dearborn Massacre*, held an unusual position at Chicago. Born in 1794 to Daniel McKillip, a British army officer, and his wife, Eleanor Lytle McKillip, Margaret grew up in Detroit. Shortly after her marriage to Lieutenant Linai Helm, a young U.S. officer, she accompanied him to Fort Dearborn. Her stepfather, John Kinzie, operated the successful trading outpost nearby with the help of her mother, Eleanor, and a large household that included Margaret's three step-siblings, French-speaking engagés, and household help, as well as several enslaved people. She was the only member of this household, aside from her stepfather, who did not spend the morning of August 15, 1812, in an open boat just off the shore from the battle.

The fallen U.S. soldier depicted in the memorial is Surgeon's Mate Isaac Van Voorhis, who had aligned himself against John Kinzie and his son-in-law Lieutenant Helm in garrison in-fighting during the first half of 1812. After receiving threats from Helm, Van Voorhis wrote the secretary of war about his "extremely unpleasant, if not truly hazardous" position at Fort Dearborn. He feared attack from other members of the U.S. garrison, as much as by Potawatomi warriors. Van Voorhis was assigned the dangerous task of accompanying the wagon loaded with women and children, and he died shortly after the battle began.

Most of the children, except those carried by their mothers, were killed near the wagons at the start of the battle. Since Margaret Helm did not have children, the child in *The Fort Dearborn Massacre* is an anomaly. She is not part of the story as told by Juliette Kinzie but does heighten the viewer's sense of savagery with her silent cry for help. An unattended child was not likely to survive this attack. The Potawatomis were unwilling to take prisoners who could not readily travel back to their villages and potentially serve some useful purpose.

The Indian posed on the right side of the monument protecting Margaret Helm is Black Partridge. Black Partridge grew up in one of the Potawatomi villages around St. Joseph River in what is now southwestern Michigan. He fought against the Americans at Fallen Timbers, but signed the Treaty of Greenville in 1795 and accepted a medal of friendship from the United States. He moved westward with his younger brother Waubansee (Foggy Day) to establish villages along the Illinois River, where he came to know Kinzie and his brother and partner, Thomas Forsyth.[13]

Wherever the Fort Dearborn memorial is relocated, it ought to be renamed in honor of Black Partridge. He is the acknowledged hero in the events surrounding August 15, 1812, and his role is confirmed in historical narratives as well as in the monument itself. Black Partridge remained loyal to his U.S. allies until just before the evacuation from Fort Dearborn. Then, after warning Captain Heald and John Kinzie that an attack was imminent, Black Partridge returned his peace medal to Heald. He was present at the Potawatomi attack on the retreating U.S. contingent and never wavered in his intent to protect the Kinzie family. From all accounts, but none more than that of Juliette Kinzie, Black Partridge showed great compassion and bravery on the morning of August 15, 1812.

While the attack at Chicago was part of a wider war of conquest, it was also a battle in which personal loyalties mattered. People acted as neighbors and friends, as well as enemies at war. Like Black Partridge, John Kinzie stood with Captain Heald not so much as an American, but rather as a good neighbor and business partner. Captain Heald understood that Kinzie's particular value was his personal networks. Not only could he distinguish between potential enemies and friends, but he worked in concert with, not against, Potawatomi leaders like Black Partridge. During the crucial moments of the battle in August 1812, Kinzie used his personal influence to keep his family and some of the American officials from harm.

Yet of all the principal actors in the events surrounding the evacuation of Fort Dearborn, Black Partridge alone was an unambiguous hero. With the reinstallation and reinterpretation of this monument, Black Partridge takes a place of honor in Chicago history. The monument would no longer memorialize a "massacre," but a defeat within a long conquest war that Chicago history (and U.S. history more generally) has been slow to acknowledge.

A NEW START TO CHICAGO HISTORY

Reinterpretation of the events of August 15, 1812, can take many different forms, depending especially on where the monument is located. We have learned here a great deal more about what happened in Chicago before 1833, but the task of changing how we remember the past remains. Can the information here help us make the "imaginative leap of perspective" that can change the past we carry around in our heads? Discussion on location, reinterpretation, and renaming of the monument provides an opportunity to move our new knowledge of the past out of the written historical record and into our landscape.[14]

Thinking about August 15, 1812, also offers an opportunity to reconsider Chicago's multiple foundation stories, with competing historical claims. Jean Baptiste Point de Sable, John Kinzie, the creation of Fort Dearborn and its destruction in 1812, the 1830 real estate plat, the Black Hawk War, and the 1833 Treaty of Chicago have all been taken as starting points for Chicago's history. I have woven these events and people into a foundation narrative that includes rather than excludes groups, individuals, and events.

This book considers several of the people and events long associated with some of Chicago's most long-lasting myths—especially the "first settler" stories. Foundation myths matter profoundly to city residents because these stories determine who are insiders, as well as who has the ultimate claim to a place. In addition to establishing identity, they legitimize groups, conflicts, and attitudes.

Including so many groups and perspectives allows us to understand the wide range of futures envisioned by people in the region. At one end were nativist leaders like Tecumseh and Tenskwatawa, who sought the removal of all Euro-American people, goods, and culture in the region, while at the other end were American settlers who fought for the removal of all Indian people. Between these two perspectives were many Indians and Euro-American settlers, including Jean Baptiste Point de Sable and John Kinzie, who sought to maintain the Indian Country in the region around Chicago where Euro-American traders and goods would remain present. By taking a look before and after the events of August 1812, and by looking both in and outside Chicago, we can highlight a past that can help us envision new and different futures.

Foundation myths tell us as much about contemporary affairs as they do about what took place in the earliest days of a place, a people, or a nation. They shape our views on politics and society today. In light of their crucial importance to the present and the future, I would encourage Chicagoans to adopt a more inclusive foundation story that encompasses the whole of the American era, one in which Chicago was part of the Indian Country of the western Great Lakes.

Jean Baptiste Point de Sable was the first non-Native inhabitant at Chicago. However, Point de Sable was never alone at Chicago. He lived with his Indian wife, Catherine, and their métis children, as well as neighbors like

Archange and Antoine Ouilmette, and Jean Lalime and his wife, Nokeno-qua. Together, they comprised a small settlement that would continue, with only a few months' hiatus after August 15, 1812, down to the present. The foundation of Fort Dearborn at Chicago in late 1803 brought a rotating group of American soldiers and officials, as well as John Kinzie and his family. Chicago, once a small outpost in Indian Country, had begun its rise as an inland metropolis as the Potawatomis and their allies ceded the last of their claims in 1833.

To mark this continuous settlement from Point de Sable to the present, as well as the transition to U.S. control of the territory in and around Chicago, I recommend that we rededicate the first star in the city's flag to honor the era when Chicago was a part of the Indian Country of the western Great Lakes. To do so would bring together disparate foundation stories to recognize a shared past instead of a divided one.

Few Chicagoans know that their flag has been an evolving symbol. In 1917, when the Chicago City Council adopted the flag, it bore just two stars—one marking the 1871 fire and the other the 1893 World's Fair.

In 1933 a third star was added in honor of the Century of Progress Exposition. Occupying a site near the new Soldier Field, this World's Fair attracted thousands of visitors to a city that was reeling from the effects of the Great Depression. Understandably, civic leaders regarded the 1933 exposition as an opportunity to focus on the future, rather than the hundredth anniversary of the end of Indian Country. Nevertheless, they provided space for a replica of the Second Fort Dearborn and a cabin identified as that of Jean Baptiste Point de Sable.[15] As the African American community grew after World War I, activists began to lobby for recognition of Point de Sable as "the first civilized human to settle in what is now Chicago." However, fair organizers rejected their efforts as emphasizing "race difference" and allowed only a small wooden cabin alongside the replica of Fort Dearborn.[16]

In the years following the 1933 exposition, African Americans continued to press for recognition of Point de Sable, with limited success. Beyond the construction of DuSable High School in 1935, no other monument, street, or library was named in his honor.[17] Indeed, when it came to chose a fourth star for the Chicago flag in 1939, the City Council selected Fort Dearborn (or the "Fort Dearborn Massacre," as one newspaper reported). While not a direct confrontation, race remained an undercurrent in the debate about memorializing early Chicago in the landscape.[18]

Figure 35. The Chicago Flag used as a backdrop for the inauguration of Mayor Rahm Emanuel, April 2011. (Betsy Keating)

Through this book, we have seen the clear connections between Fort Dearborn, John Kinzie, and Jean Baptiste Point de Sable. They are not competing myths so much as different entrance points into the early history of Chicago. There is real value in marking a first generation of people living in and around Chicago, including Point de Sable, Kinzie, Archange Ouilmette, Nathan Heald, Black Partridge, and Topinbee. These individuals endured the War of 1812 and provided the roots from which Chicago would grow. Taken together, they provide a unified foundation story. It is a story of conquest but does not make villains out of heroes. In it, John Kinzie and his neighbors are not straightforwardly heroes, victims, or villains, but women and men who, as Potawatomi leader John Low suggested, faced "difficult circumstances and choices."[19] In that, they were not unlike twenty-first-century Chicagoans seeking to protect family and investments in the face of a quickly changing world that cannot be controlled by any one individual or local place. Kinzie, like his neighbors, turned to those he most trusted to help him through troubled times and in turn extended help to those he could.

Rededicating the first star in the Chicago flag broadly to this founding era and particularly to August 15, 1812, provides a clear start to the city's history. The Battle of Chicago, known for many years as the Fort Dearborn "Massacre," should stand alongside the 1871 fire as an event that dramatically reshaped Chicago's history. The death and destruction in both 1812 and 1871 could have, but did not, crush Chicago. Instead, these events ushered in new periods of growth and development. While the Potawatomis and their allies won the day in 1812, the ground shifted in the broader war and the era of Chicago in Indian Country ended. Chicago's foundation rests in this era of multi-racial, multi-ethnic communities buffeted by international rivalries and competing visions for the future.

Notes

Introduction

1. The word "massacre" was used to describe these events as early as an October 7, 1812, letter from a Detroit judge encouraging the British to assist the prisoners taken by the Potawatomis and their allies at Chicago. See Milo M. Quaife, *Chicago and the Old Northwest, 1673–1835* (Urbana, IL, 2001), 415, 422.

2. Mrs. John H. (Juliette) Kinzie, *Wau-Bun: The "Early Day" in the North-West* (Chicago, 1932), 262. According to Kinzie, if Heald had listened to John Kinzie, the massacre could have been averted (251). The standard account of the massacre in the twentieth century was published in 1913 by Milo M. Quaife as *Chicago and the Old Northwest*. Constance R. Buckley is the first historian to take up this subject in recent years. See "Searching for Fort Dearborn: Perception, Commemoration, and Celebration of an Urban Creation Memory" (PhD diss., Loyola University, 2005). Buckley's focus is on the way that the event has been remembered, rather than the event itself. She has done the careful work of examining the many accounts of the massacre. Perhaps most helpful here is her comparison of Kinzie's first account, *Narrative of the Massacre at Chicago* (Chicago, 1844), with the first publication of *Wau-Bun* in 1856. See Buckley, especially appendix 2, 438–73.

3. The monument itself remained on display at the Chicago History Museum until 1986, when it was removed after years of protests about its depiction of Native Americans. After a brief return to Prairie Avenue, the city of Chicago removed the monument to a warehouse, where it remains today.

4. Donald R. Hickey, *The War of 1812: A Forgotten Conflict* (Urbana, IL, 1989), 151.

5. In *The Civil War of 1812: American Citizens, British Subjects, Irish Rebels, and Indian Allies* (New York, 2010), Alan Taylor provides an examination of a civil war between mobile people from the United States, Canada, and Ireland. He does not mention the destruction of Fort Dearborn in 1812 but notes the rebuilding of the fort at Chicago in 1816. Taylor extends his study westward only to Detroit and makes the case for the value of Indian "massacres" (focusing particularly on the River Raisin massacre in January 1813) to increase Republican support for the war effort. See especially pages 211–13. Other important accounts of the war include Hickey, *The War of 1812*, and J. C. A. Stagg, *Mr. Madison's War: Politics, Diplomacy, and Warfare in the Early American Republic, 1783–1830* (Princeton, NJ, 1983).

6. In a very real sense, the origins of Chicago are not depicted in William Cronon's *Nature's Metropolis: Chicago and the Great West* (New York, 1991), so much as they are from Richard White, *The Middle Ground: Indians, Empires, and Republics in the Great Lakes Regions, 1650–1850* (New York, 1991).

7. Andrew Cayton, "The Meaning of the Wars for the Great Lakes," in *The Sixty Years' War for the Great Lakes, 1754–1814*, ed. David Curtis Skagus and Larry L. Nelson (East Lansing, MI, 2001), 380–81. As Walter Nugent has recently reminded us, the U.S.-Canadian border is an international one, despite being one of the most open in the world. See *Habits of Empire* (New York, 2008). François Furstenberg posits that "the history of the trans-Appalachian West shaped the

destinies not just of Native America, nor of Mexico, Canada, and the United States, nor even of the most powerful global empires of the nineteenth century, but by extension of modern world history itself." Furstenberg, "The Significance of the Trans-Appalachian Frontier in Atlantic History," *American Historical Review* 114, no. 3 (June 2008): 677.

8. Michael A. McDonnell, "Charles-Michel Mouett de Langlade," in *The Sixty Years' War for the Great Lakes*, ed. Skagus and Nelson, 90. Coll Thrush notes the importance of beginning urban history with the indigenous in *Native Seattle: Histories from the Crossing-Over Place* (Seattle, 2007), 15.

9. On Pontiac's War, see Gregory Evans Dowd, *War under Heaven: Pontiac, the Indian Nations, and the British Empire* (Baltimore, 2002); and White, *The Middle Ground*, 262–14. On the Seven Years' War (the French and Indian War), see Fred Anderson, *Crucible of War: The Seven Years' War and the Fate of Empire in British North America, 1754–1766* (New York, 2000).

10. Henry Lewis Carter, *The Life and Times of Little Turtle, First Sagamore of the Wabash* (Urbana, IL, 1987), 28. The early history of the Miamis was compromised in 1790, when the Harmar expedition destroyed two large chests of materials that the Miamis used to tell their stories. See ibid., 12.

11. Ibid., 45. Paul A. Hutton contends that Little Turtle was born in 1751. See Hutton, "William Wells: Frontier Scout and Indian Agent," *Indiana Magazine of History* 74, no. 3 (September 1978): 186. There are many variations in the spelling of Little Turtle's Algonquian name, Meshekunnoghquoh. This is the spelling as recorded in the Treaty of Greeneville; see Carter, *Life and Times of Little Turtle*, 43.

12. There are two key secondary sources on the Potawatomis: R. David Edmunds, *The Potawatomis: Keepers of the Fire* (Norman, OK, 1978); and James A. Clifton, *The Prairie People: Continuity and Change in Potawatomi Indian Culture, 1665–1965* (Lawrence, KS, 1977). On Chicago-area Indians, see also Helen Hornbeck Tanner, ed., *Atlas of Great Lakes Indian History* (Norman, OK, 1987); Wayne C. Temple, *Indian Villages of the Illinois Country: Historic Tribes* (Springfield, IL, 1958); David B. Stout and Erminie Wheeler-Voegelin, *Indians of Illinois and Northwest Indiana* (New York, 1974); and Terry Straus, ed., *Native Chicago* (Chicago, 2002).

13. One 1812 report identified villages at 25, 30, and 100 miles from the mouth of the St. Joseph River, and another village 25 miles up the mouth from of the Elkhart (Stagheart) River. See Edmunds, *The Potawatomis*, 191. On Topinbee, see Elmore Barce, "Topenbee and the Decline of the Pottawattomie Nation," *Indiana Magazine of History* 14, no. 1 (March 1918): 3–12.

14. Tanner, *Atlas of Great Lakes Indian History*, 98–99.

15. Helen Hornbeck Tanner, "Tribal Mixtures in Chicago Area Indian Villages," in *Indians of the Chicago Area*, ed. Terry Straus (Chicago, 1989), 21.

16. John Sugden, *Tecumseh: A Life* (New York, 1997), 175; Henry H. Hurlbut, *Chicago Antiquities* (Chicago, 1881), 464; Nehemiah Matson, *Memories of Shaubena with Incidents Relating to Indian Wars and the Early Settlement of the West* (Chicago, 1890), 18–19.

17. James A. Clifton, George L. Cornell, and James M. McClurken, *People of the Three Fires: The Ottawa, Potawatomi and Ojibway of Michigan* (Grand Rapids, MI, 1986), 53.

18. The Illinois tribal population dropped from more than 6,000 in 1700 to about 2,200 by 1768 (with a continued decline after that point). Tanner, *Atlas of Great Lakes Indian History*, 63. In many ways, the federal government feared most western settlers who adopted Potawatomi-style expansion that could not be controlled by a central authority. President George Washington's reaction to the Whiskey Rebellion is a case in point.

19. C. Henry Smith, "Black Partridge: The Hero of Fort Dearborn," in *Metamora* (Bluffton, OH, 1947), 23.

20. Quoted in Dorothy Libby, "Thomas Forsyth to William Clark, St. Louis, December 23, 1812," *Ethnohistory* 8, no 2 (Spring 1961): 179–95. See also Temple, *Indian Villages of the Illinois Country*, 189; and Nancy Oestreich Lurie, "The Winnebago Indians: A Study in Cultural Change" (PhD diss., Northwestern University, 1952), 46, 56.

21. Kerry A. Trask, *Black Hawk: The Battle for the Heart of America* (New York, 2006), 3; See also Temple, *Indian Villages of the Illinois Country*, 103.

22. Trask, *Black Hawk*, 3; Milo Milton Quaife, ed., *Life of Black Hawk* (Chicago, 1916), 13.

23. Temple, *Indian Villages of the Illinois Country*, 159, 164.

24. See Tanner, *Atlas of Great Lakes Indian History*, 66, 96. On 1812 population, see also Libby, "Thomas Forsyth to William Clark, St. Louis, December 23, 1812," 181–91.

25. Andrew Cayton has suggested that the lack of interest reflects a resistance "to confront something we do not like to consider at length: the extent to which this nation's history rests on military conquest and the extent to which its history is about power as well as liberty." Cayton, "The Meaning of the Wars for the Great Lakes," 380–81.

26. Clifton, *The Prairie People*, 181. See also Clifton, "Chicago, September 14, 1833: The Last Great Indian Treaty in the Old Northwest," *Chicago History* 9, no. 2 (Summer 1980): 89; Edmunds, *The Potawatomis*, 186–88; and John Low and Paula Holley, "Treaty of Chicago—September, 1833," in *Native Chicago*, ed. Straus, 108.

27. David Curtis Skagus, "The Sixty Years' War for the Great Lakes: An Overview," in *The Sixty Years' War for the Great Lakes*, ed. Skagus and Nelson, 2. See also Peter Silver, *Our Savage Neighbors: How Indian War Transformed Early America* (New York, 2008), xxiii–xxv.

28. Quoted in Libby, "Thomas Forsyth to William Clark, St. Louis, December 23, 1812," 183.

Chapter One

1. John Swenson has recently uncovered evidence suggesting that John Kinzie might actually be the son of William Forsyth, as records indicate that the senior Kinzie died before John Kinzie was conceived. Swenson, unpublished paper on Jean Baptiste Point de Sable, 2006.

2. Kinzie's half-sister Alice married a British official, Sampson Fleming, at Detroit in 1768 and moved to New York City. According to Kinzie family histories, John attended school in New York City just before the start of the American Revolution. See Mrs. John H. (Juliette) Kinzie, *Wau-Bun: The "Early Day" in the North-West* (Chicago, 1932), 222.

3. Milo M. Quaife, "Historical Introduction," in Kinzie, *Wau-Bun*, xxxiv. See also Ulrich Danckers and Jane Meredith, *Early Chicago* (River Forest, IL, 1999), 147–48; and Henry H. Hurlbut, *Chicago Antiquities* (Chicago, 1881), 469. On Detroit, see Brian Leigh Dunnigan, *Frontier Metropolis: Picturing Early Detroit, 1701–1838* (Detroit, 2001), 70.

4. Juliette Kinzie described that at the age of ten or eleven, John Kinzie made his way to Quebec, apprenticed with a silversmith, and then returned to his family at Detroit. Kinzie, *Wau-Bun*, 223–24. The arrangement might have been something like the one that William Burnett considered for his son Isaac in Detroit in 1804. See William Burnett to James May, November 20, 1804, quoted in *Letter Book of William Burnett*, ed. Wilbur M. Cunningham (Niles, MI, 1967), 170.

5. Copy of 1785 account between John Casety and John Kinzie, John Kinzie Collection, Chicago History Museum; original at Burton Historical Society sent to the Chicago Historical Society in 1939 by Milo Quaife.

6. We have a wonderful window into the world at Kekionga and Fort Miami because Henry Hay, son of the British Indian agent at Detroit, wrote about his time there in 1789 and 1790. Hay confirms that Kinzie worked at Kekionga as a silversmith and trader. Hay described how Kinzie played "his fiddle indifferently for drinking bout and mass," and at another point in his account he noted that he "got infernally drunk last night with Mr. Abbot and Mr. Kinzie." Henry Hay, "Journal from Detroit to the Miami River," quoted in Milo M. Quaife, *Chicago and the Old Northwest* (Chicago, 1913), 145–46.

7. Alexander McKee, Matthew Elliott, and Simon Girty were longtime traders with the Shawnees in the Ohio Valley. In March 1778 all three fled Pittsburgh to Detroit and joined the British Indian service. Helen Hornbeck Tanner, "The Glaize in 1792: A Composite Indian Community," *Ethnohistory* 25, no. 1 (1978): 26–27. See also Ronald Horsman, *Matthew Elliott, British Indian Agent* (Detroit, 1964).

8. Richard C. Wade, *The Urban Frontier: Pioneer Life in Early Pittsburgh, Cincinnati, Lexington, Louisville, and St. Louis* (Chicago, 1959), 1. Wade takes up the role of the frontier in American history, arguing that cities were the spearheads of the frontier. This is a critical insight, but Wade does

not accept urban systems beyond those of the United States, leaving much of the regional map empty when, in fact, it was a rich mixture of systems within Indian Country.

9. Richard White has called the world based in the fur trade "a middle ground." See White, *The Middle Ground: Indians, Empires, and Republics in the Great Lakes Region, 1650–1815* (New York, 1991). More recently, Alan Taylor has described it as a "divided ground." See Taylor, *The Divided Ground: Indians, Settlers, and the Northern Borderland of the American Revolution* (New York, 2006). Carolyn Gilman describes the fur trade "as an example of how two radically dissimiliar cultures establish a common ground of understanding without sacrificing their unique characteristics and without annihilating one another. The fur trade is the story of how people act when they meet the Other: the stranger, the puzzling change in accepted wisdom, the rapid onslaught of the future." Gilman, *Where Two Worlds Meet: The Great Lakes Fur Trade* (Minneapolis, 1982), 1.

10. Jacqueline Peterson, "Prelude to Red River: A Social Portrait of the Great Lakes Metis," *Ethnohistory* 25, no. 1 (1978): 46.

11. Ibid., 53.

12. Ibid., 44–45.

13. Colin G. Calloway, *The Scratch of a Pen: 1763 and the Transformation of North America* (New York, 2006), 76–81.

14. For more discussion on Kakima, see Susan Sleeper-Smith, *Indian Women and French Men: Rethinking Cultural Encounter in the Western Great Lakes* (Amherst, MA, 2001), 74–85.

15. Burnett to William Hands, February 2, 1790, quoted in *Letter Book of William Burnett*, ed. Cunningham, 31–32. See also Sleeper-Smith, *Indian Women and French Men*, 91.

16. Susan Sleeper-Smith, "The American Revolution in the Western Great Lakes," in *The Sixty Years' War for the Great Lakes, 1754–1814*, ed. David Curtis Skagus and Larry L. Nelson (East Lansing, MI, 2001), 148.

17. Margaret Kimball Brown, *History as They Lived It: A Social History of Prairie du Rocher, Ill.* (Tucson, AZ, 2005), 17; Kaskaskia Manuscript Collection, Document 46:10:8:1, Randolph County Archives, quoted in (and translated by) Carl J. Ekberg, Grady Kilman, and Pierre Lebeau, *Code Noir: The Colonial Slave Laws of French Mid-America* (Naperville, IL, n.d.), 62–63. John Swenson, an intrepid researcher of the eighteenth and early nineteenth centuries in the Chicago region, first suggested that Point de Sable could be from Kaskaskia in an unpublished 2006 paper.

18. Henry H. Sibley, writing in 1830, quoted in James R. Grossman, Ann Durkin Keating, and Janice Reiff, *Encyclopedia of Chicago* (Chicago, 2004), 317.

19. Frank Reed Grover, *Antoine Ouilmette* (Evanston, IL, 1908), 4, writes that Ouilmette came to Chicago in the employ of the American Fur Company in 1790. However, the American Fur Company was not organized until 1808, so perhaps Ouilmette worked for the Northwest Fur Company, organized in 1779. See Pierre Lebeau, "Fur Trade," in Grossman, Keating, Reiff, *Encyclopedia of Chicago*, 320–21.

20. Quaife, *Chicago and the Old Northwest*, 143–45.

21. The most complete biography of Archange Ouilmette is by Katherine Hussey-Arnston, in *Women Building Chicago: A Biographical Dictionary, 1790–1990*, ed. Rima Lunin Schultz and Adele Hast (Bloomington, IN, 2001), 653–54. Danckers and Meredith, *Early Chicago*, 280, write that Archange was the daughter of François and Marianne Chevalier born at Sugar Creek, Michigan, in 1764 and a sister of both Sheshi Buisson (married to Louis) and Catherine Robinson (Catherine married Alexander in 1826). However, there is some question about the year of her birth, with 1781 being an alternative to 1764. It is curious that while Archange was married in 1796, her first child was born in 1807. Perhaps there were children born earlier who died. It also seems possible that she was not born at Sugar Creek, Michigan. It appears that she died at or near a mission at Sugar Creek, Kansas, and her birth and death place may have been confused. It seems more likely that she was born in the Calumet region.

Chapter Two

1. Anthony F. C. Wallace, *Jefferson and the Indians: The Tragic Fate of the First Americans* (Cambridge, MA, 1999), 163. As Alan Taylor has recently noted: "By repetition in documents and sub-

sequent historians, the supposed sovereign right of preemption has been naturalized: taken for granted as if it were real. In fact, preemption was imposed to benefit the regimes that invaded Indian country." See Taylor, *The Divided Ground: Indians, Settlers, and the Northern Borderland of the American Revolution* (New York, 2006), 10–11.

2. Helen Hornbeck Tanner, ed., *Atlas of Great Lakes Indian History* (Norman, OK, 1987), 70.

3. Daniel K. Richter, *Facing East from Indian Country: A Native History of Early America* (Cambridge, MA, 2001), 216–17.

4. Alexander McKee and Joseph Brant were part of the British expeditionary force to Kentucky in 1781. See Henry Louis Carter, *The Life and Times of Little Turtle, First Sagamore of the Wabash* (Urbana, IL, 1987), 82–83. The spelling of the name of the village that Wells was taken to is that in Tanner, *Atlas of Great Lakes Indian History,* 85.

5. Carter, *Life and Times of Little Turtle,* 84; Paul Hutton, "William Wells: Frontier Scout and Indian Agent," *Indiana Magazine of History* 74, no. 3 (September 1978): 184.

6. Carter, *Life and Times of Little Turtle,* 91–96.

7. Hutton, "William Wells," 189. See also Carter, *Life and Times of Little Turtle,* 115. Richard White argues that Wells "was a servant of empire but had deep loyalties to the people whose interests the country he served sought to subvert." See White, *The Middle Ground: Indians, Empires, and Republics in the Great Lakes Region, 1650–1815* (New York, 1991), 500–501.

8. Carter, *Life and Times of Little Turtle,* 134.

9. Timothy Willig, *Restoring the Chain of Friendship: British Policy and the Indians of the Great Lakes, 1783–1815* (Lincoln, NE, 2008), 248–49.

10. Ronald Horsman, *Matthew Elliott, British Indian Agent* (Detroit, 1964), 101–2.

11. White, *The Middle Ground,* 472. See also Tanner, *Atlas of Great Lakes Indian History,* 91.

12. Dwight L. Smith and Mrs. Frank Roberts, "William Wells and the Indian Council of 1793," *Indiana Magazine of History* 56, no. 3 (September 1960): 217–26.

13. They also met Constantin-François Chasseboeuf, Comte de Volney, a French scholar whose acquaintance Thomas Jefferson had made during his sojourns in Paris. Volney was particularly interested in studying Native American languages and customs. He met with Wells and Little Turtle many times. See C.-F. Volney, *A View of the Soil and Climate of the United States of America* (London, 1804).

14. Hutton, "William Wells," 203.

15. David B. Stout and Erminie Wheeler-Voegelin, *Indians of Illinois and Northwest Indiana* (New York, 1974), 407–8.

16. R. David Edmunds, *The Shawnee Prophet* (Lincoln, NE, 1983), 65.

17. Stout and Wheeler-Voegelin, *Indians of Illinois and Northwest Indiana,* 301. See also Sleeper-Smith, *Indian Women and French Men: Rethinking Cultural Encounter in the Western Great Lakes* (Amherst, MA, 2001), 87.

18. John Hay to Governor Edwards, May 31, 1812, Ninian Edwards Papers, Chicago History Museum.

19. In 1795 some of these warriors attacked a farm in southern Illinois, killing five and taking prisoners. Before the retaliation and response and further retaliation were finished, the matter involved the Spanish government at St. Louis, American officials at Kaskaskia, the Peoria Potawatomis (who were murdered by a white mob), and the Illinois Confederacy. See R. David Edmunds, *The Potawatomis: Keepers of the Fire* (Norman, OK, 1978), 134.

20. Ibid., 154, 185.

21. On Gomo and Little Turtle, see Report of Thomas Forsyth to the Secretary of War James Monroe, quoted in C. Henry Smith, *Metamora* (Bluffton, OH, 1947), 53.

22. Waubansee, or Foggy Day, was Black Partridge's younger brother, who had connections at Peoria but also a summer village on the Fox River near what is today Aurora. See Stout and Wheeler-Voegelin, *Indians of Illinois and Northwest Indiana,* 232; and Smith, *Metamora,* 24.

23. Milo M. Quaife, "Historical Introduction," quoted in Mrs. John H. (Juliette) Kinzie, *Wau-Bun: The "Early Day" in the North-West* (Chicago, 1932), xxxvi. There were about five hundred people in the town, with estimates of twelve hundred when including the farmers in the area. As

one longtime trader at Mackinac, George Meldrum, noted in 1796: "Everything has a new face . . . nothing is changed in business, but the New Appearance is not very agreeable to Many who has long breathed under the British Government." Quoted in F. Clever Bald, *Detroit's First American Decade, 1796–1805* (Ann Arbor, MI, 1948), 27–29.

24. *Collections of the Michigan Pioneer and Historical Society*, vol. 8 (Lansing, MI, 1886), 410–11. Alan Taylor presents a different view of evolving notions of citizenship in *The Civil War of 1812: American Citizens, British Subjects, Irish Rebels, and Indian Allies* (New York, 2010), 3–5, 101–3.

25. Kinzie, *Wau-Bun*, 325, 329.

26. Quaife, "Historical Introduction," xxxix.

27. Copy of marriage certification in John Kinzie Collection, Chicago History Museum. As Milo Quaife noted, "It would have been difficult to find in all America in 1795 two people who had better grounded reasons for hating and fearing the United States than John Kinzie and Eleanor McKillip." See Quaife, "Historical Introduction," xli.

28. William Burnett to Mr. Robert Innes & Co., September 26, 1797; Burnett to Innes, November 2, 1797; Burnett to Robert McKenzie, December 20, 1798. All quoted in *Letter Book of William Burnett*, ed. Wilbur M. Cunningham (Niles, MI, 1967), 86–87, 91, 114.

29. There is a possibility that Lalime was the son of Joseph Lepine dit Lalime, a Quebec trader. His wife, Marie Roy, then married Jean Corpron. See George W. Brown et al., *Dictionary of Canadian Biography* (Toronto, 1981), 142.

30. William Burnett to Messrs. Meldrum & Park, May 25, 1786, quoted in *Letter Book of William Burnett*, ed. Cunningham, 8–9. See also Burnett to William Hands, Detroit, June 30, 1786; and Burnett to John Casety, August 22, 1786, quoted in ibid., 15–16, 24–25.

31. July 18 and June 8, 1797, William Burnett Day Book, Detroit Public Library, transcribed by Gail Moreau-DesHarnais for John Swenson.

32. Burnett to Messrs. Parker Gerrard & Ogilvy, August 24, 1798, quoted in *Letter Book of William Burnett*, ed. Cunningham, 107–8.

33. Inventory of Point de Sable's property, September 18, 1800, DuSable Collection, Chicago History Museum. Soon after the sale, Burnett outfitted Point de Sable with trade goods, and he moved south, ultimately to St. Charles, Missouri. The transaction has been misrepresented in most nineteenth-century histories. Juliette Kinzie incorrectly states that Point de Sable's property was purchased by François Le Mai, not Jean Lalime.

Chapter Three

1. The standard source on Chicago in this era is Milo M. Quaife, *Chicago and the Old Northwest* (Chicago, 1913). Also, Ulrich Danckers and Jane Meredith, *Early Chicago* (River Forest, IL, 1999), provides much new information. Nineteenth-century histories are useful but should be read with an eye toward exaggeration and possible misstatements. See especially A. T. Andreas, *History of Chicago*, 3 vols. (Chicago 1884); and Henry H. Hurlbut, *Chicago Antiquities* (Chicago, 1881).

2. Anthony F. C. Wallace, *Jefferson and the Indians: The Tragic Fate of the First Americans* (Cambridge, MA, 1999), 206. Other books on Jefferson useful to thinking about the Midwest and the settlement around Fort Dearborn include Daniel K. Richter, *Facing East from Indian Country: A Native History of Early America* (Cambridge, MA, 2001); and Bernard Sheehan, *Seeds of Extinction: Jeffersonian Philanthropy and the American Indian* (Chapel Hill, NC, 1973).

3. James E. Davis, *Frontier Illinois* (Bloomington, IN, 1998) 115; Andrew R. L. Cayton, *Frontier Indiana* (Bloomington, IN, 1996), 175–76.

4. Robert M. Owens, "Jeffersonian Benevolence on the Ground: The Indian Land Cession Treaties of William Henry Harrison," *Journal of the Early Republic* 22, no. 3 (Autumn 2002): 406–7.

5. President Jefferson message to Miamis, Potawatomis, and Weas, January 7, 1802, Potawatomi File, Great Lakes Indian Archives, Indiana University.

6. Conference held with Little Turtle and other Indian chiefs (Miami, Wea, and Potawatomi), Washington, January 4–7, 1802, in ibid.

7. William Wells to Gen. James Wilkinson, October 6, 1804, in ibid.

8. Henry Louis Carter, *The Life and Times of Little Turtle, First Sagamore of the Wabash* (Urbana, IL, 1987), 15–16, 90–91.

9. William Wells to the Secretary of War, April 20, 1808 (postscript April 23, 1808), quoted in Clarence Edwin Carter, ed., *The Territorial Papers of the United States*, 26 vols. (Washington, D.C., 1939), 7:555.

10. Gerard T. Hopkins, *A Mission to the Indians from the Indian Committee of Baltimore Yearly Meeting to Fort Wayne in 1804*, Potawatomi File, Great Lakes Indian Archives, Indiana University.

11. Henry Dearborn to William Henry Harrison, June 17, 1802, in ibid.

12. William Wells to Gen. James Wilkinson Fort Wayne, October 6, 1804, in ibid.

13. Secretary of War to William Wells, May 26, 1803, quoted in Carter, *Territorial Papers*, 7:115.

14. Secretary of War to William Wells, March 27, 1804, quoted in ibid., 7:187.

15. *Baltimore Daily Intelligencer*, November 2, 1793, quoted in Alan D. Gaff, *Bayonets in the Wilderness: Anthony Wayne's Legion in the Old Northwest* (Norman, OK, 2004), 142.

16. Journal of Lieutenant James Strode Swearingen, "Remarks on the Road from Detroit to Chicago," July–August 1803, quoted in Quaife, *Chicago and the Old Northwest*, 373–77. There is no evidence that Whistler and Wells met in their travels, but both were in communication with William Burnett during the summer of 1803.

17. According to Captain John Whistler's daughter-in-law Julia, they found four trader cabins occupied by Canadian Frenchmen with Indian wives. See Hurlbut, *Chicago Antiquities*, 25.

18. President Jefferson's Third Annual Message, October 17, 1803, where he discusses the projected purchase of Louisiana and the acquisition of a large territory from the Kaskaskias in what is now Illinois. Quoted in *The Life and Selected Writings of Thomas Jefferson*, ed. Adrienne Koch and William Peden (New York, 1993), 310–11.

19. Captain John Whistler to Colonel Jacob Kingsbury, August 12, 1804; Kingsbury to Inspector's Office, February 20, 1805; Kingsbury Papers, Chicago History Museum.

20. Colonel Jacob Kingsbury to Clerk, April 26, 1805, Kingsbury Papers, Chicago History Museum.

21. George Whistler graduated from West Point at age nineteen. He eventually left the U.S. Army to build railroads in Russia. His son was the artist James Abbott McNeil Whistler. See Quaife, *Chicago and the Old Northwest*, 169.

22. Captain John Whistler to Colonel Jacob Kingsbury, July 12, 1805, Kingsbury Papers, Chicago History Museum.

23. Jane F. Babson, "The Architecture of Early Illinois Forts," *Journal of the Illinois State Historical Society* 61, no. 1 (Spring 1968): 36–37.

24. Colonel Jacob Kingsbury, June 12, 1804, Kingsbury Papers, Chicago History Museum; Arthur H. Frazier, "The Military Frontier: Fort Dearborn," *Chicago History* 9, no. 2 (Summer 1980): 82.

25. James Grant Wilson, "Chicago from 1802 to 1812," unpublished manuscript, Chicago History Museum.

26. Nathan Heald tried to deflate the rumors about how much corn Whistler grew at Chicago when he became commander at Chicago in 1810. See Captain Heald to Colonel Kingsbury, May 31, 1810, Kingsbury Papers, Chicago History Museum. Eventually, Whistler was accused of assigning a soldier to do his personal business. See Lt. Seth Thompson to Colonel Kingsbury, May 1, 1810, Kingsbury Papers, Chicago History Museum.

27. Matthew Irwin to Colonel Jacob Kingsbury, April 29, 1810, Kingsbury Papers, Chicago History Museum.

28. Lt. Philip Ostrander to Colonel Jacob Kingsbury, January 4, 1811, Kingsbury Papers, Chicago History Museum.

29. Danckers and Meredith, *Early Chicago*, 151.

30. Matthew Irwin to Colonel Jacob Kingsbury, April 29, 1810, Kingsbury Papers, Chicago His-

tory Museum. Alan Taylor discusses the problems of supply in the War of 1812 in *The Civil War of 1812: American Citizens, British Subjects, Irish Rebels, and Indian Allies* (New York, 2010), 344–47.

31. Captain Nathan Heald to Colonel Jacob Kingsbury, May 31, 1810, Kingsbury Papers, Chicago History Museum.

32. Lt. Seth Thompson to Colonel Kingsbury, May 1, 1810, Kingsbury Papers, Chicago History Museum; Captain Nathan Heald to Secretary of War William Eustis, June 9, 1811, Potawatomi File, Great Lakes Indian Archives, Indiana University. On one occasion, Captain Whistler mustered a soldier into special service as a teamster for the garrison (without extra wages), while at the same time paying another soldier extra to do the same work.

33. Milo M. Quaife, "The Story of James Corbin, a Soldier at Fort Dearborn," *Mississippi Valley Historical Review* 3, no. 3 (September 1916): 221–22.

34. Thomas Forsyth described James Leigh as having a brother-in-law and father-in-law at Chicago. Thomas Forsyth to William Clark, July 20, 1812, Potawatomi File, Great Lakes Indian Archives, Indiana University.

35. James Leigh to Colonel Jacob Kingsbury, March 30, 1811, Kingsbury Papers, Chicago History Museum; Thomas Forsyth to William Clark, July 20, 1812, Potawatomi File, Great Lakes Indian Archives, Indiana University. In addition to Russell and Leigh, another discharged soldier who stayed at Chicago was Thomas Burns, who married a widow, Mary Cooper, who lived in a house on the north bank of the Chicago River. See Quaife, *Chicago and the Old Northwest*, 212, 253.

36. Bessie Louise Pierce, *History of Chicago*, 3 vols. (Chicago, 1937), 1:17.

37. Mrs. John H. (Juliette) Kinzie, *Wau-Bun: The "Early Day" in the North-West* (Chicago, 1932), 242; Danckers and Meredith, *Early Chicago*, 56.

38. Hurlbut, *Chicago Antiquities*, 102–3, 107.

39. Head Papers, Chicago History Museum; Hurlbut, *Chicago Antiquities*, 102–3.

40. Charles Jouett to the Secretary of War, Chicago, February 20, 1807, quoted in Carter, *Territorial Papers*, 7:430. After several years of correspondence, Jouett decided that it would be wise to meet Harrison in person. Ibid. Jouett moved many annuity payments to Chicago and was so successful that that by 1807 William Wells was protesting that the Potawatomis at Fort Wayne were severely inconvenienced by having to travel to Chicago. See William Wells to Henry Dearborn, Fort Wayne, October 20, 1807, Potawatomi Archive, Great Lakes Indian Archives, Indiana University.

41. Jouett to the Secretary of War, December 1, 1807, quoted in Carter, *Territorial Papers*, 7:479.

42. Ibid.

43. Jouett to the Secretary of War, August 22, 1807, quoted in ibid, 7:472.

44. Thomas Jefferson to Foxes, Sac, and Potwatomis, January 4, 1805, Potawatomi File, Great Lakes Indian Archives, Indiana University.

45. John Mason to Matthew Irwin, September 9, 1808, quoted in ibid, 7:586.

46. Ebenezer Belknap was appointed the first factor at Chicago in 1805. He was followed by Joseph B. Varnum, the son of an influential Massachusetts congressman. Varnum moved to Mackinac in 1808, making room for Irwin's appointment.

47. Lyman C. Draper, "The Fur Trade and Factory System at Green Bay," *Collections of the State Historical Society of Wisconsin* 7 (1876): 267–68.

48. John Mason to Joseph B. Varnum Jr., September 10, 1808, quoted in Clarence Edwin Carter, ed., *The Territorial Papers of the United States*, 26 vols. (Washington, DC, 1942), 10:233; John Mason to Matthew Irwin, May 6, 1809, quoted in Carter, *Territorial Papers*, 7:35. See also Quaife, *Chicago and the Old Northwest*, 298–301.

49. John Mason to Matthew Irwin, September 9, 1808, quoted in Carter, *Territorial Papers*, 7:586.

50. Quaife, *Chicago and the Old Northwest*, 300–304.

51. Charles Jouett and Joseph B. Varnum Jr. to the Secretary of War, August 17, 1808, quoted in Carter, *Territorial Papers*, 7:583.

52. John Mason to Matthew Irwin, September 9, 1808, quoted in ibid., 7:586.

Chapter Four

1. Ulrich Danckers and Jane Meredith, *Early Chicago* (River Forest, IL, 1999), 129; *The Autobiography of Gurdon Saltonstall Hubbard*, ed. Caroline M. McIlvaine (Chicago, 1911), 29.

2. Margaret Kimball Brown, *History as They Lived It: A Social History of Prairie du Rocher, Ill.* (Tuscon, AZ, 2005), 197.

3. Captain Nathan Heald to Secretary of War William Eustis, June 9, 1811, Potawatomi File, Great Lakes Indian Archives, Indiana University; Antoine LeClair statement taken by Lyman C. Draper, Potawatomi File, Great Lakes Indian Archives, Indiana University.

4. A. T. Andreas, *History of Chicago*, 3 vols. (Chicago, 1884), 1:105.

5. Ibid.; and Danckers and Meredith, *Early Chicago*, 229.

6. Henry H. Hurlbut, *Chicago Antiquities* (Chicago, 1881), 304. Mary Hammersmith, in her chronology of the Beaubien brothers, states that he did not leave home until 1802, when he went to Mackinac. See Beaubien Papers, Naper Settlement. See also George R. Lee, *The Beaubiens of Chicago* (Chicago, 1973), 10.

7. Lee, *The Beaubiens of Chicago*, 14–15.

8. Hammersmith has her as the daughter of Chief Shabbona, while Lee, *The Beaubiens of Chicago*, 15, states she was a sister of Shabbona.

9. Robinson could not read or write, but David McKee reported that he kept accurate accounts with pencil and paper by means of characters of his own to represent quantities and that he "was a model of uprightness." See Danckers and Meredith, *Early Chicago*, 301–2.

10. Mrs. John H. (Juliette) Kinzie, *Wau-Bun: The "Early Day" in the North-West* (Chicago, 1932), 210–11.

11. Black Jim made purchases that showed up in Kinzie's ledger at least two times. The ledger also included the sale by indenture of a "negro wench." Slaves were both customers and property. Barry Transcript, Kinzie Account Books, Chicago History Museum. See Ira Berlin and Philip D. Morgan, introduction to *The Slaves' Economy: Independent Production by Slaves in the Americas* (London, 1991).

12. Antoine LeClair statement taken by Lyman C. Draper, Potawatomi File, Great Lakes Indian Archives, Indiana University.

13. Kinzie and Forsyth, Ledger A, folio 97, Felix Fountaine for February 25, 1812, shows payment for making 3½ dozen shirts; folio 102: Joseph Lafortune shows payment on February 22, 1808, for making two shirts; Thomas Forsyth Papers, Missouri Historical Society.

14. Brown, *History as They Lived It*, 191; and folio 28, September 6, 1806, to June 6, 1807, Madam Grandbois, Kinzie & Forsyth Ledger A, Thomas Forsyth Papers, Missouri Historical Society. I am indebted to Linda L. Sturtz for suggesting a close look at women's place in these ledgers. See *Within Her Power: Propertied Women in Colonial Virginia* (New York, 2002), 25. On "made-up work," see David Lavender, *The Fist in the Wilderness* (Lincoln, NE, 1998), 256.

15. *Autobiography of Gurdon Saltonstall Hubbard*, 630.

16. Thomas Forsyth to the Secretary of War, April 10, 1813, quoted in Clarence Edwin Carter, ed., *The Territorial Papers of the United States*, 26 vols. (Washington, DC, 1948), 16:310–12. See also Susan Sleeper-Smith, *Indian Women and French Men: Rethinking Cultural Encounter in the Western Great Lakes* (Amherst, MA, 2001), 74–85.

17. Kinzie mended the shoe buckle of one of Detroit's leading merchants. Copy of 1785 account between John Casety and John Kinzie, John Kinzie Collection, Chicago History Museum.

18. Barry Transcript, Kinzie Account Book, Chicago History Museum, provides the names of customers but only occasionally the items purchased. The original was destroyed in the Chicago Fire of 1871. The Kinzie and Forysth Account Book, Peoria, Thomas Forsyth Papers, Missouri Historical Society, offers a good sense of items traded.

19. Kinzie, *Wau-Bun*, 226.

20. Point de Sable signed his name with an X as did many others in this era. See Draper Collection, Series T, Forsyth Papers, microfilm reel 53, where Gurdon Hubbard described the "hieroglyphics" one trader used in his autobiography. See *Autobiography of Gurdon Saltonstall Hubbard*, 47.

21. Antoine LeClair statement taken by Lyman C. Draper, Potawatomi File, Great Lakes Indian Archives, Indiana University; Draper Collection, Series T, Forsyth Papers, microfilm reel 53.

22. Danckers and Meredith, *Early Chicago*, 102.

23. Milo M. Quaife, *Chicago and the Old Northwest, 1673–1835* (Urbana, IL, 2001), 150–51.

24. The Kinzie "mansion," in comparison, was twenty-two by forty feet. See Carter, *Territorial Papers*, 16:379–83. See also Memorial to Congress from Inhabitants of Peoria, December 20, 1813, Potawatomi File, Great Lakes Indian Archives, Indiana University. For Kinzie mansion dimensions, see Danckers and Meredith, *Early Chicago*, 218–19. The Forsyths had two more children, Thomas and Mary, born in 1815 and 1817, at St. Louis.

25. Alexander McKenzie to Thomas Forsyth, December 22, 1797, William Clark Papers, Wisconsin Historical Society.

26. *Autobiography of Gurdon Saltonstall Hubbard*, 16–17.

27. John Denis Haeger, *John Jacob Astor: Business and Finance in the Early Republic* (Detroit, 1991), 52–53.

28. Milo M. Quaife, ed., *John Askin Papers*, 2 vols. (Detroit, 1928), 1:8–9.

29. *Letter Book of William Burnett*, ed. Wilbur M. Cunningham (Niles, MI, 1967), 175–76.

30. Jeremy Adelman and Stephen Aron, "Trading Cultures: The Worlds of Western Merchants," in *Trading Cultures: The Worlds of Western Merchants*, ed. Jeremy Adelman and Stephen Aron (Tornhout, Belgium, 2001), 5.

31. Alexander McKee, Letter to the Potawatomi Indians, November 1804, Potawatomi File, Great Lakes Indian Archives, Indiana University.

Chapter Five

1. Timothy D. Willig, "Prophetstown on the Wabash: The Native Spiritual Defense of the Old Northwest," *Michigan Historical Review* 23, no. 2 (Fall 1997): 118.

2. Core texts on Tecumseh and Tenskwatawa include Gregory Evans Dowd, *A Spirited Resistance: The North American Indian Struggle for Unity, 1745–1815* (Baltimore, 1992); John Sugden, *Tecumseh: A Life* (New York, 1997); R. David Edmunds, *The Shawnee Prophet* (Lincoln, NE, 1983); and R. David Edmunds, *Tecumseh and the Quest for Indian Leadership* (New York, 1984). On Main Poc, see R. David Edmunds, "Main Poc: Potawatomi Wabeno," in *American Indian Prophets: Religious Leaders and Revitalization Movements*, ed. Clifford E. Trafzer (Sierra Oaks, CA, 1986), 21–34.

3. Edmunds, *The Shawnee Prophet*, 3; Thomas Forsyth to William Clark, January 15, 1827, in the Draper Collection, Forsyth Papers, microfilm vol. 9T52–3.

4. William Wells to the Secretary of War, April 20, 1808, quoted in Clarence Edwin Carter, ed., *The Territorial Papers of the United States*, 26 vols. (Washington, DC, 1939), 7:555.

5. Ibid.

6. Speech delivered at Le Maioutinong by the Indian chief Le Maigouis or the Trout, May 4, 1807, Potawatomi File, Great Lakes Indian Archives, Indiana University.

7. Ibid. See also Dowd, *A Spirited Resistance*, 144.

8. Constantin Volney, quoted in Anthony F. C. Wallace, *Jefferson and the Indians: The Tragic Fate of the First Americans* (Cambridge, MA, 1999), 213. For discussion on liquor and western Indians, see ibid., 211–13; and Dowd, *A Spirited Resistance*, 144. Also see Colin G. Calloway, *Crown and Calumet: British-Indian Relations, 1783–1815* (Norman, OK, 1987); and Peter Mancall, *Deadly Medicine: Indians and Alcohol in Early America* (Ithaca, NY, 1995).

9. William Wells to Secretary of War, January 7, 1808, Potawatomi File, Great Lakes Indian Archive, Indiana University.

10. William Wells to the Secretary of War, April 2, 1808, quoted in Carter, *Territorial Papers*, 7:540; and Wells to Dearborn, January 7, 1808, Potawatomi File, Great Lakes Indian Archives, Indiana University.

11. William Wells to the Secretary of War, April 20, 1808, quoted in Carter, *Territorial Papers*, 7:555.

12. Secretary of State Dearborn to William Wells, March 10, 1808, Potawatomi File, Great Lakes Indian Archives, Indiana University. William Wells claimed to have moved Main Poc

"from a dangerous man" to "a useful one to the US." See William Wells to Henry Dearborn, June 30, 1808, in ibid.

13. Jonathan Smith to William Wells, August 2, 1808, in ibid.

14. Gerard T. Hopkins, *A Mission to the Indians from the Indian Committee of Baltimore Yearly Meeting to Fort Wayne in 1804*, Potawatomi File, Great Lakes Indian Archives, Indiana University.

15. Ibid.

16. Ibid.

17. Ibid.

18. Thomas Jefferson to the Potawatomi, December 1808, Potawatomi File, Great Lakes Indian Archives, Indiana University.

19. Hopkins, *A Mission to the Indians.*

20. William Wells to the Secretary of War, April 20, 1808, quoted in Carter, *Territorial Papers*, 7:555.

21. Thomas Jefferson to the Potawatomi, December 1808, Potawatomi File, Great Lakes Indian Archives, Indiana University.

22. Thomas Jefferson, Second Inaugural Address, March 4, 1804, in *The Life and Selected Writings of Thomas Jefferson*, ed. Adrienne Koch and William Peden (New York, 1993), 316.

23. William Wells to Henry Dearborn, October 20, 1807, Potawatomi File, Great Lakes Indian Archives, Indiana University.

24. These complaints were not specific to these two treaties. See David Agee Horr, "General Nature and Content of the Series" (Garland American Indian Ethnohistory series), quoted in David B. Stout and Ermine Wheeler-Voegelin, *Indians of Illinois and Northwestern Indiana* (New York, 1974), 9.

25. Paul A. Hutton, "William Wells: Frontier Scout and Indian Agent," *Indiana Magazine of History* 74, no. 3 (September 1978): 212–13. Captain Nathan Heald and his family lived near the Geigers in Kentucky and again in Missouri after the War of 1812. See Heald Journal, quoted in Milo M. Quaife, *Chicago and the Old Northwest* (Chicago, 1913), 404–5.

26. Wayne C. Temple, *Indian Villages of the Illinois Country: Historic Tribes* (Springfield, IL, 1958), 70.

27. Robert M. Owens, "Jeffersonian Benevolence on the Ground: The Indian Land Cession Treaties of William Henry Harrison," *Journal of the Early Republic* 22, no. 3 (Autumn 2002): 432.

28. "A Treaty Between the United States of America and the Tribes of Indians called the Delawares, Pattawatamies, Miamies, and Eel River Miamies," September 30, 1809, Potawatomi File, Great Lakes Indian Archives, Indiana University.

29. William Wells to Secretary of War William Eustis, December 20, 1811, in ibid.

30. William Wells to the Secretary of War, April 20, 1808, quoted in Carter, *Territorial Papers*, 7:555. See also Edmunds, *The Shawnee Prophet*, 92; and Marshall Smelser, "Tecumseh, Harrison, and the War of 1812," *Indiana Magazine of History* 65, no. 1 (March 1969): 25–44.

Chapter Six

1. In this chapter, I have relied on the work of several scholars. On William Henry Harrison, see Andrew R. L. Cayton, *Frontier Indiana* (Bloomington, IN, 1996); Freeman Cleaves, *Old Tippecanoe: William Henry Harrison and His Time* (New York, 1939); and *Messages and Letters of William Henry Harrison*, vol. 1, ed. Logan Esarey (New York, 1975). On the U.S. Army, see Richard M. Lytle, *The Soldiers of America's First Army* (Lanham, MD, 2004). On Tippecanoe, see especially John Sugden, *Tecumseh: A Life* (New York, 1997); R. David Edmunds, *The Shawnee Prophet* (Lincoln, NE, 1983); and Alfred A. Cave, "The Shawnee Prophet, Tecumseh, and Tippecanoe: A Case Study of Historical Myth-Making," *Journal of the Early Republic* 22, no. 4 (Winter 2002): 637–73. On Governor Ninian Edwards, see Ninian Edwards, *History of Illinois from 1778 to 1833 and the Life and Times of Ninian Edwards* (Springfield, IL, 1879).

2. Although he was born in New Ipswich, New Hampshire, Heald would return to Concord regularly over the course of his adult life. New Ipswich was a growing town with hundreds of residents, who supported local churches and schools. Nathan may have received a basic education at a local academy with affiliations to neighboring Dartmouth University. Heald

served at Fort Massac for over four years, during which time he probably traveled to Vincennes and St. Louis and likely encountered Governor Harrison. See Heald Journal, quoted in Milo M. Quaife, *Chicago and the Old Northwest* (Chicago, 1913), 402.

3. Samuel Wells was born in 1754. Samuel Wells had already been married once when Rebekah was born, to Mary Rebecca Pope, who had died in childbirth. Samuel Wells was widowed a second time and subsequently married Margaret Audrain Hoffman. Wells advertised his chestnut sorrel as a stud horse in the local paper in 1802. See "The First American West: The Ohio River Valley, 1750–1820," at the American Memory website (www.memory.loc.gov).

4. For instance, in 1795 a group promised to pay a certain sum for "every Indian scalp taken in the County of Jefferson on the west of the Main Road leading from Louisville to Shepherdsville." While Sweet Breeze could have avoided this threat by staying on the family farm, it must have been difficult for her and probably for her children. Ibid.

5. Elizabeth F. Ellet, *The Pioneer Woman of the West* (Philadelphia, 1852), 283.

6. Matthew Irwin to the Secretary of War, December 30, 1809, quoted in Clarence Edwin Carter, ed., *The Territorial Papers of the United States*, 26 vols. (Washington, DC, 1948), 14:66–68. See also Lt. Seth Thompson to Colonel Jacob Kingsbury, May 1, 1810, Kingsbury Papers, Chicago History Museum.

7. Postscript in Gallatin's hand to a letter from Matthew Irwin to the Secretary of War, October 30, 1811, quoted in Carter, *Territorial Papers*, 16:179.

8. Captain Nathan Heald to Colonel Jacob Kingsbury, June 8, 1810, Kingsbury Papers, Chicago History Museum.

9. N. Heald at Fort Wayne to Col. Kingsbury, June 17, 1811; Lieut. Helm at Fort Detroit to Col. Jacob Kingsbury, March 16, 1811; L. T. Helm at Fort Dearborn to Col. J. Kingsbury, August 10, 1811. All in the Jacob Kingsbury Papers, Chicago History Museum.

10. Main Poc was injured in one raid in 1810 and spent much of the following winter recovering from his injuries. Many of Main Poc's supporters thought he was "invulnerable to all weapons." Quoted in "An Account of the Manners and Customs of the Sauk and Fox Nations of Indian Tradition by Thomas Forsyth," sent as letter from Forsyth to General William Clark, Superintendent of Indian Affairs, St. Louis, January 15, 1827, quoted in Emma Helen Blair, ed., *The Indian Tribes of the Upper Mississippi Valley and Region of the Great Lakes* (Cleveland, 1912), 2:203.

11. Edwards, *History of Illinois*, 45–47.

12. *Messages and Letters of William Henry Harrison*, 1:511; William Clark to William Eustis, July 3, 1811, Potawatomi File, Great Lakes Indian Archives, Indiana University.

13. Thomas Forsyth to General William Clark, December 31, 1812 quoted in Blair, *Indian Tribes of the Upper Mississippi Valley*, 273.

14. Sugden, *Tecumseh*, 205.

15. Edmunds, *The Shawnee Prophet*, 172.

16. *Autobiography of Black Hawk*, ed. Donald Jackson (Urbana, IL, 1972), 58. See also Sugden, *Tecumseh*, 205–8.

17. Sugden, *Tecumseh*, 209–12.

18. Marshall Smelser, "Tecumseh, Harrison, and the War of 1812," *Indiana Magazine of History* 65, no. 1 (March 1969): 37.

19. *Messages and Letters of William Henry Harrison*, 1:487–96.

20. Sugden, *Tecumseh*, 222–23.

21. *Messages and Letters of William Henry Harrison*, 1:530–31.

22. Simon Pokagan, "The Massacre of Fort Dearborn at Chicago," *Harper's New Monthly Magazine*, March 1899, 651; Sugden, *Tecumseh*, 234–36.

23. William E. Foley, *Wilderness Journey: The Life of William Clark* (Columbia, MO, 2004), 191; James E. Davis, *Frontier Illinois* (Bloomington, IN, 1998), 137.

24. William Henry Harrison to William Eustis, January 14, 1812, Potawatomi File, Great Lakes Indian Archives, Indiana University.

25. William Eustis to William Henry Harrison, January 17, 1812, in ibid.

26. Benjamin F. Stickney to Nathan Heald, Fort Wayne, April 29, 1812, quoted in Gayle Thornbrough, ed., *Letter Book of the Indian Agency at Fort Wayne, 1809–1815* (Indianapolis, 1961); William

Henry Harrison to Secretary of War Eustis, April 14, 1812, Potawatomi File, Great Lakes Indian Archive, Indiana University.

27. Jacob LaLime [sic] to Governor Howard, February 1812, quoted in Carter, *Territorial Papers*, 14:536–37; Matthew Irwin to Mason, January 3, 1812, National Archives, Great Lakes Regional Archives, March 7, 2008, T58 Letters received, Superintendent of Indian Affairs, 1806–24.

28. Jacob LaLime [sic] to Governor Howard, February 4, 1812, quoted in Carter, *Territorial Papers*, 14:536–37.

29. Thomas Forsyth to Governor Howard Peorias, February 18, 1812, quoted in ibid., 14:535–36.

30. Matthew Irwin to the Secretary of War, January 19, 1812, quoted in ibid., 16:184–85. Evidence for the purchases from the Pattinson brothers come after the War of 1812, when Kinzie & Forsyth were sued by the Pattinson brothers, who were trying to recoup the monies they had lent the partnerships.

31. Matthew Irwin to the Secretary of War, January 19, 1812, quoted in ibid.

32. Letter from Nathan Heald to Matthew Irwin, June 26 1812, Nathan Heald Collection, Chicago History Museum; Secretary of War to Matthew Irwin, April 7 1812, quoted in Carter, *Territorial Papers*, 16:210.

33. Sugden, *Tecumseh*, 260–61.

34. William Clark to Ninian Edwards, April 11, 1812, Potawatomi File, Great Lakes Indian Archives, Indiana University.

35. Matthew Irwin to the Secretary of War, March 10, 1812, in ibid.

36. Robert Forsyth to Capt. Rhea, March 10, 1812, in ibid.

37. Mrs. John H. (Juliette) Kinzie, *Wau-Bun: The "Early Day" in the North-West* (Chicago, 1932), 233; Ulrich Danckers and Jane Meredith, *Early Chicago* (River Forest, IL, 1999), 90, 120.

38. James Leigh to Colonel Jacob Kingsbury, March 30, 1811, Kingsbury Papers, Chicago History Museum.

39. Captain Nathan Heald to Captain William Wells, April 15, 1812, quoted in Carter, *Territorial Papers*, 16:47; Matthew Irwin to the Secretary of War, April 16, 1812, quoted in ibid., 16:212–13.

40. Kinzie, *Wau-Bun*, 239.

41. Ibid., 240.

42. Matthew Irwin to the Secretary of War, April 16, 1812, quoted in Carter, *Territorial Papers*, 16:212–13.

43. Matthew Irwin to the Secretary of War, May 15, 1812, quoted in ibid., 16:219–22.

44. Copy of letter from Captain Nathan Heald to William Wells, April 15, 1812, quoted in *Louisiana Gazette*, May 30, 1812, Potawatomi File, Great Lakes Indian Archives, Indiana University.

45. Matthew Irwin to the Secretary of War, May 15, 1812, quoted in Carter, *Territorial Papers*, 16:219–22.

Chapter Seven

1. Mrs. John H. (Juliette) Kinzie, *Wau-Bun: The "Early Day" in the North-West* (Chicago, 1932), 236–37. This chapter rests on the work of Gregory Evans Dowd, *A Spirited Resistance: The North American Indian Struggle for Unity, 1745–1815* (Baltimore, 1992); John Sugden, *Tecumseh: A Life* (New York, 1997); R. David Edmunds, *The Potawatomis: Keepers of the Fire* (Norman, OK, 1978); James A. Clifton, *The Prairie People: Continuity and Change in Potawatomi Indian Culture, 1665–1965* (Lawrence, KS, 1977); Timothy Willig, *Restoring the Chain of Friendship: British Policy and the Indians of the Great Lakes, 1783–1815* (Lincoln, NE, 2008); and Helen Hornbeck Tanner, ed. *Atlas of Great Lakes Indian History* (Norman, OK, 1987).

2. Tecumseh speech in "Speeches of Indians at Massassinway May 15, 1812," quoted in *Messages and Letters of William Henry Harrison*, ed. Logan Esarey, 2 vols. (New York, 1975), 1:51.

3. Governor Ninian Edwards to Secretary of War, May 12, 1812, Potawatomi File, Great Lakes Indian Archive, Indiana University.

4. Willig, *Restoring the Chain of Friendship*, 235–41.

5. William Wells provided a transcript of the council that he dated May 15, 1812, and sent to Governor Harrison. See Ross F. Lockridge, "History on the Mississenawa," *Indiana Magazine*

of History 30, no. 1 (March 1934): 38–40. See also Benjamin Stickney to Governor Hull, May 25, 1812, quoted in Gayle Thornbrough, ed., *Letter Book of the Indian Agency at Fort Wayne, 1809–1815* (Indianapolis, 1961), 126–27.

6. *Messages and Letters of William Henry Harrison*, ed. Esarey, 2:61; Sugden, *Tecumseh*, 270.

7. Thomas Forsyth to General Gibson, July 26, 1812, Potawatomi File, Great Lakes Indian Archive, Indiana University.

8. *Messages and Letters of William Henry Harrison*, ed. Esarey, 2:61; Sugden, *Tecumseh*, 270.

9. Sugden, *Tecumseh*, 272.

10. Thomas Forsyth to Governor Edwards, June 8, 1812, quoted in Clarence Edwin Carter, ed., *The Territorial Papers of the United States*, 26 vols. (Washington, DC, 1948), 16:228–31; Thomas Forsyth to General Gibson, July 26, 1812, Potawatomi File, Great Lakes Indian Archive, Indiana University.

11. Thomas Forsyth to Governor Edwards, June 8, 1812, quoted in Carter, *Territorial Papers*, 16:228–31.

12. Report of Antoine LeClair, July 14, 1812, quoted in ibid., 16:254–55; John Kinzie to Thomas Forsyth, July 7, 1812, quoted in ibid., 16:248–50.

13. Governor Ninian Edwards to Secretary of War, July 21, 1812, Potawatomi File, Great Lakes Indian Archive, Indiana University. Also Governor Ninian Edwards to the Secretary of War, July 21, 1812, quoted in Carter, *Territorial Papers*, 16:244.

14. Report of Antoine LeClair, July 14, 1812, quoted in Carter, *Territorial Papers*, 16:254–55.

15. "Some few of the Indians may have a little gunpowder yet left, but may suppose if they are not supplied shortly they will be much in want of that article in the course of a few weeks." Thomas Forsyth to Governor Edwards, June 8, 1812, quoted in ibid., 16:228–31.

16. Thomas Forsyth to General Gibson, July 26, 1812, Potawatomi File, Great Lakes Indian Archive, Indiana University.

17. Governor Ninian Edwards to Thomas Forsyth, May 24, 1812, quoted in Ninian Edwards, *History of Illinois from 1778 to 1833 and the Life and Times of Ninian Edwards* (Springfield, IL, 1879), 323.

18. Report of Antoine LeClair, July 14, 1812, quoted in Carter, *Territorial Papers*, 16:254–55.

19. Clifton, *The Prairie People*, 203.

20. Thomas Forsyth to Governor Edwards, June 8, 1812, quoted in Carter, *Territorial Papers*, 16:228–31.

21. He also recognized Wells's political power (through his Kentucky connections), as well as the support he had provided Harrison in a recent civil suit. See William Henry Harrison to the Secretary of War, April 23, 1811, quoted in *Messages and Letters of William Henry Harrison*, ed. Esarey, 1:506–7.

22. William Henry Harrison to Secretary of War, July 8, 1812, quoted in ibid., 2:67–70.

23. William Wells to William Henry Harrison, Fort Wayne, July, 22, 1812, quoted in ibid., 2:76–78.

24. Benjamin Stickney to Secretary of War William Eustis, July 8, 1812, Potawatomi File, Great Lakes Indian Archive, Indiana University.

25. William Wells to William Henry Harrison, July 22, 1812, quoted in *Messages and Letters of William Henry Harrison*, ed. Esarey, 2:76–78.

26. On Dickson, see David Lavender, *The Fist in the Wilderness* (Lincoln, NE, 1998), 26–27; and Robert Alexander Cruikshank, "Robert Dickson, the Indian Trader," *Wisconsin Historical Collections* 12 (1892): 135–38. See also Julius W. Pratt, "Fur Trade Strategy and the American Left Flank in the War of 1812," *American Historical Review* 40, no. 2 (January 1935): 246–73.

27. "Documents relating to Detroit and vicinity, 1805–1813," *Michigan Historical Collections* 40 (1929): 262–63.

28. Willig, *Restoring the Chain of Friendship*, 254–55.

29. Cruikshank, "Robert Dickson," 135–38.

Chapter Eight

1. James Grant Wilson, "Chicago from 1802 to 1812," unpublished manuscript, Chicago History Museum. I have relied on the insights of several historians in shaping this chapter, includ-

ing Ian K. Steele, *Fort William Henry and the "Massacre"* (New York, 1990); Peter Silver, *Our Savage Neighbors: How Indian War Transformed Early America* (New York, 2008); J. C. A. Stagg, *Mr. Madison's War: Politics, Diplomacy, and Warfare in the Early American Republic, 1783–1830* (Princeton, NJ, 1983); and Alan Taylor, *The Civil War of 1812: American Citizens, British Subjects, Irish Rebels, and Indian Allies* (New York, 2010).

2. Matthew Irwin to Secretary of War William Eustis, July 1812, quoted in Richard Knopf, *Document Transcriptions of the War of 1812 in the Northwest*, 10 vols. (Columbus, OH, 1957), 6:69–71.

3. John Kinzie to Lewis Cass, Detroit, July 15, 1815, quoted in James Ryan Haydon, "John Kinzie's Place in History," *Transactions of the Illinois State Historical Society* 39 (1932): 196–97.

4. Matthew Irwin to Secretary of War William Eustis, July 1812, quoted in Knopf, *Document Transcriptions of the War of 1812 in the Northwest*, 6:69–71

5. Captain Nathan Heald to Matthew Irwin, June 26 1812, Nathan Heald Collection, Chicago History Museum.

6. Isaac Van Voorhis to Secretary of War William Eustis, May 16, 1812, quoted in Knopf, *Document Transcriptions*, 6:220–21. Peter Silver points out that many American soldiers saw it "as impossible to draw distinctions between Indians." Silver, *Our Savage Neighbors: How Indian War Transformed Early America* (New York, 2008), 130.

7. Isaac Van Voorhis to Secretary of War William Eustis, May 16, 1812, quoted in Knopf, *Document Transcriptions*, 6:220–21.

8. Nathan Heald Journal, quoted in Milo M. Quaife, *Chicago and the Old Northwest* (Chicago, 1913), 403. The microfilm copy of the journal in the Draper Collection provides some sense of the pocket size of the book. See Draper Collection, 17U, microfilm reel 58. Van Voorhis was an 1808 graduate from the New York City College of Physicians and Surgeons, so he was new and inexperienced and perhaps too young to be considered to deliver Heald's baby. Also he had alienated Heald by siding with Irwin. For more on midwivery in this era, see Laurel Thatcher Ulrich, *A Midwife's Tale: The Life of Martha Ballard Based on Her Diary, 1785–1812* (New York, 1990).

9. Matthew Irwin to John Mason, October 16, 1812, quoted in Clarence Edwin Carter, ed., *The Territorial Papers of the United States*, 26 vols. (Washington, DC, 1942), 10:411–15.

10. Quaife, *Chicago and the Old Northwest*, 212–14.

11. Lalime had been witness to many of the important documents during the Fort Dearborn era, but he was not present for this. See Clarence Edwin Carter, ed., *The Territorial Papers of the United States*, 26 vols. (Washington, DC, 1948), 16:221–22.

12. Deposition of Francis Reheaum, May 1, 1812, quoted in Clarence Edwin Carter, ed., *The Territorial Papers of the United States*, 26 vols. (Washington, DC, 1949), 14:574–75.

13. Matthew Irwin to John Mason, October 16, 1812, quoted in ibid., 10:411–15.

14. Matthew Irwin to the Secretary of War, May 15, 1812, quoted in ibid., 16:221–22.

15. Robert Alexander Cruikshank, "Robert Dickson, the Indian Trader," *Wisconsin Historical Collections* 12 (1892): 139.

16. Matthew Irwin to the Secretary of War, May 15, 1812, quoted in Carter, *Territorial Papers*, 16:221–22.

17. Ibid.

18. Date and time for the fight is confirmed in Isaac Van Voorhis to Secretary of War William Eustis, June 30, 1812, quoted in Knopf, *Document Transcriptions*, 6:67–68. Young John Harris Kinzie remembered his father's preparations. They were related by J. H. Kinzie's son Arthur M. Kinzie in a letter to G. S. Hubbard, February 5, 1884, John Kinzie Manuscript Collection, Chicago History Museum. The nineteenth-century accounts of these events are inconsistent. Not surprisingly, Mrs. John H. Kinzie (Juliette), *Wau-Bun: The "Early Day" in the North-West* (Chicago, 1932), does not mention the Jean Lalime's death at all. Joseph Kirkland, *The Chicago Massacre of 1812: A Historical and Biographical Narrative of Fort Dearborn (Now Chicago)* (Chicago, 1893), gives the story considerable coverage, including a photo of Lalime's exhumed remains. Van Voorhis's and Irwin's accounts of Lalime's murder were unknown well into the twentieth century, so were unavailable to earlier historians, including Quaife, *Chicago and the Old Northwest*, who gives these events only passing mention.

19. A. T. Andreas, *History of Chicago*, 3 vols. (Chicago, 1884), 1:105.

20. Captain Nathan Heald to Matthew Irwin, June 26 1812, Nathan Heald Collection, Chicago History Museum.

21. Reminiscences of John Kinzie Clark, Head Collection, Chicago History Museum.

22. Matthew Irwin to Secretary of War William Eustis, July 1812, quoted in Knopf, *Document Transcriptions*, 6:69–71.

23. Isaac Van Voorhis to Secretary of War William Eustis, June 30, 1812, quoted in ibid., 6:67–68; Matthew Irwin to Secretary of War William Eustis, July 1812, quoted in ibid., 6:69–71.

24. Gurdon Hubbard, a longtime friend of the Kinzie family who arrived in Chicago six years after the murder, stated in an 1881 letter: "The fact has always been firm in my mind that Lalime made the attack, provoking the killing, in self-defense." Letter from Hubbard to John Wentworth, June 25, 1881, quoted in Kirkland, *The Chicago Massacre of 1812*, 188–89.

25. Matthew Irwin to Secretary of War William Eustis, July 1812, quoted in Knopf, *Document Transcriptions*, 6:69–71.

26. Ibid.

27. Ibid.

28. *Chicago*, 3, no. 7 (September 1956): 16.

29. Irwin explained that in the immediate aftermath of the murder, "the Citizens were anxious an inquest should be held in the body, but a file of soldiers headed by Lt. Helm carried it away by force." See Matthew Irwin to Secretary of War William Eustis, July 1812, quoted in Knopf, *Document Transcriptions*, 6:69–71.

30. Captain Nathan Heald to Matthew Irwin, June 26, 1812, included as an enclosure in letter from Irwin to Secretary of War Eustis, July 1812, quoted in ibid., 6:69–71.

31. Matthew Irwin to Secretary of War William Eustis, July 1812, quoted in ibid., 6:69–71.

32. Matthew Irwin to John Mason, October 16, 1812, quoted in Carter, *Territorial Places*, 10:411–15.

33. Matthew Irwin to Secretary of War William Eustis, August 6, 1812, Potawatomi File, Great Lakes Indian Archive, Indiana University.

34. Isaac Van Voorhis to Secretary of War Eustis, May 16, 1812, quoted in Knopf, *Document Transcriptions*, 6:220–21; Isaac Van Voorhis to Secretary of War William Eustis, June 30, 1812, quoted in ibid., 6:67–68.

35. Burnett would marry a Potawatomi woman whose name was Notanoquay. She was likely Nokenoqua, the widow of Jean Lalime. See *Letter Book of William Burnett*, ed. Wilbur M. Cunningham (Niles, MI, 1967), xxii–xxiii; and Susan Sleeper-Smith, *Indian Women and French Men: Rethinking Cultural Encounter in the Western Great Lakes* (Amherst, MA, 2001), 204n80.

36. Matthew Irwin to Secretary of War William Eustis, July 1812, quoted in Knopf, *Document Transcriptions*, 6:69–71.

37. The two American citizens were identified as "Mr. Bunnell [Burnett] of Detroit and Mr. High [Leigh] of this place." Quoted in ibid., 6:67–71.

38. *Autobiography of Black Hawk*, ed. Donald Jackson (Urbana, IL, 1972), 66.

39. Thomas Forsyth to the Secretary of War, September 29, 1817, quoted in "Letter Book of Thomas Forsyth, 1814–1818," *Wisconsin Historical Collections* 11 (1888): 351.

40. Forsyth journeyed to Chicago to consult with his brother about this. See Thomas Forsyth to William Clark, May 27, 1812, Potawatomi File, Great Lakes Indian Archive, Indiana University.

41. Forsyth had agreed to meet with Clark at St. Louis in April 1812 but was delayed because of the attack at the Leigh farm, and Clark left to journey eastward without a meeting. See Thomas Forsyth to William Clark, May 27, 1812, Potawatomi File, Great Lakes Indian Archive, Indiana University.

42. Governor Ninian Edwards to Secretary of War Eustis, May 12, 1812, in ibid.

43. Governor Ninian Edwards to Secretary of War Eustis, May 26, 1812, in ibid.

44. However, Forsyth sought a substantial salary (at least $500), more than the $70 per year offered him as a subagent by William Clark at St. Louis. Illinois Governor Edwards was willing

to pay him more out of his private funds, especially since Forsyth seemed "determined to go to Detroit on his private business." By going to Detroit, Forsyth would lose his value to the Illinois governor and the Indian agent at St. Louis, and perhaps offer his services instead to the British outside Detroit.

45. Henry Lewis Carter, *The Life and Times of Little Turtle, First Sagamore of the Wabash* (Urbana, IL, 1987), 230.

46. R. A. Cruikshank, *Documents Relating to the Invasion of Canada and the Surrender of Detroit 1812* (Ottawa, ON, 1912), 54–55.

Chapter Nine

1. For a broad perspective on these events, see David Curtis Skagus and Larry L. Nelson, eds., *The Sixty Years' War for the Great Lakes, 1754–1814* (East Lansing, MI, 2001); Timothy Willig, *Restoring the Chain of Friendship: British Policy and the Indians of the Great Lakes, 1783–1815* (Lincoln, NE, 2008); Richard White, *The Middle Ground: Indians, Empires, and Republics in the Great Lakes Region, 1650–1815* (New York, 1991); Helen Hornbeck Tanner, *Atlas of Great Lakes Indian History* (Norman, OK, 1987) ; J. C. A. Stagg, *Mr. Madison's War: Politics, Diplomacy, and Warfare in the Early American Republic, 1783–1830* (Princeton, NJ, 1983); and Alan Taylor, *The Civil War of 1812: American Citizens, British Subjects, Irish Rebels, and Indian Allies* (New York, 2010).

2. Victoire Mirandeau Porthier related that her "father took him to Milwaukee where he stayed till his shoulder got well and he found he wouldn't be troubled if he came back." Quoted in A. T. Andreas, *History of Chicago*, 3 vols. (Chicago, 1884), 1:104.

3. John Kinzie to Thomas Forsyth, July 7, 1812, and Antoine LeClair Report, July 14, 1812, quoted in Clarence Edwin Carter, ed., *The Territorial Papers of the United States*, 26 vols. (Washington, DC, 1948), 16:248–50. Kinzie wrote that he was suspected by the Indians at Milwaukee "until my affairs was known to them on the fourth day." It is likely that LeClair then was able to vouch for Kinzie. There are few extant letters from Kinzie. Forsyth forwarded this letter to Governor Ninian Edwards, who in turn forwarded it to the secretary of war.

4. John Kinzie to Thomas Forsyth, July 7, 1812, quoted in ibid.

5. Ibid.

6. *Michigan Pioneer and Historical Collections* 16 (1890): 327–41. It is possible that Robert Forsyth, brother of Thomas Forsyth and John Kinzie, also was part of this group.

7. Kinzie & Forsyth Ledger A, Peoria, Folio 160, Thomas Forsyth Collection, Missouri Historical Society. The last entry in the ledger is Billy Caldwell for July 15, 1812 (pipe and smoked deerskins, no prices listed).

8. Governor Ninian Edwards to Thomas Forsyth, May 24, 1812, quoted in Ninian Edwards, *History of Illinois from 1778 to 1833 and the Life and Times of Ninian Edwards* (Springfield, IL, 1879), 323. Edwards wrote Forsyth: "You will take every means in your power to ascertain when Main Pock will return and what his disposition may be towards the US and if hostile, what forces he will likely to raise."

9. A series of letters, with information from each man, was sent on to Governor Ninian Edwards in the middle of July and provides us with insight into their views. Thomas Forsyth addresses a letter directly to Edwards on July 21, 1812, with two enclosures, letters from Billy Caldwell and Antoine Leclair. Forsyth also appears to have forwarded a letter to him from his brother John Kinzie on July 7, 1812, as he made his way from Chicago to Milwaukee and then south to Peoria, in search of Thomas Forsyth after Lalime's murder. All landed in the territorial papers. See Carter, *Territorial Papers*, 16:247–53.

10. Matthew Irwin to Secretary of War Eustis, August 6, 1812, Potawatomi File, Great Lakes Indian Archive, Indiana University.

11. Carter, *Territorial Papers*, 16:247–53.

12. Thomas Forsyth to General Gibson, July 26, 1812, Potawatomi File, Great Lakes Indian Archive, Indiana University.

13. Thomas Forsyth to Governor Edwards, July 13, 1812, quoted in Carter, *Territorial Papers*, 16:250.

14. Jeremy Adelman and Stephen Aron, "Trading Cultures: The Worlds of Western Merchants," in *Trading Cultures: The Worlds of Western Merchants*, ed. Jeremy Adelman and Stephen Aron (Tornhout, Belgium, 2001), 5.

15. Thomas Forsyth to General Gibson, July 26, 1812, Potawatomi File, Great Lakes Indian Archive, Indiana University.

16. James A. Clifton, *The Prairie People: Continuity and Change in Potawatomi Indian Culture, 1665–1965* (Lawrence, KS, 1977), 205.

17. It appears that there was an inquest into the murder of Jean Lalime held under Heald at Fort Dearborn in July 1812 while Kinzie is still absent. Van Voorhis wrote: "A Garrison order has been posted permitting Mr. Kinzie to return & live unmolested with his family, until the civil authority takes him up." Isaac Van Voorhis to Matthew Irwin, July 13, 1812, Chicago History Museum.

18. John Kinzie to President Monroe, Chicago, April 4, 1817, National Archives, RG94, letters received by Adjutant General. The letter is included (without citation) in James Ryan Haydon, "John Kinzie's Place in History," *Transactions of the Illinois State Historical Society* 39 (1932): 185–87. Haydon was a Chicago newspaper reporter who would go on to write a strong anti-Kinzie account: *Chicago's True Founder, Thomas J. V. Owen: A Pleading for Truth and for Social Justice in Chicago History* (Lombard, IL, 1934).

19. John Kinzie to President Monroe, Chicago, April 4, 1817, National Archives, RG94, letters received by Adjutant General. See also Thomas Forsyth to the Governor of Louisiana Territory [a copy of this letter was forwarded to the secretary of war], September 7, 1812, quoted in Carter, *Territorial Papers*, 16:261–65.

20. Alongside Kinzie's 1817 account of these events, Thomas Forsyth wrote about them in a September 7, 1812, letter to the governor of Louisiana. While they generally agree, there are differences. It is important to keep in mind who they were writing to and why they wrote. The account closest to the event is Forsyth's secondhand account and places William Wells in a more central role. Kinzie also provides a second account in 1820 that deviates somewhat from his own 1817 account. See Mentor L. Williams, "John Kinzie's Narrative of the Fort Dearborn Massacre," *Journal of the Illinois State Historical Society* 46 (Winter 1953): 347–49. In addition, Gurdon Salstonhall Hubbard and Juliette Kinzie wrote accounts based on the stories they heard from family members about these events. Yet another account was written by John Kinzie's son-in-law Lieutenant Linai Helm in 1814 but remained unknown to researchers until the early twentieth century.

21. There are some differences among existing accounts of the return of Kinzie's group. Thomas Forsyth recounted that Kinzie's party returned as a group to Chicago, while in 1817 Kinzie remembered that the Indian leaders returned to their villages. While only a slight difference, it changes the composition of the Indians outside Fort Dearborn in the days before August 15, 1812. If Forsyth's account is to be believed, then the leaders most likely to be American allies were present at Fort Dearborn with William Wells, while in Kinzie's account, the Indian leaders leaning toward the Americans (or at least not toward Tecumseh and/or the British) had gone home and were not present throughout the days leading to the evacuation and attack.

22. Ninian Edwards to the Secretary of War, July 21, 1812, quoted in Carter, *Territorial Papers*, 16:247. Thomas Forsyth got this letter to Illinois territorial governor Ninian Edwards, who immediately forwarded it to the secretary of war. By then the United States had declared war against Great Britain.

23. General Hull to Secretary of War Eustis, July 29, 1812, *Michigan Historical Collections* 40 (1929): 424–26.

24. Captain Nathan Heald to Thomas H. Cushing, Adjutant General, U.S. Army, October 23, 1812, typescript copy, Chicago History Museum. While some have focused on whether Heald's orders were in Hull's hand, this did not affect the outcome of events.

25. Clifton, *The Prairie People*, 177.

26. Kinzie account quoted in Williams, "John Kinzie's Narrative," 347–49.

27. "Defends His Father: The Story of the Fort Dearborn Massacre Retold," *Chicago Tribune*, April 23, 1892, in the Chicago Massacre of 1812 Collection, Chicago History Museum.

28. Mrs. John H. (Juliette) Kinzie, *Wau-Bun: The "Early Day" in the North-West* (Chicago, 1932), 249.

29. The only other account comes from James Corbin, an enlisted solder who escaped Indian captivity after the battle. Corbin had the longest connection to Fort Dearborn of any of these observers—he came with the original troops who built the fort and was in his third five-year term of enlistment in August 1812. His account was taken down in 1826 to help this illiterate veteran gain an army pension. Corbin quoted in Milo M. Quaife, "The Story of James Corbin, a Soldier at Fort Dearborn," *Mississippi Valley Historical Review* 3, no. 3 (September 1916): 219–28.

30. In the Helm account, Heald got General Hull's order for evacuation on August 8, 1812, and William Wells arrived four days later (a day before what the Heald account says). Helm relates contentious discussions between U.S. officers and Wells. According to Helm, Heald intended to distribute all of the goods to the surrounding Potawatomis, as he "observed that it was not sound policy to tell a lie to an Indian." But Kinzie, Helm, and Wells prevailed in convincing Heald that the ammunition and muskets must be destroyed. According to Helm, they were destroyed "on the night of the 13th." L. T. Helm to Augustus Woodward, June 6, 1814, typescript copy, Chicago History Museum.

31. Williams, "John Kinzie's Narrative," 347–49.

32. While some accounts do not have Wells arriving at Fort Dearborn until after the liquor and ammunition have been destroyed, there can be little doubt of his view on this subject. Juliette Kinzie has Captain Wells arrive on August 14, after the destruction of the arms and liquor. See Kinzie, *Wau-Bun*, 254.

33. Captain Nathan Heald to Thomas H. Cushing, Adjutant General, U.S. Army, Pittsburgh, PA, October 23, 1812, from a typescript copy, Chicago History Museum.

34. Kinzie, *Wau-Bun*, 251; "Report of the Committee of claims on the petition of Kinzie and Forsythe, December 31, 1812," Washington, DC, 1814, Chicago History Museum. Milo M. Quaife, *Chicago and the Old Northwest* (Chicago, 1913), 246n, contains the January 1813 letter from Forsyth to Captain N. Heald concerning the Kinzie & Forsyth claims.

35. The wording here is interesting. Kinzie did not destroy his own property—the government did with his permission. This is important in the petition to Congress made by Kinzie & Forsyth for reimbursement of their lost goods. They needed to have it clear that the U.S. government was responsible for the destruction of their goods—that it was not their own choice. See "Report of the Committee of claims on the petition of Kinzie and Forsythe, December 31, 1812," Washington, DC, 1814, Chicago History Museum.

36. Kinzie, *Wau-Bun*, 252, 254.

37. Williams, "John Kinzie's Narrative," 352; "Defends His Father," in the Chicago Massacre of 1812 Collection, Chicago History Museum.

38. Simon Pokagan, "The Massacre of Fort Dearborn at Chicago," *Harper's New Monthly Magazine*, March 1899, 651.

39. Quaife, "The Story of James Corbin," 219–28.

Chapter Ten

1. Heald quotation in Milo M. Quaife, *Chicago and the Old Northwest* (Chicago, 1913), 417. The work of several historians influenced this chapter: Evan Haefeli and Kevin Sweeney, *Captors and Captives: The 1704 French and Indian Raid on Deerfield* (Amherst, MA, 2003); James A. Clifton, *The Prairie People: Continuity and Change in Potawatomi Indian Culture, 1665–1965* (Lawrence, KS, 1977); Helen Hornbeck Tanner, *Atlas of Great Lakes Indian History* (Norman, OK, 1987); J. C. A. Stagg, *Mr. Madison's War: Politics, Diplomacy, and Warfare in the Early American Republic, 1783–1830* (Princeton, NJ, 1983); and Alan Taylor, *The Civil War of 1812: American Citizens, British Subjects, Irish Rebels, and Indian Allies* (New York, 2010). There are three standard historical accounts of the battle that do not agree: Mrs. John H. (Juliette) Kinzie, *Wau-Bun: The "Early Day" in the North-West* (Chicago, 1932); Joseph Kirkland, *The Chicago Massacre of 1812: A Historical and Biographical Narrative of Fort Dearborn (Now Chicago)* (Chicago, 1893); and Quaife, *Chicago and the Old Northwest*. Quaife was most dismissive of Juliette Kinzie's account, which I have found here to be of great value, if used carefully. None of these sources had access to two accounts of the battle by

John Kinzie. James Ryan Haydon uncovered the first in "John Kinzie's Place in History," *Transactions of the Illinois State Historical Society* 39 (1932): 183–89; and the second is Mentor L. Williams, "John Kinzie's Narrative of the Fort Dearborn Massacre," *Journal of the Illinois State Historical Society* 46 (Winter 1953): 347–49. Constance R. Buckley has worked her way through many of these accounts. See "Searching for Fort Dearborn: Perception, Commemoration, and Celebration of an Urban Creation Memory" (PhD diss., Loyola University, 2005), esp. 30–79 and appendix 2.

2. The problems with translation were evident at the time. See Samuel Levering to Governor Ninian Edwards, August 12, 1811, quoted in Clarence Edwin Carter, ed., *Territorial Papers of the United States*, 26 vols. (Washington, DC, 1948), 16:178: "Perhaps the difficulty of communicating with the Potowatomi through the French language, into English does measurably prevent the meanings."

3. Ninian Edwards to the secretary of war, July 21, 1812, quoted in ibid., 16:244.

4. Nehemiah Matson, "Sketch of Shau-be-na, a Potawatomie Chief," *Collections of the State Historical Society of Wisconsin* 18 (1908): 417–18.

5. Frank Reed Grover, *Antoine Ouilmette* (Evanston, IL, 1908), 10.

6. Kinzie, *Wau-Bun*, 251.

7. Quaife, *Chicago and the Old Northwest*, 193.

8. Simon Pokagan quoted in "Fort Dearborn Massacre from an Indian's Point of View," *Chicago Sunday Tribune*, February 7, 1897.

9. President Thomas Jefferson to the Potawatomi, December 1808, Potawatomi File, Great Lakes Indian Archive, Indiana University.

10. There were other family ties. Billy Caldwell was Wabinewa's son-in-law. Billy Caldwell's first wife was "a Roman Catholic girl named La Nanette daughter of Wabinewa (White Sturgeon) whose brother was Neskotnemek (Mad Sturgeon)." See James A. Clifton, "Personal and Ethnic Identity on the Great Lakes Frontier: The Case of Billy Caldwell, Anglo-Canadian," *Ethnohistory* 25 no. 1 (Winter 1978): 75; also in Ulrich Danckers and Jane Meredith, *Early Chicago* (River Forest, IL, 1999), 93.

11. Susan Sleeper-Smith, *Indian Women and French Men: Rethinking Cultural Encounter in the Western Great Lakes* (Amherst, MA, 2001), 87.

12. C. Henry Smith, "Black Partridge: The Hero of Fort Dearborn," in *Metamora* (Bluffton, OH, 1947), 24.

13. Ninian Edwards, *History of Illinois from 1778 to 1833 and the Life and Times of Ninian Edwards* (Springfield, IL, 1879), 48.

14. Ibid.

15. Thomas Forsyth to the Governor of Louisiana Territory, September 7, 1812, quoted in Carter, *Territorial Papers*, 16:261.

16. Thomas Forsyth to Governor Edwards, June 8, 1812, quoted in ibid., 16:230. Forsyth reported that Gomo said, "There must be a change among the Indians, otherwise he would abandon them and live and die among the White people of this place."

17. Thomas Forsyth to the Governor of Louisiana Territory, September 7, 1812, quoted in ibid., 16:262.

18. Clifton, *The Prairie People*, 174.

19. Ibid., 174–75.

20. Simon Pokagan, "The Massacre of Fort Dearborn at Chicago," *Harper's New Monthly Magazine*, March 1899, 653. Kinzie received the same warning from Topinbee early on the morning of August 15. See R. David Edmunds, *The Potawatomis: Keepers of the Fire* (Norman, OK, 1978), 186.

21. John Kinzie to President Monroe, April 4, 1817, National Archives, RG94, letters received by Adjutant General.

22. Kinzie, *Wau-Bun*, 270.

23. Ibid., 257. Jean Baptiste Chandonnai's mother, Chip-pe-wa-gua, was a sister of Topinbee, a Potawatomi village leader from the St. Joseph area, as well as of Kakima, the wife of St. Joseph trader William Burnett.

24. Williams, "John Kinzie's Narrative," 352. Captain Heald gave the time of departure as

nine o'clock, while other accounts gave ten o'clock, including James Van Horne, a retreating soldier. See Van Horne, "Narrative," Fort Dearborn Collection, Chicago History Museum.

25. Kinzie, *Wau-Bun*, 258.

26. Ibid., 121.

27. Kirkland, *The Chicago Massacre of 1812*, 21.

28. Chicago History Museum Reference Report, Fort Dearborn Massacre, June 20, 1960.

29. Milo M. Quaife, "The Story of James Corbin, a Soldier at Fort Dearborn," *Mississippi Valley Historical Review* 3, no. 3 (September 1916): 222. See also the Aunt Maryann version of the Chicago battle, copy from the Draper Collection as found in Fort Dearborn Collection, Chicago History Museum. Aunt Maryann was the daughter of Alexander Robinson.

30. Captain Nathan Heald to Thomas H. Cushing, October 23, 1812, typescript copy, Fort Dearborn Collection, Chicago History Museum.

31. Van Horne, "Narrative," Fort Dearborn Collection, Chicago History Museum.

32. Williams, "John Kinzie's Narrative," 352.

33. There do not appear to be any extant accounts of the attack from any native participants. The closest comes from Simon Pokagan, the son of a Potawatomi leader, who arrived the day following the battle: "When whites are killed it is a massacre . . . when Indians are killed it is a fight." Quoted in "Fort Dearborn Massacre from an Indian's Point of View."

34. Clifton, *The Prairie People*, 176–77.

35. Ibid., 177. On the location of the attack, see H. A. Musham, "Where Did the Battle of Chicago Take Place?" *Journal of the Illinois State Historical Society* 36, no. 1 (March 1943): 21–40. Mushman places the attack at Twelfth Street and provides compelling evidence.

36. Captain Nathan Heald to Thomas H. Cushing, October 23, 1812, typescript copy, Fort Dearborn Collection, Chicago History Museum.

37. Kinzie quoted in Williams, "John Kinzie's Narrative," 349.

38. Clifton, *The Prairie People*, 177.

39. Pokagan, "The Massacre of Fort Dearborn at Chicago," 653.

40. Kinzie quoted in Williams, "John Kinzie's Narrative," 349.

41. Henry R. Schoolcraft, *Narrative Journal of Travels*, ed. Mentor L. Williams (East Lansing, MI, 1953), 256.

42. Kinzie quoted in Williams, "John Kinzie's Narrative," 349.

43. Thomas Forsyth to the Governor of Louisiana Territory, September 7, 1812, quoted in Carter, *Territorial Papers*, 16:261–65.

44. Thomas Forsyth put the number of Potawatomi warriors killed at three, with three additional casualties. Captain Nathan Heald to Thomas H. Cushing, October 23, 1812, typescript copy, Fort Dearborn Collection, Chicago History Museum.

45. "Defends His Father: The Story of the Fort Dearborn Massacre Retold," *Chicago Tribune*, April 23, 1892, in the Chicago Massacre of 1812 Collection, Chicago History Museum.

46. Quoted in Quaife, *Chicago and the Old Northwest*, 411.

47. Kinzie, *Wau-Bun*, 269.

48. Williams, "John Kinzie's Narrative," 350.

49. Smith, "Black Partridge," 21–59.

50. John Kinzie to President Monroe, Chicago April 4, 1817, National Archives, RG94.

51. Margaret Helm revised her story over time, making her role more heroic. Kinzie, *Wau-Bun*, 122.

52. Darius Heald account, quoted in Quaife, *Chicago and the Old Northwest*, 411–12.

53. Clifton, *The Prairie People*, 207; and Williams, "John Kinzie's Narrative," 351.

54. Because of this, Kawbenaw "saved the badly wounded Mrs. Heald, and gained the new war name—Captain Heald." Clifton, *The Prairie People*, 207.

55. Jean Baptiste Chandonnai, Kinzie's chief clerk, had a dense kin network in the region. His mother was a sister of Topinbee, a Potawatomi village leader from the St. Joseph region, and had been raised by Charlotte and Charles Chandonett. Chandonnai also was related to the Laframboises, as another of his aunts (Madeleine) had married Joseph Laframboise, a trader. See Sleeper-Smith, *Indian Women and French Men*, 92–93. John B. Lalime, son of Noke-no-qua, and

Jean B. Chandonnai, son of Chip-pe-wa-gua, both received land settlements at St. Joseph as a result of the 1821 Treaty of Chicago. Henry H. Hurlbut, *Chicago Antiquities* (Chicago, 1881), 194. It might be that the two men are related, perhaps cousins.

56. Kinzie, *Wau-Bun*, 269.

57. Kirkland, *The Chicago Massacre of 1812*, 37–38.

58. Williams, "John Kinzie's Narrative," 350.

59. Ibid., 352.

60. Clifton, *The Prairie People*, 176.

61. Benson J. Lossing, *The Pictorial Field-Book of the War of 1812* (New York, 1868), 309, the standard nineteenth-century account of the war, places LeClair with Captain Heald.

62. Captain Nathan Heald to Thomas H. Cushing, October 23, 1812, typescript copy, Fort Dearborn Collection, Chicago History Museum. Darius Heald said about his father: "But for his surrender, the Chicago Massacre would have been, on a small scale, the fore-runner of the great Custer slaughter, where not a white man lived to tell the tale." Quoted in Kirkland, *The Chicago Massacre of 1812*, 33.

63. Williams, "John Kinzie's Narrative," 350.

64. Quaife, *Chicago and the Old Northwest*, 431. See also Linai Helm to Augustus B. Woodward, June 6, 1814, Fort Dearborn Collection, Chicago History Museum.

65. Linai Helm to Augustus B. Woodward, June 6, 1814, Fort Dearborn Collection, Chicago History Museum.

Chapter Eleven

1. Frank Reed Grover, *Antoine Ouilmette* (Evanston, IL, 1908), 5, states that Ouilmette came to Chicago in 1790, in the employ of the American Fur Company, but the American Fur Company did exist until 1808. He may have worked for one of the AFC antecedents, perhaps the Northwest Fur Company. However, this connection suggests that Ouilmette's connections were to Great Britain, though he was a francophone. All of this, plus the death of Archange's Potawatomi grandfather, Naunongee, at American hands on August 15, 1812, probably aligned the family with the British.

2. Henry R. Schoolcraft, *Narrative Journal of Travels*, ed. Mentor L. Williams (East Lansing, MI, 1953), 256. The absence of the Indian perspective in early historical accounts of the battle at Fort Dearborn is telling but not unusual. In the past three decades, historians have addressed this absence; see, for instance, Daniel K. Richter, *Facing East from Indian Country: A Native History of Early America* (Cambridge, MA, 2001); James Axtell, *Natives and Newcomers: The Cultural Origins of North America* (New York, 2001); and Frederick E. Hoxie, Ronald Hoffman, and Peter J. Albert, eds., *Native Americans and the Early Republic* (Charlottesville, VA, 1999). The role of captives has been explored in a number of historical works in recent years. I have relied most on the perspectives of John Demos, *The Unredeemed Captive: A Family Story from Early America* (New York, 1994); and Evan Haefeli and Kevin Sweeney, *Captors and Captives: The 1704 French and Indian Raid on Deerfield* (Amherst, MA, 2003). My work on this chapter is very much influenced by Carl Smith, *Urban Disorder and the Shape of Belief: The Great Chicago Fire, the Haymarket Bomb, and the Model Town of Pullman* (Chicago, 1995); and Kevin Lynch, *What Time Is This Place?* (Cambridge, MA, 1972).

3. Moses Morgan narrative, quoted in William R. Head Papers, Chicago History Museum.

4. Head Papers, Chicago History Museum.

5. Joseph Kirkland, *The Chicago Massacre of 1812: A Historical and Biographical Narrative of Fort Dearborn (Now Chicago)* (Chicago, 1893); Milo M. Quaife, *Chicago and the Old Northwest* (Chicago, 1913), 48. See also the Aunt Maryann version of the Chicago battle, copy from the Draper Collection, Fort Dearborn Collection, Chicago History Museum. Aunt Maryann was the daughter of Alexander Robinson.

6. "Alexander Robinson, Death of Pottawatomie Chief near Chicago," *Chicago Tribune*, May 14, 1872.

7. Grover, *Antoine Ouilmette*, 7. See also Mrs. John H. (Juliette) Kinzie, *Wau-Bun: The "Early Day" in the North-West* (Chicago, 1932), 277–78.

8. Kinzie, *Wau-Bun*, 264–65.

9. Mentor L. Williams, "John Kinzie's Narrative of the Fort Dearborn Massacre," *Journal of the Illinois State Historical Society* 46 (Winter 1953): 350.

10. Captain Nathan Heald to Thomas H. Cushing, October 23, 1812, typescript copy, Fort Dearborn Collection, Chicago History Museum.

11. The soldiers who were tortured included James Latta, Jacob Landon, Richard Gardner, Prestly Andrews, Micah Dennison, and Thomas Burns. See James Van Horne, "Narrative," Fort Dearborn Collection, Chicago History Museum. Also see Quaife, *Chicago and the Old Northwest*, 234.

12. Head Papers, Chicago History Museum.

13. Captain Nathan Heald to Thomas H. Cushing, October 23, 1812, typescript copy, Fort Dearborn Collection, Chicago History Museum.

14. Kinzie, *Wau-Bun*, 271.

15. Ibid.

16. Letter from Thomas Forsyth to William Wolden, December 9, 1826, quoted in Milo M. Quaife, "The Story of James Corbin, a Soldier at Fort Dearborn," *Mississippi Valley Historical Review* 3, no. 3 (September 1916).

17. Kinzie, *Wau-Bun*, 282.

18. Kinzie account, quoted in Williams, "John Kinzie's Narrative," 350; and John Kinzie to President Monroe, Chicago, April 4, 1817, National Archives, RG94.

19. Kinzie account, quoted in Williams, "John Kinzie's Narrative," 351.

20. Ibid.

21. Nehemiah Matson, "Sketch of Shau-be-na, a Potawatomie Chief," *Collections of the State Historical Society of Wisconsin* 18 (1908): 417–18.

22. Thomas Forsyth to the Governor of Louisiana Territory, September 7, 1812, quoted in Clarence Edwin Carter, ed., *Territorial Papers of the United States*, 26 vols. (Washington, DC, 1948), 16:261–65.

23. The third clothbound book of Kinzie ledgers was destroyed during the Chicago Fire, but the Barry Transcript, containing all the names in the ledger, as well as some transactions, includes August 18 with the following names: Charles Chandonnet, John Burnett, Peter Gassellens, J. Chosie, Goslans, Thomas Ines, and Billy Caldwell. This would suggest that these men traded with Kinzie in the days immediately following the battle. There are also entries for September 9, 1812, from St. Joseph and from Detroit in January 1813. See Barry Transcript, John Kinzie Collection, Chicago History Museum.

24. Kinzie account, quoted in Williams, "John Kinzie's Narrative," 351; Kinzie, *Wau-Bun*, 272.

25. Thomas Forsyth to Nathan Heald, January 2, 1813, quoted in Quaife, *Chicago and the Old Northwest*, 246.

26. Kinzie, *Wau-Bun*, 273–74.

27. Ibid., 274.

28. Matson, "Sketch of Shau-be-na," 417–18.

29. Backing this up is Caldwell's appearance in the Barry Transcript of the Kinzie & Forsyth ledger on August 18, 1812. However, in several other accounts, Caldwell and Waubansee fought alongside Tecumseh in early August outside Detroit. There is no way to resolve this at the moment. James A. Clifton, "Personal and Ethnic Identity on the Great Lakes Frontier: The Case of Billy Caldwell, Anglo-Canadian," *Ethnohistory* 25, no. 1 (Winter 1978): 76, notes: "Whether or not he [Caldwell] actually interceded after the battle to rescue the Kinzie family will always be uncertain, although he apparently told both Alexander Robinson and his brothers that he had done [so]. However, it is certain that if he did, it was the action of a loyal, long-service employee of John Kinzie." See also James A. Clifton, "Merchant, Soldier, Broker, Chief: A Corrected Obituary of Captain Billy Caldwell," *Journal of the Illinois State Historical Society* 71, no. 3 (August 1978): 185–210.

30. Ouilmette wrote a letter in which he described damages received during the Winnebago hostility in 1827. However, it is quite possible that Ouilmette is remembering the destruction that came as a final chapter in the Fort Dearborn attack, on or after August 20, 1812. The Winnebago War, in 1827, was not fought at Chicago. Letter presented in full in Grover, *Antoine*

Ouilmette, 6. Ouilmette was illiterate, so the letter was dictated and he made his mark, not his signature. The original letter was furnished to Mrs. Eleanor Kinzie Gordon of Savannah, Georgia, a daughter of John H. Kinzie (and mother of the founder of the Girl Scouts in the United States, Juliette Gordon Low).

31. Kinzie, *Wau-Bun*, 276.

32. Kinzie account, quoted in Williams, "John Kinzie's Narrative," 351.

33. Kinzie, *Wau-Bun*, 279.

34. Simon Pokagan felt that when whites were killed, it was considered a massacre, but when Indians were killed, it was called a battle. He also opined: "In this wholesale slaughter not one white man stretched out a hand to save a single soul. Your own historians, true to their trust, have recorded the cruelty of their own race." Simon Pokagan, "The Massacre of Fort Dearborn at Chicago," *Harper's New Monthly Magazine*, March 1899, 656. On Pokagan, see David H. Dickason, "Chief Simon Pokagan: 'The Indian Longfellow,'" *Indiana Magazine of History* 57, no. 2 (June 1961): 127–40.

35. See Smith, *Urban Disorder*, 6.

Chapter Twelve

1. Joseph Kirkland, *The Chicago Massacre of 1812: A Historical and Biographical Narrative of Fort Dearborn (Now Chicago)* (Chicago, 1893), 37–38. The experiences of prisoners of war is a central one in the Chicago region in 1812—Eleanor Kinzie, Keziah Forsyth, and William Wells were all captives in their youth. In *The Civil War of 1812: American Citizens, British Subjects, Irish Rebels, and Indian Allies* (New York, 2010), Alan Taylor has made the treatment of prisoners an important part of his history: "Histories usually emphasize battles and treat prisoners as mere byproducts. In this war, however, the management of prisoners became pivotal." Preceding Taylor, other historians have thought carefully about the experience of captivity. See Larry L. Nelson, ed., *A History of Jonathan Alder: His Captivity and Life with the Indians* (Akron, OH, 2002). See also John Demos, *The Unredeemed Captive: A Family Story from Early America* (New York, 1994); and Evan Haefeli and Kevin Sweeney, *Captors and Captives: The 1704 French and Indian Raid on Deerfield* (Amherst, MA, 2003).

2. The family friend, Benjamin O'Fallon, was the nephew of General William Clark. Rebekah Heald dictated her story before her death in 1856, but the manuscript was lost during the Civil War. See "Defends His Father: The Story of the Fort Dearborn Massacre Retold," *Chicago Tribune*, April 23, 1892, in the Chicago Massacre of 1812 Collection, Chicago History Museum.

3. Darius Heald's narrative of the events around August 15, 1812 (son of Captain Nathan Heald and Rebekah Wells Heald), as told to Lyman C. Draper in 1868, quoted in Milo M. Quaife, *Chicago and the Old Northwest* (Chicago, 1913), 414; See also Disability Report for Nathan Heald, June 18, 1828, by A. Wilson; and receipt submitted to U.S. Army for medical care, prepared by Nathan Heald, Louisville, Kentucky, January 4, 1812 (should be 1813). Both in the Draper Collection, 8U, microfilm reel 56.

4. Mrs. John Harris (Juliette) Kinzie, *Wau-Bun: The "Early Day" in the North-West* (Chicago, 1932), 281–82.

5. Heald would later submit a copy of the receipt for this trip to the U.S. Army for reimbursement. See receipt from September 7 (or 17), 1812, witnessed by William Griffith, in the Draper Collection, 8U, microfilm reel 56.

6. Captain Nathan Heald to Thomas H. Cushing, October 23, 1812, typescript copy, Fort Dearborn Collection, Chicago History Museum. See also Nathan Heald, September 17, 1812, pledge, and Adjutant General's Office, Washington City, January 18, 1813, General Orders, Draper Collection, 8U, microfilm reel 56.

7. For a painstaking discussion on the fate of soldiers, see Quaife, *Chicago and the Old Northwest*, 428–36.

8. James A. Clifton, *The Prairie People: Continuity and Change in Potawatomi Indian Culture, 1665–1965* (Lawrence, KS, 1977), 276.

9. Eunice Williams, captured during the 1701 raids at Deerfield, presents a case of one young captive who chose not to return to Massachusetts. See Demos, *The Unredeemed Captive*.

10. L. T. Helm to Augustus Woodward, June 6, 1814, typescript copy, Fort Dearborn Collection, Chicago History Museum.

11. John D. Barnhart, "A New Letter about the Massacre at Fort Dearborn," *Indiana Magazine of History* 41, no. 2 (June 1945): 187–99. Milo Quaife initially dismissed Jordan's account, in *Chicago and the Old Northwest*, 394–96. However, the discovery of substantiating letters from the Jordan family now lend credibility to his account.

12. Milo M. Quaife, "The Story of James Corbin, a Soldier at Fort Dearborn," *Mississippi Valley Historical Review* 3, no. 3 (September 1916): 222.

13. James Van Horne, "Narrative," Fort Dearborn Collection, Chicago History Museum; Corbin, quoted in Quaife, "The Story of James Corbin," 223.

14. Van Horne, "Narrative," Fort Dearborn Collection, Chicago History Museum.

15. Ibid.; Corbin, quoted in Quaife, "The Story of James Corbin," 223.

16. Quaife, *Chicago and the Old Northwest*, 236, provides other accounts: William Nelson Hunt froze to death in the winter of 1812–13; Irishman Hugh Logan was too tired to walk and was tomahawked, as was August Mott, a German.

17. Ibid., 236.

18. Van Horne, "Narrative," Fort Dearborn Collection, Chicago History Museum.

19. Quaife, *Chicago and the Old Northwest*, 260–61.

20. Kinzie, *Wau-Bun*, 284–86.

21. Quaife, *Chicago and the Old Northwest*, 253. In 1820 Mrs. Burns and her two daughters were living in Detroit, and Sergeant Griffith tried to get them a pension, because her husband had been in the Chicago militia—there is no record of whether they were successful.

22. Quaife, *Chicago and the Old Northwest*, 247–48.

23. Ibid., 248–49. "The last eye-witness of the Fort Dearborn massacre in 1812 died a short time ago in Santa Ana, California. She was Mrs. Susan Simmons Winans, the daughter of a non-commissioned officer in the U.S. Army who was stationed at the fort at the time of the terrible Indian outbreak." "Eye-Witnesses Gone," *Chicago Tribune*, September 26, 1902, Fort Dearborn Collection, Chicago History Museum.

24. Rhea to Meigs, Fort Wayne, August 19, 1812, National Archives, RG107.

25. General William Henry Harrison to Secretary of War, August 28, 1812, *Messages and Letters of William Henry Harrison*, ed. Logan Esarey, 2 vols. (New York, 1975), 2:98–99.

26. Alan Taylor makes the point that Indian massacres—whether actual, threatened, or embellished—raised public support for the War of 1812. The battle at Fort Dearborn seems to have followed this pattern. See Taylor, *Civil War of 1812*, 203–13.

27. Quaife, *Chicago and the Old Northwest*, 236.

28. Ibid., 237.

29. Augustus Woodward to Colonel Proctor, October 7, 1812, Fort Dearborn Collection, Chicago History Museum.

30. Quaife, *Chicago and the Old Northwest*, 237.

31. Quaife, "The Story of James Corbin," 224n; Thomas Forsyth to Nathan Heald, April 10, 1813, quoted in Quaife, *Chicago and the Old Northwest*, 236.

32. Quaife, *Chicago and the Old Northwest*, 249–50. Incredibly, she was not yet out of danger, as Indians attacked and killed her sister and her family on a nearby farm in late 1813, just months after Susan Simmons had made her way home.

33. Van Horne, "Narrative," Fort Dearborn Collection, Chicago History Museum.

34. Thomas Forsyth to Nathan Heald, April 10, 1813, quoted in Quaife, *Chicago and the Old Northwest*, 236.

35. Barry Transcript, Kinzie Account Book, Chicago History Museum.

36. Quotes from Kinzie, *Wau-Bun*, 279–80. See also John Kinzie to President Monroe, Chicago, April 4, 1817, National Archives, RG94.

37. Brian Leigh Dunnigan, *Frontier Metropolis: Picturing Early Detroit, 1701–1838* (Detroit, 2001), 132.

38. Milo M. Quaife, ed., *John Askin Papers*, 2 vols. (Detroit, 1928), 1:11.

39. James R. Forsyth, nephew of John Kinzie, letter to Lyman Draper, July 13, 1882, Detroit,

quoted in the Draper Collection, , 8YY, microfilm reel 119. See also Quaife, "Historical Introduction," in Kinzie, *Wau-Bun*, xli.

40. Quaife, *John Askin Papers*, 1:280–81. Robert Forsyth, brother of John Kinzie and Thomas Forsyth, initially chose to remain a British subject after the Jay Treaty. He later changed his mind and on May 15, 1812, was formally admitted to U.S. citizenship. Robert Forysth shared information with the commander at Fort Wayne in the spring of 1812, in a move not at all unlike that made by Thomas Forsyth with Ninian Edwards. See Robert Forsyth to Capt. Rhea, March 10, 1812, Potawatomi File, Great Lakes Indian Archive, Indiana University.

41. Upon the death of James Forsyth in 1816, John Kinzie, his stepbrother, was appointed administrator of his estate. At the time of the appointment (March 21, 1816), Kinzie was living in Detroit, but in July he removed to Chicago and in 1819 was dismissed by the court on the ground that he was neglecting his duties as administrator. At the time of his death, Forsyth owned a Detroit city lot and 694 acres of surrounding land. James R. Forsyth, nephew of John Kinzie, letter to Lyman Draper, July 13, 1882, Detroit, quoted in the Draper Collection, , 8YY, microfilm reel 119.

42. Kinzie, *Wau-Bun*, 289–90. The last bargain was made by Black Jim and one of the children, who redeemed the slave of a Kentucky militiaman with an old horse.

Chapter Thirteen

1. Thomas Forsyth to Governor Howard, September 7, 1812, quoted in Clarence Edwin Carter, ed., *Territorial Papers of the United States*, 26 vols. (Washington, DC, 1948), 16:264. While traditional accounts of the War of 1812—like Donald R. Hickey, *The War of 1812: A Forgotten Conflict* (Urbana, IL, 1989)—consider the battle at Fort Dearborn as part of the conflict between the United States and Great Britain, it was also part of a related war, between the United States and western Indians. Richard White and Alan Taylor both describe this western conflict—although it is not the center of either of their books. Alan Taylor, *The Civil War of 1812: American Citizens, British Subjects, Irish Rebels, and Indian Allies* (New York, 2010), 435; Richard White, *The Middle Ground: Indians, Empires, and Republics in the Great Lakes Region, 1650–1815* (New York, 1991), 516–17. The western Indian conflict is considered in detail by Helen Hornbeck Tanner, ed., *Atlas of Great Lakes Indian History* (Norman, OK, 1987); see map, 106–7, and a list of hostile actions, 108–15. Peter Silver, *Our Savage Neighbors: How Indian War Transformed Early America* (New York, 2008), discusses the unchecked violence in the western Indian wars. See also Julius W. Pratt, "Fur Trade Strategy and the American Left Flank in the War of 1812," *American Historical Review* 40, no. 2 (January 1935): 246–73.

2. When Thomas Forsyth arrived at Chicago after the battle, Indians there told him "that Fort Wayne would be attacked about the 20th of August by a great number of Indians." See Thomas Forsyth to Governor Howard, September 7, 1812, quoted in Carter, *Territorial Papers*, 16:261–65.

3. Zachary Taylor wrote William Henry Harrison: "Tecumseh was preparing a considerable force to strike an important blow somewhere against the white people." Taylor to Harrison, August 9, 1812, quoted in *Messages and Letters of William Henry Harrison*, ed. Logan Esarey, 2 vols. (New York, 1975), 2:82–83. See also "The Expedition of Major-General Samuel Hopkins Up the Wabash, 1812: The Letters of Captain Robert Hamilton," *Indiana Magazine of History* 43, no. 4 (December 1947): 393–402.

4. Tanner, *Atlas of Great Lakes Indian History*, 109.

5. John Sugden, *Tecumseh: A Life* (New York, 1997), 315. See also R. David Edmunds, *The Shawnee Prophet* (Lincoln, NE, 1983).

6. "Dearborn Raid, a Great Orator," *Chicago Tribune*, August 17, 1952; R. David Edmunds, *The Potawatomis: Keepers of the Fire* (Norman, OK, 1978), 189.

7. See James A. Clifton, *The Prairie People: Continuity and Change in Potawatomi Indian Culture, 1665–1965* (Lawrence, KS, 1977), 207; Edmunds, *The Potawatomis*, 189–91; Sugden, *Tecumseh*, 313; and Benson J. Lossing, *The Pictorial Field-Book of the War of 1812* (New York, 1868), 315.

8. Several nineteenth-century historians, including Joseph Kirkland, dismissed Jordan's ac-

count as a hoax. Jordan account from the *Niles' Register*, May 8, 1813, which included Jordan's letter to his wife dated October 19, 1812, Fort Wayne.

9. Tanner, *Atlas of Great Lakes Indian History*, 109.

10. Edmunds, *The Potawatomis*, 190–91.

11. Ibid., 191.

12. Tanner, *Atlas of Great Lakes Indian History*, 117.

13. Ibid., 109.

14. Edmunds, *The Potawatomis*, 191.

15. Ibid., 198.

16. Sugden, *Tecumseh*, 317.

17. "The main effect of the American counterattacks was to throw needy Indian communities upon British supplies, thus increasing the alliance with the redcoats and to redistribute Indian populations." Ibid.

18. Colonel Campbell, December 25, 1812, quoted in Ross F. Lockridge, "History on the Mississinewa," *Indiana Magazine of History* 30, no. 1 (March 1934): 43–44. See also Sugden, *Tecumseh*, 317.

19. Hickey, *The War of 1812*, 85.

20. Edmunds, *The Potawatomis*, 193.

21. Thomas Forsyth to the Governor of Louisiana Territory, September 7, 1812, quoted in Carter, *Territorial Papers*, 16:264.

22. *Black Hawk: An Autobiography*, ed. Donald Jackson (Urbana, IL, 1964), 66.

23. Governor Ninian Edwards to the Secretary of War, September 21, 1812, quoted in Carter, *Territorial Papers*, 16:265.

24. Tanner, *Atlas of Great Lakes Indian History*, 117.

25. Sugden, *Tecumseh*, 317.

26. C. Henry Smith, "Black Partridge: The Hero of Fort Dearborn," in *Metamora* (Bluffton, OH, 1947), 40.

27. Ibid., 46.

28. There is some discrepancy in the sources regarding the attack on Black Partridge's village. Helen Tanner places Black Partridge's village out of the range of these attacks in 1812—at the confluence of the Des Plaines River where it becomes the Illinois River. Certainly these attacks did take place, but the one identified as at Black Partridge's village may in fact have taken place at Pemwatome's village (Kickapoo).

29. Smith, "Black Partridge," 46. See also the reminiscence of General Reynolds, quoted in ibid., 42; and General Whiteside reminiscence, quoted in ibid., 46.

30. Ibid., 46.

31. Thomas Forsyth to the Secretary of War, St. Louis, April 10, 1813, quoted in Carter, *Territorial Papers*, 16:310–12.

32. Forsyth to Governor Howard, September 7, 1812, quoted in ibid., 16:264.

33. Thomas Forsyth to the Secretary of War, St. Louis, April 10, 1813, quoted in ibid., 16:310–12.

34. Memorial to Congress from Inhabitants of Peoria, December 20, 1813, quoted in ibid., 16:379–83.

35. Smith, "Black Partridge," 47. Gomo came to the rescue of the white women and children left behind by Craig's forces. The men were later released by order of Governor Edwards, but not until many of them had lost all their property (including Kinzie & Forsyth).

36. Thomas E. Craig to Governor Edwards, Shawneetown, Illinois Territory, December 10, 1812, quoted in *The Edwards Papers* (Chicago, 1884), 86–90.

37. Thomas Forsyth to the Secretary of War, St. Louis, April 10, 1813, quoted in Carter, *Territorial Papers*, 16:310–12.

38. Sugden, *Tecumseh*, 317–18; Edmunds, *The Potawatomis*, 195.

39. Edmunds, *The Potawatomis*, 199.

40. Shabbona was among the Potawatomi warriors from the Illinois River willing to leave

his family, based in his strong allegiance to the nativism spread by Tecumseh. Nehemiah Matson, "Sketch of Shau-be-na, a Potawatomie Chief," *Collections of the State Historical Society of Wisconsin* 18 (1908): 416–18.

Chapter Fourteen

1. In many general histories of the War of 1812, what happened in the West is immaterial to the war itself. Donald R. Hickey notes: "Jackson's victories in the Southwest, coupled with those of Perry and Harrison in the Northwest, greatly increased American security on the western frontier. The only problem with these victories was that they occurred in regions too remote to have a decisive effect on the outcome of the war." Donald R. Hickey, *The War of 1812: A Forgotten Conflict* (Urbana, IL, 1989), 151. In Alan Taylor's recent account of the War of 1812, Chicago and Fort Dearborn are not even on his base map. See Alan Taylor, *The Civil War of 1812: American Citizens, British Subjects, Irish Rebels, and Indian Allies* (New York, 2010).

2. Hickey, *The War of 1812*, 85–86.

3. James A. Clifton, "Personal and Ethnic Identity on the Great Lakes Frontier: The Case of Billy Caldwell, Anglo-Canadian," *Ethnohistory* 25, no. 1 (Winter 1978): 76. See also William Hickling, "Caldwell and Shabonee," June 1877, in the Draper Collection, 9YY, microfilm reel 119.

4. Robert Alexander Cruikshank, "Robert Dickson, the Indian Trader," *Wisconsin Historical Collection* 12 (1892): 142–43.

5. James Ryan Haydon, "John Kinzie's Place in History," *Transactions of the Illinois State Historical Society* 39 (1932): 186.

6. Ibid.

7. R. David Edmunds, *The Potawatomis: Keepers of the Fire* (Norman, OK, 1978), 200.

8. Cruikshank, "Robert Dickson," 144–45.

9. Ibid.

10. Ibid., 147.

11. Ibid., 148; "Court of Inquiry, 1815," transcript in *Michigan Pioneer and Historical Society* 16 (1910): 333.

12. Haydon, "John Kinzie's Place in History," 186.

13. "Court of Inquiry, 1815," 332–33.

14. Mrs. John H. (Juliette) Kinzie, *Wau-Bun: The "Early Day" in the North-West* (Chicago, 1932), 293–94.

15. Helen Hornbeck Tanner, ed., *The Atlas of Great Lakes Indian History* (Norman, OK, 1987), 118; Gurdon Hubbard to Lyman Draper, February 16, 1883, in the Draper Collection, 9YY, microfilm reel 119.

16. Hickey, *The War of 1812*, 135.

17. C. Henry Smith, "Black Partridge: The Hero of Fort Dearborn," in *Metamora* (Bluffton, OH, 1947), 50; Edmunds, *The Potawatomis*, 200.

18. Governor Ninian Edwards to Thomas Forsyth, January 5, 1812, quoted in the Draper Collection, Series T, Forsyth Papers, microfilm reel 53.

19. Thomas Forsyth to the Secretary of War, St. Louis, April 10, 1813, quoted in Clarence Edwin Carter, ed., *Territorial Papers of the United States*, 26 vols. (Washington, DC, 1948), 16:310–12.

20. Thomas Forsyth to Benjamin Howard, St. Louis, May 7, 1813, quoted in ibid., 16:324–26.

21. Carter, *Territorial Papers*, 16:324–26.

22. Ibid.

23. *Black Hawk: An Autobiography*, ed. Donald Jackson (Urbana, IL, 1964), 66.

24. See "Letter Book of Thomas Forsyth, 1814–1818," *Wisconsin Historical Collections* 11 (1888): 316, 354; Smith, "Black Partridge," 52; and R. David Edmunds, "The Illinois River Potawatomi in the War of 1812," *Journal of the Illinois State Historical Society* 62, no. 4 (Winter 1969): 359–61.

25. Governor Ninian Edwards to Secretary of War, June 15, 1813, quoted in Carter, *Territorial Papers*, 16:343.

26. Edmunds, *The Potawatomis*, 201.

27. Edmunds, "The Illinois River Potawatomi in the War of 1812," 341–62.

28. Smith, "Black Partridge," 52.

29. Captain Bullock to General Proctor, Michilimackinac, September 25, 1813, quoted in *Wisconsin Historical Collections* 12 (1892): 110.

30. Edmunds, *The Potawatomis*, 201.

31. "Court of Inquiry, 1815," 331.

32. John Kinzie to President Monroe, Chicago, April 4, 1817, National Archives, RG94; Governor Lewis Cass to John Kinsey [sic], September 4, 1814, quoted in Clarence Edwin Carter, ed., *Territorial Papers of the United States*, 26 vols. (Washington, DC, 1942), 10:477.

33. Edmunds, *The Potawatomis*, 201.

34. "Court of Inquiry, 1815," 331.

35. Edmunds, *The Potawatomis*, 203.

36. Governor McArthur to the Secretary of War, September 26, 1814, quoted in Carter, *Territorial Papers*, 10:486.

37. Ibid.

Chapter Fifteen

1. R. David Edmunds, "Main Poc: Potawatomi Wabeno," *American Indian Quarterly* (Summer 1985): 268–69.

2. Helen Hornbeck Tanner, ed., *Atlas of Great Lakes Indian History* (Norman, OK, 1987), 120–21.

3. Ibid.

4. C. Henry Smith, "Black Partridge: The Hero of Fort Dearborn," in *Metamora* (Bluffton, OH, 1947), 52; Tanner, *Atlas of Great Lakes Indian History*, 120–21; R. David Edmunds, *The Potawatomis: Keepers of the Fire* (Norman, OK, 1978), 205.

5. James A. Clifton, "Chicago, September 14, 1833: The Last Great Indian Treaty in the Old Northwest," *Chicago History* 9, no. 2 (Summer 1980): 91. See also James A. Clifton, *The Prairie People: Continuity and Change in Potawatomi Indian Culture, 1665–1965* (Lawrence, KS, 1977), 181; and Francis Paul Prucha, *American Indian Treaties: The History of a Political Anomaly* (Berkeley, CA, 1994), 133.

6. Kerry A. Trask, *Black Hawk: The Battle for the Heart of America* (New York, 2006), 26. See also Tanner, *Atlas of Great Lakes Indian History*, 120–21.

7. Major Thomas Forsyth, Indian Agent, "Journal of a Voyage from St. Louis to the Falls of St. Anthony in 1819," quoted in *Report and Collections of the State Historical Society of Wisconsin*, 10 vols. (Madison, 1872), 6:189.

8. Clifton, "Chicago, September 14, 1833," 91.

9. John Kinzie to William Woodbridge, April 1815, quoted in James Ryan Haydon, "John Kinzie's Place in History," *Transactions of the Illinois State Historical Society* 39 (1932): 194–95.

10. John Kinzie to Lewis Cass, Detroit, July 15, 1815, quoted in ibid., 196–97.

11. "1822 Treaty with the Sac and Fox," quoted in Charles J. Kappler, *Indian Affairs: Laws and Treaties*, 7 vols. (Washington, DC, 1904), 2:202–3.

12. Prucha, *American Indian Treaties*, 135–36.

13. Edmunds, *The Potawatomis*, 217.

14. Ibid., 218.

15. Clifton, "Chicago, September 14, 1833," 92.

16. John Low and Paula Holley, "Treaty of Chicago—September, 1833," in *Native Chicago*, ed. Terry Straus (Chicago, 2002), 96–97.

17. Henry R. Schoolcraft, "A Journey up the Illinois River in 1821," quoted in Milo M. Quaife, ed., *Pictures of Illinois One Hundred Years Ago* (Chicago, 1918), 122–26. Schoolcraft was an eyewitness to the 1821 Treaty of Chicago.

18. Ibid., 125–26.

19. Ibid., 125–27.

20. Ibid., 132–33, 129, 164–68.

21. Ibid., 164; Edmunds, *The Potawatomis*, 224.

22. Of course, others received grants whose connections to Kinzie were not as straightforward including Joseph LaFramboise and Charles and Medare Beaubien. See Schoolcraft, "A Journey up the Illinois River," 164.

23. Edmunds, *The Potawatomis*, 226.

24. Ibid., 228.

25. James A. Clifton, "Personal and Ethnic Identity on the Great Lakes Frontier: The Case of Billy Caldwell, Anglo-Canadian," *Ethnohistory* 25, no. 1 (Winter 1978): 81–82.

26. Colonel G. S. Hubbard's Narrative, quoted in William Hinkling, *Caldwell and Shabonee* (Chicago, 1877), 46, in Draper Collection, 9YY, microfilm reel 119. See also Alta P. Walters, "Shabonee," *Journal of the Illinois State Historical Society* 17, no. 3 (October 1924): 381–97.

27. LaFramboise identified as "Indian Chief" in the 1839 Chicago City Directory—see Ulrich Danckers and Jane Meredith, *Early Chicago* (River Forest, IL, 1999), 230.

28. His granddaughter Mrs. Katherine Boettcher remained on the property until her house burned in 1955. "Oldest Schiller Citizen, Indian Descendant Dies," *Schiller Park Independent*, Franklin Park, Illinois, December 9, 1965, article filed at the Elmwood Park Public Library.

29. Caldwell's father died in 1818 and in his will acknowledged his illegitimate oldest son while disinheriting him. See James A. Clifton, "Merchant, Soldier, Broker, Chief: A Corrected Obituary of Captain Billy Caldwell," *Journal of the Illinois State Historical Society* 71, no. 3 (August 1978): 185–210; quote in Clifton, "Personal and Ethnic Identity," 77.

30. Colonel G. S. Hubbard's Narrative, quoted in Hinkling, *Caldwell and Shabonee*.

31. Peter Schrake, "Chasing an Elusive War: The Illinois Militia and the Winnebago War of 1827," *Journal of Illinois History* 12, no. 1 (Spring 2009): 27–52.

32. Frank Reed Grover, *Antoine Ouilmette* (Evanston, IL, 1908), 10–11, 23.

33. However, these grants were not easily sold, as this required the specific permission of the president of the United States. See Frank Strauss, "Monee," in *Native Chicago*, ed. Terry Straus (Chicago, 2002), 131.

34. "Treaty, July 29, 1829, Treaty with the Chippewa, etc.," in Kappler, *Indian Affairs*, 2: 297–300.

35. Strauss, "Monee," 132–33.

Chapter Sixteen

1. Jacqueline Peterson, "Founding Fathers," in *Native Chicago*, ed. Terry Straus (Chicago, 2002), 51.

2. It is not entirely clear that John Kinzie retained ownership of their property at Chicago. See letter from Ramsey Crooks, American Fur Company, to John Kinzie, July 31, 1817, in the American Fur Company Collection, Chicago History Museum. Jacqueline Peterson is the historian who has focused her attention on Chicago in this era. See Peterson, "The People in Between: Indian-White Marriage and the Genesis of a Metis Society and Culture in the Great Lakes Region, 1680–1830" (PhD diss., University of Illinois, Chicago, 1981); and Peterson, "Wild Chicago: The Formation and Destruction of a Multi-Racial Community on the Midwestern Frontier" (MA thesis, University of Illinois, Chicago, 1977).

3. Forsyth to the Secretary of War, St. Louis, September 29, 1817, quoted in "Letter Book of Thomas Forsyth, 1814–1818," *Wisconsin Historical Collections* 11 (1888): 351.

4. Sale signed by both John and Eleanor Kinzie. Bond of Mortgage Received for record October 10, 1815, Fort Dearborn Papers, Chicago History Museum. See also Peterson, "Founding Fathers," 51. The last mention of Black Jim was in Detroit in early 1814. See Mrs. John H. (Juliette) Kinzie, *Wau-Bun: The "Early Day" in the North-West* (Chicago, 1932), 290.

5. The following year, on June 26, 1816, this curious bail arrangement was terminated, in another legal document drawn up and recorded by George McDougall, operating as attorney for Richard and Hugh Pattinson. The document stated: "Having been directed by Richard Pattinson as his attorney to discontinue his actions against Kinzie and Forsyth and to release them from all mortgages, I hereby acknowledge satisfaction of the bond mortgage here recorded. George McDougall for self and as attorney for Richard Pattinson and Hugh Pattinson." Bond of Mortgage Received for record October 10, 1815, Fort Dearborn Papers, Chicago History Museum.

6. Report of the Committee of claims on the petition of Kenzie and Forsythe, December 31, 1812, (Washington, DC, 1814), Fort Dearborn Papers, Chicago History Museum.

7. Ibid.

8. Thomas Forsyth to Nathan Heald, April 10, 1813, in Draper Collection, 24U, microfilm reel 59; Captain Heald deposition, December 2, 1817, Draper Collection, Series T, Forsyth Papers, microfilm reel 53.

9. Memorial to Congress from Inhabitants of Peoria, December 20, 1813, quoted in Clarence Edwin Carter, ed., *Territorial Papers of the United States*, 26 vols. (Washington, DC, 1948), 16:379–83.

10. Forsyth discussed Indian administration with Secretary of War John C. Calhoun. See Thomas Forsyth, "Documents: The French, British and Spanish Methods of Treating Indians &c," *Ethnohistory* 4, no. 2 (Spring 1957): 210. See also Thomas Forsyth to the Secretary of War, September 29, 1817, quoted in "Letter Book of Thomas Forsyth," 351–52.

11. *Black Hawk: An Autobiography*, ed. Donald Jackson (Urbana, IL, 1964), 95.

12. Kerry A. Trask, *Black Hawk: The Battle for the Heart of America* (New York, 2006), 59.

13. John Kinzie to President James Madison, April 4, 1817, Chicago, National Archives, M566.

14. Governor Cass to Acting Secretary of War, July 10, 1815, quoted in Clarence Edwin Carter, *Territorial Papers of the United States*, 26 vols. (Washington, DC, 1942), 10:567.

15. Milo Milton Quaife, *Checagou: From Indian Wigwam to Modern City, 1673–1835* (Chicago, 1933), 168–69.

16. For more on Jouett, see A. T. Andreas, *History of Chicago*, 3 vols. (Chicago, 1884), 1:87; John Kinzie to President James Madison, April 4, 1817, Chicago, National Archives, M566; Charles Jouett to President James Madison, April 3, 1817, Chicago, National Archives, M566. See also Secretary of War to Governor Cass, quoted in James Ryan Haydon, "John Kinzie's Place in History," *Transactions of the Illinois State Historical Society* 39 (1932): 188.

17. Alexander Wolcott to Governor Cass, November 14, 1819, quoted in Carter, *Territorial Papers*, 10:885.

18. *The Autobiography of Gurdon Saltonstall Hubbard*, ed. Caroline M. McIlvaine (Chicago, 1911), 139.

19. These sentiments seem to come from both John and Eleanor Kinzie. John's older stepsister married well in New York City. Alice Haliburton married Sampson Fleming and then Nicholas Low. See Milo M. Quaife, "Historical Introduction," in Kinzie, *Wau-Bun*, xxxiii–xxxiv.

20. Journal of Jacob B. Varnum of Petersburg, Virginia, 1864, Chicago History Museum.

21. John D. Haeger, "The American Fur Company and the Chicago of 1812–1835," *Journal of the Illinois State Historical Society* 61, no. 2 (Summer 1968): 124.

22. Haydon goes on to criticize Kinzie for pleading poverty when he is in fact working for the American Fur Company. See Haydon, "John Kinzie's Place in History," 189.

23. In 1825 Kinzie was one of the principal taxpayers in Chicago and paid $4 taxes that year upon property valued at $400, as appears on the tax roll, dated July 25, 1825. With one exception, none of the fourteen taxpayers of that year owned property in excess of $1,000. John Kinzie's holdings appear on the same roll as worth $500, while those of John B. Beaubien are set down at $1,000; the lowest man on this list is Joseph LaFramboise, who paid fifty cents on property valued at $50, and Ouilmette's taxes appear considerably above the average in amount. Reprinted in Rufus Blanchard, *Discovery and Conquest of the North-West, with the History of Chicago* (Chicago, 1896), 517, 519.

24. John Kinzie to John H. Kinzie, August 19, 1821, John Kinzie Collection, Chicago History Museum.

25. Ibid.

26. *Autobiography of Gurdon Saltonstall Hubbard*, 29.

27. Terry Straus, "Founding Mothers," in *Native Chicago*, ed. Terry Straus (Chicago, 2002), 70.

28. Ouilmette's grandson I. J. Martell to Frank R. Grover, August 22, 1905, quoted in Frank Reed Grover, *Antoine Ouilmette* (Evanston, IL, 1908), 25.

29. Helen Hornbeck Tanner, ed., *Atlas of Great Lakes Indian History* (Norman, OK, 1987), 140.

30. Colbee C. Benton, *A Visitor to Chicago in Indian Days: Journal to the Far-Off West* (Chicago, 1957), 79–80.

31. John Denis Haeger, *John Jacob Astor: Business and Finance in the Early Republic* (Detroit, 1991); Kenneth Wiggins, *John Jacob Astor: Business Man*, 2 vols. (New York, 1966).

32. "Exclusion of British Traders," April 29, 1816, quoted in Francis Paul Prucha, ed., *Documents of United States Indian Policy* (Lincoln, NE, 2000), 28; Secretary of War John C. Calhoun to Michigan Governor Lewis Cass, March 25, 1818, quoted in ibid., 29; Governor Lewis Cass to Acting Secretary of War A. J. Dallas, July 20, 1815 quoted in ibid., 25–26.

33. David Lavender, *The Fist in the Wilderness* (Lincoln, NE, 1998), 232, 303.

34. Ibid., 266; Prucha, *Documents of United States Indian Policy*, 33.

35. Frank Strauss, "Monee," in *Native Chicago*, ed. Straus, 125–26.

36. Lavender, *The Fist in the Wilderness*, 280.

37. *Autobiography of Gurdon Saltonstall Hubbard*, 15.

38. Robert Crooks to John Kinzie, August 11, 1819, American Fur Company Collection, Chicago History Museum.

39. *Autobiography of Gurdon Saltonstall Hubbard*, 27.

40. The $1,174 that Chandonnai owed the American Fur Company would live on for many years, finally to be settled in the 1833 Treaty of Chicago. See Ramsey Crooks, American Fur Company, to John Kinzie, September 19, 1818, American Fur Company Collection, Chicago History Museum.

41. Lavender, *The Fist in the Wilderness*, 287.

42. Bessie Louise Pierce, *History of Chicago*, 3 vols. (Chicago, 1937), 1:28–29.

43. John Kelley, "1822 Chicago: From Tales of an 1822 Chicagoan, Some Memoirs of the Late Alexander Beaubien," *Journal of the Illinois State Historical Society* 14, nos. 3–4 (October 1921–January 1922): 408.

44. Quaife, "Historical Introduction," in Kinzie, *Wau-Bun*, xiv.

45. Haeger, "The American Fur Company," 128.

46. Lavender, *The Fist in the Wilderness*, 289, 303.

47. Haeger, "The American Fur Company," 130.

48. Major Irwin to Colonel McKenney, October 6, 1821, quoted in *Report and Collections of the State Historical Society of Wisconsin*, 10 vols. (Madison, 1876), 7:280.

49. Lavender, *The Fist in the Wilderness*, 316–17. Another related episode with liquor occurred 1824, with national attacks on the American Fur Company's use of whiskey involving William H. Wallace, a company trader in Indiana. See ibid., 355–56.

50. Quaife, *Checagou*, 163.

51. Robert Stuart to John Kinzie, September 11, 1825, American Fur Company Papers, Chicago History Museum.

52. Haeger, "The American Fur Company," 132–33.

53. Trask, *Black Hawk*, 9.

54. Tanner, *Atlas of Great Lakes Indian History*, 125.

55. Haeger, "The American Fur Company," 133–34. John Jacob Astor was not in the fur trade exactly—he was looking for places to extract wealth—and he did so by following the U.S. government around in their treaties and extracting debt payments before Indians got monies— transfer of great wealth that went to New York City did not stay as a fund for Indians for future generations; instead it fueled the real estate boom in New York that would in turn fuel commercial development of the United States.

56. John Kinzie plan of peace, dated at Detroit, April 1815, to Lewis Cass, quoted in Haydon, "John Kinzie's Place in History," 192.

Chapter Seventeen

1. A. T. Andreas, *History of Chicago*, 3 vols. (Chicago, 1884), 1:97. It is not clear where the Kinzie family lived when John Kinzie died. It is also possible that the Kinzies moved into the Le Mai house—a few doors down the way from their original house. It may be that Kinzie was able to purchase this house at some point, and this might provide some explanation for the confusion

regarding the purchase of Point de Sable's house from Jean Lalime (not François Le Mai, as is often stated in nineteenth-century sources).

2. Mrs. John H. (Juliette) Kinzie, *Wau-Bun: The "Early Day" in the North-West* (Chicago, 1932), 217.

3. Ibid., 214.

4. Jacqueline Peterson, "Founding Fathers," in *Native Chicago*, ed. Terry Straus (Chicago, 2002), 45–46. They came to Chicago after John Kinzie died, but Eleanor Kinzie was still present. This may help to explain the *Wau-Bun* stories that completely excise this part of the family. This is a place where *Wau-Bun* seems unreliable.

5. John W. Hall, *Uncommon Defense: Indian Allies in the Black Hawk War* (Cambridge, 2009), 253.

6. Helen Hornbeck Tanner, ed., *Atlas of Great Lakes Indian History* (Norman, OK, 1987), 122.

7. Peterson, "Founding Fathers," 50.

8. See Kerry A. Trask, *Black Hawk: The Battle for the Heart of America* (New York, 2006).

9. Thomas Forsyth, quoted in *Black Hawk: An Autobiography*, ed. Donald Jackson (Urbana, IL, 1964), 109. Lyman C. Draper notes: "After the war, Major Forsyth was many years Indians agent for the Sauks and Foxes; and had been continued over them, it is believed, the Sauk war of 1832 would never have occurred." Editorial note in "Journal of a Voyage from St. Louis to the Falls of St. Anthony in 1819," by Major Thomas Forsyth, Indian Agent, quoted in *Report and Collections of the State Historical Society of Wisconsin*, 10 vols. (Madison, 1872), 6:188.

10. Hall, *Uncommon Defense*, 8.

11. William Hinkling, *Caldwell and Shabonee* (Chicago, 1877), in Draper Collection, 9YY, microfilm reel 119.

12. Hall, *Uncommon Defense*, 137.

13. "Recollections of Apta-ke-sic (Half Day)," quoted in a letter from Henry Blodgett to Hon. A. H. Burley, January 23, 1893, Henry Blodgett Collection, Chicago History Museum.

14. John Low and Paula Holley, "Treaty of Chicago—September, 1833," in *Native Chicago*, ed. Straus, 107.

15. James A. Clifton, "Chicago, September 14, 1833: The Last Great Indian Treaty in the Old Northwest," *Chicago History* 9, no. 2 (Summer 1980): 91–92. See also Clifton, "The Potawatomi Removal of 1833," *Indiana Magazine of History* 68, no. 3 (September 1972): 240–53.

16. Francis Paul Prucha, *American Indian Treaties: The History of a Political Anomaly* (Berkeley, CA, 1994), 188–89.

17. John D. Haeger, "The American Fur Company and the Chicago of 1812–1835," *Journal of the Illinois State Historical Society* 61, no. 2 (Summer 1968): 135.

18. "1833 Treaty of Chicago," quoted in Charles J. Kappler, *Indian Affairs: Laws and Treaties*, 7 vols. (Washington, DC, 1904): 2:323.

19. Haeger, "The American Fur Company," 136–37.

20. "1833 Treaty of Chicago."

21. James A. Clifton suggests, "All those who had worked to make Chicago an American place, rather than a Potawatomi or a French or an English district, were being rewarded." Clifton, "Chicago, September 14, 1833," 95.

22. "1833 Treaty of Chicago."

23. R. David Edmunds, *The Potawatomis: Keepers of the Fire* (Norman, OK, 1978), 250–52.

24. William Hinkling, *Caldwell and Shabonee*, quoted in Draper Collection, 9YY, microfilm reel 119.

25. Ibid.

26. " . . . Last Eye-witness to the Chicago Massacre," *Chicago Tribune*, May 14, 1872.

27. "Alexander Robinson, Death of Pottawatomie Chief near Chicago," *Chicago Tribune*, May 14, 1872.

28. The Ouilmettes are also mentioned in the Treaty of 1833. Josette Ouilmette, "the little bound girl" of Waubun, was "personally provided for," probably at the demand of the Kinzies, in the following words: "To Josette Ouilmette (John H. Kinzie, Trustee) $200." The other children did not fare so well, for the treaty further provided "to Antoine Ouilmette's children $300." See Frank Reed Grover, *Antoine Ouilmette* (Evanston, IL, 1908), 9.

29. Ouilmette Papers, Evanston Historical Society.

30. Grover, *Antoine Ouilmette*, 20. From the reminiscence of Benjamin F. Hill, who lived in Evanston and was interviewed by Grover in 1901 (he died in 1905 in Milwaukee).

31. Archange and Antoine both died at Council Bluffs, Iowa, in 1840 and 1841. However, their eight children were successful in selling the property in 1847. See Ouilmette Papers, Evanston Historical Society.

32. Jacqueline Peterson, "Goodbye, Madore Beaubien: The Americanization of Early Chicago Society," *Chicago History* 9, no. 2 (Summer 1980): 108–9.

33. Kathy Gourley, "Locations of Sauk, Mesquakie, and Associated Euro-American Sites, 1832–1845: An Ethnohistoric Approach" (PhD diss., Iowa State University, 1990), 44–47.

Epilogue

1. Carl Becker, 1931 Presidential Address, American Historical Association, www.historians .org. My thanks to Joe Bigott for reintroducing me to Carl Becker and his pragmatic approach to history.

2. John N. Low, quote from the July 13, 2009, press release by Tina Feldstein, president of the Prairie Avenue Neighborhood Alliance.

3. Jerry Crimmins, the author of a recent young adult fiction on Fort Dearborn, opposed the renaming. He suggested, "Historical revisionism typically takes heroes from the past and makes villains of them." Crimmins promised, "So long as I write about it, I'm going to call it the Fort Dearborn Massacre." Quoted in Ron Grossman, "Another Ft. Dearborn Skirmish at Park," *Chicago Tribune*, August 14, 2009. While Crimmins has taken a principled stand against what he sees as historical revisionism, he has no problem muddying the line between fiction and nonfiction in his novel in the tradition of Allen Eckhart.

4. Constance Buckley noted in her study of Fort Dearborn's history that "new evidence in the form of unearthed documentation or a fresh analysis is often dismissed if it does not conform to accepted knowledge—contrary to other disciplines, such as medicine, in which revisionist knowledge is embraced as a cure, not a challenge." See Constance R. Buckley, "Searching for Fort Dearborn: Perception, Commemoration, and Celebration of an Urban Creation Memory" (PhD diss., Loyola University, 2005), 6.

5. H. A. Musham, "Where Did the Battle of Chicago Take Place?" *Journal of the Illinois State Historical Society* 36, no. 1 (March 1943): 22. For more on Musham, see Buckley, "Searching for Fort Dearborn," 357.

6. *Webster's New Universal Unabridged Dictionary* (New York, 1996), 1182.

7. Simon Pokagan, "The Massacre of Fort Dearborn at Chicago," *Harper's New Monthly Magazine*, March 1899, 653; 1973 quote in Buckley, "Searching for Fort Dearborn," 389.

8. For example, see Carl Smith, *Urban Disorder and the Shape of Belief: The Great Chicago Fire, the Haymarket Bomb, and the Model Town of Pullman* (Chicago, 1995); Dolores Hayden, *The Power of Place: Urban Landscapes as Public History* (Cambridge, 1995); Christine Boyer, *The City of Collective Memory: Its Historical Imagery and Architectural Entertainments* (Cambridge, MA, 1994); and Brian Ladd, *Ghosts of Berlin: Confronting German History in the Urban Landscape* (Chicago, 1997).

9. After a fifty-year sojourn within the Chicago Historical Society walls, the monument was returned to Prairie Avenue for fourteen years, until it was again removed in 1998 to make way for the Hillary Clinton Women's Park.

10. Chicago Historical Society, *Ceremonies at the Unveiling Bronze Memorial Group of the Chicago Massacre of 1812* (Chicago, 1893), 7.

11. Kicking Bear and Short Bull also worked in the European tour of Buffalo Bill's Wild West instead of serving prison time. See Buckley, "Searching for Fort Dearborn," 227; and Theodore Karamanski, "Monuments to a Lost Nation," *Chicago History* 33, no.1 (Spring 2004): 13–15.

12. George Pullman to E. G. Mason, June 19, 1893, quoted in *Ceremonies at the Unveiling Bronze Memorial Group of the Chicago Massacre of 1812*, 5–6. See also the address at the unveiling by former President Benjamin Harrison, esp. 17.

13. Waubansee, or Foggy Day, was Black Partridge's younger brother, who had connections at Peoria but also a summer village on the Fox River near what is today Aurora. See David B.

Stout and Erminie Wheeler-Voegelin, *Indians of Illinois and Northwest Indiana* (New York, 1974), 232; and C. Henry Smith, "Black Partridge: The Hero of Fort Dearborn," in *Metamora* (Bluffton, OH, 1947), 24.

14. Michael A. McDonnell, "Charles-Michel Mouett de Langlade," in *The Sixty Years' War for the Great Lakes, 1754–1814*, ed. David Curtis Skagus and Larry L. Nelson (East Lansing, MI, 2001), 90.

15. Thomas O'Shaughnessy organized local Catholic college and high school women to lobby successfully for a replica of the cabin inhabited by Father Pere Jacques Marquette, S.J., during the winter of 1674–75 also on display at the 1933 exposition. Other Catholic groups lobbied for recognition of Thomas J. V. Owen, who came to Chicago in 1829 and was instrumental in its incorporation. See James Ryan Haydon, *Chicago's True Founder, Thomas J. V. Owen: A Pleading for Truth and for Social Justice in Chicago History* (Lombard, IL, 1934).

16. Christopher R. Reed, "'In the Shadow of Fort Dearborn': Honoring De Sable at the Chicago World's Fair of 1933–1934," *Journal of Black Studies* 21, no. 4 (June 1991): 402.

17. Ibid., 398–413.

18. "Fort Dearborn Sets a Star on Chicago's Flag," *Chicago Daily Tribune*, December 22, 1939. See also Buckley, "Searching for Fort Dearborn," 360. In 1961 Dr. Margaret Burroughs founded the DuSable Museum of African American History, memorializing Point de Sable as Chicago's first settler. In 1987 Mayor Harold Washington dedicated DuSable Park at the mouth of the Chicago River, and in 2010 the City Council renamed the Michigan Avenue Bridge after DuSable.

19. John N. Low, quote from the July 13, 2009, press release by Tina Feldstein, president of the Prairie Avenue Neighborhood Alliance.

Index

Page numbers followed by an *f* indicate figures.

Adams, John, 40; inaugurated (1797), ix
Adams, John Quincy, 40; inaugurated (1825), ix
Agency House (Chicago), 61–65, 62*f*, 213, 223
agriculture, 5, 28–29, 51, 53, 80. *See also* farming
alcohol. *See* liquor
Algonquians, 8, 10–11, 15, 24–25, 45, 54, 136, 164, 237, 250n11
Allen, Susan Randolph. *See* Jouett, Susan Randolph Allen
American frontier, 22–23, 34–35, 87, 167, 252n8, 276n1
American Fur Company, 205, 207, 214, 216–21, 230, 233, 252n19, 270n1, 280n40, 280n49
American partisans, 75, 128
American Revolution (1776–83), ix, 16, 25, 27, 30, 33, 251n16, 252n9. *See also* Revolutionary War (1776–83)
ammunition: destruction of, 1, 133–34, 157, 211, 267n30, 267n32; for militias, 100; secured for war, 105–10, 174–75, 186, 236; shortages, 94; as trade goods, 18. *See also* weapons
anti-American sentiment, 40–41, 46, 62, 81, 126, 140, 158, 173, 176–77, 181–82, 192. *See also* pro-American sentiment
Apekonit. *See* Wells, William (Apekonit)
Aptakisic (Half-Day), 216, 227
assimilation, xx, 92
Astor, John Jacob, 216–18, 280n55
Athena (enslaved woman in Kinzie household), xiv, 69–70
Au Glaize, vii, 36–37, 43, 251n7
Au Glaize River, 139

Bailey, Jonathan, 223
Bailly, Joseph, xiii, 67–68, 108, 155, 191–92, 204, 208, 217
Bailly, Marie, 67
Bailly, Monee, 208
Baker, Daniel, 212–13
Barry Transcript: of Kinzie & Forsyth ledger, 257n11, 257n18, 271n23, 271n29, 273n35
battledore (game similar to badminton), 103–4, 114
Battle of Chicago. *See* Battle of Fort Dearborn (August 15, 1812)
Battle of Fort Dearborn (August 15, 1812), x,

130–50; aftermath, 153–62; allies and protectors, 141–43, 147–49; captors and captives/ prisoners of war, 1, 155–56, 162–72, 272–74n; on city flag, 2, 246, 247*f*, 248; coda to battle, 159–61; departures and arrivals, 156–59; map, 144*f*; "massacre," use of word/term, 1–2, 235–38, 244, 248, 249n1; plaque, 241*f*; Potawatomi attack, xix, 1, 5, 130, 143–47, 236–37, 244, 267–70n; surrender, 149–50, 270n62. *See also* War of 1812; Western War (1811–15)
Battle of Fort Dearborn Park (Chicago), 235, 241
Battle of the Thames (1813), 188, 190–91
Battle of Tippecanoe (November 1811), ix, 87–100, 110, 136, 140, 237–38, 259–61n; Chicago after, 95–98; and Harrison, 92–96, 131; and Leigh farm, 98–100; retaking Indian Country, 90–92. *See also* Tippecanoe
Beaubien, Charles, 67, 278n22
Beaubien, Jean Baptiste, xiii, xv, 67–68, 100, 124, 191, 208, 215, 219–20, 223, 226, 230
Beaubien, John B., 279n23
Beaubien, Josette LaFramboise, xv, 67, 100, 142
Beaubien, Madore, 67
Beaubien, Mah-naw-bun-no-quah, xiii, 67
Beaubien, Marie, 67
Beaubien, Mark, 223
Beaubien, Medare, 278n22
beaver, 8, 24, 75, 75*f*. *See also* fur trade
Becker, Carl, 235, 282n1
Belknap, Ebenezer, 256n46
Benton, Thomas Hart, 217
Big Foot, 206
Blackbird (Siggenauk), 40–42, 82, 85–86, 91, 107, 124, 130, 155–56, 161, 175, 188, 229; and Battle of Fort Dearborn, 137–41, 145, 147, 149–50; loyalty medal, 138*f*
Black Hawk, 15, 92, 107, 121, 181, 226–28, 228*f*
Black Hawk War (1832), x, 226–28, 245, 281n5
Black Jim (enslaved man in Kinzie household), xiv, 69–70, 142,157, 257n11, 274n42, 278n4
Blackmeat (enslaved man in Jouett household), 62
Black Partridge (Mucktypoke), xiii, xix–xx, 36–37, 40, 42, 45, 78, 107, 179–80, 182, 191, 195–96, 206, 215, 216, 229, 240*f*, 275n28, 282–83n13; and Battle of Fort Dearborn, 1, 3, 137, 139–41, 147–48, 156–57, 159–60, 162, 167, 169–70, 177, 237, 240*f*, 242–44, 247; friendship/peace

INDEX